Midnight Matinees

A SPECIAL SALUTE TO 'SCARJO': No actress appears more often in this volume than Scarlett Johansson, who alternates roles in cult films with others in mainstream movies; and, as "Black Widow" in *Captain America The Winter Soldier*, stars in modern films that bridge the gap between the two.

Midnight Matinees

Cult Cinema Classics
(1896 to the present day)

by Douglas Brode

BearManor Media
2021

Midnight Matinees: Cult Cinema Classics (1896 to the present day)

© 2021 Douglas Brode

All rights reserved.

With special thanks to the entire team at the Sundance Print Center in San Antonio, TX for their tireless support.

No portion of this publication may be reproduced, stored, and/or copied electronically (except for academic use as a source), nor transmitted in any form or by any means without the prior written permission of the publisher and/or author.

Published in the United States of America by:

BearManor Media

1317 Edgewater Dr. #110
Orlando, FL 32804

BearManorMedia.com

Printed in the United States.

ISBN—978-1-62933-785-2

DEDICATION:

for

Dr. Richard Lawrence Miller
"Old friends are the best friends!"

Contents

Once Upon a Time At the Movies… 1

Abbott & Costello Meet Frankestein to *Atomic Café* 17

Babes In Toyland to *Buckaroo Banzai* 33

The Cabin In the Woods to *The Crow* 89

Dakhtari Dar Sab Tanha Be Xane Mirvas to *Duel* 119

Easy Rider to *Eye of the Devil* 143

Faster, Pussycat! Kill! Kill! to *From Dusk Till Dawn* 159

The Gang's All Here to *Gun Crazy* 175

Hairspray to *Hugo* 191

Ichi the Killer to *I Walked With a Zombie* 219

Le Jetee to *Juno* 231

Kanashimi no Beradonna to *Kubo and the Two Strings* 237

The Last Seduction to *Lucky* 249

Mad Love to *Mystery Train* 265

The Naked Kiss to *The Nutty Professor* 301

Office Space to *The Outlaw* 315

Pandora's Box to *The Puppetoon Movie* 323

Quadrophenia to *The Queen of Space* 343

Re-Animator to *Rushmore* 347

Saw to *Switchblade Sisters* 367

Tab Hunter Confidential to *Two-Lane Blacktop* ...397

Under the Skin to *The Usual Suspects* 427

Valerie a Tyden Divu to *Videodrome* 429

Walkabout to *Written On the Wind* 433

Yi Yi 457

Zero Woman to *Zombieland* 459

About the Author 463

Once Upon a Time At the Movies...
The Myth and Meaning of Cult Cinema

AUTUMN, 1961: The first month of college at a small state university in upstate New York. At three in the morning, several freshmen remain wide awake in their dorm room, discussing guy stuff: sports, music, and most of all movies. Current favorites include *Spartacus*, which recently played at the local bijou. Vividly, they recall the gladiatorial bout between Kirk Douglas and Woody Strode. The former a mainstream

FROM THE RIDICULOUS TO THE SUBLIME: Cult films range from 'so bad they're great' items like *Showgirls* with Elizabeth Berkeley to the intellectual/existential box-office flop *Fight Club* starring Brad Pitt.

movie star whom they, like most everyone else in the world, adore. The latter? lesser known to the mainstream. All the same, special to those who seek out his performances, if often in supporting roles. And derive additional fun from discussing these with like-minded friends.

Strode *afficionados*. And, though they likely have not heard this term yet, a *cognoscenti* of Woody devotees. An unofficial 'following' for a singular and special performer.

In time, the discussion turns to films that stand-out amid memories of the mid-1950s. When, as boys, they grew up in towns far from one another. While listening to the same music (early rock 'n' roll), playing the same sports, and also watching that single set of Hollywood movies which then passed through their individual corners of the country. From the weekly succession of science-fiction and fantasy flicks they eagerly flocked to—*War of the Worlds, The Thing (From Another World), It Came from Outer Space,* etc.—one in particular comes to mind. A creepy little chiller that played matinees only, likely paired with an Abbot and Costello comedy or some Audie Murphy oater. About a kid (not unlike one of those in the audience of any seedy local Rialto) who goes to sleep one night and dreams that the Martians have invaded. In vivid, glossy, headache-inducing colors, the film chronicles his nightmarish fantasy about adults (parents included) who turn into zombies, much as they would several years later in another memorable item, *Invasion of the Body Snatchers*. A huge whirlpool of dirt out back near the winding road sweeps the unwary down into the bowels of the earth. Once there, sucking them into a metallic mother ship, commanded by a silent head held steady in what appears to be an upside-down fishbowl. At least, when the movie is viewed in retrospect. Back then, though, children in the audience bought it, believing that what happened to little Jimmy Hunt might someday overtake them.

While watching, these ordinary, everyday guys could not guess that a couple of geniuses were, far removed from them and one another, also experiencing the phantasmagoria. And did so, to borrow from A.A. Milne, while we were very young. Alive to The Movies, as to life itself, as we are at no other point in our existences. For in due time, Steven Spielberg would recreate that remote pathway with its oddly shaped fence in *Close Encounters of the Third Kind* (1977). George Lucas recalled that strange face when he invented 'Yoda' for his second *Star Wars* (1980) venture. Then, those regular onetime college kids, now early-middle-aged and long since out of touch with one another, each sensed a wave

AUTHENTIC CULT STARS: Woody Strode developed a devoted following of action fans who appreciated his remarkable presence in such films as *Sergeant Rutledge* and *Spartacus* (both 1960) and, seen here, Richard Brooks' The *Professionals* (1966); while mature Eisenhower-era adults preferred Audrey Hepburn, Grace Kelly, or Marilyn Monroe, the first wave of American teen-agers adored declasse low-budgeters featuring Mamie Van Doren.

of nostalgia for half-forgotten pop-culture totems. Experiencing them again a quarter of a century later, in redux form. Sitting beside kids of their own. Enjoying the movie almost as much as they enjoyed watching their young children's enjoyment. On some level sensing that, as the romantic poet William Wordsworth noted about nostalgia in 1804:

> Though nothing can bring back the hour
> Of splendour in the grass, of glory in the flower;
> We will grieve not, rather find
> Strength in what remains behind;
> In the primal sympathy
> Which having been must ever be...
> In years that bring the philosophic mind.

Even as what were flicks created for kids and teenagers, and those rare, unique adults of marginal or 'fringe' tastes, overtook the American mainstream. Spielberg, Lucas, and others bringing such half-recalled joys to the public at large. And, in due time, Quentin Tarantino

(1963–) doing so with the darker, more threatening realms of film noir, Asian martial arts action and other elements of what may be called Transgressive Cinema.

But back once more to that small college. Or any of a hundred similar schools where much the same conversation also occurred. For as James Barrie informed us as the beginning of 'Peter and Wendy' (1911), *all this has happened before, and all this will happen again…*

"Y'know, there was a movie I saw once with Robert Mitchum. He played a crazy preacher who has the letters L-O-V-E tattooed on the fingers of his right hand… and H-A-T-E on the left. Jesus, did *that* creep me out!"

"I remember it!" a roommate chimes in. "Mitchum would hand-wrestle himself as he spoke in public to the poor people in the Deep South, terrifying them with his sermons."

"What I recall is Shelley Winters, after Mitchum murders her. In that old car, deep under the water… her long hair reaching up toward the surface along with the weeds."

"I'd give anything if only I could think of the title," the first fellow sighs.

"Well, you know: There's a guy rooming just across the way who never stops talking about movies. He loves them."

"We *all* do."

"Not like this guy. He lives and *breathes* 'em. *He*'d know."

"Well? Let's head over and ask him."

So the three step out of their room, quietly crossing the hall, rapping on an adjacent door. No answer. They knock again, a little louder. Then, the sound of someone stirring inside.

"Who is it?" the fellow coughs. "What do you want?"

Cracking the unlocked door open, one roommate sticks his head in, whispering: "Hey, man. Sorry to wake you. But we're going nuts, trying to come up with the name of a movie."

"Okay… "

The noir-ish sequence is repeated. Before the speaker can finish, the guy inside responds: "*The Night of the Hunter.*"

"Right, right! Thanks."

"Oh, and by the way…" Another roommate hovering near asks about that odd fantasy film discussed earlier.

"*Invaders from Mars.*"

"Yes!"

They cross back to their room, a small community united by stirred memories, common to each, now shared.

One might call them a cult.

And when, a month later, *Night of the Hunter* happens to show up on local late-late night TV, all four gather around a small black and white set in the dorm basement to share it.

To their surprise, others in residence show up. Not everyone in residence. Just a handful, who were biding their time to again experience the eerie delights offered by *The Night*...

Students from other dorms arrive. Most of the guys back in their own rec rooms chose to watch some variety TV show. Though perhaps the 'normals' would have been willing to turn the dial if the late-night movie had been *From Here to Eternity*, a beloved memory movie to every member of their generation. The same with High *Noon, The Seven Year Itch*, and *East of Eden, Singin' in the Rain*...

Virtually every student on campus (and elsewhere) could recall those. And would happily watch them again.

This was something else entirely. But... *what*?

Once upon a time, all movies were cult films. During the later years of the nineteenth century, experimental artists like Brit-born Californian Eadweard Muybridge (1830–1904) created the illusion of movement by juxtaposing a succession of images of racehorses. These were projected onto a makeshift screen in a beam of light, the apparatus modelled on Magic Lanterns which had relied on sketches before the advent of photography. Small groups gathered together to see the results in screening rooms.

Most people passing on the street outside could have cared less. That would soon change.

Shortly, films produced by Thomas Edison in New Jersey and New York, the street realism featurettes of the Lumiere Brothers and experimental sci-fi fantasies of George Melies in Paris, and dramatized documentaries of London's William Friese-Greene would offer visual diversions to intrigued consumers of early cinema. At Big City Nickelodeons and sleazy Peep Shows, garish beach-side boardwalks and the midways of rural carnivals, respectable people dared one another to 'gaze' at some fascinating if forbidden image, glimpsed in the eerie daylight darkness of a canvas tent or a side-street venue.

In retrospect, the flickering movement of a body-builder flexing his muscles, a leggy lady showing off her stuff with gams displayed in

NICKELODEON DAYS: In the beginning, all vulgar 'flickers' were considered cult items, including *The Kiss* and *What Happened on Twenty-third St,, New York*.

seamed stockings, a couple kissing in close-up or an English queen losing her head to the axe may strike us as nothing more than quaint and curious. That was not the case way back when. These moments to remember were as shocking in their time as Linda Lovelace or Marilyn Chambers performing fellatio in 1970s X-rated fare at post sexual revolution grindhouses.

No semblance of cinema in the late Victorian Era more effectively captures the allure of motion-pictures in their earliest form than the all-important mid-point sequence of Francis Ford Coppola's *Bram Stoker's Dracula* (1992). A scene written not by the long-deceased author but the leading L.A. auteur as his unique contribution to the vampire legacy. At the century's cusp, Vlad Tsepish (Gary Oldman) arrives in London. His mission: Track down and seduce Mina Murray (Winona Rider), a decent young lady of the solid white-collar-working/aspiring middle-classes. The Count discovers her not in one of London's more respectful neighborhoods, which she hails from, rather in Piccadilly Circus. Where nice people go to mingle with the miscreants when in the mood to toy with something… naughty.

Mina Murray is a momentary transgressor, willingly wandering away from the solid (or seemingly so) civilization around them. She slips into a downscale theatre. There, silhouettes of devil-men and wicked women dance about on a screen… much to the delight of she and others who dare partake, hoping against hope fiancées and friends will not learn of this dalliance.

Originally, movies were considered by the self-appointed arbiters of respectability to be the devil's work. And so the situation remained until 1915 when the release of D.W. Griffith's *The Birth of a Nation* and other feature films played to mass audiences, conveying conventional values of those times. Thus allowing the commercial movie to compete with live theatre as suitable entertainment. During the 1920s, families queued up outside a motion picture palace, these lavishly constructed theatres asserting by their elegance that the movies were now acceptable escapism. Like attending a baseball game or riding bicycles through a park where a band concert commenced. And if some Hollywood films did on occasion offend, this would become shortly apparently be eliminated once the Breen/Hays Office appeared early in the 1930s to scrupulously censor films, at least those submitted for the all-important official endorsement.

That, however, was not true of all movies. Others were produced for private screenings in out of the way venues. Grindhouses, folks called them. Low-level dives, seedy in appearance, catering to divergent moviegoers eager to catch films that had not received the Motion Picture Code's Approval Rating. And perhaps had not even been submitted, then turned down. In some cases, such Forbidden Cinema played unannounced (to the public) at midnight showings at those same theatres that presented middlebrow entertainment during daylight hours. If some members of that mainstream secretly gathered to share those officially restricted sights (and after 1927) sounds.

Nudity. Violence. Whatever you had been told that you could not watch, as hungrily longed for as Eden's forbidden fruit.

AUTUMN, 1966: The onetime 17-year-old movie lover is now a teaching assistant at a major university. He stands in front of a class of some 25 freshman, leading a discussion of Jonathan Swift's *Gulliver's Travels* (1925). Focusing on the difficult Fourth Book so often ignored by polite society, with monstrous half-human (at best) things: ill-formed Houyhnhnms and Yahoos, monstrosities with immense appetites that can never be sated.

The 22-year-old instructor notices that, in the room's back row of seats, one student uncontrollably smirks. Though intuiting the answer to his unspoken question, the instructor asks what the freshman found so humorous. Initially, the embarrassed student declines. Then, after some genial encouragement, he answers.

"What you were saying reminded me of—"

"—*The Little Shop of Horrors*?"

"Yeah!"

At that point, a third of those present laugh out loud, in on 'the joke.' The edgier students; the ones for whom 'watching movies' is not (as with most underclassmen) limited to catching *Dr. Zhivago, Hawaii*, or *The Singing Nun* at a mainstream theatre. Instead or in addition to such middle of the road fare, they recall that time while still in high school when a Saturday matinee featured Roger Corman's 1961 low-budgeter in which an appealingly unconvincing creature called "Audrey II" commanded its nebishy creator: "Feed me!" Watching it again (and again) at the midnight hour on a frat house TV, calling out those words even as the monster did. For by now they know the film by heart.

Is there a clear, simple, absolute definition of a cult film? Yes and no, depending less on any individual movie than the context in which it is received and experienced. Let's try to make some sense out of this... by considering a feature that might have been included here... indeed, a dozen or so years ago, would *necessarily* have been... but is not now.

A Christmas Story (1983): The delightfully nostalgic low-to-medium budget project which Canada's Bob Clarke shaped from Jean Shepherd's *In God We Trust, All Others Pay Cash* (1966)—a collection of his anecdotal pieces that originally appeared in *Playboy* and other publications. The book itself rated as a cult novel during the following decade, much loved among college students who read it more than once before passing the slim volume on to close friends. That held true too of other novels, notably *Candy* (1958) by Terry Southern, though that like Henry Miller's *Tropic of Cancer* (1934), printed by something called The Underground Press, had to be secretly sold in most cities.

Banned in Boston and other locales.

Which reveals the true, wide spectrum of cult culture. The form (if it is a form) ranges from the G-rated memoirs of a boy growing up in 1940s middle America to the under the counter misadventures of a transgressing underage Lolita. From the wild and whacky to the sweet and sentimental. Significantly, cult consciousness came roaring out of the closet in the 1960s.

To understand how drastically our social revolution (the Sexual one included but not the whole of it) of the Sixties in fact was, do note that the 1968 film version of *Candy* was not some B movie project like its predecessor, *Sex Kittens Go to College* (1960). What a difference a decade makes! In 1968, the blockbuster Hollywood film (a Christmastime release, no less) was headlined by superstars Marlon Brando and Richard Burton. Despite that, the film failed at the box-office less owing to its transgressive elements (Future Shock had dimmed the once potent controversy over the past five years), or even that the public had already become jaded (this though was in fact the case)... rather as it happened to be awful.

And, in time, became something of a cult film. Few things qualify a big movie for cultdom as much as commercial failure. Also, some viewers believed *Candy* to be so bad it was good... in a reversal of the earlier meanings of those terms. Lest we forget, at mid-decade radical cultural critic Susan Sontag had created the term 'camp' in intellectual circles. Most members of the public at large didn't know that term but had already experienced the concept. ABC debuted *Batman* not as a matinee kiddie show (like *Superman* in the 1950s, when the as yet

ONCE, THEY WERE CULT FILMS: Cult status is not necessarily a permanent position in popular culture: *The Wizard of Oz* (1939) and *A Christmas Story* have been elevated to the status of American classics.

untitled notion of camp existed in an unconscious state) but in prime time. With everything purposefully played way over the top, the creators winking at a knowing audience. Even as comic books in general, once thought to be the lowest level of popular culture, came into their own as upscale graphic novels.

Yesterday's lowbrow is today's highbrow and tomorrow's middlebrow. For proof, just consider Shakespeare's plays.

Or opera.

Cultish cinema, then, may be of a daring order (likely when most mainstream fare is middle of the road); or lull us into a warm mood (likely when sex and violence have become The New Normal). So here is one possible definition of a cult film: It is abnormal in one way or another for the time period during which it was released. It pleases those who embrace the unexpected.

When *A Christmas Story* opened in early December 1983, just before the holiday blockbusters appeared, then-popular critics Roger Ebert and Gene Siskel agreed on their TV show "*everyone* will go see this film or *no one* will." Here was a little movie that would swiftly earn a cult following and, in time, rightful status as a true American classic. Broadcast all day long on various channels Christmas day, virtually everyone watching.

At which point *A Christmas Story* ceased to be a cult film, now an acknowledged American classic.

CHRISTMAS EVE (ACTUALLY, EARLY IN THE WEE HOURS OF THE MORNING ON CHRISTMAS DAY, 1971: That aforementioned college student/movie devotee is now a college professor. Hired as an English teacher, he had been asked to create the school's first film studies course. Entertainment of the past now accepted as what Rudolf Arnheim once dared to hail as 'an original art form.' Recently, international favorites like *Blow-up* (1967) paved the way for a new sort of mainstream movie that combined the joys of Hitchcock's suspense-thrillers with Existential themes so prevalent in European cinema. At this moment, the distinction between Hollywood product and international cinema waned. And, during the 1970s, ceased to be.

But back to that late December night, after the presents had been opened, the stockings stuffed, the family fed. And, finally, everyone went to bed. Except that rare person who sits up until the late late movie

FROM THE ARTHOUSE TO THE GRINDHOUSE: During the 20th century, cult films popped up in classy theatres such as Long Island's most revered in the elegant Hamptons or the low-rent 42nd St. venues that featured oddball items for 'discriminating' viewers.

is over and the local station signs off. (This a decade before 24/7 became the rule for TV). An old black and white feature would be run to fill the allotted time slot. From one of the great Hollywood moviemakers, Frank Capra, no less. The film buff had seen many of that master's most famous films over the years: *It Happened One Night*, *Mr. Deeds Goes to Town*, *Mr. Smith Goes to Washington*, and *Meet John Doe* acknowledged classics.

And, indeed, had recently taught some of them to his first wave of Cinema Studies students. Here, though, was a lesser known item: *It's a Wonderful Life* (1946).

Something special then happened, for that lone viewer in a darkened house and others of his ilk everywhere in America. A magical one-of-a-kind movie—part realistic drama, part comedy of the screwball variety, but metaphysical fable—unwound its unique tale of a typical/ordinary small-town fellow (James Stewart) whose once vivid ambitions have (as is so often the case) turned to dust. The Great American Dream of success by luck and pluck, Horatio Alger fashion, has somehow eluded him. And, on a depressing Christmas Eve, he considers taking his own life. Until an odd little angel named Clarence arrives to save the day, transforming this into a Disney fable for grown-ups.

A million or more other nighthawks similarly observed in fascination. Film fanatics like to talk with their fellows; serious journals about cinema all at once replaced the old mainstream movie star magazines. And, shortly, the forgotten *It's a Wonderful Life* spontaneously became a cult classic owing to public domain status. The distributors hadn't considered it important enough to renew the copyright, so anyone who came across a copy could show it. TV stations did precisely that.

The cult spread… and spread… until that term no longer applied. Once NBC began broadcasting the Capra piece (by this time better known, ironically, than those aforementioned agreed upon classics), the piece rates as mainstream.

Sometimes, cultdom lasts forever. But not always. Which adds to the difficulty of applying the term. Explaining why *It's a Wonderful Life*, like *A Christmas Story*, is not included in this volume. Or, for that matter, the once cultish *The Wizard of Oz* (1939). Here is a collection of movies that continue to maintain cult (a relatively small following) status at this juncture in time. If this book had been written five years ago or hence, the selection might be markedly different.

THE FIFTIES FOREVER! No single actor more perfectly captured the tone of the supposed 'happy days' than James Dean, seen here in *Rebel Without a Cause*; though a major movie star, Robert Mitchum dared take on the role of a crazed serial killer (not many A listers would have even considered to do so) in *The Night of the Hunter*.

Things change. Here are 500* of those films which, as we enter the third decade of the 21st century, once played either as matinee fare or midnight movies. Drastically different from one another, but with this in common: once experienced, never forgotten.

Cult films!

GENIUS AT WORK I: The films that were produced, written, and directed by (as well as starring) Orson Welles (1915–1985) lacked appeal for the mass audience but locked in his reputation as the first (and greatest) cult filmmaker of all time.

WHEN THE MORONS MET THE MONSTERS: The team of Bud Abbott and Lou Costello still maintain a huge cult following, though their most loved midnight movie or weekend matinee flick also featured Universal's standout creatures 'The Frankenstein Monster' (Glenn Strange), the Wolfman (Lon Chaney Jr.), and Dracula (Bela Lugosi).

ABBOTT AND COSTELLO MEET FRANKENSTEIN (1948)

Cult-Comedy Rating: *****

Lugosi Cult Rating: *****

Bud and Lou Cult Rating: *****

Charles Barton, dir.; Robert Lees, Frederic I. Rinaldo, John Grant, scr.; Robert Arthur, pro.; 1.37:1; B&W; 83 min.; Universal International.

With the 1950s Big Bug/UFO quickies looming on the horizon, U.I. executives decided to call it quits with the monster movies they had been churning out since 1931. Taking a chance on one final last go-around, Dracula (Bela Lugosi, 1882–1956), Frankenstein's monster (Glenn Strange, 1890—1973), and The Wolf Man (Lon Chaney Jr., 1906–1973) 'met' the comedy duo (Bud, 1895–1974); Lou (1906–1959) that dominated during the Forties but likewise was running out of steam. Despite an ultra-low budget (for fear of box-office failure), *A.A.C.M.F.* reaped bountiful box-office rewards with the finest horror comedy until Mel Brooks *Young Frankenstein* (1974). Notably, for the first time in an American film, the vampire's kiss is played for dark eroticism. When Lugosi bites into the neck of Lenore Aubert, her obsessed eyes suggest an on-screen orgasm. Notable too: Quentin Tarantino (1963–) cites this as the film that convinced him horror and comedy could be mixed.

ABENTEURER DES PRINZEN ACHMED, DIE (1926)

Animation cultists: *****

Lotte Reiniger, dir.; Reiniger, Carl Koch, scr.; Reiniger, Koch, prod.; 35 mm; B&W/C; 81 min.; Comenius-Film GmbH.

During the 1930s, Max and Dave Fleischer had engaged in a race with Walt Disney to see who would be first to release a full-length animated film in color, *Gulliver's Travels* (1938/39) or *Snow White and the Seven Dwarfs* (1937/38). But a husband and wife team of European artists earlier accomplished that with this marvel, released in the U.S. as *The Adventures of Prince Achmed.* Many beloved Arabian Nights tales are collapsed into one adventure as the hero flies on a winged horse to win the hand of a princess (with the aid of Aladdin) while opposing a witch and a magician. The genius is in conceptualist L.R.'s (1899–1981) approach: Silhouette Animation, which can be dated back to the silent era. Reininger and collaborator C.K. carefully cut caricatures of varied figures from cardboard, then—in between shooting any single image at 1/24 f.p.s.—moved these ever so slightly against glossily tinted backdrops painted on illuminated glass planes. Many fans prefer the simple beauty achieved here to the more elaborate "full animation" of W.D.

ABOUT SCHMIDT (2002)

Edgy cult comedy Rating: *****

Alexander Payne, dir.; Payne, Jim Taylor, scr.; Michael Besman, Harry Gittes, pro.; 1.85:1; C; 125 min.; New Line.

Retirement! What does a Norman Normal kind of guy do when he has no reason to get up in the morning? For 'Schmidt' (Jack Nicholson, 1937–), your typical Rush Limbaugh listener in Omaha, there is an option: Drive his RV to Denver and attend the upcoming marriage of his estranged daughter (Hope Davis). Along the way, Schmidt encounters a diversity of people and, without realizing, becomes broader and deeper as a person. A.P. (1961–) destroys any still-existing boundaries between comedy and drama to create a remarkable sense of life itself, crystalized in the most unpretentious sort of cinematic art. If the journey recalls that of Art Carney in *Harry and Tonto* (1974), J.N.'s performance is equalled only by Bill Murray in *Lost in Translation* as the greatest character study in an American film of the 21st century so far. Happily, the ending retains the low-key approach so essential to this film's success. From a novel by Louis Begley, combined with A.P.'s own concepts. Co-producer H.G. (1936–2017) had earlier provided inspiration for the gumshoe portrayed by J.N. in *Chinatown* (1974).

ABRES LOS OBOS (1997)

Arthouse Cult Rating: *****

Alejandro Amenabar, dir.; Amenabar, Mateo Gil, scr.; Fernando Bovaira, Jose Luis Cuerda, pros.; 1.85:1; C; 117 min.; Canal + Espana.

In Madrid, a self-centered playboy (Eduardo Noriega) meets a woman (Penelope Cruz) he knows at first sight will be 'the one.' Yet he allows a mysterious man-eater (Najwa Nimri) to coax him into her car. This devil-in-the-flesh crashes through a barrier to commit suicide; he survives, disfigured. But all that may be a dream. A self-proclaimed 'monster,' he seeks out plastic surgeons; this may be an extension of the previous dream, *if* that crash ever happened—which is impossible to know. That's the beginning of an endless succession of twists and turns. Influences on Amenabar (1972–) include Shakespeare and his life is but a dream within a dream motif; Sigmund Freud's theories on the relationship of dreams to the psyche; Rod Serling's *Twilight Zone*; Cocteau's *Orpheus*, featuring a femme fatale who incarnates the poet's desire for the fall; Hitchcock's *Vertigo*, as to the fear of heights; *Seconds*, which dramatized every person's desire to go back and do it all over again; and the complete works of Philip K. Dick (1928–1982). *A.L.O.'s* auteur absorbed those elements without imitating anyone. Happily, his film stands as an absolute original.

ADAPTATION (2002)

Cult classic Rating: *****

Spike Jonze cult Rating: *****

Spike Jonze, dir.; Charlie Kaufman, scr. Kaufman, Jonathan Demme, Edward Saxon, Vincent Landay, prod.; 1.85:1; C; 114 min.; Propaganda Films/Columbia.

Orchids and The Meaning of Life, if indeed life does have a meaning. That's one theme in *A.*, which offers a meditation on the title: Why adapt a work that is perfect as is into another medium as this can only corrupt the beauty of the original? Nicolas Cage (1964–) plays writer Charlie Kaufman (1958–) and his twin (C.K. does not have a sibling, this a projection of the author's alter-ego) assigned to turn "The Orchid Thief" by Susan Orlean (1955–) into a script. Problem is, everything that was best about the book gets lost in transition. The beleaguered screenwriter tries to fictionalize the title character, John Laroche (1962–), played by Chris Cooper (1951–) Should a crowd-pleasing romance be created between a denizen of the Everglades and the female lead (Meryl Streep, (1949–)?

A movie about movies and, more significantly, life itself. And, yes, life's *meaning*! Cult worthy persons who appear in small but memorable cameo roles include Catherine Keener, John Cusack, John Malkovich, and Maggie Gyllenhaal.

AGUIRRE, DER ZORN GOTTES, aka *AGUIRRE, THE WRATH OF GOD* (1972)

Arthouse Rating: *****

Werner Herzog Cult Rating: *****

Klaus Kinski Cult Rating: *****

Werner Herzog, dir.; Herzog, scr.; Herzog, Hans Pescher, pros.; 1.37:1; C; 95 min.; Heissicher Rundfunk.

 Where does genius end and insanity begin? That difficult question underlines the great films of W. H. (1942–). The Bavarian-born *wunderkind* knocked out the screenplay in less than three days while travelling by bus with a soccer team, then shot his epic on a tight budget with a skeleton crew, as obsessed with completing this as his anti-hero is with his own impossible dream. Don Lope de Aguirre (1510–1561) numbered among the Spanish conquistadors dispatched by Pizarro to explore the Andes, navigating the Amazon in search of fabled El Dorado. In this film as in life, Aguirre is secretly intent on reigning as lord and master of a lost world by creating an empire composed of surviving Incans. The inspired/mad actor Klaus Kinski (1926- 1991) in his first collaborative effort with W.H., exudes the charisma of a born leader able to rally others to follow him on what may be a one-way journey. Mostly, this was organically filmed; W.H. tossed away pages of the script, allowing his actors to improvise their scenes in spectacular settings. A meditation on the ways in which a less than benign Quixote-like character can impose his harsh inner vision on the world around him, at least briefly.

L AMOUR FOU: 'Crazy love' remains one of the great themes of the dark cult films, including this 'forbidden' Asian item about a man and a woman planning for his self-willed strangulation even as he brings her to orgasm.

AI NO KORIDA, aka IN THE REALM OF THE SENSES (1978)

Erotic film fan Rating: *

Nagisa Oshima cult Rating: *****

Nagasi Oshima, dir.; Oshima, Koji Wakamatsu, scr.; Anatole Dauman, pro.; 1.50:1; C; 109 min. (uncut); Argos Film.

  Among the 50 films written and directed by Japan's Oshima (1932–2013), *A.N.K.* ranks as the best known, universally praised and damned. Here is a fact-based story about a 1936 sexual scandal that rocked the island nation where the focal female (Sada Abe, 1905–1971) remains a mythic figure. Played by Eiko Matsuda (1952–2011), S.A. was a prostitute turned hotel maid. Her 'master' (Tatsaya Fuji) raped her repeatedly, she a willing participant. The balance of power shifted: Sada the dominatrix, he ever more eager for her to devour him. This concluded with Sada strangling her willing victim to death at his moment of orgasm, then castrating the corpse. For Asian feminists, should Abe be considered a heroine for her conquest or a retro-woman owing to her early submission? The most graphic 'serious'/ mainstream art film made until then. But should it be damned as porn when at no point is there a hint of eroticism? Long banned in such diverse countries as Germany, Israel, the U.S.… and even its native Japan!

AKIRA (1988)

Animee/Manga Cult Rating: *****

Katsuhiro Otomo Rating: *****

Katsuhiro Otomo, dir.; Otomo, Izo Kashimoto, scr.; Shunzo Kato, ryonel Suzuki, pros.; 1.85:1; C; 124 min.; TMS Ent.

  Gradually, 'Tetsuo' grasps that he is not merely one more of the lost, lonely individuals wandering around Neo-Tokyo but the Chosen One, picked to oppose the title organization. As a 'Horatio' to Tetsuo's 'Hamlet' we meet 'Kaneda,' an oblivious biker drawn into a Marxist dialectic

EXPERIMENTS IN ANIMATION: Some of the greatest cult cartoons were created in far flung countries: *Akira* (Japan) and *Allegro Non Tropo* (Italy) remain two of the finest.

of revolution/oppression. 'Bullet-time' was the technical/aesthetic breakthrough used to heighten the action for thrill-seeking modern audiences. In the tradition of Sam Peckinpah, many bloodbaths balance with intellectual musings on the death of individuality in modern life. Maximum detailed imagery is undercut cut by a minimalist use of music. One of those rare occasions when the avatar of the original Manga, Otomo (1954–), was allowed full creative control over the corresponding Anime. The film only gradually made its way to international markets via bootleg VHS copies and word of mouth among aficionados of dystopian fiction. O. has said that his inspirations were *Rebel Without a Cause, Bonnie and Clyde,* and *2001: A Space Odyssey.* Likewise, the Wachowski Bros. cited *A.* as an inspiration for *The Matrix.*

ALLEGRO NON TROPO (1976/1977)

Cult Animation Rating: *****

Bruno Bozzetto, dir.; Bozzetto, Maurizio Nichetti, Guido Manuli, scr.; Bozzetto, pro.; 1.66:1; CB&W/C; 85 min.; Roxy International/Speciality Films.

Walt Disney's *Fantasia* (1941) rates as the greatest feature-length cartoon ever made. *A.N.T.,* the cinematic equivalent of a jazz 'riff' on that masterwork, has become a classic among animation buffs. In B.B.'s (1938–) cult classic an oblivious filmmaker (Maurizio Michell) in rural Italy explains his Dream Movie: Classical music in relationship to contemporary images. Gulping hard, friends explain: a famous American accomplished that 35 years ago. Not to be dissuaded, this 'artist of the beautiful' sets to work, kidnapping an animator when no one agrees to take the job and assembling an orchestra composed of geriatrics. Ward Kimball (1914–2002), one of Disney's greatest team members, claimed that other than their own projects, this was his best loved movie. Most memorable among the sequences: Maurice Ravel's "Bolero" comes to life with such sound and fury, every second of onscreen animation vividly corresponding to each note, that this now rates as the milestone moment against which all other such animated work must be measured.

THE FIRST 'POST GROUPIE': Kate Hudson (previously known as the daughter of Star Goldie Hawn) shot to superstardom thanks to her complex role as a fact-based character.

ALMOST FAMOUS (2000)

Rock 'n' Roll Movies Cult Rating: **** ½

Late 1970s/Early 1980s Cultist Rating: **** ½

Cameron Crowe, dir.; Crowe, scr.; Crowe, Ian Bryce, pros.; 1.85:1 C; 122 min. (theatrical release), 152 min. (extended cut), 162 min. (director's cut); Columbia/DreamWorks.

'Stillwater' (*not* a depiction of the brief-lived rock group) sets out on a make-it-or-break-it tour; tagging along is a 15-year old journalist (Patrick Fugit), based on filmmaker Crowe (1957–). In addition to depicting ups and downs on the road, celebrating each other in public yet turning nasty when alone, *A.F.* has much to say about the press: Will the idealistic reporter maintain his integrity and tell the truth or be sucked in by all the neon glitz? Charismatic performer 'Russ Hammond' (Billy Crudup, 1968–) offers a crazy combination of Glenn Fry of *the Eagles*, Robert Plant of *Led Zeppelin*, Greg of *The Allman Bros. Band*, and Eddie Vedder of *Pearl Jam*. His guitar stylings resemble those of Peter Frampton, who taught Crudup to play. Memorable roles include Frances McDormand (1957–) as the lead's dominating mother; future *New Girl* star Zooey Deschanel (1980–) as his stressed-out sister, the late-great Philip Seymour Hoffman (1960–2014) as real-life music critic Lester Bangs, and a transcendent Kate Hudson (1970–) as 'Penny Lane,' a seemingly carefree, inwardly troubled "post-groupie." However much beloved by rock movie cultists, the film was on its initial run a box-office disaster.

AMELIE, aka *LE FABULOUS DESTIN D'AMELIE POULAIN* (2009)

French Feel-Good Film Rating: *****

Jean-Pierre Jeunet, dir.; Jeunet, Guillaume & Jean Pirre Laurant, scr.; Claudie Ossard, pro.; 2.39:1; C/B&W; 122 min.; Union Generale Cinematographique.

Like *Being There* (1979), this tale (set in Paris) concerns a child raised in isolation who, to compensate, creates her own world of imagination. Once on her own in actuality, 'Amelie' (Audrey Tatou, 1976–) sees everything through rose (as well as green and yellow) colored (invisible) glasses, setting out on the day after Princess Diana's death (8/31/1997) to help anyone less fortunate and, perhaps, find love along the way. A joyous celebration of life as to theme and aesthetically for cinema as an art form thanks to Jeunet's (1953–) surreal hues added to realistic settings, color-drenched visuals offset by minimalist use of music, stop-motion photography and radical swish-pans by the camera, odd angles and brief cutaways to black and white. These purposefully deconstruct the story, forcing us into an awareness of the joys of 'film as film.' Though written with Emily Watson in mind, it's impossible to picture anyone but Tatou in the role: Pixie-ish, with the slightest hint of Goth owing to her black garb, this undercut by eager eyes as big as those in a Keane painting. *Charmant!*

ANDY WARHOL'S BAD (1977)

Conventional Entertainment Rating: NO STARS

Camp Rating: *****

Warhol completist Rating: ****

Jed Johnson, dir.; Pat Hackett, George Abagnalo, scr.; Andy Warhol, Jeff Tornberg, pros.; 35 mm; C; 105 min.; The Factory.

'Bad' means 'good,' cultural critic Susan Sontag claimed in 1964, if only when presented in a knowing context. A.W. (1928–1987) signed his name on Campbell's soup cans; in so doing he transformed that everyday item from mass produce to campy art. Such an edgy aesthetic permeates *Bad*, calculated to offend middlebrow moviegoers. In a ticky-tacky Long Island suburban house 'Helen,' seemingly normal enough, runs a small beauty salon in her living room. Several clients earn extra money while escaping the oppressing boredom by hiring out as hit women. Hideous looking females slowly stab adorable dogs to death and toss innocent babies from rooftops. If ours is an absurdist age, *why not?* At least in a 'harmless' home movie produced by a distant genius in his Factory for turning out terrible (i.e., great) *objets d'art*. Washed up Hollywood star Carroll Baker (1931–) has the lead. Middle-of-the-road reviewers described *A.W.B.* as: "depraved," "sadistic," "sick," "anarchic," "nihilistic," and "revolutionary." Warhol and his collaborators accepted such attacks as compliments.

APOCALYPSE NOW (1979)

Film Classics Rating: *****

Coppola Cult Rating: ******

Brando Cult Rating: *****

Francis (Ford) Coppola, dir.; Coppola, John Milius, Michael Herr, scr.; Coppola, Eddie Romero, pro.; 2.39:1; C; 147 min., 103 min.; 330 min.; American Zoetrope/UA.

"Making a movie is like owning a piece of real estate," F.F.C. (1939–) told the press on the eve of A.C.'s release. "You can cut it up in many different ways." The various run-times that his Vietnam epic would appear in over the following decades (theatrical release and re-releases, Home Video, Cable, Blue-Ray, DVD, Streaming, etc.) proved his point. F.F.C. had here produced the most demanding work of Hollywood cinema since Eric von Stroheim's *Greed* (1924) and, before that, D.W. Griffith's *Intolerance* (1916). The premise of Joseph Conrad's *Heart of Darkness* (1899) was revamped for then-recent history. A naïve officer (Martin Sheen (1940–) heads off to relocate man of genius 'Kurtz' (Marlon Brando, 1924–2004) who vanished after arriving in the jungle. Sent to civilize the indigenous people, he was instead drawn into their primitive world. In theatres between such then-emergent popcorn pictures as *Star Wars* (1978) and *Raiders* (1981), *A.N.* had a hard row to hoe with its bizarre combination of documentary realism and wild hallucinogenic imagery. A modest success in its time, the film would not go away: Cut after cut would give way to the next, each eagerly awaited not by the mainstream (as with future cuts of 'The Godfather Saga') but a cult of devotees insisting that this, not those commercial hits, is F.F.C.'s masterwork.

ARMY OF DARKNESS (1992)

Cult Dystopian Future Rating: ****

Sam Raimi Cultist Rating: **** 1/2

Bruce Campbell Cult Rating: *****

Sam Raimi, dir.; Raimi, Ivan Raimi, scr.; 1.85:1; C; Rob Tagert, Bruce Campbell, pros.; 96 min. (director's cut), 88 min. (international release print), 81 min. (original U.S. Theatrical); Universal/Renaissance.

Following up on *The Evil Dead*, director Raimi (1959–) and fellow Michigan-born moviemaker Campbell (1958– , co-producer as well as

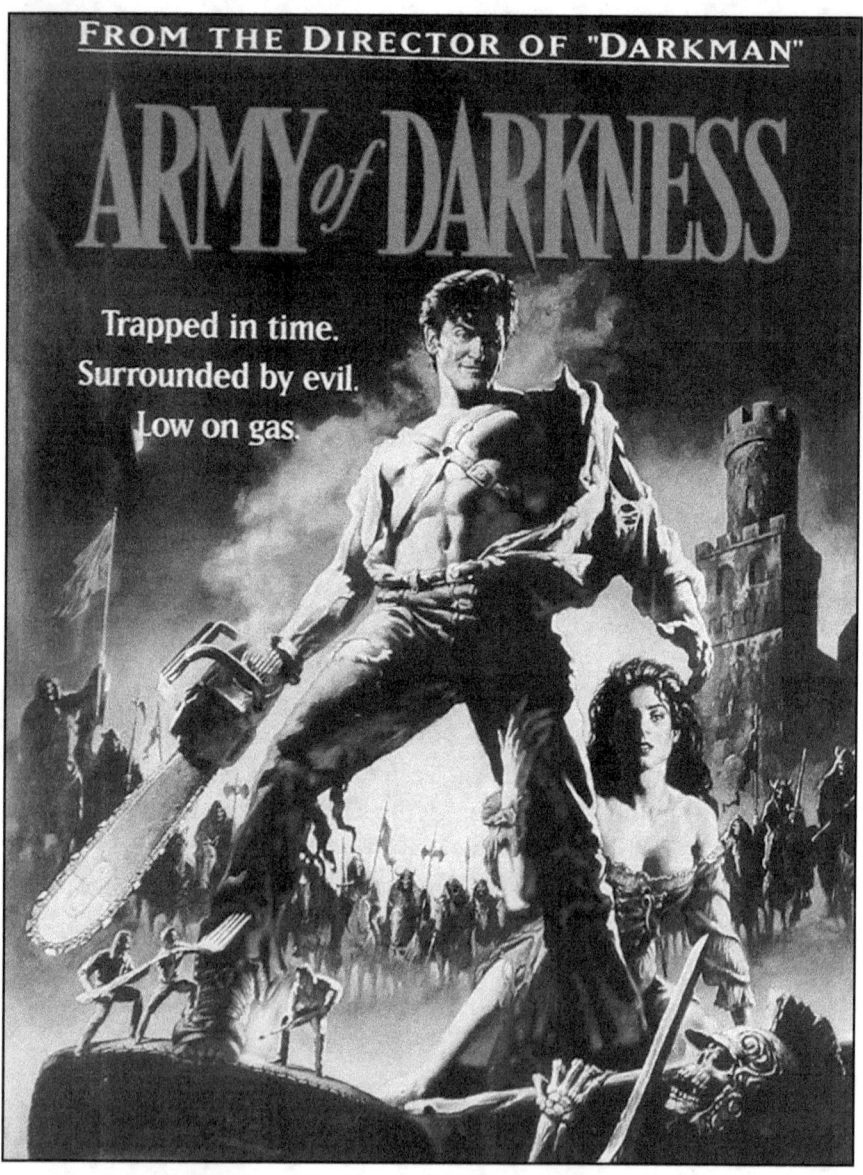

IS THAT CHARLIE SHEEN HAVING A BAD HAIR DAY?: Nope, cult star Bruce Campbell in an early collaboration with cult director Sam Raimi.

star) bring their beloved (by geeky teenage boys) 'Ash' back across the centuries to a fantasy conception of medieval times that has more to do with the so-named dinner-show than anything historical. With a budget big enough to hire lots of extras for battle scenes and a succession of engaging monsters, the collaborators created a high-level junk movie, played tongue-in-cheek. The visual scheme recalls those garish aesthetics of Dark Horse comics. Raimi lovingly spoofs films that influenced him while young, ranging from *The Day the Earth Stood Still* (Robert Wise, 1951), with its great catchphrase "Klaatu barada nikto"; Ray Harryhausen's army of skeletal warriors in *Jason and the Argonauts* (1963); and the title piece of equipment in Tobe Hopper's *The Texas Chainsaw Massacre*. Raimi later cast B.C. as 'Autolycus' in *Hercules: The Legendary Journeys* and *Xena: Warrior Princess*. Embeth Davidtz (1965–) is the damsel in distress, Bridget Fonda (1964–) Ash's girl in the modern story. An appealingly self-conscious tribute to the joys of mindless action movies

ASSAULT ON PRECINCT 13 (1976)

Urban-Action Rating: *****

John Carpenter Cultist Rating: *****

John Carpenter, dir.; Carpenter, scr.; J. Stein Kaplan, pro.; 2.35:1; C; 91 min.; CKK/Astral Films.

Lauded for horror and science-fiction, Carpenter (1948–) has always insisted that he really wanted to make Westerns. His most loved: *Rio Bravo* (1959), Howard Hawks' tale of a marshal (John Wayne, 1907–1979) and his companions besieged in a jail by outlaws. Hoping to mount an unofficial remake, Carpenter's miniscule budget did not allow for period trappings so he shot *A.O.P.13* on contemporary settings. An old police precinct is about to be closed on New Year's Eve. Phones have been shut off as officers make ready to escort the last prisoners to another location. Outside, a gang member is killed; his cohorts enact revenge on those within. Additional Western element: Carpenter directed 'star' Darwin Jonson to mimic Charles Bronson (1921–2003) in *Once Upon a Time in the West*. The gang members are modelled on zombies in *Night of the Living Dead*. Here is quality on a shoestring. Suspense and characterizations are superb; violence, in the tradition of Hitchcock's *Psycho*, more suggested than shown. Carpenter also supplied the sync score, influenced *Dirty Harry* (1971). He edited, under an assumed name: Wayne's *John T. Chance.*

ATOMIC CAFÉ (1982)

Socially Relevant Rating: **** ½

Kevin & Pierre Rafferty, Jayne Loader, dir.; scr.; pro.; 1.33:1; C/B&W; 86 min.; The Archives Project.

The worst way in which a documentary filmmaker can communicate central ideas for his/her film is to speak them—loud, clear, simple, and obviously—via a narrator on the soundtrack. Sadly this approach is most often employed, as it is the easiest way to make a point. But if people wanted didacticism, they'd head for a church, a school, or a political rally. Contrarily, the best: Soviet montage, allowing bits and pieces of imagery to appear onscreen unexplained, yet driving home your ideology by the way in which each clip relates to the one that precedes and follows it. Which explains why this cinematic collage may be the finest documentary ever, as well as the beloved cult film for anti-nuke activists for nearly 40 years. Historical footage of The Bomb's development shares time with hysterical in more ways than one) government propaganda movies that were, as Stanley Kubrick would wisely/comically state in 1965, made to help our citizenry "stop worrying and *love* the bomb." The 1952 nine-minute short "Duck and Cover," appears here; this was endlessly shown to schoolchildren nationwide in hopes of convincing Cold War kids that if a nuclear weapon were to explode nearby, all they had to do was hop under their desks while holding a piece of paper over their heads. What was once taken seriously is here, owing to genius-level juxtaposition, rendered absurdist: Make no mistake about it, this is a comedy!

B

PERFECT PARTNERS: The whole world loved Mr. Laurel and Mr. Hardy and their Yin/Yang relationship; *Big Business* (1929) and *The Music Box* (1932) rate as their greatest shorts, while *Babes in Toyland* is the feature length film most often revived.

BABES IN TOYLAND, aka *MARCH OF THE WOODEN SOLDIERS* (1934)

Laurel and Hardy Cult Rating: *****

Christmastime Cult Movie Rating: *****

Gus Meins, Charlie Rogers, dirs.; Frank Butler, Nick Grinde, scr.; Hal Roach, pro.; 1.37:1; B&W; 73 min. (theatrical cut); 77 min. (director's cut); MGM.

The UK's diminutive Stan Laurel (1890–1965) and the U.S.'s pleasingly plump Oliver Hardy (1892–1957) loved doing silent short-subjects, their mime-like artistry front-and-center. During the early sound era, they were reduced to a speciality act in large-scale musical comedies. The one among them that clicks is this supposedly family-friendly film that openly embraces grotesquerie. In Storyland, when sweet 'Bo-peep' (Charlotte Henry, 1914–1980, a year earlier the lead in *Alice in Wonderland*) is kidnapped by 'Barnaby' (Henry Kleinbach Brandon, 1912–1990), 'Stannie Dum' and 'Ollie Dee' set out to save her. Like *Snow White and the Seven Dwarfs* and *The Wizard of Oz*, this fairy-tale farce ran into censorship problems. In the UK, monstrous 'Bogeymen' were considered too terrifying for children; in the U.S., nearly seven minutes had to be excised before the film was okayed by the Breen Office. Yet Walt Disney (who would remake *B.I.T.* in 1961) allowed "Who's Afraid of the Big Bad Wolf" from "Three Little Pigs" (1933) to be included, along with studio icon Mickey Mouse! Several Hal Roach (1892–1992) Little Rascals appear here.

BABY DOLL (1956)

Conventional comedy-drama Rating: ****

Nymphette Cult Cinema Rating: **** ½

Carroll Baker Cult Rating: *****

Elia Kazan, dir.; Kazan (uncredited), Tennessee Williams, scr.; Kazan, pro.; 1.37:1; B&W; 114 min.; Newtown Prods.; WB.

How do you follow up an Oscar-winning mainstream masterpiece like *On the Waterfront*? (1954), Kazan (1909–2003) surprised everyone by filming a Deep South (in this case, Mississippi) fable. Credited to playwright Tennessee Williams (1911–1983), with whom Kazan had collaborated on *A Streetcar Named Desire*, Middle-aged 'Archie' (Karl Malden,

1912–2009) weds White Trash 'Baby Doll' (Carroll Baker, (1931–), repressing his hunger for carnal knowledge until she turns twenty. Baby Doll sleeps in a crib, sucking her thumb, wearing sexy nymphette P.J.s. Devilish Latino 'Silva' (Eli Wallach, 19015–2011) hopes to pluck her before the couple's oncoming consummation. When NYC's Cardinal Francis Spellman condemned this as indecent (today it barely merits a PG), he inadvertently transformed a modest release into a box-office phenomenon. Its success helped lessen the impact of the Hays/Breen Code for 'decency' as to Hollywood films that had been in effect since 1933. Marilyn Monroe hoped to win the lead but was deemed 'too old.'

BAD BLONDE (1953)

Barbara Payton Cult Rating: *****

B Noir Rating: * ½

Reginald le Borg, dir.; Guy Elmes, Richard H. Landau, scr.; Anthony Hinds, pro.; 1.37:1; B&W; 89 mins.; Hammer Films/ Lippert Prods.

Luridly luscious well describes Barbara Payton (1927–1967), the flaming candle blonde born into a lower-class MN. family. She headed to Hollywood, hoping to make it in The Movies. Payton won female leads in 'A' pictures opposite James Cagney (*Kiss Tomorrow Goodbye*, 1950), Gary Cooper (*Dallas,* (1950), and Gregory Peck (*Only the Valiant*, 1951). Next up? Hmmm! *Bride of the Gorilla* (1951) with Raymond (pre-*Godzilla/Perry Mason*) Burr (1917–1993). What happened? Payton cheated on classy fiancée Franchot Tone with sleazy lover Tom Neal (1914–1972). When they got caught, Neal beat Tone so fiercely the star had to be hospitalized. From then on it was bottom of the barrel productions. Here B.P. is typecast as the unfaithful wife of an aging Italian fight promoter in London. She seduces a naïve boxer (Tom Wright). From a Bus Station book by Max Cato that rips off more serious works such as Clifford Odets' *Golden Boy* and James Cain's *Double Indemnity*. A co-production of Robert L. Lippert's (1909–1976) indie outfit with England's Hammer. B.P. wallowed in alcoholism, prostitution, and criminal activities. Title of her 1963 autobiography: *I Am Not Ashamed*.

RE-THINKING THE RURAL OUTLAW GENRE: If Arthur Penn romanticized his 1930s characters in *Bonnie and Clyde* (1967), Terrence Malick took a more realistic route in the 1950s-set *Badlands*.

BADLANDS (1973)

American-arthouse Rating: *****

Malick Cult Rating: *****

Terrence Malick, dir.; Malick, Edward R. Pressman, prods.; 95 min.; C; 1.85:1; Warner Bros.

'Uncompromising' is the key term critics employ to describe Malick (1943–), a maverick who turn out boutique films rather than play the Hollywood game. *Badlands*, his first feature, is in concept not unlike *Bonnie and Clyde* (1967), *Pretty Poison* (1968), and *Bloody Mama* (1970), which create sympathy for attractive young criminals, glamorizing them. Malick's movie is bleak, distanced, and as cold-blooded as the boy (Martin Sheen, 1949–) and girl (Sissy Spacek, 1949–). Subdued music and stark images of the Southwest add to the understated impact. Always, though, this is less about story or setting than character: mis-matched lovers, neither likely to go bad were it not for the stroke of fate that throws them together. He's a garbage collector who resembles James Dean; she, a fifteen-year-old cheerleader wannabe. Without warning they murder her father (Warren Oates, 1928–1982), then set off cross-country. Her silly, sentimental perception of events, rendered in a monotone voice-over, provides ironic contrast to their lurid actions. Influenced as much by Jean-Luc Godard's *Breathless* as the Charles Starkweather/Carol Ann Fugate case.

BAD SEED, THE (1956)

Patty McCormack cult Rating: *****

Stage to Screen Adaptation Rating: *

Mervyn LeRoy, dir.; John Lee Martin, scr.; LeRoy, pro.; 1.85:1; B&W; 129 min.; Warner Bros.

"I've got the nicest Mommy in the whole world," adorable li'l 'Rhoda' (Patty McCormack, 1945–) tells her upper-middle class mother, before the wicked 10-year-old kills a classmate, a meddling handyman, and… First, as a 1954 novel by John Lee Mahin, then adapted to the stage by

THEY DON'T COME ANY 'BADDER'!: Barbara Payton lived up (down?) to her low-life image in films like *Bad Blonde*; Patty (Patricia) McCormack shed her child serial killer icon from *The Bad Seed* and emerged as a highly respected stage, film, and TV actress.

Maxwell Anderson ((1888–1959), the piece offers a realistic horror story with a wide-eyed, cold-blooded villainess. A cult has long surrounded P.M.'s performance, a no-holds-barred vision of pure evil in the guise of a young angel. The film offers an odd stage-to-screen translation, keeping the Broadway cast all but intact; lesser name Nancy Kelly portrayed the mother though superstars Betty Davis and Rosalind Russell were eager to do so. The one-set (a living room) approach was left largely intact, as were (more surprisingly) the curtain calls. The Production Code insisted the ending (in which Rhoda lives to kill again) be altered by a *deus-ex-machina* strike of lightning. Liberalism of the post-war era insisted that nurture overrides nature: a child of a murderer adopted by decent people would reflect their values. This drama says 'no' to that: Heredity, not environment, rules.

BALLAD OF BUSTER SCRUGGS, THE (2018)

Cult comedy cowboy Rating: *** ½

Coen Bros. Completist Rating: ****

Joel & Ethan Coen, dir., scr.; Coens, Robert Graf, Sue Naegle, pro.; 1.85: C; 133 min.; Annapurna Pictures.

The Big Lebowski opened with an image of the American West as accompanied by the Sons of the Pioneers' version of "Tumbling Tumbleweeds." *T.B.O.B.S.* likewise features a visual of the Old Frontier along with "Cool Water," performed by Buster Scruggs though written by the Pioneers' Bob Nolan, who replaced Roy Rogers as their lead vocalist. Clearly, the Coens enjoy kidding Cowboy Culture as much as they do honoring it in classics like *No Country for Old Men* and *True Grit* (2010). Here's an anthology of six tales including the one that lends this film its title, featuring Tim Blake Nelson as the last of the singin' cowboy heroes. A small cult of fans enjoys arguing as to which of the anecdotes works best and/or worst. In truth, only a smattering of the gags really 'click.' Two tales are based on previous ones by wilderness writers Jack London and Stewart Edward White. The literary references include ones to Percy Bysshe Shelley, Shakespeare, and the Old Testament. Among the guest stars are James Franco and Tom Waits. Notable as the first Coen Bros. project to be Digitally shot.

BARBARELLA (1968)

Sci-fi/erotic rating **** ½

Early Jane Fonda Cult Rating: *****

Graphic Novel to Film Rating: **** ½

Roger Vadim, dir.; Vadim, Claude Brule, Terry Southern, Tudor Gates, many others, scrs.; Dino De Laurentiis, pro.; 2.35:1; C; 98 mins.; Marianne Prods./Paramount.

FROM 'COMIC BOOKS' TO 'GRAPHIC NOVELS': Roger Vadim's international sex-ploitation flick marked the first time a previously unappreciated story-telling form received A budget movie-status rather than as a children's cliffhanger or series of B pictures.

The Gallic sensibility understood that comic books/graphic novels could be employed for adult narratives as well as time-killers for kids. In 1962, Jean-Claude Forest (1930–1998) created an adults-only character combining the spiritual innocence of Cinderella with the sexual freedom of Brigitte Bardot, setting his character in a fantasy world drawn from *Flash Gordon*. The pop-art movement that swept the U.S. at mid-decade paved the way for the first ever major studio's big budget adaptation of such a 'sub-literary' venue in comparison to comic book cliff-hangers in the past. (Not coincidentally *Batman* then premiered on network TV.) Vadim (1928–2000) transformed then-current wife Jane Fonda (1937–) from deb/princess to international sex kitten while drawing on imagery from *The Wizard of Oz*, filtering such visuals through the psychedelic lens of the late 1960s 'scene'. He borrowed concepts for larger-than-life set-pieces for the villain's lair from the James Bond feature *Goldfinger* (1964). Pop-rock group Duran Duran derived their name from the bad-guy (Milo O'Shea). Nudity and softcore porn might have cursed *Barbarella* with an 'X' so Paramount released it *sans* rating. A key predecessor to today's superhero spectacles.

BATMAN RETURNS (1992)

Tim Burton Cult Rating: **** ½

Michelle Pfeiffer Cult Rating: *****

Bob Kane's 'Selina Kyle' Cult Rating: *****

Tim Burton, dir.; Sam Hamm, Daniel Waters, scr.; Burton, Denise Di Nova, pros; 1.85:1; C; 126 min.; Polygram/W.B.

This follow-up to Burton's *Batman* (1989), a popular hit in its time, now rates cult status. Here, T.B. (1958–) pushes the levels of violent surrealism beyond what was then considered family-friendly, causing W.B. to replace him for the next franchise entry. Two villains plagued the Caped Crusader (Michael Keaton, 1951–): 'Penguin' (Danny De Vito, 1944–), a diminutive/cartoonish creep; and 'Catwoman,' the complex tragic anti-heroine. 'Selina Kyle' (Michelle Pfeiffer, 1958–) adding a love/hate relationship for 'Bruce Wayne.' Originally introduced in Spring 1940 by Bob Kane (1915–1998) as 'The Cat,' a seductive femme worthy of 'The Dragon

GENIUS AT WORK II: Bob Kane (1915–1998) proudly displays his original artwork for what became an international franchise; films with strong, sexy villains such as Selina Kyle/"Catwoman" (here embodied by Michelle Pfeiffer) are the ones with enduring cult appeal.

Lady' in Milt Caniff's *Terry and the Pirates*, (The) Catwoman evolved into something far more fascinating: a multi-sided woman within whom good and bad are always at odds. While men appreciated Catwoman as a sex symbol, women perceived her as a strong feminist role model. Her sadomasochistic relationship with Bruce is fully developed here, minus the tongue-in-cheek shenanigans of the earlier over the top TV series.

BATMAN: THE MOVIE (1966)

Comic Book to 'Camp' Film Rating: ****

Leslie H. Martinson, dir.; Lorenzo Semple Jr., scr.; William Dozier, pro.; 1.85:1; C; 105 min.; Greenlawn Prods./20th Century Fox.

In the mid-1960s, ABC suffered a ratings decline when their once popular 'adult westerns' ran their course. Likewise, 20th Century Fox lurched toward on the verge of bankruptcy owing to cost over-runs on *Cleopatra* (1963). As the world of high art embraced both campy humor and sentimental nostalgia, the two corporate giants revived a half-forgotten superhero, created by Bob Kane (1915–1998) half a century earlier. Adam West (1928–2017) and Burt Ward (1945–) were encouraged to play Batman and Robin in a self-consciously silly manner. Cartoon action, wonderfully awful dialogue, and outrageous set designs left no doubt this was tongue in cheek, as appealing to adults as to kids. This movie was to have played theatres before the series premiered early in 1966. When the show was jump-started, *B.T.M.* was held back until the summer, "introducing" heroes and villains that were already well known. Cult-worthy actors portrayed comical evildoers: Caesar Romero as the Joker (it should have been Milton Berle!), Burgess Meredith and Frank Gorshin pluperfect as Penguin and Riddler, with Lee Merriweather substituting for Julie Newmar as Catwoman on TV. The presence of superheroes in our ongoing popular culture derives from this film/series.

BATURO ROWAIARU, aka *BATTLE ROYALE* (2000)

Violent cult film Rating: *****

Asian action film Rating: *****

Kinji Fukasaku, dir.; Fukasaku, scr.; Fukasaku, many others, prods.; 1.78:1; C; 114 min. (edited print); 122 min. (director's cut); AM Associates.

For three days, a group of ninth grade students are isolated on an island. Provided with food, water, and weapons, they are ordered to kill one another until only one remains alive. Moral opponents of the film insist it is nothing more than a cleverly crafted work of violent exploitation, far more dangerous owing to its tween/teen appeal. Defenders claim this addresses the very issue of violence, specifically as it expanded in Japan in the 21st century, if now with a necessary emphasis on youth. Fans and foes alike admit *B.R.* is deeply disturbing, noting the intense eroticization of the gorgeous underage females inflicting pain, then killing one another while dressed in dainty school-girl uniforms. Not dissimilar to the Hollywood commercial franchise *The Hunger Games* though that pales in comparison. From Koushun Takami's graphic novel, banned in its homeland for years. Fukasaku (1930–2003) died before he could complete the terribly disappointing sequel.

BEACH BLANKET BINGO (1965)

Surfer Cultist Rating: ****

Mid-Sixties Music Rating: *****

William Asher, dir.; Asher, Leo Townsend, scr.; Samuel Z. Arkoff, James H. Nicholson, pros.; 2.35:1; C; 98 min.; Alta Vista Prods.; American International Pictures.

When the first bikini exploitation flick *Beach Party* (1963) was released, everyone at A.I.P. worried that the display of female flesh might cause their quickie to be banned from its target audience: teens. Squeaky clean former Mouseketeer Annette Funicello (1942–2003), loyal to Walt Disney, insisted that title aside she wear a simple one-piece. When complaints proved non-existent, the film's success spurred a mainstreaming of that once condemned revealing swimsuit. Even Annette agreed to wear a modest two piece for *Muscle Beach Party* (1964), then a more daring one in *Bikini Beach* (1964). All five B.P. films offer mindless fun; *B.B.B.* rates as the best. Daringly for the time, adult actor Paul Lynde (1926–1982) performed his openly gay night-club humor. As 'Eric Von Zipper,' Harvey Lembeck (1923–1982) parodied Marlon Brando in *The Wild One*. Timothy Carey shared his raving madman persona with the young set; a nympho was added to the cast of clean-cut kids via Donna Michelle (1945–2004) as 'Animal.' Most important, the music (and accompanying gyrating by the girls on the beach) are notably more frenetic than what was allowed only two years earlier. As Dylan claimed: The times they are a-changin'!

BEASTS OF THE SOUTHERN WILD (2012)

One-of-a-kind Cult Rating: *****

Ben Zeitlin, dir.; Zeitlin, Lucy Alibar, scr.; Dan Janvey, Michael Gottwald, pro.; 1.85:1; C; 93 min.; Cinereachi.

"The entire world depends on everything fitting together just right." So says 'Hushpuppy' (Quvenzhane Wallis, 2003– ; the youngest actress

ON THE BEACH: In a series that defined the mid-1960s even as The College Musicals did the mid-1940s, Annette Funicello initially showed as little skin as possible while the blonde beach girls made the once controversial bikini suit that defined 'dangerous' Brigitte Bardot a part of the all-American clean-cut scene.

ever nominated for a Best Actress Oscar): a child of The Bathtub, a Third World community (fictional if fact-based) existing within the continental U.S.: the remote islands of rural Louisiana. Hushpuppy has seen nothing of the country surrounding her corner of existence but knows what she knows: in a half-forgotten past, mammoth-sized beasts known as Urus, with the body of an ox and snout of a wild boar, roamed through the omnipresent mud here; in the near future, melting ice caps in a strange, virtually mythic place called the South Pole will drown everything on earth, including her own hidden kingdom filled with disease and poverty; in the present, the man she calls 'father' (Dwight Henry, 1963–) hopes to teach his child necessary survival skills before passing away. Few movies about indigenous cultures have succeeded so remarkably at allowing us to not only peer into such a self-contained way of life but enter the mind, and share the sensibility, of a child coming of age there. Shot in Terrebonne Parish by the brilliant Wesleyan grad Ben Zeitlin (1982–). (Is *The Vikings*, 1958, with Kirk Douglas, his all-time favorite film?) A request: Will somebody please put this one in a time capsule?

BEAT THE DEVIL (1953)

Bogart Cult Following Rating: *****

Huston Cult Following Rating: *****

Tongue in Cheek Movie Parody Rating: *****

John Huston, dir.; Huston, Truman Capote, Claude Colburn, scr.; Huston, Bogart, Capote, Jack Clayton, pros.; 1.37:1; B&W; 89 min.; Romulus Films/Santana Pictures/U.A.

During the Golden Age, Huston (1906–1987) guided superstar Bogart (1899–1957) through some of his best cynical tough-guy roles at W.B.: in *The Maltese Falcon* (1941), *Across the Pacific* (1942), etc. During the 1950s, esteemed directors and actors went indie, shooting films without interference from fading movie moguls. The two collaborated on this unofficial remake of *T.M.F.*: here Bogart's team of rogues race with a seemingly normal British couple to claim a fortune in Africa. Peter Lorre (1904–1964) replays his anxious little-guy; Sydney Greenstreet (1879–

GORGEOUS IF MISLEADING 'POSTER ART': Despite an attempt to sell *Beat the Devil* as the last of the old-fashioned Bogie entertainments, the film offered something entirely out of the mainstream.

1954), bedridden, was replaced by Robert Morley (1908–1992). Newcomer Gina Lollobrigida (1927–) and old-timer Jennifer Jones (1919–2009), in a blonde wig, are Bogart's wife and married mistress. Huston hired Capote (1924–1984) to make this a self-spoofing parody: A Camp classic if before the mainstream was ready for such innovation. In the 1960s, while Bond films were projecting a light-hearted attitude toward sex and violence, this achieved cult status.

BEFORE SUNRISE (1995)

Richard Linklater Cult Rating: *****

Richard Linklater, dir.; Linklater, scr.; Anne Walker-McBay, prod.; 1.55;1; C; 101 min.; Castle Rock.

Imagine watching *Murder on the Orient Express* with love (at first 'romantic,' then true'), not killing as the subject, and you have this deeply sensitive yet never sentimental tale of a one night stand or, perhaps, something more. On June 16, 1994, U.S. tourist 'Jesse' (Ethan Hawke, 1970–) and French student 'Celine' (Julie Delpy, 1969–) meet on the train from Budapest to Vienna, then spend a day together. A major influence: James Joyce's *Ulysses* (1922), the definitive stream of consciousness novel of several people exploring Dublin in one afternoon; also, Linklater (1960–) drew on an incident from his own youth. Hawke and Delpy were encouraged to toss out dialogue they did not think worked, writing their own as the characters became 'organic' if not 'improvised.' The better part of 20 years later, R.L. reassembled his team for a sequel, in *Before Midnight* (2013). Rather than a treacly follow-up, this equally fine film scrutinizes the relationship after a fresh encounter gives way to the reality of early middle-class life.

BEHIND THE GREEN DOOR (1972)

Porn Rating: *****

Cult Rating: *****

Artie and James Mitchell, dirs..; anonymous scr.; Mitchell Bros, prods.; 1.37:1; C; 72 min. Jartech/Cinema 7.

ONCE, SHE WAS PURE AS IVORY SNOW: Marilyn Chambers made an abrupt transition from the spokesperson for family-style soap products to the leading blonde female porn star of her generation.

B.T.G.D. opened at Adults Only theatres shortly after *Deep Throat* scored with middle-Americans eager to see Porno Chic. Here was an X film that could be taken seriously. Brothers (Artie, 1945–1991; James, 1943–2007) based the script on a long-standing urban legend: a free-living debutante—played by Marilyn 'Chambers' (Briggs, 1952–2009)—is kidnapped and drugged, then forced to submit to rape onstage for an audience of masked men and women. Unlike the artless filmmaking in *D.T.*, here the stylistics are as fascinating as the subject, offering a nightmare scenario that could randomly happen to any girl who finds herself in the wrong place at the wrong time. Some critics wondered: Was M.C. 'acting' or were these her honest sexual responses? More fascinating: Was Marilyn, like 'Gloria,' getting 'into it'—enjoying initially forced submission as a bizarre sort of freedom? Johnnie Keyes (1948–), as the well-hung African American stud, became a new sort of sex symbol. Owing to her Cybil Shepherd-like beauty M.C. became the most highly paid porn star of the 1970s.

BEING JOHN MALKOVICH (1999)

Spike Jonze cultists: *****

Charlie Kaufman cultists: *****

John Malkovich cultists: *****

Spike Jonze, dir.; Charlie Kaufman, scr.; Kaufman, Steve Golin, Vincent Landay, Sandy Stein, Michael Stipe, pros.; Gramercy/Propaganda/Astralworks.

Where does genius end and insanity begin? That issue is often raised as to Charlie Kaufman (1958–), his scripts appealingly quirky, uniquely absorbing, and subtly subversive. *B.J.M.*, was brought to the screen by music-video director Jonze (1969–) as his first feature. This odd tale concerns a self-destructive, self-pitying (if talented) puppeteer (John Cusack, 1966–). When his wife (Cameron Diaz, 1972–) forces him to find a 'real' job, he becomes a file clerk on the scaled-down 7 1/2th floor of an otherwise normal office building. His boss (Orson Bean, 1928–2020) might be an insane asylum escapee; a co-worker (Catherine Keenan, 1959–) eats men alive for breakfast. The anti-hero (a combination of Woody Allen, Lenny Bruce, and of course C.K.) discovers a portal leading into the mind of actor John Malkovich (1953–). Everyday life becomes a surreal nightmare in this comedic variation on a Franz Kafka theme. Objective reality is deconstructed, then destroyed. Issues of human identity and gender-bending are also presented in the guise of a purposefully paradoxical light-hearted comedy.

BELLE DU JOUR (1967)

Luis Bunuel Cultists; *****

Catherine Deneuve Cultists: *****

S&M/Bondage Cinema Cultists: *****

Luis Bunuel, dir.; Bunuel, Jean-Claude Carrier, scr.; Raymond and Robert Hakim, pro.; 1.55:1; C; 100 min.; Paris Film Prod./ Allied Artists.

    This Parisian import by a Spanish-born director (1900–1983) maintains the audacity of Luis Bunuel's early *avant-garde* experiment *An Andalusian Dog* while bringing surrealism to the public at large. Married to a successful doctor (Jean Sorel), 'Severine Seizy' (Catherine Deneuve, 1943–) cannot express her deep, confused sexual urges within such a conventional lifestyle. The blonde slips away from her home to become 'a girl of the afternoon': A prostitute at an expensive bordello owned by a knowing madame (Genevieve Page). S.S. submits to bondage and discipline, sadomasochism, even violent rape. Later, she returns to a lovely neighborhood to play the role of a perfect domestic wife in all places but the bedroom. Severine may be fantasizing such walks on the wild side. Or could the prostitute be dreaming about an alternative upscale existence? An iconoclast, Bunuel insists that if something is real in your own mind, it is indeed real… to *you*. One of several movies that transformed *C.D.* into the Gallic Grace Kelly, all ice on the outside if with a terrifying fire burning below that sedate surface. In the U.S., distributors were so terrified of the piece that A.A., lowest on the ladder, picked up what became their greatest box-office hit.

BELLE ET LA BETE, LA (1946)

French Arthouse Rating: *****

Fairy-tale on Film Rating: *****

Jean Cocteau, dir.: Cocteau, Rene Clement, scr.; Andre Paulve, pro.; 2.38:1; B&W; 80 min.; DisCina.

ARTHOUSE EXTREMES: In the mid-1960s, Luis Bunuel presented the Sexual Revolution onscreen in *Belle du Jour*; two decades earlier, Jean Cocteau offered a predecessor to Walt Disney's animated classic featuring a 'Belle' of a kinder, gentler order.

It isn't easy to question the artistic triumph of Disney's *Beauty and the Beast* (1991). Yet if one issue can be raised, it's this: the aesthetic approach is 'borrowed' (in the 'great filmmakers 'borrow,' bad filmmakers 'steal' sense.) Uncle Walt (1901–1966) considered doing a B&B film in the post-war years, dropping the project when he screened this and sensed it was the interpretation he would have chosen. Gallic avant-garde artist Cocteau (1889–1963; revered for *Orphee*, 1950, likewise starring Jean Marais) maintains the fairy-tale concept while mounting a movie for adult audiences about realistic 'people' rather than cliched stick-figures employed for Children's Theatre. For the believable setting where Belle (Josette Day) lives, J.C. modelled the farming village on pastoral paintings by Johannes Vermeer (1632–1675), the hidden palace on Gustave Dore's (1832–1883) mystical/mythical creations. Candles light themselves; arms protruding from walls pass a light down the hallway. Yet we care about the principles as we do while watching films set in 'the real world.' Cocteau subscribed to the 'Art Film' concept: *B&B* knows that it offers something more than temporal entertainment; this is one for the ages.

BIG HEAT, THE (1953)

Fritz Lang Rating: *****

Off-the-wall 1950s Noir Rating: *****

Fritz Lang, dir.; Sydney Boehm, scr.; Robert Arthur, pro.; 1.37:1; B&W; 89 min.; Columbia.

Parallel to film noirs depicting seedy detectives and foul criminals, the 'police procedural' followed the paths of law officers down mean streets in our post-war asphalt jungles. One stood out then and still does today. Glenn Ford (1916–2006) plays an easy-going cop whose wife steps out of their suburban home and is blown to pieces by a car bomb intended for him. The baby-faced hero transforms into a lone wolf, uncertain whether he will bring evildoers to justice or murder them in a rage of vengeance. Under F.L.'s (1890–1976) taut direction, Ford perfectly conveys the transformation. Still, the film belongs to two supporting actors: Lee Marvin (1924–1987), delivering the first of many psycho-killers he would vividly portray; and Gloria Graham (1923–1981) as his moll, a wisecracking hipster. To punish her, the out-of-control mobster tosses a pot of blazing hot coffee at her face. From the film's mid-point, she resembles that Batman villain Two Face: one half normal, even beautiful, the other scarred beyond our ability to peek at it through fingers covering our eyes. For years, many indie TV stations refused to air *T.B.H.* for fear of viewer complaints.

A NEW LEVEL OF VIOLENCE IN THE FIFTIES: Glenn Ford arrests Lee Marvin in one of the most mean-spirited police-procedural noirs of the decade thanks to Fritz Lang.

BIG SICK, THE (2017)

Dramedy Rating: **** ½

Michael Showalter, dir.; Emily V. Gordon, Kumail Nanjlani, scr.; Judd Apatow, Barry Mendel, pro.; 1.85:1; C; 120 min.; Filmnation.

    Where to begin? Let's start with the script, written by husband-and-wife team Nanjlani (1978–) and Gordon (1979–), based on the early days of their romance. Here, the two (he plays himself while Zoe Kazan embodies Emily) meet in Chicago where he hopes to score in stand-up comedy. The fear is that their different ethnicities—he was born in Pakistan, she in the U.S.—may raise issues with their respective families. The choice between one's 'blood of my blood' and the stirrings of the individual heart is at the basis of what comes across as cute and charming rather than nasty and cynical, the trouble with so many of today's self-consciously offbeat comedies. Yet there's drama too when Emily experiences a coma while in the hospital and Kumail must transform this daily horror into his creative autobiographical monologues. Not that *T.B.S.* is a docudrama: in particular the parents of Emily (played by Ray Romano and Holly Hunter) are, she insists, quite unlike their actual counterparts. The change was made to render the film funnier. On a more serious note, Kumail's ambition was to offer a clear alternative to Muslim stereotypes in current films while still portraying the ethnic characters with a comic edge… no small feat! Showalter (1970–), best known for his TV work including *Search Party* and the two *Wet Hot American Summer* TV series, found precisely the right tone while realizing the concept on film.

BIG TROUBLE IN LITTLE CHINA (1986)

John Carpenter Rating: **** ½

Retro Action/Popcorn Film Rating: **** ½

John Carpenter, dir.; Gary Goldman, David Z. Weinstein, W.D. Richter, scr.; Larry J. Franco, pro.; 2.35:1; C; 99 min.; C; 20th Century Fox.

HIGH ADVENTURE ON A LOW BUDGET: Like the Spielberg/Lucas A movie revivals of old-fashioned movie cliffhangers, John Carpenter's smaller film captured the spellbinding sense of bygone popcorn features: from left to right, Kim Cattrall, Kurt Russell, Dennis Dun and Suzee Pai.

J.C. opens this light-hearted adventure as hero 'Jack Burton' (Kurt Russell, 1951–) arrives in the title San Francisco neighbourhood. He's a contemporary cowboy: a trucker, that blue-collar working man elevated to heroic status in the 1970s (TV's *Movin' On* with Claude Akins, 1974–1977; theatrically, *Breaker Breaker* with Chuck Norris, 1977; *Convoy* starring Kris Kristofferson, 1978). Jack then friendly fights an Asian pal (Dennis Dun) even as John Wayne and Monty Clift did at the end of one of Carpenter's favorites, Howard Hawks' *Red River* (1948). When contemporary heroes set out to rescue a kidnapped girl they enter into a kingdom that recalls Sax Rohmer tales from the silent and sound era: Dr. Fu Manchu's alternative land of evil magic and forbidden eroticism. Images of flying duellists precede their glorious counterparts in *Crouching Tiger, Hidden Dragon* (2000). Though this resembles *Star Wars* and *Raiders* in reviving nostalgic cliff-hanger clichés, if now with a knowing wink, *B.T.I.L.C.* never quite clicked with the mass audience. Cheesy F/X add to the appealingly tacky cult aura.

BILL & TED'S EXCELLENT ADVENTURE (1989)

Eighties Teen Flick Rating: **** ½

Keanu Reeves Cult Rating: *****

Stephen Herek, dir.; Chris Matheson, Ed Solomon, scr.; Scott Kroopf, Michael S. Murphey, Joel Soisson, pro.; 2:35:1; C; 90 min.; De Laurentiis/ Orion.

On the eve of this slacker comedy's release, all involved hoped it would recoup a modest $6.5 million investment. While *B&T* didn't become an instant classic (like the similarly themed *Back to the Future*; Robert Zemeckis, 1985) money poured in, causing all to realize that they had come up with a cult film for that moment in time. More amazing still: over the years, then decades, this did not fade into a pleasing memory but developed a remarkably loyal following. A sequel,… *Bogus Journey* (1991) a pair of TV series, comic books and a videogame, and even an annual Halloween event at Universal, Orlando made clear that even young people of the 21st century could relate to these seemingly dated Eighties' Dudes. (A breakfast cereal did not do as well). Aficionados already anticipate a planned third feature that brings "William S. Preston' (Keanu Reeves, 1964–) and 'Theodore Logan' (1965–) into middle-age. Whether a replacement will fill the role of time traveller 'Rufus' (George Carlin, 1937–2008) is not yet known. Though generally considered a genial 'turn-your-mind-off' gag-fest in which the music-loving pals meet historical figures including Joan of Ark, Billy the Kid, and Napoleon, an appreciation for the 'causal loop' concept that was the basis of *Twilight Zone* allows for an undercurrent of intelligence rather than mere escapism.

BLACK CAT, THE (1934)

Edgar G. Ulmer Cultists: *****

Karloff Cultists: *****

Lugosi Cultists: *****

Edgar Allan Poe Cultists: *

Edgar G. Ulmer, dir.; Ulmer, Peter Ruric, Tom Kilpatrick, scr.; Carl Laemmle Jr., pro.; 1.37:1; B&W; 61 min.; Universal.

At Universal, head-honcho Carl Laemmle Jr. (1908–1979) thought to team his new horror stars, Bela 'Dracula' Lugosi and Boris 'Frankenstein' Karloff; recent German emigre Ulmer (1904–1972) received the green-light to make the first of eight films (initially for Universal, later at R.K.O.-Radio) featuring the pair. Here Lugosi (1882–1956) is 'Dr. Vitus Werdegaust'; fifteen years following WWI he travels to the remote Hungarian castle of his betrayer in life and love, 'Hjalmar Poelzig' (Karloff, 1887–1969). A young honeymooning American couple (David Manners, Julie Bishop) find themselves caught between feuding fiends as they fight to the death over a young blonde (Lucille Lund), daughter of the woman each oddball long ago loved. The role of witchcraft in contemporary Europe, with a Black Mass conclusion, is accurately portrayed. Images of sadism and torture (including a man skinned alive) abound; the Hays/Breen office took scissors to the print which initially ran more than 80 mins. Memorably shot in a timely style that references Art Nouveau

WHERE RETRO DECO MET MODERN NOUVEAU: Movie posters which were discarded as junk back in the 1930s are now considered legitimate works of art.

from the 1910s and more recent Art Deco of the 1920s. A chiaroscuro effect for the lighting of richly detailed images cinches its eerie, unsettling appeal.

BLACK CAULDRON, THE (1985)

Edgy Animation Rating: ****

Ted Berman, Richard Rich, dirs.; Berman, Rich, David Jonas, many others, scr.; Ron Miller, Joe Hale, prods.; 2.20:1; C; 80 min.; Walt Disney Films.
    Walt had passed in 1966. Disney's then head-honcho Ron Miller (Disney's son-in-law) hoped to revive their fading animation work with *T.B.C.*, from a novel by Lloyd Alexander. A peasant boy transforms into a hero for his mythic kingdom by rescuing the magical title object from a monster. Audiences found this hero-figure cold and uninvolving. At one point there

was talk of bringing Ralph Bakshi (*Wizards*, 1978) aboard for a far darker vision than ever in a Disney project. The studio pulled its punches, assigning two of old pros, resulting in a work that proved too grim for their loyal audience but not dark enough for the new generation of fantasy fans. Despite a then unheard of $44 million investment, *T.B.C.* returned less than half that. In Japan, however, this hit big-time, inspiring many young artists to create *Animees*. *T.B.C.* has become a cult fav with animation aficionados who believe the problem was that a daring film arrived ahead of its time.

BLACK MAMA, WHITE MAMA (1973)

Women in Prison Cult Rating: **** ½

Margaret Markov Cult Rating: *****

Pam Grier Cult Rating: *****

Philippino-lensed Junk Movie Rating: *****

WELCOME TO THE PHILIPPINES: Filmmaker Eddie Romero introduces American actresses Pam Grier and Margaret Markov to the unique world of ultra-low budget filmmaking.

Eddie Romero, dir.; H.R. Christian, Joe Violan, Jonathan Demme, scr.; Romero, John Ashley, pro.; 1.85:1; C; 87 min. A.I.P.

While working on A.I.P.'s Philippines-lensed Women in Prison exploitation flicks, future Oscar winner Demme (1944–2017) had an inspiration: Why not do a chase-action film about two women who, like Sidney Poitier and Tony Curtis in *The Defiant Ones* (1958), escape shackled together? "Chicks in Chains" is how *B.M.W.M.* was marketed, a huge money-maker booked into two alternative venues: Pam Grier (1949–) had become a huge sensation at downtown theatres showcasing black-oriented action movies; Margaret Markov (1948–) likewise was now a box-office sensation at rural Drive Ins. Super-villain Sig Haig (1939–2019), who alternated between both genres, played the snarling villain. *B.M.W.M.* features something for everyone hooked on the guilty pleasures of junk movies: a lesbian warden (Lynn Borden, 1937–2015) who tries to seduce Grier in stir and pays dearly; cat-fights between the two leads; and large if incompetently staged action by Eddie Romero, aka Enrique Moreno, (1924–2013) the most prolific director of Philippines-lensed grindhouse flicks. Much admired by Tarantino.

BLACK SNAKE MOAN (2006)

Poor White Southern Trash Cult Rating: ****

Samuel L. Jackson Cult Rating: **** ½

Christina Ricci Cult Rating: *****

Craig Brewer, dir.; Brewer, scr.; John Singleton, Stephanie Allain, Ron Schmidt, prods.; 2.35:1; B&W/C; 116 min.; Southern Cross/New Deal.

Former child-star Christina Ricci (1980–) in chains: That's what posters distributed by Paramount Classics presented as *B.S.M.'s* lure. In truth, that's a minor element. Despite the suggestive (some might claim sexist and racist) title, here is a surprisingly sensitive character study. Two of life's losers uplift one another: Samuel L. Jackson (1948–) plays an over-the-hill blues musician now performing menial work. Ricci is a small-town tramp, left for dead on a rural road by abusers. 'Lazarus' (yup, that's his name) brings 'Rae' to his home for tender mercies. Occasionally recalls *Poor White Trash*, re-imagined as a modern indie art film in the radical tradition of 1961's *Something Wild*. Ricci wears cowboy boots, Baby Doll short-shorts, an off-the-rack jeans jacket, and what may be the naughtiest panties ever. One of those 'Deep South Psychos in the Summer-time' flicks. A fine follow-up for Brewer (1971–) after *Hustle and Flow*; The *Footloose* remake (2011) bombed.

BLADE RUNNER (1982)

Original Theatrical Release Rating: *** ½

1991 Revised Cut: **** ½

2007 'Final Cut': *****

Ridley Scott, dir.; Hampton Fancher, David Webb Peoples, scr.; Michael Deeley, pro; 2.35:1; C; 112 min. (U.S. theatrical release print); 116 min (revised print); 117 (final cut); Ladd Company/W.B.

The U.K.'s Ridley Scott (1937–) helmed this $30 million version of Philip K. Dick's *far*-out-of-the-mainstream sci-fi novel *Do Androids Dream of Electric Sheep* (1968). To expand the slight narrative, Scott oversaw the creation of elaborate visuals, designed as miniatures and pre-C.G. matte shots, all influenced by *Metropolis* and neo-noir (*Chinatown*, 1974). Harrison Ford (1942–) embodies a hunter of outlawed synthetic people, they desperate to survive by blending into society. He falls in love with a more advanced cyborg (Sean Young,1959–), coming to wonder if he might be one of 'them' himself. Vividly conveying Dick's theme—what *does* constitute 'humanity'?—Scott's four hour cut was deemed un-releasable. A theatrical version, featuring an awful tacked-on ending and a witless voice-over, caused critics to label *B.R.* a failed/intriguing work. Over the years, fans crusaded to bring Scott's version/vision to the public. Recut more than once, *B.R.* won a reputation as one of the all-time great dystopian fiction films. The term 'replicant' replaced the earlier *android* owing to this movie.

THE SHAPE OF THINGS TO COME: 'Pris' (Daryl Hannah) is the future's sexiest cyborg killer; 'Deckard' (Harrison Ford) tracks down another illegal half-human.

BLADE RUNNER 2049 (2017)

Dystopian Future Flick Rating: *****

Sequel to Classic Sci-Fi Rating: *****

Dennis Villeneuve, dir.; Hampton Fancher, Michael Green, scr.; Ridley Scott, Bud Yorkin, Cynthia Sykes, Broderick Johnson, numerous others, prod. 2.39:1; C; 164 min.; Columbia.

Though *Blade Runner* is widely considered the greatest single sci-fi film of the 1980s, disappointing box-office results caused it to for decades be considered a cult flick. At last receiving due respect as a sci-fi classic, Columbia came to believe a sequel, if 'done right,' might finally be in order. The good news: director D.V. (1967–), who had cinched his reputation for near future noir with *Arrival* (2016), delivered the goods. Thirty years after Decker's abrupt disappearance, a replicant Blade Runner named 'K' (referencing a Kafka literary anti-hero, played by Ryan Gosling), eliminating rogues of his own race, discovers proof that his predecessor and that man's replicant lover 'Rachael' (Sean Young) had a child. Powerful forces attempt to halt him in a quest to locate this golden child, as biological offspring would destroy social values by erasing the final distinction between replicants and people. *B.R.2049* was hailed by diehard *B.R.* fans and international critics. Like its predecessor, this proved to be a box-office bomb. For like the original, this is one of the great cult sci-fi films, not a mainstream movie like *Star Wars* or *Trek*.

BLONDE VENUS (1932)

Dietrich Cult Rating: *****

Von Sternberg Cult Rating: *****

Hollywood Pre-Code Pan-Sexual Rating: *****

Josef von Sternberg, dir.; von Sternberg, Jules Furthman, S.K. Lauren, scr.; von Sternberg, pro.; 1.37:1; B&W; 93 min., director's cut; 85 min., Post-Code theatrical release.

THE FETISHISTIC IMAGE: Not satisfied with Marlene Dietrich's natural beauty, Josef von Sternberg insisted on turning her into an otherworldly blonde mannequin in their Svengali/Trilby self-consciously 'formal' films.

"If light allows for clarity," J.V.S. (1894–1969) once said, "then shadow provides the realm of mystery." This held true for the films in which he directed actress/songstress Marlene Dietrich (1901–1992), beginning with the Berlin-produced *The Blue Angel* (1930). That early talkie introduced M.D. as an amoral seductress ("men cluster to me, like moths around a flame, and if their wings burn, I know I'm not to blame"). Its success led to a joint Paramount contract for this modern contemporary Svengali-Trilby. *B.V.* casts M.D. as a demure, innocent German girl who marries a dull American (Hebert Marshall) at his insistence. Back in the states, she pays for the ill man's doctors by performing at a cabaret, charming her handsome boss (Cary Grant). A pre-Code classic, *B.V.* begins with an extended nude swimming sequence, cut after 1933. Marlene cross-dresses in a white silk tuxedo, goes native in a politically non-correct Voodoo routine, and kisses a female admirer on her lovely lips. The term *divine decadence* may derive from this movie. Feminist film historian Marjorie Rosen argued that Dietrich "re-vamped the Vamp" by having such a woman of the night reveal herself to be a devoted wife and loving mother at home. Alternately elegant and lurid.

BLOOD FEAST (1963)

Drive-In Sex/Horror Rating: NO STARS

Herschel Gordon Lewis Cult Rating: *****

Herschel Gordon Lewis, dir.; Allison Louise Downe, scr.; Lewis, David F. Friedman, pro.; 1.85:1; C; 67 min.; Box Office Spectaculars.

Simultaneous with Russ Meyer, H.G.L. (1926–2016) tossed his hat into the exploitation ring, attempting to knock late-1950s mini-movie magnates Roger Corman and Ed Wood out of the ring. Whereas they had opted for mild product with bizarro titles, the newcomers dared push further. R.M.'s desire to show female nudity (notably, large breasted women) did not hold true for Lewis. His first hit did star *Playboy*'s June 1963 "Playmate of the Month" Connie Mason (1937–) yet the former college

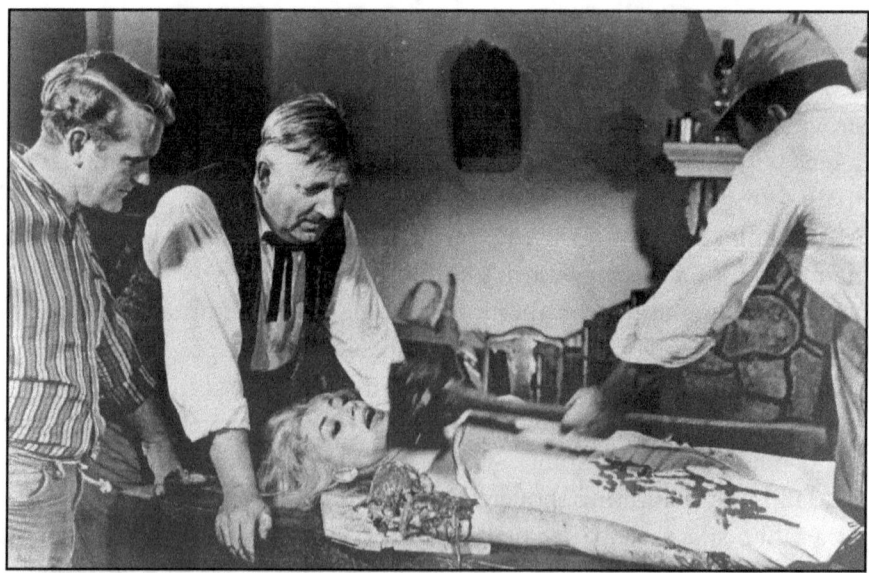

GRINDHOUSE GORE-FEST: The early-1960s Drive-In Circuit allowed Herschel Gordon to escape censorship so long as he featured no actual female nudity.

prof. turned director, writer, cinematographer, and musical scorer made certain that even when the girl appeared naked, the audience could see nothing of her 'private parts.' Something always covered her: suds when in a bathtub, more often blood. Insisting on violence rather than sex, H.G.L. skirted the censors, on the lookout for the latter. Plot? A serial killer serves up women's body parts (displayed in close-up, perhaps inspiring the career of David Cronenberg) to an ancient evil deity, earning Lewis the nickname "Godfather of Gore." Many observers believe *B.F.* to be the first Splatter Flick. On an investment of less than $25,000, H.G.L. and partner D. F.F. (1923–2011) netted more than $4 million in pure profit.

BLOOD SIMPLE (1984)

Southwestern Noir Rating: *****

Coen Bros. Rating: **** ½

Joel and Ethan Coen, dir(s).; Coen Bros., scr.; Coen Bros, pros.; 1.85;1; C; 99 min. (theatrical release), 96 min. (the director's cut), Rover Road/Foxton/Circle Films.

Growing up in Minneapolis MN, the Coens—Ethan, (1957–); Joel (1954–)—determined to be moviemakers. Going from house to house, they convinced everyday people to invest, raising the necessary amount to shoot this small film. The brothers loved Noir, but their budget did not allow for filming in a big city. So they shifted the genre to rural Texas, inadvertently creating modern southwest neo-Noir. A sleazy P.I. (M. Emmet Walsh, 1935–) is hired by the downbeat owner (John Getz, 1946–) of a dismal diner to discover if his wife (Frances McDormand, 1957– ; married Joel C.) is cheating with a worker (Dan Hedaya (1940–). Plots give way to counterplots; nasty conspiracies to ever more vicious trysts. The ripe-with-sex 'n' violence indie smartly comments on the dangers of acting on one's assumptions, always with disastrous results. This theme ties all Coen films into a singular body of work or, as cinema college profs call it, an *oeuvre*. Critical acclaim launched the Coens on their way to upcoming classics: *Fargo* (1996), *No Country for Old Men* (2007), *True Grit* (2010).

SWINGIN' LONDON: Michelangelo Antonioni took international viewers on a psychedelic tour of the post-Beatles city in this Hitchcock inspired psychological thriller.

BLOW-UP (1966)

European Art Film Rating: *****

Swingin' Sixties Cult Rating: *****

Michelangelo Antonioni, dir.; Antonioni, Tonino Guerra, scr., Julio Cortazar (short story); Carlo Ponti, pro.; 1.85:1; C; 111 min.; MGM/Bridge Films.

In trendy post-Beatles London, a photographer (David Hemmings, 1941–2003) strolls through a quiet park on a sunny day, spots a woman (Vanessa Redgrave, 1937–) kissing a man, and snaps a few shots. Shortly, she pursues the cynical antihero, begging him to turn over the pictures. Back in his studio, he blows up the images, realizing she murdered her 'lover.' Forsaking his earlier oblique/obscure arthouse films (*L'Avventura*, 1960; *La Notte*, 1961) M.A. (1912–2007) updated/revitalized Hitchcock level suspense. Released in the U.S. prior to *The Graduate* and *Bonnie and Clyde*, B.U. initiated the New Cinema with radical international aesthetics for an emergent youth audience, challenging (and soon destroying) the Production Code via taboo themes (drug-use, group sex) and graphic nudity, each presented in a non-exploitive/artsy manner. Scintillating entertainment qualities are underlined by a philosophic sub-text: Is all reality subjective? What does human perception have to do with what in truth surrounds us? The cast included supermodel Veruschka von Lehndorff (1939–), hippie princess Jane Birkin (1946–), and Jeff Beck, Jimmy Page, and The Yardbirds. *B.U.* provided the tip of the iceberg for Woodstock-era filmmaking.

FAMILY-STYLE NOIR?: Shirley Temple's legion of fans did not take well to this, the most unsettling of all her musical films; edgier film fans become devotees of this one.

BLUE BIRD, THE (1940)

Shirley Temple Mainstream Rating: *

Oddball children's film cultists Rating: **** ½

Walter Lang, dir.; Ernest Pascal, Walter Bullock, scr.; Daryl F. Zanuck, pro.; 1.37:1; B&W/C; 88 min. (original theatrical print), 74 min. (abridged TV release); 20th Century Fox.

 It wasn't wise to say 'no' to the bubbly, diminutive superstar of Depression-era Hollywood films. Fox's mogul Daryl F. Zanuck (1902–1979) learned this the hard way when he failed to manage negotiations that would have allowed his studio's beloved box-office attraction Shirley Temple (1928–2014) to star in MGM's *The Wizard of Oz*. Apologetic D.Z. mounted an ambitious version of a symbolist play for children by Berlin's acclaimed Maurice Maeterlinck (1862–1949). Gale Sondergaard (1899–1985), who turned down The Wicked Witch of the West role, here plays a Catwoman as dark as that DC villainess yet to come. But the girl 'hero' is no 'Dorothy,' rather a notably nasty child. The idea was to introduce a whole new dimension to S.T. but such reverse-typecasting was despised by the mass audience, this one of her few b.o. flops. The ultra-gloomy alternative world through which S.T. passes in her search for the title object (a symbol of happiness) failed to charm anyone. A financial disaster, the film ended S.T.'s Star Era. Today it's thought of as a misunderstood masterpiece by devotees of quirky films.

BLUES BROTHERS, THE (1980)

John Belushi Cult Rating: *****

American Pop/Rock Music Rating: *****

John Landis, dir.; Landis, Dan Aykroyd, scr.; Robert K. Weiss, pro.; 1.85:1; C; 133 min. (theatrical), 148 min. (director's cut), Universal.

 With *Animal House*, J.L. (1950–) tested the theatrical waters as to whether TV's 'Not Ready for Prime Time Players' might be the zaniest comedy stars since those crazy clowns at the Mack Sennett studio during

SOUL MEN: The popular *Saturday Night Live* TV skit became a big screen hit and, ever since, a cult film for music buffs thanks to the string of great artists including Ray Charles.

Silent Days. The film's surprise success caused this far more ambitious (budget-wise) follow-up to be greenlighted at the same studio. Drawn from a memorable skit on what had now emerged from a late-night cult sensation into an American comedy institution, the loose, leisurely plot follows 'Joliet Jake' (John Belushi, 1949–1982), just released from prison, and his brother 'Elwood' (D.A., 1952–) as they set out on "a mission from GAHD!" to save their beloved Catholic school from closure by raising the necessary money through a series of musical club bookings. This allows for a Who's Who of legendary American blues, rock, jazz and honkytonk greats to perform, Cab Calloway, James Brown, Aretha Franklin, Ray Charles, and John Lee Hooker among them, their performances marbled with clever gags. Adding to the cultishness: cameos by SNL/SCTV/Laugh-In veterans John Candy and Henry Gibson, also Twiggy, Paul Reubens, Frank Oz and Carrie Fisher.

BLUE VELVET (1986)

Lynch Cult Rating: *****

Dennis Hopper Rating: *****

Erotic thriller Rating: *

David Lynch, dir.; Lynch, scr.; Fred C. Caruso, pro.; 2.35;1; C; 120 min. (theatrical release print); 172 min. (director's cut); De Laurentiis Ent.

An appealing pair of teens (Kyle MacLachlan, 1959–); Laura Dern, 1967–) giddily stroll along a quiet street in the all-American town of Lumberton, which resembles Main Street, USA in a Disney theme park. Their idyllic mood shatters at the sight of an ant-covered human ear in the green grass. Like Teresa Wright in Hitch's *Shadow of a Doubt* (1943), David Lynch's (1946–) inspiration, the innocent kids explore a previously unnoticed shadow-world on the edges of what they naively accepted as their brightly lit ideal village. A talentless singer (Isabella Rossellini,

WELCOME TO LYNCH-LAND, U.S.A.: Dennis Hopper plays his greatest villain role opposite Isabella Rossellini's redux of her mom Ingrid Bergman's aura in 1986's most controversial release; this marked the pre-Tarantino 'collapsing' of grindhouse, arthouse, and mainstream movies into one another.

1952–) is being held captive by 'Frank Booth,' a brutally insane villain. However right for the role Dennis Hopper (1936–2010) may be, he was cast only after friend Harry Dean Stanton (1926–2017) turned the part down owing to extreme violence, ranging from vicious beatings to a ritualized rape. The title references a Bobby Vinton record, considered in such poor taste that it qualifies as 'good' according to the New Norm. Several critics included *B.V.* on both their Best *and* Worst Films of the Year lists!

BONE TOMAHAWK (2015)

Cult Western/Horror Hybrid Rating: *****

S. Craig Zahler, dir./scr.; Jack Heller, Dallas Sonnier, prod.; 2.35:1; C; 132 min; Caliber Media/Platinum Pictures.

During the early decades of the 21st century, one approach to old Hollywood genres (to keep them alive while consciously avoiding time-worn conventions) is to combine several in a single film. There have been several Western/ horror hybrids, though none so artistically successful as this. S.C.Z. (1973–)—previously a caterer, rock band member, journalist, and novelist—opens his first film, about the fading frontier, in the most authentic manner possible. As the attention to detail recalls John Ford, and the catalyst involves a white woman abducted by savages, we might guess this will be a redux of *The Searchers* (1956). Hardly! A dark sense of the supernatural descends as a tired sheriff (Kurt Russell, challenging Clint Eastwood for status of Last Great Cowboy Star) leads a small posse into ever more surreal terrain. With startling success, the film changes horses in mid-stream, transforming into a *Cannibal Holocaust* stomach-churner. How important that, in our era of political correctness, the abductors are not Indians but Troglodytes, a pre-human race of the sort encountered in Arthur Conan Doyle's *The Lost World* (1912), as well as varied books by Edgar Rice Burroughs and H. Rider Haggard.

EVERYTHING OLD IS NOUVEAU AGAIN: Arthur Penn's rural gangster epic allowed Fay Dunaway to revive the old noir style of Marie Window in the 1950s.

BONNIE AND CLYDE (1967)

Definitive 1960s Cool Rating: *****

Michael J. Pollard Cult Rating: *****

Arthur Penn, dir.; David Newman, Robert Benton, Robert Towne, scr.; Warren Beatty, pro.; 1.85:1; C; 11 min.; Warner Bros.

 1967 was the year when American movies changed forever, in part owing to this ultra-violent (for its time) fact-based tale about Prohibition-era gangsters Clyde Barrow (Warren Beatty, 1937–) and Bonnie Parker (Faye Dunaway, 1941–). The "ballet of blood" with which the film ends so sickened studio boss Jack L. Warner (1892–1978) that he sent this off to the grindhouse/Drive In circuit. Establishment reviewers largely dismissed *B&C* as bloodthirsty junk. A new breed of critics, writing for alternative (i.e. 'Underground') papers, hailed it as a metaphor for the then-current Youth Movement. Originally, producer Beatty (a star who insisted on seizing control of his career) hoped to lure Jean-Luc Godard or Francois Truffaut to America. Penn (1922–2010) studied their Nouvelle Vogue work, bringing such innovations as slow- and fast-motion, referencing of earlier movies, and a new freedom (minor nudity, rough action) to the screen Michael J. Pollard (1939–2019) became a sensation owing to his portrayal of sidekick "C.W. Moss," a goofy redneck. Virtual unknown Dunaway (1941–) was picked to play Bonnie only after Tuesday Weld, Jane Fonda, and Natalie Wood turned it down. F.D.'s costumes (including a sassy beret) influenced women's fashions during the hippie era, a time when everything old (like granny-glasses) seemed new again.

BOOGIE NIGHTS (1997)

Paul Thomas Anderson Rating: **** ½

Heather Graham Cult Rating: *****

Paul Thomas Anderson, dir.; Anderson, scr., Anderson, Lloyd Levin, Paul Thomas Anderson, pro.; 2.35:1; C; 155 min.; New line Cinema.

    The best big studio movie ever made about the porn industry. P.T.A. (1970–) relates the story of an all-American boy (Mark Wahlberg, 1971–) drawn into X-rated filmmaking by a sleazy 'director' (Burt Reynolds, 1936–2018), achieving a limited sense of stardom (as 'Dirk Diggler') owing to his immense member. More than an unsparingly accurate 'docudrama' of a sordid industry, *B.N.* depicts hard-core filmmaking as a metaphor for the 1970s. Porno Chic (and with it Cocaine Chic) is portrayed as inseparable from Disco music and what the social critic Christopher Lasch tagged 'The Culture of Narcissism' as hedonism replaced a late 1960s' commitment to serious social causes. Focuses on that brief juncture in time when porn appeared about to be accepted as a pop art form, destroyed by the changeover from film to videotape. Heather Graham (1970–) provides a point-on performance apparently based on real-life Ginger Lynn, sleaziest of all female porn stars. Industry veterans Nina Hartley (1959–) and Veronica Hart (1956–) appear. Remarkably, P.T.A. managed to maintain his edginess and iconoclasm after shifting to more easily accessible Oscar-nominated work: *Magnolia* (1997); *There Will Be Blood* (2007).

THE LAST AMERICAN HERO VS. THE BADDEST BIKERS EVER: Tom Laughlin first introduced his continuing half-Indian hero in one of the more thoughtful post-*Wild Angels* biker flicks, which he anonymously wrote and directed himself.

BORN LOSERS, THE (1967)

Biker flick appeal: *****

T.C. Frank (Tom Laughlin), dir.; James Lloyd (Elizabeth James), scr.; Delores Taylor, prod.; C; 35 mm; 113 mins.; Fanfare Films.

    The mid-Sixties Drive-In craze for outlaw biker flicks was at its height when Tom Laughlin (aka Frank, 1931–2013) directed and starred in this unique variation of their already tired theme. Once more, the meanest motorcycle maniac imaginable (Jeremy Slate) pursues a bikini-clad beauty (Elizabeth James, aka Lloyd, 1944–) down the Pacific Coast Highway. For once (and here was the key to this artlessly shot film's impact), the chase and eventual rape is related from the woman's point-of-view—appropriate at a time when modern feminism reached the mainstream. As to pop culture, *B.L.* helped re-ignite the James Dean cult; bad bikers congregate beneath a huge poster-image of that deceased rebel star. Shot by the director's family, including his wife Taylor, for $360,000, this reaped in $36 million and allowed Laughlin to expand his half-Native American Vietnam vet anti-hero into the Billy Jack franchise. Written in the style of a Stanley Kramer 1950s message movie.

BOUT DE SOUFFLE, A, aka *BREATHLESS* (1960)

The Film That Changed Film Forever Rating: *****

Jean-Luc Godard, dir.; Francoise Truffaut, scr.; George de Beaurgard, pro.; 1.37:1; B&W; 90 min.; Les Films Imperia.

    French New Wave avatars Godard (1930–) and Truffaut (1932–1984) dedicated this early entry in their emergent school of filmmaking to Monogram and Mascot, Hollywood's lowest studios in the Poverty Row category. They reveled in the supposed 'incompetence' of Z budget noirs in comparison to the more staid/conventional Hollywood product of The Majors. *Breathless* is modelled on inexpensive junk that had been re-analyzed as gems by young critics for *Cahiers du Cinema*, the Parisian journal where J.G. and F.T. expounded the auteur theory of a director's dominance before becoming filmmakers themselves. Bad boy Jean-Paul

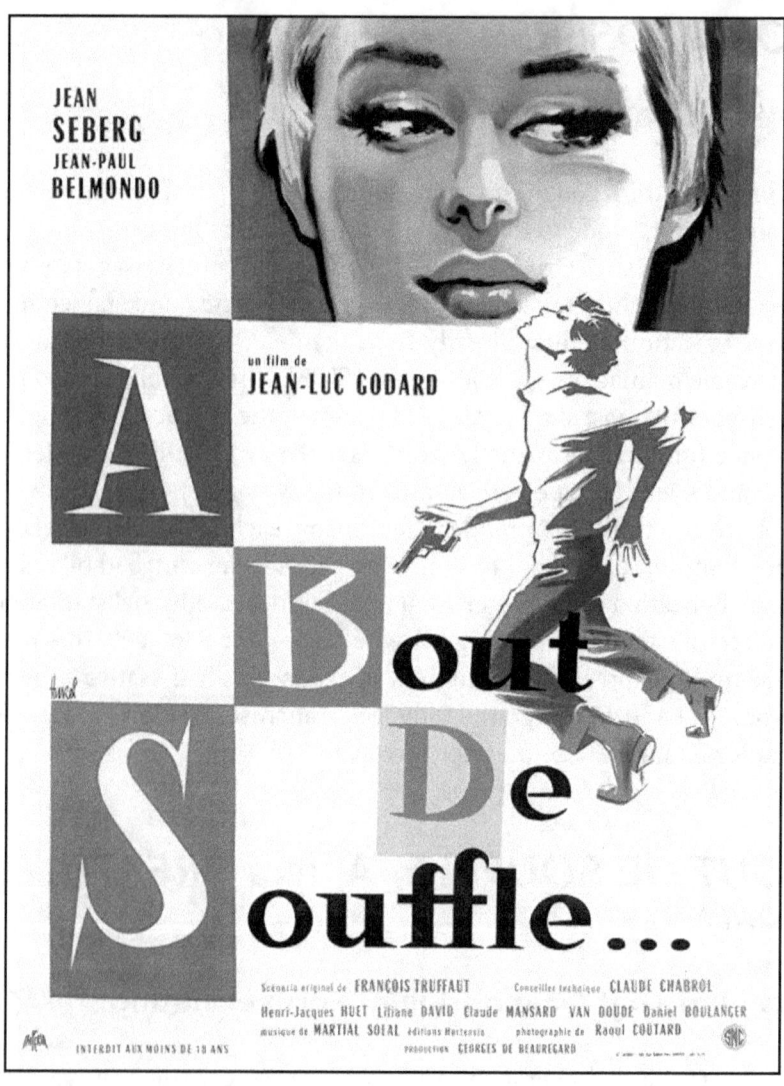

INTRODUCING THE FRENCH NEW WAVE: Jean-Luc Godard's acclaimed experiment in liberation of the camera was drubbed by old-fashioned movie critics as "offensively amoral" during its initial release.

Belmondo (1933–) is a sociopathic criminal who idolizes gangsters as once portrayed by Humphrey Bogart. Nihilistically he kills a cop, heading for Paris to hide out with his American expatriate girlfriend (Jean Seberg, 1938–1979). Purposefully, all the rules of 'good' filmmaking are broken, even destroyed: the hand-held camera offers a jerky image that would soon be called Cinema Verite. The editing is disorienting thanks to sudden 'jump cuts'; the dialogue, mostly improvised. By decade's end, such 'awful' approaches would become accepted in America (via films such as *Easy Rider*) as a bold new aesthetic. Antic, radical, anarchic.

BOWLING FOR COLUMBINE (2002)

Cult Documentary Rating: *****

Michael Moore Aficionado Rating: *****

Michael Moore, dir.; Moore, scr.; Moore, Charles Bishop, Jim Czarnecki, pros.; 1.85:1; B&W/C; 120 min.; U.A.

A high-school shooting in Colorado on April 20, 1999 left 15 people (a teacher, students, the perpetrators) dead. In a knee jerk reaction, conservatives blamed everything from rock 'n' roll to violent video games to action flicks. Moore (1954–) offered an equally absurd idea, if in irony: as the killers were rumoured to have gone bowling earlier that day, could the sport be held responsible? Ever controversial—attacking G.M. corporate C.E.O. Roger B. Smith for destroying Flint MI by downsizing the plant in *Roger and Me* (1989); holding Pres. George W. Bush responsible for the destruction of America's international alignments in *Fahrenheit 9/11* (2004)-—Moore's most consistent target is the conventional documentary/TV film which proffers ridiculously simplistic solutions to complex problems. *B.F.C.* expands into a study of America's culture of violence and need for gun control. Significant interviews with actor/NRA president Charlton Heston (1923–2008) and "The God of Grotesque Rock" performer Marilyn Manson (1969–). As with other examples of New Journalism, the ultimate subject of any Moore "documentary" is Moore. He offers not 'the' truth but his 'truth' in works that are *intended* to be subjective.

BOY AND HIS DOG, A (1975)

Cult dystopian fiction: ****

L.Q. Jones Cultists: **** ½

L.Q. Jones, Jones, scr.; Jones, pro.; 2.35:1; C; 91 min.; LQ/JAF Prods.

One more arid, inhospitable stretch of desert; yet another male loner, brandishing a rifle, accompanied by a dog. This is the opening image in *Mad Max: The Road Warrior* (1981) and, earlier, *Hondo* (1955). Jones's modern turn on such a bleak landscape revealing a post-apocalyptic world was introduced in a novella by sci-fi writer Harlan Ellison (1934-2018), who penned the greatest original *Star Trek* story, "The City on the Edge of Forever" (4/6/1967). Here is the only film directed by actor L.Q. (1927– ; real name, Justin Ellis McQueen). Don Johnson (1949–), before achieving stardom with *Miami Vice*, is able to telepathically communicate with his canine companion, 'Blood' (played by Tiger). Sequences set below ground, in a cavern filled with misanthropic survivors (Jason Robards as the leader) borrows from *Beneath the Planet of the Apes* (1970). Feminists rejected this low-budget item owing to the anti-hero's casual rape of each woman he meets, the latest Suzanne Benton. This initiated cannibalism as a popular riff.

BOYHOOD (2014)

DIY Filmmaking Rating: *****

Richard Linklater, dir, scr.; Linklater, Anna Walker McBay, many others, pro.; 1.85:1; C; 165 min.; Detour Prods./IFC.

During the first two decades of the 21st century, DIY transformed in the industry in general and the Cult Film most specifically. In the past, indie films often looked like precisely what they were: intriguing personal projects that in truth resembled home movies more than Hollywood product. Now, owing to advances in technical apparatus, anyone can be an auteur whose films look every bit as slick as a Hollywood product and be released to a mass audience. That does not necessarily mean they are 'good,' this as always determined by talent or lack of it. So far at least the most outstanding project has been this wonderfully odd creative experiment, taking the 'coming of age' story to a whole new dimension. Over 12 years, Linklater annually brought a cast together, even as Michael Apted did in his remarkable Seven Up series. That, however, was a documentary. This is a fiction film with Ellar Coltrane (1994–) playing 'Mason,' cult-worthy stars Ethan Hawke and Patricia Arquette as the parents. Seamlessly, a five-year-old child passes through the ever changing American social, political, and cultural scene, readying to enter college at eighteen. So self-assured and subtly satisfying that full recognition of the one-of-a-kind accomplishment has never been forthcoming; R.L. makes the near impossible seem easy.

BRAZIL (1985)

Terry Gilliam Cultists: **** ½

Dystopian Future Cultists: ****

Terry Gilliam, dir.; Gilliam, Top Stoppard, Charles McKeown, scr.; 1.85:1; C; 132 min. (theatrical), 140 min. (director's cut) Embassy Int.

Imagine Franz Kafka's *The Trial*, George Orwell's *1984*, and James Thurber's "The Secret Life of Walter Mitty" collapsed together and filtered through the sensibility of visionary genius Gilliam (1940–). The result? *Brazil*. That title refers less to the country than a sweet, sensuous, sentimental song from the 1940s; also, an aura that surrounded such easygoing music ('cool' back then, 'campy' today) from a golden age when romance filled the air. Contrast that with a dystopian world and it's easy to grasp why one lonely, misunderstood white-collar worker (Jonathan Pryce, 1947–) retreats to nostalgic recesses of his imagination. There, he romances a dream-girl (Kim Greist); one day she steps out of their blue-sky fantasy and into his drab surroundings. Robert De Niro (1943–) has a cameo as a bug-like fellow whose problems become inextricably connected to the hero's. A script by Tom Stoppard (1937– ; author of *Rosencrantz and Guildenstern are Dead*) relies on derivative ideas for this critique of technocracy. Monty Python's Michael Palin (1943–) plays a key role.

BREAKFAST CLUB, THE (1985)

Eighties Youth Cult Rating: *****

Indie Cult-Film Rating: *** ½

John Hughes, dir.; Hughes, scr.; Hughes, Ned Tanen, prods.; 1.85:1; C; 97 min.; A&M Films/Universal.

Most of the films written, directed, and or produced by John Hughes (1950–2009) were commercial blockbusters: *National Lampoon's Vacation* (1983), *Ferris Bueller's Day Off* (1986), and *Home Alone* (1990) among

UPDATING THE YOUTH FILM: The late John Hughes revived and reoriented teen flicks about bad boys and girls with *The Breakfast Club* and the mainstream hit *Ferris Bueller's Day Off* (1986).

them. But for his second feature, Hughes went the 'ambitious indie' route: a half-dozen or so people trapped in a self-made hell on earth (essentially, Jean Paul Sartre's *No Exit* updated for contemporary America), shot on a tight one million budget. Five students at a suburban Chicago high school must spend eight hours detention-time on a Saturday morn: a clean-cut athlete (Emilio Estevez, 1962–), a pampered pretty princess (Molly Ringwald, 1968–), a brainy nerd (Anthony Michael Hall, 1968–), an often mute basket-case (Ally Sheedy, 1962–), and a juvenile delinquent (Judd Nelson, 1959–) as the now-legendary 'Bender.' Initially despising one another more than their proctor (Paul Gleason), they form a community based on the one thing they have in common: Youth. Impressive soul-searching moments for each were improvised under Hughes' guidance. Occasionally, the comedy gets too raucously silly. What 'works' over-rides any complaints.

BREWSTER McCLOUD (1970)

General Cult Rating: *****

Altman aficionado Rating: *****

Bud Cort Cultist Rating: *****

Robert Altman, dir.; Doran William Cannon, scr.; Lou Adler, John Phillips, pros.; 2.35:1; C; 105 min.; Lion's Gate/MGM.

Had *M*A*S*H* (1970) not turned out to be a surprise commercial hit for Robert Altman (1925–2000), that edgy, offbeat 'service comedy' would have qualified as a Cult Film. Less than a year later, *B.M.* did no business but achieved such status. A dark, bizarre contemporary fairy-tale for grown-ups, this concerns an intelligent, obsessive youth (Bud Cort, 1948–) who hides from society in a forgotten abscess in Houston's Astrodome. His dream: assemble a pair of immense wings, then fly over a shocked crowd. Brewster finds a worthy inamorata in 'Suzanne' (Shelley Duvall, 1949–), this her film debut. R.A. made this off-the-wall premise work by tossing away Cannon's script; he had previously written *Skidoo!* (1968), arguably the worst comedy of that decade. Alternately charming and cruel, *B.M.* rates as the first release by the long-lived Lion's Gate indie company, which Altman founded. He cited this radical 'comedy' as his

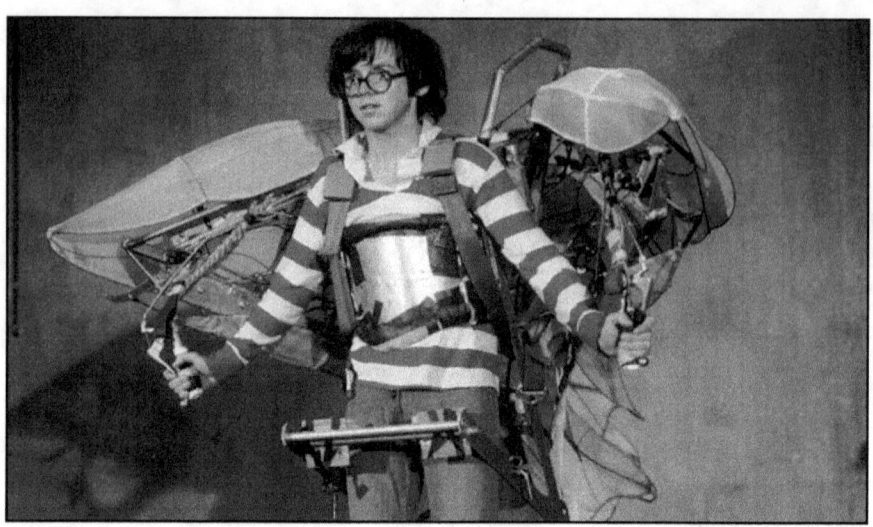

YOU'LL BELIEVE A BOY CAN FLY: Character actor Bud Cort sailed to cult stardom in Robert Altman's most offbeat film.

own fav among his work. As the despicable 'Daphne Heap,' witchy Margaret Hamilton (1902–1985) wears a pair of ruby slippers all but identical to those in *The Wizard of Oz*.

BRICK (2005)

Conventional Teen Flick Rating: ****

Cult Rating: **** ½

Rian Johnson, dir.; Johnson, scr.; Mark G. Mathis, Ron Bergman, pros.; 1.85:1; C; 110; Bergman Lustig Prods.

    The greatest 21st.Century example (so far) of a major talent without connections overseeing a personal project from its inception through release, thereby winning a spot on the L.A. A-list. Johnson (1973–) imagined an old-fashioned noir reset in his contemporary San Clemente high school. When a beautiful blonde (Emile de Raven) goes missing, her former boyfriend (Joseph Gordon-Levitt, 1981–) determines to find out what happened and why. Assorted low-life teens go only by nicknames (Brain, Pin, Tugger) in homage to Howard Hawks' *Rio Bravo* (1959) though they more resemble the villains in *Blue Velvet*. Other pop-culture references include *The Birds* (Seagulls contrasted with pretty girls), Gilbert and Sullivan's *The Mikado*, and TV's edgy animated *Cowboy Bebop*. There's a femme fatale (Nora Zehetner) named after Gene Tierney's 'ghost' in *Laura* (1944). This is a post-Tarantino/ post-modernist film with a *Lock, Stock, and Two Smoking Barrels* (1998) approach to time and space. The tightly budgeted (under half a million) indie was edited on a home-computer. Its ever-expanding cult won Johnson work on *Star Wars: The Last Jedi* (2017).

BRIDE OF FRANKENSTEIN (1935)

Traditional Monster movie appeal: ** ½

Black comedy appeal: *****

James Whale Cult Appeal: *****

Karloff Cult Appeal: *****

James Whale, dir.; Robert Florey, William Hurlbut, John L. Balderston, scr.; Carl Laemmle Jr., pro.; 1.37:1; B&W; Universal.

When *Frankenstein* (1931) attained classic status, Universal hungered for a sequel. Director Whale (1889–1957) agreed to guide Boris Karloff (1887–1969) through the motions once more only if granted total artistic freedom. Laemmle agreed; J.W. mounted not a traditional horror film but a one-of-a-kind set-piece of outrageous flamboyance That paved the way for *The Rocky Horror Picture Show* and Mel Brooks *Young Frankenstein* (1974). In addition to the remarkably sustained tone of black humor combined with ancient fairy-tale motifs (creating the screen's first Camp classic thirty years before that term came into existence), there are stunning tableaus: Mary Shelley (Elsa Lanchester, (1902–1986) relating her tale to poets Byron and Shelley on a dark and stormy night; 'Dr. Pretorius' (Ernst Thesiger, 1879–1961) with his fruity mannerisms and miniature people 'under glass'; a lower-class harridan (Una O'Connor, 1880–1959) tearing through the streets, screaming for help; the Christ-like blind hermit (O.P. Heggie, 1877–1936) offering succor to a much-maligned monster; the title character (also Lanchester) moving and hissing like a swan; Colin Clive (1900–1937) re-imagining his "It's alive… *alive!*" line. The score by

STRANGELY SEDUCTIVE: Elsa Lanchester plays the title character with Ernest Thesiger stealing the show as "Dr. Praetorius" in James Whale's off-the-wall combination of Universal horror and dark comedy.

Franz Waxman (1906–1967) proved so memorable, with its subtle satire on classics of 19th century symphonies, it was reused for *Flash Gordon*. Sir Ian McKellan plays Whale planning this project in *Gods and Monsters* (1998).

BRING ME THE HEAD OF ALFREDO GARCIA (1974)

Peckinpah cultist Rating: *****

Oates cultist Rating: *****

Sam Peckinpah, dir.; Peckinpah, Frank Kawalski, Gordon (T.) Dawson, scr.; Martin Baum, pro.; 1.37:1; C; 112 min.; U.A.

Fans of Old Sam (1925–1984), whose best movies combine the elegiac aspect of John Ford's 1960s Westerns with the hard-edged pessimism and random violence of Quentin Tarantino's 1990s southwestern sagas, love to argue whether Peckinpah was a genius or madman. This film proves he was indeed both. The maverick, devastated when his Hollywood financed movies (*Major Dundee*, 1965; *Pat Garrett* and *Billy the Kid*, 1972) were cut to ribbons by the studios to render them palatable for mainstream audiences wandered to Mexico for a low-budget indie. The only film for which S.P. contracted for the all-important final cut (even his masterpiece *The Wild Bunch* lacks several sequences). His anger, bitterness, melancholy, and nihilism are expressed in this bizarre Road Movie/Buddy Buddy flick (here, one of the 'buddies' is dead) featuring elements of John Huston's *The Treasure of Sierra Madre* (1948) and Francois Truffaut's *Tirez Sur le Pianiste* (1960). Ambiguously gay bounty hunters (Gig Young, Robert Webber) search for the elusive title figure; a depressed loner (Warren Oates) sets out to locate the dead man's body and deliver Alfredo's head to a Mexican warlord for the reward. Sam and Oates were, while shooting, fuelled by alcohol/cocaine. It shows onscreen. Madly, and brilliantly.

BRONSON (2008)

One of a Kind Cult Rating: *****

Nicolas Winding Refn, dir.; Refn, Brock Norman Brock, scr.; Danny Hansford, Rupert Preston; 1.85:1; C; 92 min.; Vertigo.

    When asked what he might have become had a writing career not emerged, young Woody Allen replied: "likely, a criminal." His first auteurial effort, *Take the Money and Run* (1969), cast Woody as a character based on himself (same birth date) who follows in John Dillinger's footsteps. So! Is there any truth to the theory that if violent impulses are redirected toward creative expression, the result may well be a genius rather than a menace to society? No film has raised that issue more effectively than this fact-based piece about Michael Gordon Peterson (1952– ; played by Tom Hardy), sent to prison for a short time owing to a robbery. He soon proved so brutal (a bare-knuckles fighter who violently seized hostages) that, named England's most dangerous person, he spent three decades in solitary. To survive, M.G.P. assumed an alternate identity: movie star Charles Bronson (1921–2003), eventually shedding every aspect of his own personality to live a more rewarding life within his mind. Critics complained about over-use of Wagnerian music to pump up the volume. Danish-born director Refn (1970–) employs Bronson's eventual focus on drawing as a means to raise issues for his audience's consideration.

BROTHER FROM ANOTHER PLANET (1984)

John Sayles Cult Rating: *****

John Sayles, dir.; Sayles, scr.; Peggy Rajski, Maggie Renzi, pro.; 1.85:1; C; 108 min.

    Imagine a cross between Nicholas Roeg's *The Man Who Fell to Earth* and Steven Spielberg's *E.T.* (1982), done in the style of a 1970s Urban Actioners if with a self-satirizing element, and you have a sense of what this low-budget ($350,000) comedic piece of social criticism is up to. Joe Morton (1947–) plays the title character, a gentle alien whose black coloring cause the residents of New York to assume he's Afro-American and treat him according to their prejudices. Writer-director J.S. (1950–) is yet another of those intellectual Ivy League grads allowed an opportunity to enter the movie biz by working on R.C.'s popular junk films. Always though Sayles knew what he really wanted to do: make serious-minded (if often comic in tone) indie pictures. There are those who believe that the inexpensively produced *Return of the Secaucus Seven* (1979) comes closer to capturing the failed dreams of 1960s radicals than Lawrence Kasdan's popular *The Big Chill* (1983). Other impressive Sayles films include the nostalgia fest *Baby It's You* (1983) and the southwestern crime drama *Lone Star* (1996). Sometimes cited as the first film to present 'Men in Black' (no pun intended) as an element in contemporary sci-fi cinema.

BUBBA HO-TEP (2002)

Elvis Completist Cult Rating: **** ½

Bruce Campbell Cult Rating: *****

Don Coscarelli, dir.; Coscarelli, Joe R. Lansdale, scr.; Coscarelli, Jason R. Savage, pro.; 1.85:1; C; 92 min.; Silver Sphere Corp.

Elvis Lives! At least in Lansdale's (1911–) award winning story and the low-budget, high-impact film that Coscarelli (1954–), best known for his *Phantasm* franchise, derived from it. Now elderly, the King is committed to an Old Folks' home. Nurses in charge accept him as a geriatric with dementia who believes himself to be Elvis. As we watch this zany project, with comedic shifts in style from burlesque to surprisingly smart-sophisticated dialogue, an audience goes back and forth, accepting the hero's story for a while, then wondering if the Miss Ratched-worthy head nurse is right. To make matters more complex, there's an Afro-American patient who claims to be JFK. The two join as elderly super-heroes to combat an evil Egyptian force that slips into the building, though that may be a shared fantasy of two likeable insane people. Originally, the hope had been to include Elvis music as well as clips from the musical travelogues as Bubba watches TV, but with a budget of little more than half a million, that was not possible. A great fav at edgy sci-fi film festivals, and yet another feather in the hat of reigning cult action-comedy star Bruce Campbell (1958–), in the role that he was born to play.

BUCKAROO BANZAI, aka, ADVENTURES OF BUCKARBOO BANZAI ACROSS THE 8th DIMENSION (1984)

Cult Rating: *

W.D. Richter, dir.; Earl Mac Rauch, scr.; Richter, Neil Canton, prod.; 2.35;1; C; 103 min.; Sherwood Prods./20th Century Fox.

Imagine that supercool 1960s spoofy spy 'Flint' (James Coburn) re-created as a low-key hipster/geek some two decades later and you'd have B.B. played by Peter "RoboCop" Weller (1947–). A downbeat, even lethargic contemporary Renaissance man, B.B. casually drifts from playing guitar in a garage band to a nearby hospital where he perform brain surgery, then takes off with his team, The Hong Kong Cavaliers, to save the world from supervillain 'Lizardo' (John Lithgow, 1945–) and other evil invaders. Producer Canton mistakenly thought that he would be creating another Indiana Jones for the mass popular audience; Writer W.D.R. (1945–) imagined the piece as a droll cinematic equivalent of a Thomas Pynchon novel. Vapid, transparent even, the film is so smug and self-satisfied that it failed to find an audience with aficionados of less cynical, laid-back fare. Attempts at humor feel forced; the plot twists are facile. Plays like a self-conscious caricature of true cult movies.

CABIN IN THE WOODS, THE (2011)

Teens Menaced in a Small Place Rating: ****

Drew Goddard, dir.; Goddard, Joss Whedon, scr.; Whedon, pro.; 2.40:1; C; 95 min.; Lionsgate.

 Alter "Don't open that door!" to "Don't look in the cellar!" while retaining teenagers so stupid that they don't deserve to live and you have this effective (for many, surprisingly so!) horror item. Goddard (1975–) and Whedon take a subgenre of contemporary horror that appeared with the new freedom of the screen circa 1969/1970 and manage to breath new life into it, with appreciated support from David Julyan's intricately eerie musical score and Peter Deming's ability to bring a primitive Gothic sensibility to what seemingly is a tranquil setting. An anti-Romantic (the arts movement, not love stories) sensibility sets in as five teens head into the woods for fun and games only to find themselves the prey of part zombie, part werewolf, part vampire things. For once, the monsters are intriguingly individualized. Kristen Connolly is the pretty girl who reads from the book of the dead, unwittingly unleashing horror. Director Goddard (no relationship to Jean-Luc, his last name spelled with one 'd') went on to make the effective neo-noir *Bad Time at the El Royale* (2018); star Chris Hemsworth (1983–) became "Thor."

CAGED HEAT (1973)

Philippino Exploitation Flick Rating: *****

Barbara Steele Cult Rating: *****

Jonathan Demme, dir.; Demme, scr.; Roger Corman, Evelyn Purcell, Samuel W. Gelfman, pros.; 1.85:1; C 83 min. Artisan Ent./New World.

"White hot desires melt cold prison steel!"; a rich baritone bellows this mantra over seamy images in the film's Drive-In preview. With on-screen nudity accepted for five years, now no longer a shocker, Corman needed something more titillating to draw in his jaded audience. S&M, B&D were obviously the way to go. He revived Women's Prison Pictures, setting his stories in the Philippines. Demme (1944–2017) wrote the first (and one of the best), *The Hot Box* (1972) with cult blonde Margaret Markov (1948–), then made his directorial debut here. The beauties on view include raven-haired Erica Gavin (1947–), star of Russ Meyer's early nudie *Vixen* (1969); and Barbara Steele, making her transition from vampire girls to vicious matrons. Rough-hewn feminism (this was the era when Women's Liberation made its impact) appears as diverse girls put petty arguments aside to form an all-female community, exacting revenge on male guards who raped them. Demme would cross-over to the mainstream (but bring his exploitation flick roots with him), winning a Best Director Oscar for *Silence of the Lambs* (1991).

CANNIBAL HOLOCAUST (1980)

Cannibal Cult Film Rating: *****

Ruggero Deodato, dir.; Gianfranco Clerici, scr.; Franco Palaggi, Franco Di Nunzio, prods.; 1.85:1; C; 95 min.; F.D. Cinematografica.

Italy's Deodato (1939–) turned out an exploitation flick that explores the movie medium's full range of possibilities. He relished the Mondo Cane venue of weirdo documentaries (partly staged, partly real), the stylized, artistically rendered violence in Giallos, and the degree to which TV news footage may be faux. *C.H.* concerns an American anthropologist (Robert Kinman) who travels to the frontier between Brazil and Peru in search of a missing camera crew; he returns with found footage (this two decades before *Blair Witch*). Part shockumentary, part horror flick, and (some claim) part Snuff Film, this spectacle of in-your-face brutality to humans (and animals) has been banned in 50+ countries. Some critics consider *C.H.* the most offensive grindhouse piece ever; others 'read' it as a wry, ironic social comment in which 'civilized' interlopers prove themselves more ruthless than the Amazonian world.

CAPTIVE WILD WOMAN (1943)

Gorgeous Female Monster Movie Rating: ** ½

Acquanetta Cult Rating: *****

Edward Dmytryk, dir.; Griffin Jay, Henry Sucher, Ted Fithlan, Neil P. Varnick, scrs.; Ben Pivar, pro.; 1.37:1; B&W; 61 min.; Universal.

Following *The Wolf Man*, Universal had difficulty coming up with new monsters. Then a team of four writers devised this original if ghastly idea: yet another mad scientist (John Carradine, 1906–1988), obsessed by recent experiments with human glands, transfers his nurse's brain into the body of a female gorilla. The result: 'Paula Depree,' an exotic beauty, mysterious in her muteness. P.D. surrenders to her dark animal instincts when a blonde (Evelyn Keyes, 1916–2008) attracts the man (Milburn Stone) Paula lusts after. As the beauty *and* the beast, Acquanetta (1924–

THE BEAUTY IS A BEAST: Despite this mis-leading staged publicity shot, in the film Acquanetta and the ape are one and the same character.

2004) was billed as The Venezuelan Volcano. Her birth name: Mildred Davenport; she hailed from Ozone WY. Acquanetta played Paula again the next year in *Jungle Captive*, then moved on to *Tarzan and the Leopard Woman* (1946). Nearly a third of this circus-set opus featured stock footage from *The Big Cage* (1933) with lion-tamer Clyde Beatty (1903–1965). Character actor Stone (1904–1980) was cast as the lead because he physically resembled C.B.

CARNIVAL OF SOULS (1962)

Ultra-Low Budget Horror Cult Rating: ****

Candace Hilligoss Fan Rating: **** ½

One Shot Wonders of Commercial Filmmaking Cult: *****

Herk Harvey, dir.; John Clifford, scr.; Harvey, pro.; 1.85:1; B&W; 91 min. (initial release print), 94 min. (director's cut), 78 min. (original TV release print); Harcourt Prods./ Herts-Lion.

The best low-budget thriller ever filmed in Salt Lake City. A year earlier, businessman H.H.. (1924–1996) drove from Cal. (where he'd shot an industrial film) home to Lawrence KS. As he passed abandoned Saltaire amusement park, a ghost story took form in his mind. Once back, he convinced fellow Centron employee J.C. to pen a story about a woman (Candace Hilligoss, 1935–) who nearly dies in a KS car accident, then moves to UT where a hideous Angel of Death (H.H.) follows her everywhere. That tale may have been 'borrowed' from a classic *Twilight Zone*, "The Hitchiker" (1/22/1960); it would be 'recycled' by M. Night Shamalayan for *The Sixth Sense* (1999). Harvey raised a modest $20,000, then shot *C.O.S.* over his two-week vacation. A low-level distributor picked it up; the film sank at the box-office. When *C.O.S.* played on late-night TV horror movie shows it engendered a cult following that continues to this day.

CAT PEOPLE (1942)

Cult B Horror Rating: *****

Simone Simon Cultist Rating: *****

Jacques Tourneur, dir.; DeWitt Bodeen, scr.; Val Lewton, pro.; 1.37:1; B&W; 73 min.; RKO.

At RKO Lewton (1904–1961), assigned to produce a string of horror films, decided to go the opposite route from Universal with its 'seen' monsters: Dracula, Frankenstein, The Mummy, etc. His filmmaking unit cut costs by relying on our instinct to fear the dark, the unknown, the *un*seen: Nothing that could be projected onscreen could compare to the horror lurking just beyond the screen's edge… or what the recesses of a human mind can project onto a black slate. *C.P.* offers a modern fable about an average guy (Kent Smith) who meets a Serbian émigré (the eerily enigmatic Simone Simon, 1916–2005) at the zoo. A hasty wedding results in an unconsummated marital situation; she fears a kiss may turn her into a kill-crazy creature. Bodeen (1908–1988) opted for a balance between a tale of terror and a candid study of female frigidity. J.T. (1904–1977) employed the studio-bound *faux* city street-set to his advantage, endowing the piece with an 'other worldly' aura. A notable predecessor to all the post-war movies featur-

TO THE DEVIL, A DAUGHTER: Like her father Klaus, who played many Satanic roles including Dracula, Natassja Kinsky projects a deadly power over mortal men.

ing a psychiatrist even crazier than his patients, here played by Tom Conway. Two haunting sequences: the stalking of a normal woman (Jane Randolph) on a late-night Manhattan avenue; her desperation while, taking a swim in her apartment-house pool, strange shadows and shrill sounds test her sanity.

CAT PEOPLE (1982)

Paul Schrader Auteurist Rating: NO STARS

Natassja Kinski Cult Queen Rating: *****

Paul Schrader, dir.; Schrader (unbilled), Alan Ormsby, scr.; Charles W. Fries, pro.; 1.85:1; C; 118 min.; Universal.

Schrader (1946–) brought his ingrained Calvinist sensibility to Tinseltown, rendering him the worst possible candidate to helm sex-oriented movies: *Hardcore* (1979), *American Gigolo* (1980), and this worse-than-awful remake of one of the most appealingly erotic (by implication) horror-noirs. By shifting the story from New York to the voodoo haunts of New Orleans, Schrader eliminated the essence of DeWitt Bodeen's concept: This could happen in any city. The best sequences are shot-by-shot replays of set-pieces from the 1942 version: a normal woman (Annette O'Toole, 1952–) stalked on late-night city-street, then in a swimming pool. What elevates this disaster to cult status: the enigmatic presence of Natassja Kinski (1961–), daughter of the creepy German actor Klaus and onetime protege of ever-edgy Roman Polanski. Barely 16, K.K. had already appeared nude with older man Marcello Mastroianni in *Stay As You Are* (1979). When a shot at A-list stardom in *Tess* (from Thomas Hardy's novel) failed to 'take,' she drifted into diverse roles, none so memorable as her appearance here.

CAT-WOMEN OF THE MOON (1953)

Low Budget 1950s Sci-Fi Rating: NO STARS

Low Camp Weird Humor Rating: *****

Marie Windsor Cult Rating: **** ½

Arthur Hilton, dir.; Ray Hamilton, scr.; Al Zimbalist, Jack Rabi, pros.; 1.85:1; B&W; 64 min.; Astor Pictures.

In Astor's low-budget, zestfully idiotic *C.W.O.T.M.*, a team of astronauts discover that while the moon is not made of green cheese, inhabitants are would-be fashion models running around a faux cave in hot black leotards. Female lead Marie Windsor (1919–2000) does not play their queen but an earth scientist. Among her fellow voyagers are Sonny Tufts (1911–1970), teen-heart-throb of the 1940s. Special effects include a giant spider descending on ropes that were obvious even to little kids watching this in 3-D. Touches of quality are present in the score by young Elmer Bernstein (1922–2004; his name mis-spelt 'Bernstien' in the credits. Several imaginative matte shots of the lunar surface are by gifted artist Chesley Bonestell (1888–1986). How sad, though, to see a great character actor, Victor Jory (1902–1982), reduced to a supporting role as an alcoholic space cadet. Remade as *Missile to the Moon* (1958). The first in a genre (Bad Girls in Heavenly Situations) that would be eventually burlesqued in *Amazon Women of the Moon* (1987).

CHANGE OF HABIT (1969)

Casual Elvis Fans' Rating: *

Hardcore/diehard Elvis Aficionado Rating: ****

William A. Graham, dir.; James Lee, S.S. Schweitzer, John Furia, scr.; Joe Connelly, pro.; 1.85:1; C; 93 min./NBC-Universal.

Elvis' 1960s musical travelogues are a staple of mainstream cable viewing, each constantly rerun—with one exception. This, the last Presley screen vehicle, isn't easy to locate, yet its small cult insists this amateurish piece (not a musical but a drama with music, including "Rubberneckin',") contains the key that unlocks The King's essential appeal. Made at the same time a considerable number of people began to think of E.P. (1935–1977) as God, his fan base a religion, he plays 'Carpenter': an idealistic doctor who forsakes the big bucks of a suburban practice for the bleakest slum (the film released soon after his hit record "In the Ghetto") to attend the poor. One assisting nun is played by popular songstress Barbara McNair (1934–2007). The other, Mary Tyler Moore (1936–1977), though she's incognito and, seeming a civilian, attracts and is attracted to the Jesus-like healer. Throughout the film she must choose between loving Christ or

THE SECOND COMING OF ELVIS: After more than ten years of playing bad boys in such films as *Jailhouse Rock* (1957), Elvis evolved toward the end of his movie career into a Christ-like figure.

Carpenter, only to grasp in the final shot that they are one and the same. You have to see this one to believe it; *Viva Las Vegas* (1964), it ain't!

CHIEN ANDALOU, UN, aka ANDALUSIAN DOG, AN (1929)

Surrealist Cult Rating: *****

Must-See Silent Cinema Rating: *****

Luis Bunuel, dir.; Bunuel, Salvador Dali, scr.; Man Ray, prod.; 1.33:1; B&W; 16 ½ mins.; no company listed.

Aware they could not continue living in their native Spain owing to oppressive conservative values, *avant garde* artists Bunuel (1900–1983) and Dali (1904–1989) headed for Paris, a Bohemian demi-monde where arts and free-thinking flourished. The two collaborated on this surreal 'dream film' in which narrative, the basis of most movies, is aggressively attacked: title cards purposefully confuse us as to the time (or space) in which ever more bizarre events occur. *T.A.D.*'s opening image became infamous: a woman's eye (in truth a sheep's) slashed by a razor. An arthouse item, the film also set the pace for Grindhouse slasher flicks! Simone Mareuil and Pierre Batcheff play young lovers in a wild spoof of heterosexual romance. Images of rotting animal bodies and a classic grand piano are set in grotesque tandem with ants crawling out of a hole in a human hand. Are these resonant with meaning or sick put-ons? The auteurs would not say. Their film wordlessly ridicules all religion, Catholicism in particular, echoing Karl Marx's condemnation: "the opiate of the masses." Nearly two decades later, Alfred Hitchcock (1899–1980) hired Dali to recreate the eyeball sequence for his edgy mainstream psycho-drama *Spellbound* (1945). Among other distinctions, this rated as the the favorite film of musician David Bowie (1947–2016).

CHILDREN OF MEN (2006)

Intellectual Near Future Sci-Fi Rating: *****

Alfonso Cuaron Cult Rating: *****

Alfonso Cuaron, dir.; Cuaron, Timothy J. Sexton, David Arata, scr.; Mark Abraham, Tilary Shor, prod.; 1.85:1; C; 109 min.; Strike Ent./Universal.

98 • *Midnight Matinees: Cult Cinema Classics*

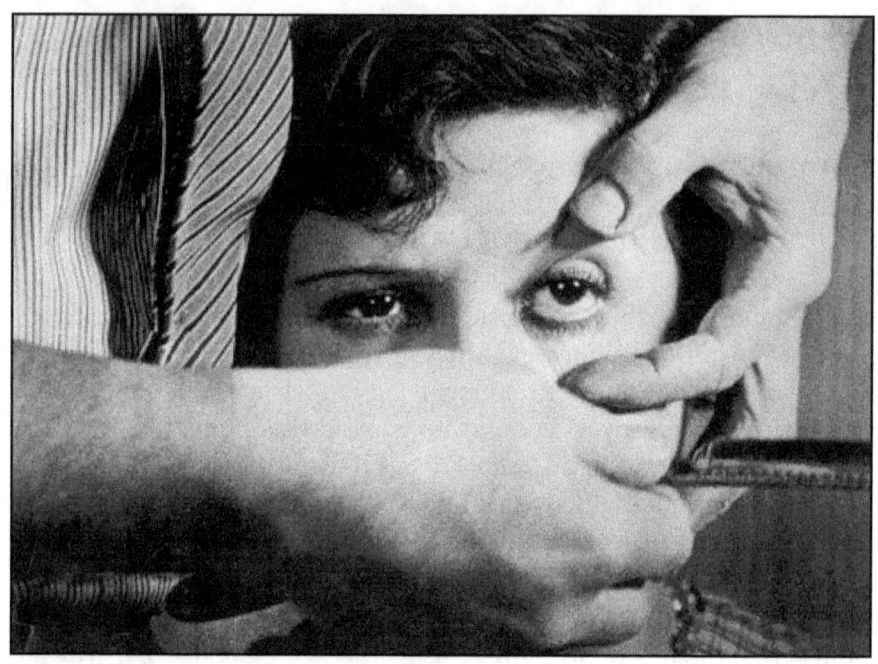

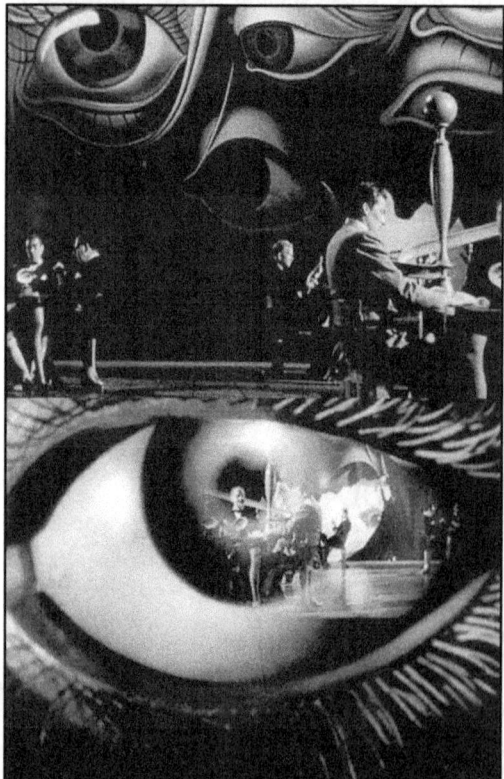

GIVEN WORLD ENOUGH AND TIME, FORBIDDEN CINEMA GOES MAINSTREAM: In the 1920s, only arthouse films or grindhouse flicks would dare to feature an opening sequence in which an eyeball is severed by a razor; mainstream movie-goers were spared such Theatre of Cruelty assaults an audience's sensibility… for the time being, at least; twenty years later, Alfred Hitchcock would cautiously mainstream this concept (with full cooperation from Salvador Dali) for his postwar classic *Spellbound* (1945).

This is how the world ends, poet T. S. Eliot predicted, not with a bang but with a whimper. Though many sci-fi films have been made about the former (think *Armageddon*) only one (*World Without End*, (1956–) opted for the approach taken here: all is about to end owing to the sudden state of infertility among women of the world. The female leader (Julianne Moore, 1960–) of a non-violent radical organization The Fishes (symbol of the Jesus Movement 2,000 years earlier) requests that her former husband (Clive Owen, 1964–) aid them in a top-secret plan to spirit a girl called 'Kee' (Clare-Hope Ashitey, 1987–) to the seaside, then out of England. Kee is pregnant: her child may herald The Second Coming and/or humankind's last hope for survival. A hand-held camera technique allows for the illusion that we are watching TV news footage of the events, while color has been dissipated from the imagery to suggest a life-in-death day-after-tomorrow existence, Kee providing a final ray of hope. From a novel by England's P.D. James; (Mexico's most famous auteur A.C. (1961–) would eventually score a commercial as well as critical hit with *Gravity* (2013).

CHOCOLAT (2000)

Cult Charmer Rating: *****

Lasse Hallstrom, dir.; Robert Nelson Jacobs, scr.; David Brown, many others, pro.; 1.85:1; C; 121 min.; Miramax.

Before *Amelie*, there was *Chocolat*: a modest box-office hit on the arthouse circuit that so endeared itself to upscale movie-goers almost everyone who saw it purchased a VHS or later DVD copy so the delightful comedy-drama would always be available. Far from sophisticated Paris, a young woman (Juliet Binoche, 1964–) arrives in an ultra-traditionalist small town and opens a candy shop. Ordinarily, that would hardly be worth noting—except that residents are so conservative that they fear any 'guilty pleasure,' even one as seemingly innocent as dessert, might send them to hell for eternity. Hallstrom's style here (as in his earlier *My Life as a Dog*, 1987) is best described as 'magical realism': stories occur in what appears to be an actual place yet there's always a hint of pixie-dust hanging in the air. Think: Disney for adults; a Gallic take on our own Frank Capra (*It's a Wonderful Life*, 1946) that exudes a delicate aura of goodwill to all, via a cockeyed/charming sense of optimism that can induce, at the end, a bittersweet tear. Zen Buddhists might ask after watching: What is the sound of one of Tinker Bell's wings flapping, and if this happens off in the forest with no one is around, was there a noise? Irresistible supporting performances from Judy Dench, Alfred Molina, Carrie Ann Moss, and a young Johnny Depp.

CHOPPING MALL (1986)

No Budget Exploitation Flick Rating: **** ½

Jim Wynorsky, dir.; Wynorski, Steve Mitchell, scr.; Julie Corman, pro.; 1.85:1; C; 95 min. (initial release), 77 min. (re-release); Concorde/Trinity Pics.

Talk about an exploitation move with all the elements! Take the sex-crazed kids from *Porky's* (1981), set them down in the late-night mall from *Dawn of the Dead* (1978), add menacing robots like Yul Brynner in *Westworld* (1973) which resemble the cute title character in *Short Circuit* (1986), throw in some sumptuous T&A courtesy B-movie babes Suzee Slater and Kelly Maroney as a Final Girl who fights as boldly as Sigourney Weaver in *Alien* (1979)… so, how to explain why this Z-budget flick didn't initially score? Simple: Bad marketing, wrong title (*Killbots*). Edited to a tighter running time, redistributed with a youth cult horror-humor audience in mind, J.W.'s (1950–) second feature as director achieved the sort of limited if intense devotion it deserved. Performers adding to the film's cult status include Paul Bartel and Mary Woronov (referencing *Eating Raoul* in their dialogue), Dick Miller ad Mell Welles (long-time Corman regulars). Roger's wife produced.

CIDEDAD DE DEUS, aka CITY OF GOD (2002)

Rio-lensed cult cinema Rating: *****

Fernando Meirelles, Kafia Lund, dir.; Braulio Mantoani, scr.; Andre Barata Ribeiro, Maurice Andrada Ramos; prod.; 1.85:1; C; 135 min. (director's cut), 130 mi. (international release print); 02 Films.

Boys to Men: three companions grow up in Rio's most horrific slum: 'Li'l Ze' (Leonardo Firmina), who dreams of becoming one of the gangsters he idolizes; 'Rocket' (Alexandra Rodriguez), searching for a way up and out owing to his creative gifts; and 'Bene' (Phellipe Haagensen), a follower who must choose between the two. On one level, this is akin to watching Martin Scorsese's gangland trilogy—*Mean Streets* (1973), *GoodFellas*, and *Casino* (1995)—condensed into an epic about one set of characters as they gradually age without necessarily maturing over three decades. As is so often the case with Scorsese, onscreen imagery at first appears grimly realistic, underlined by a subtle touch of the surreal. Intense onscreen brutality led to a discussion as to whether this was a work of art about the impact of violence on the young or an out of control, over the top example of exploitation, justifying and even inciting further street brutality. Based on an autobiographical novel by Paulo Lins; Rocket shares that author's vivid memories and attitudes toward the lifestyle he was born into and managed to escape, if hardly unscathed, to tell this cautionary tale.

CINEMA PARADISO, aka *NOUVO CINEMA PARADISO* (1988)

Movie buff Rating: *****

Giuseppe Tornatore, dir.; Tornatore, Vanna Paoli, scr.; Franco Cristaldi, prod.; 1.66:1; C/B&W; 123 min.; Les Films Ariane.

A revered international film director (Jacques Perrin) makes a sentimental journey to the small town in Sicily where he came of age. First stop: The local bijou where he spent the happy moments of his youth falling under the spell of cinema and the unique alternative worlds that open up to a delighted viewer. His mentor was the projectionist (Philippe Noiret), seen in flashbacks as we share the central character's initial love for, and eventual total obsession with film, as well as the eternal bond forged with his unique companion in devotion to what England's Penelope Gilliatt once described as Sight and Sound. Occasionally recalls Federico Fellini's memory movie *Amarcord* (1973), if here the focus does not wander far from the thrills of learning about life by viewing Technicolor alternatives to everyday reality. Here is a film able to delight mainstream viewers while speaking directly to die-hard *Cineastes*: international fans who do not merely enjoy catching a flick but live, breath, watch, devour, re-watch and talk about their common love for the celluloid experience. The great Ennio Morricone (1928–) provided a fitting soundtrack.

GENIUS AT WORK, III: J(i)ri Trinka labored long hours in his studio to create his unique and remarkable visions; here he works on a Czech puppet animation version of Shakespeare's *A Midsummer Night Dream*.

CISARUV SLAVIK, aka EMPEROR'S NIGHTINGALE, THE (1949)

Animation Cultist Rating: *****

J(i)ri Trnka Cultist Rating: *****

J(i)ri Trnka, Miles Makovec, dir.; Trnka, Viezslav Nezval, scrs.; Trnka, pro. (uncredited); 1.37:1/35 mm; 72 min. (director's cut), 55 min. (U.S. TV version).

Trnka (1912–1969) built a puppet theatre to enchant Czech children. He alternated that labor of love with his chosen profession: illustrating books for young people. Falling in love with cinema, Trnka realized this medium would allow him to share his unique vision with kids worldwide. Following a series of delightful short subjects, he and colleagues at Prague's leading art school set out to make feature length movies in a stop/motion technique. The surviving masterpiece of that era was based on a 1843/1844 tale by Denmark's Hans Christian Andersen (1805–1875); a Chinese emperor delights in the music of his living nightingale. When given a bejewelled mechanical bird, the ruler forgets that flesh and blood is more precious than gilt or technology. To render the tale meaningful for contemporary kids, J.T. devised a framing device similar to those at the beginnings of *The Never Ending Story* and *The Princess Bride*. For the American market, the film was accompanied with an eerie narration by Boris Karloff.

CLERKS (1994)

Kevin Smith Cult Rating: *****

Kevin Smith, dir.; Smith, scr.; Scott Mosier, pro.; 1.37:1; B&W; 102 min. (director's cut), 92 min. (theatrical release print); View Askew/Miramax.

"Just because they *serve* you," the best line in this low-budget indie insists, "doesn't mean they *like* you." The focus is on 'Dante' (Brian O'Halloran), an employee at the Quick Stop Convenience store in a small New Jersey town. He covers for a friend who failed to show for his shift; as the hours drag by Dante sells cigarettes, rents out videos, and whines about his current girlfriends. The most important subject of discussion with equally desperate customers: *Star Wars*. These are 'get a life' slackers in their early twenties who see no means to escape their unsatisfying existence. Smith's (1970–) droll if dark comedy, shot in a grainy docudrama style, is filled with offhand dialogue that accurately and humorously captures a dead end existence. No plot per se, as the movie's message is similar to TV's *Seinfeld*: This is a movie about *nothing*, if on a notably lesser level of social status. Smith and Jason Mewes (1974–) introduced the lovable losers they would recreate in future films: 'Silent Bob,' energetic 'Jay.' Shot by former film student Smith for $230,000. Deadpan hipster minimalism.

CLOCKWORK ORANGE, A (1971)

Kubrick Cult Rating: *****

Near Future Dystopian Sci-Fi: *****

Stanley Kubrick, dir., scr., pro.; Kubrick, scr.; 1.66;1; C/B&W; 136 min.; Hawk Films/Warner Bros.

When in 1962 Anthony Burgess wrote the novel on which this film was based, he wished to express a fear of the 'Teddy Boys' roaming London's streets, expressing rage at The Machine through random violent acts. His literary approach: dystopian fiction, employing near-future sci-fi to depict how horrible the contemporary situation would, if not challenged, become. No one in the film business so much as considered a motion picture version then, as graphic sex and violence couldn't be openly portrayed onscreen before 1967. That was then; this, 'now.' Expatriate genius Kubrick (1928–1999) cast Malcolm McDowell (1943–) in the lead role of 'Alex.' S.K. shot on pre-existing locations to imply that this was anything but fantasy, though lighting each sequence in a phantasmagoric manner. Controversy ensued when the box-office smash led to copycat crimes, irresponsible audience members accepting The Droogies as role models rather than cautionary figures. Still, when Alex is brainwashed by society and repelled by violence, he seems less human (if in the lowest sense of that term) than before: a once organic being (an 'orange') reduced to flesh and blood technology (i.e., clockwork). A combination of commercial and critical success upon initial release has been followed by equally intense cult worship ever since.

CLOUD ATLAS (2002)

One of a Kind Cult Rating: *****

Tom Tykwer, Lana and Andy (aka Lilly) Wachowski, dirs..; Tykwer, Wachowskis, scr.; Tykwer, Wachowskis, Stefan Arndt, Grant Hill, Alex Boden, prod.; 2.35:1; C; 172 min.; X-Filme.

How to top *The Matrix*? For Lana (1965–) and Andy (Lilly) (1967–) Wachowski, the answer appeared when Natalie Portman suggested they adapt David Mitchell's 2004 combination of sci-fi and philosophy, an epic on the order of Frank Hebert's *Dune* (1965). N.P. hoped to play 'Sonmi-451,' the first among equals in a sprawling cast of characters existing in far-flung places and differing eras (perhaps alternative dimensions) but are tied together by coincidence and/or fate. With friend T.T. (1965-) aboard, the brothers spent four years developing a script and raising the more than $100 million necessary. (At the time of release, this rated as

THE MOST EXPENSIVE CULT FILM EVER MADE? Despite an A list cast of actors that included Halle Berry and Tom Hanks, among many others, this remarkable movie did not find a large audience... though devotees hail it as a mistreated masterpiece, which it is.

the most expensive indie ever.) Superstars Halle Berry and Tom Hanks were so fascinated by the piece's complexity that each signed on to play multiple roles, though Portman had to drop out owing to pregnancy. (The role of that titular soft-spoken radical was beautifully played by Donna Bae, 1979–). The spectacular results recall previous masterpieces by Alejandro Amenabar and Alejandro G. Inarritu. This critically lauded release failed to return a quarter of its cost. (On the international market *C.A.* fared better). One of the greatest movies most people have never heard of, much less seen, other than a devoted cult following.

COBRA WOMAN (1944)

Color 'Camp' Rating: *****

Maria Montez Cultist Rating: *****

Robert Siodmak, dir.; George Lewis, Richard Brooks, Scott Darling, scr.; George WaGGner, pro.; 1.37:1; C: 71 mins; Universal.

Between 1941–1945, Hollywood performed a balancing act between support-the-war-films and garishly colourful escapist movies. As to the latter: In this mesmerizing bad-taste B movie a bold hero (Jon Hall, 1915–1979) and his trustworthy young sidekick (Sabu, 1924–1963) journey to an isle of death to rescue the princess (Maria Montez, (1912–1951) from her wicked snake-worshipping twin sister (also Montez). Siodmak ((1900–1973) and his crew took a serious approach to the silly material, turning out an early Camp classic. Most memorable sequence: Montez (born in the Dominican Republic and Tinseltown's 1940s "Queen of Technicolor") as the bad beauty dancing wildly in her hidden Temple, randomly/whimsically picking which of her helpless citizens will be sacrificed to the phallic King Cobra. Sabu had recently appeared in Zoltan Korda's mainstream masterpieces *The Thief of Bagdad* (1940) and *The Jungle Book* (1942). Lon Chaney Jr., who starred for Siodmak in *Son of Dracula* two years previous, adds his hulking presence to the inspired madness. This gaudy guilty pleasure is the best loved film of moviemaker/author *(Hollywood Babylon)* Kenneth Anger.

THEY DON'T MAKE 'EM LIKE THIS ANYMORE: In mainstream products that today are considered 'camp,' moviemakers had the opportunity to shoot entertainment for the masses that rang with S&M themes; star Maria Montez emerged as a cult queen in the 1960s thanks to the new mantra: "So bad it's good!"

COCKFIGHTER (1974)

Monte Hellman Cult Rating: *****

Warren Oates Cult Rating: *****

Monte Hellman, dir.; Charles Willeford, scr.; Roger Corman, pro.; 1.85:1; C; 83 min.; Artists Ent./New World.

    What *Nightmare Alley* did for the Deep South's geek shows, this version of C.W.'s Bus Station book proffers for a sport that remained legal only in Georgia and two other states when this was shot. M.H. (1929–2021) persuaded Corman to back the risky project owing to loyalty earned when they collaborated on junk movies a decade and a half earlier. Warren Oates (1926–1982), the Jason Robards of cult cinema, has his greatest single non-Peckinpah lead (we're not forgetting *Dillinger*, 1973) as a silently ruthless trainer of brutal roosters. An eccentric cast includes Hollywood has-beens Troy Donahue and Millie Perkins as his 'family.' Much of the impact owes to Nestor Almendros' (1930–1992) cinematography.

LIVIN' ON THE EDGE: Cult star Warren Oates accepted the title role in what may have been the most disturbing film since *Nightmare Alley*, though with the new freedom of the screen this Monte Hellman feature was considerably more graphic in depicting its forbidden 'profession.'

His unique approach: forsake electric lights when possible for natural lighting, then shoot specific sequences only when the current weather is precisely right for that dramatic moment. The capturing of cockfighting's sleazy appeal for a remarkably wide (if often anonymous) audience led to A list assignments including *Days of Heaven* (1978), for which N.A. won an Oscar. Animal rights activists divide as to whether this is the worst example of infuriating exploitation or a long overdue/necessary expose.

THE FEMALE SUPERSTAR OF BLACK-EXPLOITATION: Pam Grier created a new kind of kick-ass post-feminist woman in the early 1970s.

COFFY (1973)

Urban Crime Rating: ****

Pam Grier Cultist Rating: ***** 1/2

Jack Hill, dir.; Hill, scr.; Samuel Z. Arkoff, Buzz Feltshans, pros.; C; 1.85:1; 91 min.; American International Pictures.

    Hill (1933–) proved himself a Renaissance man at A.I.P. thanks to an adeptness at horror flicks, car racing sagas, women's prison pictures, and low-budget epics. When Arkoff gave up on Beach Party projects for 'black-exploitation,' Hill made the transition with the first female-oriented example of this urban-action genre. 'Coffy' (Pam Grier, 1949–) works as a nurse by day, transforming into a chintzy glamor-queen ("Miss Teeque") by night. An avenger, she kills drug dealers (black as well as white) with shotguns, as unsparing on a murder spree as she is sensitive while in the hospital. Sid Haig (1939–2019), a B movie regular, offers a deplorable villain with bald pate and black beard. Boffo box-office (as *Variety* used to say) led to two follow-ups (*Foxy Brown*, 1974; *Friday Foster*, 1975). Neither in a league with the original. Q.T. revived Pam's career with *Jackie Brown* (1997), a big-budget retro-tribute to this short-lived if vividly recalled genre.

COMPANY OF WOLVES, THE (1984)

Fairy-tale on Film Rating: **** 1/2

Neil Jordan, dir.; Jordan, Angela Carter, scr.; Chris Brown, Stephen Woolley, pro.; 1.66:1; C; 95 min.; I.T.C.

    Fairy-tales are horror stories scaled down for children while retaining the same threatening material. 'Little Red Riding Hood,' then, is best understood as a werewolf encounter. Here is the first modern movie to acknowledge this. A girl on the edge of becoming a young woman (the sad-eyed Sarah Peterson, 1972–) gazes out a window, senses a sudden pain deep inside below the belt, and falls into a cryptic dream about meeting a stranger in the woods while on her way to the home of Granny (Angela Lansbury, 1925–). Drawing heavily on old fables by Charles Perrault (1628–1703), Jordan (1950–) returned that master's unsettling sensibility to stories too often watered down for modern suburban kids. In so doing, he set the pace for *Into the Woods* and other film and stage plays that revive C.P.'s original edginess (violence, sexuality, etc.). Terence Stamp (1938–) replaced an ailing Andy Warhol as The Devil.

DUKE, AS YOU'VE NEVER SEEN HIM BEFORE OR SINCE: John Wayne as Genghis Khan at the low-point of his career in a project that resulted in death for many of its ' cursed' cast and crew.

CONQUEROR, THE (1956)

Mainstream Ancient World Epic Rating: NO STARS

John Wayne Camp Classic Rating: *****

Dick Powell, dir.; Oscar Millard, scr.; Powell, Howard Hughes, pros.; 2.55:1; C; 111 min.; RKO.

"I don't act," John Wayne once claimed, "I *react*." That was certainly true in John Ford's classic *The Searchers* (1956). Sadly, Wayne failed to take his own advice earlier that year, talking Powell 1904–1963) into casting him as Temujin (1162–1227), the wise warrior who united Mongols into an empire, he then re-named Genghis Khan. Made up to appear Asian with slant eyes, The Duke (in a ridiculous costume) takes but one look at Susan Hayward (playing a princess) and announces: "I feel this Tartar woman is for me, and my blood says: '*Take her!*'" Folks laughed out loud at the time and still do today, claiming it's 'so bad it's great.' Producer Hughes (1905–1976) tried to hide *T.C.* away in a vault but it's out there. On a tragic note: This was shot near Yucca Flats NV not long after a nuclear bomb test; one after another of the cast and crew died of cancer. Three cult-worthy 'Heavies' stalk about: Ted de Corsia, Lee Van Cleef, and Leo (V.) Gordon. Wayne's career survived. RKO did not; the film's losses killed it off.

CONVERSATION, THE (1974)

Cult Thriller Rating: *** ½

Early-1970s Watergate Cinema Rating: **** ½

Gene Hackman cult Rating: *****

Francis Ford Coppola cult Rating: *** ½

Francis Ford Coppola, dir.; Coppola, scr.; Coppola, Fred Roos, prods.; 1.37:1; C; 113 min.; American Zoetrope/Paramount.

In-between the Oscar-winning blockbusters *The Godfather* (1972) and *The Godfather: Part II* (1976), Coppola (1939–) chose to do a purposefully small film. A cross between an American arthouse/serious item and those tightly budgeted thrillers he once knocked out for Corman, this ultra-contemporary tale from F.F.C.'s indie company American Zoetrope focuses on 'Harry Caul' (Gene Hackman, 1930–), a professional "secretive surveillance expert." He records a wife's (Cindy Williams, 1947–) ill-timed meeting with a lover (Frederic Forrest, 1936–) at the bequest of her rich, powerful husband (Robert Duvall, 1931–). New York critics were overwhelmed, perhaps more so than they ought to have been. Beginning with the street mime, including an 'open your eyes' (in this case 'ears") theme (reality is subjective, not set in stone) much is 'borrowed' from Michelangelo Antonioni's *Blow-Up*. Yet Hackman's role is among the most fully developed characters in contemporary cinema, a 'Willy Loman' for the modern age in which privacy is a dead-end issue. The most warmly remembered of Hackman among all his many diverse roles, and rightfully so.

COOL WORLD (1992)

Edgy animation fan Rating: ** ½

Kim Basinger fan Rating: *****

Ralph Bakshi cult Rating: ***

Ralph Bakshi, dir.; Michael Grais, Mark Victor, scr.; Frank Mancuso Jr., pro.; 1.37:1; C; 102 min.; Paramount.

Imprisoned, a desperate cartoonist (Gabriel Byrne) tries to keep his mind focused by creating the ultimate comic book bad blonde. Then she develops a mind and will of her own, coldly seducing her creator by pulling him into her imaginary world, allowing her an opportunity to escape into reality. If the concept sounds much like that of the remarkable *Ex Machina* yet to come, the execution does not satisfy. Bakshi, who has never been able to tell a coherent story, allows his material to go out of control and over the top, involving a complex war of the worlds when he might better have focused on the leads. Yet cult status was a natural, owing to mesmerizing Holly Wood, one of the great fantasy femme fatales. Kim Basinger (1953–), a near perfect beauty in the Marilyn Monroe sense, is here idealized by the rotoscoping technique in which a person

HOLLY WOULD! Kim Basinger was rotoscoped by Ralph Bakshi to create the most memorable character in his sexy/surreal fantasy.

is first filmed, the animation-auteur then further enhancing her image. Arguments between Bakshi and the studio resulted in an uncertain tone, no one involved able to determine whether this would be a slightly edgier version of *Who Framed Roger Rabbit?* (Robert Zemeckis, 1988, or a nasty work of mainstream porn on the order of Frank Miller's yet to come *Sin City* (2005).

CORPSE BRIDE (2005)

Tim Burton Cult Rating: *****

Stop Action/Puppet Animation Rating: *****

Tim Burton, dir.; Burton, Carlos Grangel, John August, Caroline Thompson, Pamela Peltier, scr.; Burton, Allison Abbate, pros.; 1.85:1; C; 72 min.; Warner Bros.

When Disney prepared to release *A Nightmare Before Christmas* in late fall, 1993, executives feared Burton's (1958–) edgy puppet animation piece might be too dark for the mainstream. Their $18 million investment resulted in a return of $75 mill. A dozen years later, W.B. hoped lightning might strike twice as *C.B.* reached the theatres. A $40 million investment (owing to more meticulous stop-action work with pliable and convinc-

IS THERE LIFE AFTER DISNEY? Tim Burton struck out on his own in order to create a far darker puppet-animation film than Uncle Walt's company would allow.

ing doll heads) netted only $50 million in the U.S. Victorian England: an anxious boy from the nouveau riche is about to marry a girl from the old penniless aristocracy when he's spirited off to the land of the dead by a female corpse. Burton regulars Johnny Depp and Helena Bonham Carter voice the living lovers; Emily Watson does the honors for the title character; guest voices include Albert Finney, Michael Gough, Christopher Lee, and Tracey Ullman. Includes homages to Disney's *Skeleton Dance* (1929), Peter Lorre (rather than Vincent Price, for once) via a memorable cockroach, and even Burton's own *Frankenweenie* (1984) with another delightful dead dog.

CRASH (2004)

Rating: *****

Paul Haggis, dir.; Haggis, scr.; Haggis, Don Cheadle, many others, pros.; 2.35:1; C; 112 (theatrical release); 115 (dir. Cut); DEJ Prods.; Bull's Eye Ent.

Though *C.* brought in nearly $100 mill. on a budget of $6.5 mill., it's considered more a cult film than an acclaimed classic. In part this has to do with the film's status as one of the least popular at the box office Oscar winners for Best Picture. Complaints were raised that many Academy voters had a failure in courage by not acclaiming *Brokeback Mountain* ("the gay cowboy movie") as the top picture. However important (and well crafted) that movie may be, *Crash* is more ambitious and successful aesthetically. During three days, Angelinos—be they wealthy, middle-class, or poor—intersect in a city suffering a racial identity crisis. To his credit, Haggis (1953–) does not simplify characters, despite a large ensemble cast. Their meetings may seem convenient plotting to those who fail to grasp this is not based on realistic coincidence but a Greek sense of destiny. Despite depressing occurrences, Haggis opts for a flicker of optimism at the finale. The objective view of racism has been damned by politically correct critics, upset that ethnic characters are displayed as less than perfect. Stand-out roles include Don Cheadle as a mother-dominated cop and Sandra Bullock as a desperate housewife.

CROW, THE (1998)

Offbeat Avenger Film Rating: **** ½

Alex Proyas, dir.; David J. Schow, John Shirley, scr.; Jeff Most, Edward R. Pressman, prods.; 1.85:1; C; 102 min. (director's cut), 98 min. (edited for mainstream cut); Miramax.

When James O'Barr (1960–) created the title character for a graphic novel series, he hoped to outdo The Dark Knight as to an obsessive avenger. Here, that figure returns from the grave to exact retribution on villains who murdered him and his girlfriend. Brought to the screen with reasonable fidelity if not outright reverence by Egyptian-born, Australian-raised Proyas (1963–), this uneven if enticing movie features an oddball assortment of grotesque bad-guys on the order of those in Chester Gould's *Dick Tracy* Sunday funnies. Sadly, it's a cursed movie: disasters during production included the accidental death of star Brandon Lee (1965–1993). That the actor's famed father Bruce Lee also died young added to the intrigue. To complete filming, digital recreations of The Crow were devised. A.P. brought the flashy techniques he designed while shooting TV commercials and music videos to this Gothic piece which often references the writings of Edgar Allan Poe.

DAKHTARI DAR SAB TANHA BE XANE MIRVAD, aka *GIRL (WHO) WALKS HOME ALONE AT NIGHT, A* (2014)

Undefinable Film Experience Rating: *****

John Begnaue, Sina Savyah, Elijah Wood, pro.; 2.35:1; B&W; 101 min.; Logan Pictures/Say Ahh productions.

    Vampires are lonely creatures. Not only those who haunt bleak hillsides in Rumania but others in the East, often referred to as Lamia. Sheliah Vand (1985–) plays just such a figure, wearing an open black chador as "Dracula or 'Carmilla Karnstein' might a body-covering cape. She seeks out men in the hideous ghost-town (in more ways than one!) of 'Bad City' in Iran though this film was shot entirely in Taft, CA. First time director Ana Lily Amirpour, an English-born Iranian who identifies herself as an American director, shot this story in one form of the Persian language, hoping to create (in her own words) "a vampire/Spaghetti Western" about the cinema's first ever skateboarding succubus. Black and white cinematography, which purposefully threatens to suffocate characters and their setting, recalls Stephanie Rothman's 1960s bloodsucker tale. Some interpret the unnamed vamp's refusal to kill male victims if they reveal emotion and empathy as a feminist statement. The implication that 'the girl' can only love without killing a boy if they avoid sex recalls the more commercial *Twilight* series. Word of mouth among goths contributes to the small but intense and growing cult for this anti-sensual work.

DANCER IN THE DARK (2000)

Fans of the edgiest cult films Rating: ***

Bjork fanatics Rating: ***

All others: NO STARS

Lars von (Van) Trier, dir.; von (Van) Trier, scr.; Vibeke Windelo, pro.; 2.35:1; C; 140 min.; Zentropa.

"I have always depended on the kindness of strangers," 'Blanche DuBoise' earnestly insists in Tennessee Williams A Streetcar Named Desire. The title character in this Danish musical (or is it a subtle arthouse horror film with music?) doesn't say that but certainly could. A sad-faced Czech immigrant living in the Pacific Northwest, she labors in a tool factory, cares for her ten-year old son, bravely faces the fact that she is going blind, and trusts in others, particularly a concerned mentor (Catherine Deneuve, 1943–). Even as her eyesight dims, the bird-like girl discovers that her sense of hearing grows ever keener. The slightest sound can spark an imaginary song and dance fantasy in her mind. Tragically the real world comes crashing down on this delicate creature. The purposeful craziness of the choreography suggests a collaboration between Gene Kelly and Federico Fellini; 'surreal' doesn't fully do the job of describing what occurs here. Yet another case of the public at large hating a film which develops a dedicated cult. Bjork (1965–) plays the lead and provided the… let's say… unconventional music. To put it mildly!

DARK CRYSTAL, THE (1982)

Cult puppet animation Rating: ** ½**

Jim Henson, Frank Oz, dirs.; Henson, David Odell, scr.; Henson, Gary Kurtz, pro.; 2.35;1; C; 93 min.; Universal.

Epic fantasy films thrived in the early 1980s: *Legend* (1985), *The Labyrinth* (1986) and by far the best. T.D.C. Henson (1936–1990) had already established himself as the most beloved puppet-master in America since the golden age of George Pal with child-friendly Muppets on *Sesame*

Street (1969–) and the now all but forgotten "Land of Gorch" on *Saturday Night Live* (1975–1976). Top collaborator Oz (1944–) oversaw a transition to theatrical films with *The Muppet Movie* (1979). They united with designer Brian Froud (1947–) to develop this project that would entice kids and parents. 'Jen' and 'Kova' are adorable Geldings who risk all to track down the title shard and save the universe. Unique among entertainments of its time as the first live-action movie in which no humans appeared onscreen (though people did provide voices). A routine, mostly derivative story transformed into a much-loved (over many generations) family-fable owing to the fine craftsmanship.

DARKMAN (1990)

Oddball Superhero Rating: ****

Sam Raimi cult Rating: ****

Sam Raimi, dir.; Sam & Ivan Raimi, Joshua and Daniel Goldin; Chuck Pfarrer, scr.; Rob Tapert, prod.; 1.85:1; C; 96 min; Renaissance/Universal.

Growing up, Raimi (1959–) adored Batman and The Shadow, dark comic anti-heroes; and was deeply moved by the silent *Phantom of the Opera*. Adult Raimi set out to collapse all three into an original concept for a movie (and hoped-for TV series that never was.) Not based on any pre-existing graphic novel, *D.* vividly expresses that print medium's aesthetics. The story concerns a well-intentioned scientist experimenting in hopes of creating synthetic skin for scarred people. He becomes one himself when badguys invade the lab. Casting Liam Neeson (1952–) opposite Frances McDormand (1957–) elevated this above other B movies. To support Raimi's edgy project, other cult directors, The Coen Brothers among them, accepted cameo roles. Raimi's early star Bruce Campbell appears in the final shot. For music, Danny Elfman (1953–) provided a far bleaker score than for Tim Burton projects while maintaining a sense of eerie playfulness. Other major influence were mad scientist laboratories from Universal's 1930s horror films as well as Vincent Price in Andre de Toth's *House of Wax* (1954).

THE HERO WHO LOOKS LIKE A VILLAIN: Liam Neeson in the title role, bringing to life Sam Raimi's Phantom of the Opera-like scarred victim.

DARK STAR (1974)

John Carpenter Cult Rating: **** ½

Low Budget Sci-Fi Rating: *** ½

John Carpenter, dir.; Carpenter, Dan O'Bannon, scr.; Carpenter, pro.; 1.85:1; C; 70 min. (theatrical release), 71 min. (director's cut), 83 min. (expanded cut), Jack H. Harris Enterprises.

During the late 1960s and early 1970s, the most sure-fire way to break into Hollywood was by graduating from one of the top film schools, then producing a low-budget hit. *D.S.*, shot for $60,000, represents a successful cross between a student film and a low-budget commercial movie. This spaced out adventure—featuring a dead commander who speaks from a deep freeze to shipmates struggling to defeat smart bombs—won raves for its appealing combination of inexpensive special effects and a satirical sense of humor as to genre clichés. D.O. (1946–2009) co-scripted while imagining a more ambitious version to be called "Star Beast"; this would morph into the classic *Alien* (Ridley Scott, 1979). D.O. also played 'Pinback'; Nick Castle (1947–), who would later co-script *Escape from New York*, plays the creature. Other talents who broke into The Biz include Jim Danforth (1940–); his matte paintings led to him being hired by Ray Harryhausen for *Clash of the Titans* (1981).

DARK TOWER, (THE) (2017)

General Rating: *** ½

Nikolaj Arcel, dir.; Arcel, Akiva Goldsman, Jeff Pinkner, Andew Thomas Jensen, scrs.; Goldsma, Erica Huggins, pro.; 2.39:1; C; 95 min.; Columbia/Sony.

Most ticket-buyers (there weren't many) didn't dislike *D.T.*; they *despised* it! Most had arrived expecting (from the title) all eight volumes of Stephen King's (1947–) dazzling mixture of science-fiction and epic fantasy plus a grand saga of good vs. evil, compressed into a single movie. Instead they were treated to a brief 'prologue' for a franchise that supposedly would include sequels and a TV series, offering bits and pieces of the saga that made little sense for anyone who had not read (and re-read) the series. This film seems like a sketch where a full portrait was required for those who had. Idris Elba (1972–) is the Old West Gunfighter who must go up against a mystery man in black (Matthew McConaughey, 1969–) for the symbolic soul (the title icon) of the cosmos itself, while a Golden Child from NYC, 'Jake' (Tom Taylor, 2001–), enters the fray taking place in Mid-Earth. Generally regarded as chintzy (Manhattan settings were shot in L.A.), dull other than several conventional action sequences, and unsatisfyingly paltry. Yet the film has developed a small, loyal cult following that insists this is the best King film adaptation ever!

DAZED AND CONFUSED (1993)

Cult Rating: ****

Richard Linklater, dir.; Linklater, scr.; Linklater, James Jacks, Sean Daniel, prods.; 1.85:1; C; 102 min.; Gramercy.

    D.A.C. is to Spring 1976 (May 28, to be precise) what George Lucas' *American Graffiti* (1973) was to Fall 1963, offering a recreation of teenagers on a long day's journey into night. In the era of Aerosmith, innocence has long since given way to cynicism. Male jocks and mean girls "haze" members of the incoming freshman class. While Deep Purple songs play, a Greek chorus of knowing observers (CAC Goldberg, Anthony Rapp, Marissa Ribisi) comment on students as diverse as a DeadHead Stoner (Rory Cochrane), an athlete (Jason London), and the one girl (Michelle Burke) who possesses a touch of sensitivity. As in Lucas's classic, *D.A.C.* is point-on as to its slightly caricatured if all-too-real vision of High School as Hell, any hint of weakness turning a person into prey. Ben Affleck and Matthew McConaughey early-on revealed their star qualities; Parker Posey (1968–) emerged as a cult figure. Shot in Austin TX but set in Anytown U.S.A. More even than *Slacker* (1991) or *A Scanner Darkly* (2006), here is the film Linklater (1960–) cultists re-watch again and again.

DEATH RACE 2000 (1974)

Bartel Cult Rating: ****

David Carradine Completist Rating: *****

Corman Drive In Action Flick Rating: *****

Paul Bartel, dir.; Robert Thom, Charles (B.) Griffith, scrs.; Roger Corman, Jim Weatherill, pros.; 1.85:1; C; 80 min.; New World Pictures.

 In 1975, Oscar-winner Norman Jewison's *Rollerball* flopped owing to its humourless portrayal of a violent futuristic sport. One year earlier, a B film drove the same theme home via over-the-top thrills and B flick black-comedy. David Carradine (1936–2009) is 'Frankenstein,' scarred superstar of a New York to L.A. marathon custom-car competition. He's challenged by 'Machine Gun Joe Viterbo' (a pre-*Rocky* Sylvester Stallone, 1946–). Drivers are encouraged to kill pedestrians, earning extra points (children and elderly worth the most). Corman had hoped to make this a bone-crunching drama, deciding brutality might be less offensive if presented spoof-style. Ever-campy Paul Bartel (1938–2000) directed, bringing pal (and eventual *Eating Raoul* co-star) Mary Woronov (1943–) on-board as an empowered right-wing feminist. Bringing in more than $8 million on a less than $300,000 budget, mostly at Drive-Ins, *D.R.* set the pace for imitations ranging from the low-budget *Gumball Rally* (1976) to the all-star *Cannonball Run* (1981).

DECLINE OF WESTERN CIVILIZATION, THE (1981)

Cult music Rating: ****

Penelope Spheeris, dir.; Spheeris, Alice Bag (uncredited), scr.; Spheeris, Jeff Prettyman, pros.; 35 mm.; B&W/C; 100 min.; Image Ent.

 The Punk Scene began in London, born out of alienated youth's repulsion at the early 1970s Thatcher Regime. The Sex Pistols and The Clash made former angry rockers (The Rolling Stones, the Animals) resemble The Four Preps. When repressive politics reached America, Manhattan bore witness to the popularity of The Ramones and New York Dolls. Punk reached its head in Los Angeles as the decade came to an end when Alice Bag (1958–) brought feminism and ethnicity into play; her band The Bags (known early-on for masking their identities under brown paper to convey marginalization) added a Chicano flavor. Spheeris (1945–) was in town, making music videos in her Rock 'n Reel studio. She turned the cameras on a counter-counter-culture as world-weary nihilism replaced flower-power naivete. No movie captures The Scene so fully. A follow-up *The Metal Years* failed to impress. After gaining mainstream success with the punk/garage band influenced *Wayne's World* (1992) P.S. sold out, directing weak commercial pap (*The Little Rascals*, 1994).

DEEP THROAT (1972)

Conventional Rating: NO STARS

Cult Porn Rating: *****

Gerard Damiano, dir.; Damiano, scr.; Louis Peraino, pro.; C; 61 min.; Bryanston Distributing.

Established in 1968, the X rating initially indicated nudies (*Vixen*, 1969) or serious arthouse items like the Oscar-winning *Midnight Cowboy* (1969). Then came *Deep Throat*, and all such movies were re-labelled 'R.' How could they remain in the same category with a work that featured penetration and fellatio? 'Linda' (Linda Boreman Lovelace, 1949–2002), an unsatisfied nympho, discovers that her clitoris is located in her throat. Previously, suburbanites were mostly loath to even speak of oral sex. Then this hard-core feature caught on; a cheapjack production shot in Florida by Damiano (1928–2008) over six days for less than $25,000 earned more than $100 million during its initial release. The result: 'porno chic,' a new freedom for sexual experimentation in which ordinary people watched such films, particularly after VHS introduced late night home-viewing. D.T. changed America's vision of what was not only permissible but accepted as The New Normal, providing a nickname for the anonymous source in the era's Watergate scandal. Male lead 'Harry Reems' (Herbert Streicher, 1947–2013) was, like auteur Damiano, a Bronx native.

DEMENTIA 13 (1963)

Ultra-low-budget thriller Rating: *****

Corman/Coppola Cultist Rating: *****

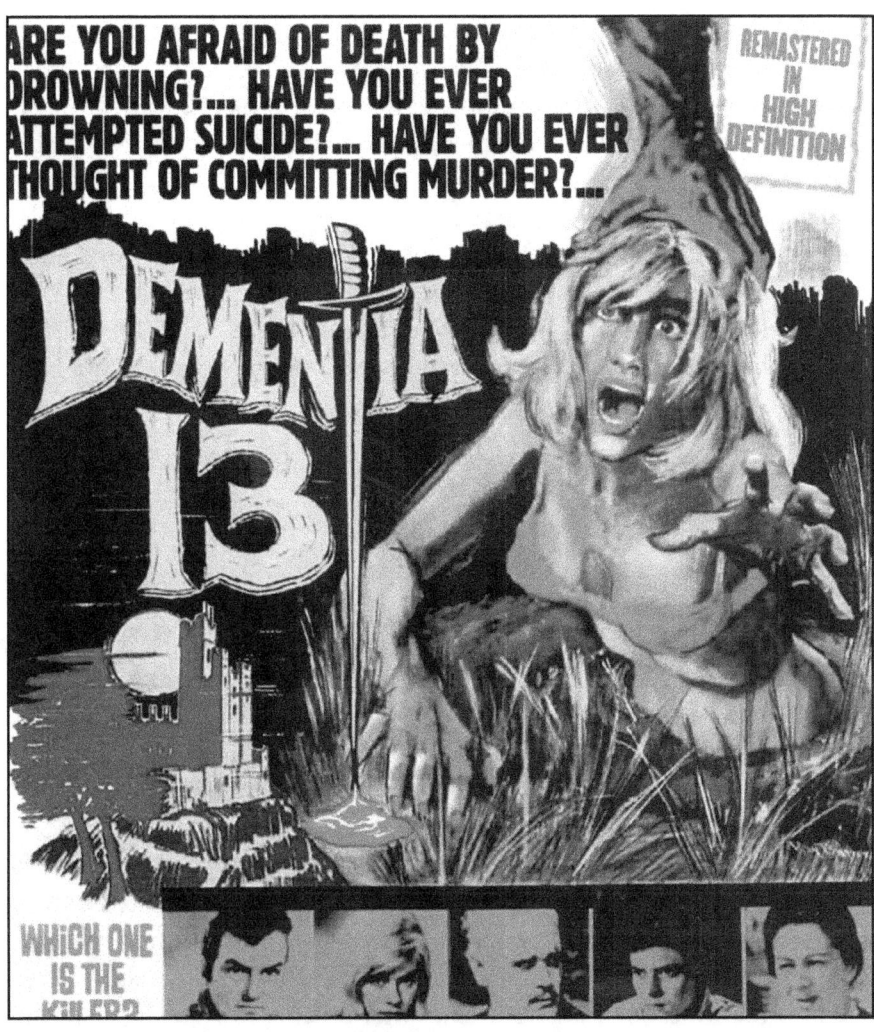

FROM THE DIRECTOR WHO WOULD GIVE US 'THE GODFATHER': Like so many other aspiring filmmakers, Francis Ford Coppola received an early shot as an auteur with this ultra low-budget (but at times brilliant) *Psycho* rip-off.

Francis (Ford) Coppola, dir.; Coppola, Jack Hill, scr.; Marianne Wood, pro.; 1.66:1; B&W; 75 min.; Roger Corman Prods.

After leaving A.I.P., Corman (1926–) shot his own tightly budgeted films including *The Young Racers* (1963) in Ireland. His assistant, a Hofstra University grad named Coppola (1939–), made the schlock-meister an offer R.C. could not refuse: Francis and another team-member, Hill, would pen a *Psycho*-inspired thriller, filming virtually without cost on the sets and with the same cast as *T.Y.R.* For the next nine days F.F.C. established himself as a top talent who would, as the saying goes, move on to bigger (though in truth not always better) projects. Killing off his female lead at mid-movie is 'borrowed' from Hitch's *Psycho* shower scene; here, it occurs in a river. During this memorable sequence, Luana Anders' (1938–1996) panties change color, shape, and style two times. The Ghost-child imagery was influenced by Jack Clayton's recent adaptation of Henry James' 1898 *Turn of the Screw*, *The Innocents* (1961). Star William Campbell (1923–2011) was at the time married to Judith Exener; back in the states, she engaged in simultaneous affairs with JFK and mob boss Sam Giancana.

DESCENT, THE (2005)

Spelunker's Cult Horror Film: **** ½

Neil Marshall, dir.; Marshall, scr.; Christian Colson, pro.; 2.35:1; C; 99 min., 100 min. (director's cut); Celada Films.

Haunted by the accidental death of her husband and daughter a year earlier, still-mourning Sarah (Shauna Macdonald) joins five other young women on a trip into Appalachia for the purpose of exploring a frightfully deep cave. Once deep down in this giant natural vagina, they come face to face with "crawlers": ghostly throwbacks to horrid early primates. Totally convincing though no caves were, for safety's sake, used; the film was shot on a series of 21 complimentary sets in the U.K.'s Pinewood Studio. Here's the film that does for claustrophobia what Hitchcock's *Vertigo* achieved for the fear of heights: Whether a viewer has such a condition before watching, chances are they'll suffer from it afterwards. Director Marshall (1970–) cut his teeth on the semi-successful *Dog Soldiers* (2002) set in the Scottish wilderness; his effective manipulation of cinematic technique to insure that the fear is fully felt by audiences was enhanced by the appropriately discomforting music of David Julyan, who would likewise do the honors for *The Cabin in the Woods*. A 2009 sequel by another director does not come close to the original.

DETOUR (1945)

B Noir Rating: *****

Ulmer Cult Rating: *****

Edgar G. Ulmer, scr.; Martin Goldsmith, scr.; Leon Fromkess, pro.; 1.37:1; B&W; 67 min.; Producer's Releasing Corporation.

   In 1992 the Library of Congress' National Film Registry, choosing socially/aesthetically important movies to restore, did something previously unheard of: Members picked a low-budget grindhouse item for inclusion, officially acknowledging what Tarantino implied through his culture-bending projects: yesteryear's supposedly worthless junk films sometimes prove to be mistreated masterpieces. Ulmer (1904–1972), working for a low level Poverty Row company, turned the proverbial sow's ear into a silk purse through technical wizardry that he brought to this nihilistic tale about life's losers. A broke NYC musician (Tom Neal, 1914–1972), hitchhiking to L.A., teams up with the first (some would say greatest) of post-war femme fatales, Ann Savage (1921–2008). Music by Chopin and Brahms were employed to avoid paying for a score. An aura of despair hangs over this relentlessly bleak piece. Much admired by such arthouse auteurs as Jean-Luc Godard and Wim Wenders.

DISASTER ARTIST, THE (2017)

Franco Cult Rating: *****

Wiseau Cult Rating: NO STARS

James Franco, dir.; Scott Neustadter, Michael H. Weber, scr.; 2.39:1; C; 109 min.; Good Universe/New Line.

   Is it possible for a great director to make a great movie about a terrible director making a terrible one? Yes! Tim Burton proved that in 1994 with *Ed Wood* starring Johnny Depp as the eponymous hero, undertaking *Plan 9 from Outer Space*. Lightning struck twice as actor-director J.F. (1978–) created this semi-fictionalized salute to Tommy Wiseau (1955–), the eccentric auteur of *The Room*, which may be the most expensive van-

EVERYTHING OLD IS NEW AGAIN: The grindhouse classic by Edgar G. Ulmer would in time be unofficially remade as an arthouse item by Jean-Luc Godard, retaining not only the story and characters but key images.

ity project ever filmed in the U.S. Franco's young brother Dave (1985–) appears as Greg Sestero (1978–), Wiseau's top 'star' and co-author (with Tom Bissell) of the book upon which this strange comedy (perhaps) was based. Cult-worthy stars in supporting/cameo roles include Seth Rogan, Sharon Stone, Zac Effron, Melanie Griffith, Judd Apatow and, via stock footage, Tommy's lifelong idol, James Dean, 1931–1955). Key question: Is this intended as a celebration of T.W. or a mockery? In our post-irony world (as Jon Stewart noted immediately after 9/11), it doesn't matter much. Point is, when you watch *Rebel* after seeing this, you can't hear him scream "You're tearing me apart!" without also thinking of T.W.!

DJANGO (1966)

Cult Rating: ***

Sergio Carbucci, dir.; S. and Brano Carbucci, Jose Gutierrez Maesso, scr.; S. Carbucci, Bruno Frasca, pros.; 1.66:1; C; 92 min (director's cut), 88 min. (original theatrical print); B.R.Z. Produziona/Tecisa.

With *A Fistful of dollars* (1964) and its sequels, Italy's Sergio Leone brought the then-distaff Spaghetti Western to the America mainstream, proving that what had been written off as downscale entertainment could lead to cinematic art. Yet another Sergio took the other route: S. Carbucci (1926–1990) embraced junk movie aspects of such violent Neo-Westerns for an international (mostly Third World) audience. As the title character, European heart-throb Franco Nero drags his 'goods' around in a coffin; Django, like the Leone/Eastwood 'Man With No Name,' is derived from Toshiro Mifune's performances as a Samurai warrior. The plot here raises a Civil Rights theme: persecution of Latin people by evil Anglos must finally end. If Leone's films look like John Ford epics re-imagined for a new era, Carbucci's suggest just what raunchy Russ Meyer might have produced had he ever worked in this genre. Beloved by many rockers, specifically members of Acid. Tarantino's *Django Unchained* (2012) implies by its title that, however much Q.T. loves Leone, Carbucci most clearly "speaks" to him. The title references American jazz artist Django Reinhardt (1910–1953).

DOLOMITE IS MY NAME (2019)

Streaming Cult Rating: *****

Craig Brewer, dir.; Scott Alexander, larry Karaszewski, scr.; John Davis, John Fox, pro.; 2.00:1; C; 118 min.; Netflix.

D.I.M.N. joins *Ed Wood* and *The Disaster Artist* as an example of an emergent genre: a high-quality (even 'art') film about the making of one of the worst movies ever. In this case, it's *Dolomite* (1975), an ultra-low-budget junk movie from one of cinema's least likely auteurs, Rudy Ray Moore (1927–2008). The Arkansas-born misfit knew from an early age that he wanted to be a star, though precisely in what venue was another issue: actor, writer, musician, club MC, stand-up comic, filmmaker… the precise label did not matter, only that he 'made it' in Show Biz and on his own terms. That finally occurred when the struggling performer was inspired to wrap all those elements together in a makeshift Urban Action flick. These had become popular during the past few years at once opulent, now decaying downtown theatres as panicky resident Anglos had fled to the suburbs. Martial arts proved to be the key to making this work, though R.R.M. was not like Bruce Lee a devotee. Survival and success happened, if on a limited level—though that proved to be enough. Premiering at a film festival, then blessed with a limited theatrical run, this comeback flick for Eddie Murphy (1961–) enjoyed its largest audience when digitally streamed on Netflix. As such it introduces the shape of things to come in which the once fine line between theatrical features and made-for-TV movies grows ever more difficult to determine.

DONNIE DARKO (2001)

Cult Rating: ****

Richard Kelly; dir.; Kelly; scr.; Nancy Juvonen, Adam Fields, Sean McKittrick, prod.; 2.35:1; C; 113 (original release print), 133 min. (director's cut); Pandora.

Like the character played by James Stewart in the old chestnut *Harvey* (1950), Donnie Darko (Jake Gyllenhaal, 1980–) sees and speaks to an immense invisible rabbit. In this dark allegory, set during the autumn

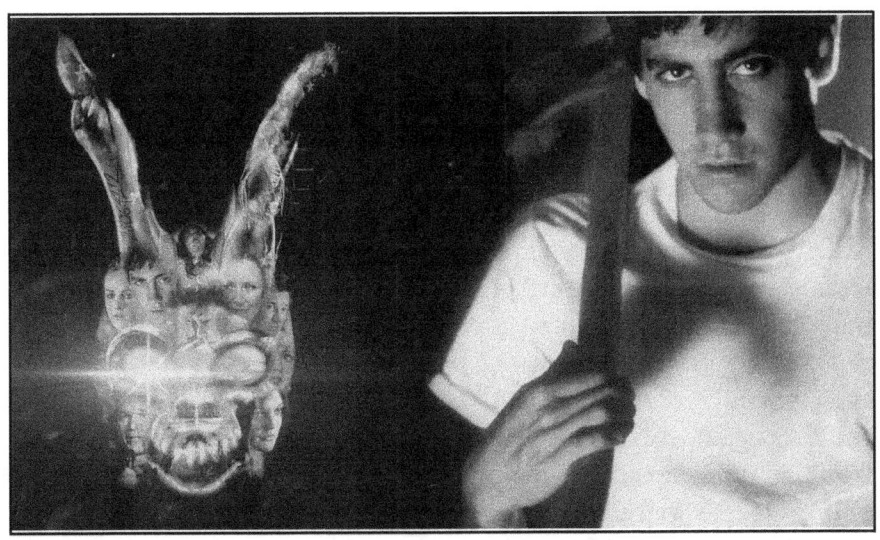

A NEW DIRECTION FOR TEEN HORROR: Cult favorite Jake Gyllenhaal plays the title character in a thriller with intellectual as well as emotional substance.

of 1988, long-eared 'Frank' informs D.D. that Apocalypse will occur in 28 days. So Donnie must deal with everyday problems like high school bullies but also odd elements including portals in the time-space continuum. Such significant topics as suicide among emotionally marginalized teens alternate with political commentary on the presidential election then taking place. Includes sci-fi elements though this does not fit neatly into that genre. Drew Barrymore (1975–), who plays a sympathetic teacher, co-produced. The film's alternative-to-theatrical-release success suggested Kelly (1957–) would immediately join a small but prescient group of filmmakers—Charles Kaufman, Spike Jonze, David Fincher, and Darren Aranofsky among them—who in the early 21st century furthered the breakdown between mainstream movies and cult cinema. His career abruptly ended with *The Box* (2009).

DONOVAN'S BRAIN (1953)

1950s Low Budget Sci Fi Rating: *****

Felix F. Feist, dir.; Feist, Hugh Brooke, scr.; Tom Gries, pro.; 1.37:1; B&W; 84 min.; Dowling Prods.

Known for films as great as *The Wolfman* (1941) and as awful as *Bride of the Gorilla*, Curt Siodmak (1902–2000) also wrote the far ahead of its time sci-fi novel *Donovan's Brain* (1942). He hoped to direct this film version from indie Dowling Prods. but was replaced on the eve of shooting with Feist (1910–1965), known for bringing in movies on time and under-budget. A well-intentioned doctor (Lew Ayres, 1908–1996) preserves the brain of a recently deceased millionaire in fluids, hoping to achieve good for humanity. Instead, the evil organ possesses him. A better than average programmer, this briefly played in theatres, then disappeared. Like many B pictures of the early 1950s *D.B.* was sold to independent TV stations and constantly rerun to fill time. Many millions of people watched it over and over again, eventually knowing every line and shouting them while watching. Filmed earlier as *Lady and the Monster* (1942), again as *The Brain* (1962) as well as endless rip-offs. The quiet wife is played by Nancy Davis Reagan. (1921–2016).

DON'T LOOK BACK (aka, *BOB DYLAN: DON'T LOOK BACK*) (1967)

Dylan Cultist Rating: *****

Rock Movie Cultist Rating: *****

Experimental Documentary Rating: *****

D.A. Pennebaker, dir; Pennebaker, scr.; Albert Grossman, John Albert Grossman, John Court, pro.; 1.37:1; 96 min.; Leacock-Pennebaker Films.

On 7/25/1965, Bob Dylan (Robert Zimmerman; Duluth MN, 1941–) set his acoustic guitar aside, embracing electronic music. B.D. displayed through example that Pete Seeger's 'pure' folk sound could be combined with rock 'n' roll, Beatles style. As Dylan embarked on his tour of the U.K., he chose Pennebaker (1925–2019) to document this journey. Transforming from a cult figure for dedicated folkies into a pop star a la John Lennon, Dylan is seen (and heard) in concert, also mixing with fans (whom he loves) and mainstream reporters (he despises them). In addition to take-your-breath-away renditions of songs like "Subterranean Home-sick Blues," B.D.'s offstage existence, as captured by the camera, alternatively

THE 1960s RE-INVENTION OF ROCK 'N' ROLL: D.A. Pennebaker's documentary offered a depiction of Bob Dylan's changeover from retro-folk to folk rock; Oliver Stone's retrospective docudrama chronicled the self-invention of Jim Morrison (Val Kilmer) and The Doors.

reveals the artist as engaging and perceptive, then nasty and cruel. An unsparing vision offered without narrative voice-over, allowing each viewer to come to his/her own conclusions.

DOORS, THE (1991)

Val Kilmer Fan Rating: *****

Jim Morrison Fan Rating: ****

Doors (The Band) Fan Rating: ** ½

Oliver Stone directorial Rating: *

Oliver Stone, dir.; Randall Johnson, scr.: Bill Graham, A. Kitman Ho, prod; 2.39:1; C; 140 min.; Carolco.

The emergence of psychedelic rock as musical accompaniment to the Hippie Movement (1966–1971) is addressed here, though O.S. (1946–) merely scratches the surface. Likewise (and the title aside) he only sketches in the band's origination in Venice CA. Stone's focus is on lead singer Jim Morrison (1943–1971), hailed as a charismatic cross between the mythic Lizard King and Brit poet William Blake (1957–1827). Even here O.S. misses the point by concentrating on the dark side of a person known to be a Jekyll and Hyde personality: sweet, sensitive, and shy until he reached for alcohol. Martin Scorsese might have made a great Doors film. Yet T.D. remains a cult item for fans of Morrison who watch it regularly for fabulous performances of "Light My Fire" and "Break on Through." among others. Kilmer (1959–), employing pure Method acting, doesn't 'portray' J.M.; he *becomes* him, even singing all the songs.

DRACULA (1931)

Vampire Completists Rating: *****

Horror Movie Rating: *** ½

Erotic Horror Cultists Rating: **** ½

Lupita Tovar Cult Rating: *****

George Melford Jr., dir.; Baltasar Tovar Avalos, scr.; Carl Laemmle, Jr., pro.; 1.20:1; B&W; 104 min.; Universal.

During the early sound-era, Hollywood studios regularly shot foreign-language versions of their latest projects to cash in on the international market, favouring Spanish owing to the immense worldwide Latin population. Once Todd Browning shot sequences for *Dracula* with Bela Lugosi, a different cast and crew arrived for all-night work, employing the same sets and costumes. Melford (1877–1961), an undistinguished director, employed a script which like the English version borrowed more from the 1924 play by Howard Deane and John Balderston than Bram Stoker's 1897 novel. Actor Carlos Villarias (1892–1976) offers a pale imitation of Bela. The standout performance is delivered by actress Lupita Tovar (1910–2016), a flamboyant sex symbol. She emphasized eroticism in her portrayal of the Count's prey—surprisingly so as Mexico, a devoutly Catholic country, frowned on such stuff. Considered lost for decades; a quality print was unearthed in 1975.

DRACULA, MINUS LUGOSI: Universal shot an alternative version of their first sound horror film for the Latin American audience; Lupita Tovar achieved cult status south of the border.

DRAGONSLAYER (1981)

Rating: **** ½

Matthew Robbins, dir.; Robbins, Hal Barwood, scr.; Barwood, prod.; 2.39:1; C; 108 min.; Paramount/Disney.

The 1980s witnessed a renaissance for epic fantasy films of varied quality and differing budgets: *Clash of the Titans*, *The Beastmaster*, *Conan the Barbarian*, and *Krull* among them. Most performed decently at the box-office with the exception only of *Dragonslayer*, one of the finest examples of its type and considered a cult classic today. Robbins (1945-) and Barwood (1940-) had written excellent scripts for leading directors Steven Spielberg (*The Sugarland Express*, 1974) and John Badham (*The Bingo Long Travelling All-Stars and Motor Kings* (1976). They struck out on their own with a variation of England's St. George and the Dragon myth: an Obi-Won Kenobi type mentor (Ralph Richardson, 1902–1983) leads a sorcerer's apprentice (Peter MacNichol, (1954-) into a fabled world (exteriors shot on location in Wales) in hopes of ending the sacrifice of virgins to a monster. If the plot sounds tired, the approach is fresh: For once, the hero arrives too late to save the princess. Genre fans tend to agree that the wicked worm on view, Vermithrax Pejorative, is the definitive screen dragon.

DR. STRANGELOVE OR: HOW I LEARNED TO STOP WORRYING AND LOVE THE BOMB (1964)

Black Comedy Rating: *****

Stanley Kubrick, dir.; Kubrick, Terry Southern, scr.; Kubrick, Lee Minoff, pro.; 1.66:1; B&W; 95 min.; Hawk Films/Columbia.

Kubrick, (1928–1999), working with counter-cultural novelist Southern (1924–1995 of *Candy* fame, adapted Peter George's apocalyptic novel *Red Alert*, reinvented the End of the World form by playing the Apocalypse as a crazed burlesque filled with dark comedy. Shot in London (where Kubrick had gone to film the verboten *Lolita*, 1962), *Stran-*

'DARK' COMEDY GOES MAINSTREAM: By emerging as a commercial as well as critical success, Stanley Kubrick's comedic depiction of the world's end predicted the major shift that commercial cinema would undergo during the 1960s; three decades earlier, the four Marx Bros. attempted to do much the same thing though a Depression-era audience was not keen to experience such a nihilistic burlesque.

gelove rate as the greatest political spoof since *Duck Soup*. Peter Sellers (1925–1980) went the Marx Bros. one better, playing three key roles: America's wussy president 'Muffley,' the RAF's 'Mandrake,' and mysterious wheelchair bound ex-Nazi 'Dr. Strangelove.' George C. Scott and Sterling Hayden were cast as caricatured generals the latter named 'Jack D. Ripper.' Slim Pickens (1919–1983) is a cowboyish B-52 bomber pilot who, in the most iconic image, rides a nuclear bomb down on 'the Russkies' as if it were a wild mustang. John Wayne was offered that role but declined. When Columbia agreed to distribute this in the U.S. executives feared a public backlash against such an anti-patriotic film. Instead, the movie's popularity spread from the arthouse to mainstream theatres, ushering in a new era of edgy projects.

DRUGSTORE COWBOY (1989)

Druggie Cult Flick Rating: ****

Gus Van Sant (Jr.), dir.; Van Sant, Daniel Yost, scr.; Cary Brokaw, Karen Murphy, Nick Wechsler, prods.; 1.85:1; C. 102 min.; Avenue Pictures/Artisan Ent.

Published in 1990, *D.C.* by James Fogle (1936–2012) became an immediate Underground bestseller. Autobiographical, the piece was written in prison, the author serving time for pharmacy robberies to support his drug habit. This harrowing film by Gus Van Sant (1952–), later to direct the mainstream classic *Good Will Hunting* (1997), offers an inside understanding of the highs and lows of addiction. Sly 'Bob' (Matt Dillon, 1964–), his sex-and-drug starved girlfriend 'Diane' (Kelly Lynch), their witless pal 'Rick' (James Le Gross, 1962–), and a flaky post-hippie blonde 'Nadine' (Heather Graham, 1970–) indulge in any 'stuff' they locate. *D.C.* combines elements of message-movies, Road films, buddy-buddy flicks, and docudrama. Critics complained about the light-hearted tone of the first half, though this was necessary to set up the spiral downward during the second. Beat Generation author (*Naked Lunch*, 1959) William S. Burroughs (1914–1997) plays 'Priest.'

DUCK SOUP (1933)

Madcap Comedy Rating: *****

Marx Bros. Cult Rating: *****

Leo McCarey, dir.; Bert Kalmar, Harry Ruby, Nat Perrin, scr.; Herman J. Mankiewicz, pro.; 1.37:1; B&W; 68 min.; Paramount.

This has as little to do with ducks as *Un Chien Andalou* did with dogs. A purposeful misnomer, *D.S.* was tacked on at the last minute by director McCarey (1898–1969), attempting to bless his work of magical madness with a memorable title. (The term then referred to pleasant living and haute cuisine.) A previously unknown hybrid—intellectualized burlesque—best describes this inspired comedic nightmare once 'Rufus T. Firefly' (Groucho) becomes president of Fredonia. Ferociously anti-patriotic; even Paul Revere's ride is parodied. Anti-war and anti-Establishment, with matronly Margaret Dumont (1882–1965) embodying a clueless variation on high society's Grand Dames. Pro-anarchic, pro-adultery, pro-absurdism, anti-middle-American. *D.S.* daringly presents a *menage a trois* between a single man, a married woman, and a horse. *D.S.* became a cult classic on the college circuit, most notably at Fredonia in upstate New York. Minnie Marx's sons were 'Chico' (Leonard, 1887–1961); 'Harpo' (Adolph, 1888–1964); 'Groucho' (Juius, 1890–1977), and 'Zeppo' (Hebert, 1901–1979). Forget Gummo!

DUEL (1971)

Made for TV Movie Cultists: *****

Spielberg Completists: *****

Southwestern rural thriller Rating: *****

Steven Spielberg, dir.; Richard Matheson, scr.; George Eckstein, pro.; 1.33:1; C; 74 min. (original TV print), 85 min. (expanded print), 90 min. (theatrical print).

During the early 1970s, Made-For-TV movies were shot on the same budget ($400,000) as theatrical B flicks with a similar two week schedule. Most lacked the sudden flashes of sex and violence that characterized Drive-In junk, a *no-no!* as to TV's far stricter censorship rules. Most were mediocre; one, brilliant. A veteran of episodic TV (*Columbo*, *Name of the Game*), S.S. (1946–) made his feature debut with a script by the great R.M.. Here (like *Jaws* several years later) is a relatively realistic thriller that edges up to fantasy: an ordinary salesman, symbolically named 'David Mann' (Dennis Weaver), finds himself menaced by an enormous truck on an isolated southwestern highway. Director and writer agreed the driver (played by stunt legend Carey Loftin, 1914–1997) should be seen as little as possible so that the truck would take on a demonic quality: as motiveless a malignancy as Bruce the Shark. Home viewers were held spellbound; Universal requested that S.S. shoot ten more minutes of footage so *D.* could be theatrically released. Sadly, the additional scenes play as padding, slowing down the originally taut proceedings.

E

EASY RIDER (1969)

Late 1960s Counter-Culture Relic Rating: **** ½

Dennis Hopper, dir.; Hopper, Peter Fonda, Terry Southern, scr.; Bob Rafelson, pro.;1.85:1; C/B&W; 95 min.; Pandora Co.

The Loners served as working title for a tale of two hippie-ish bikers (Peter Fonda, 1940–2019); Dennis Hopper, 1936–2010) employing money from a drug sale to finance their cross-country trip. The project rose above its exploitation roots to become the most important American indie flick of all time. "This used to be a great country," an alcoholic lawyer (Jack Nicholson, 1937–) sighs as they sit by a campfire. "*What went wrong?*" In truth, everyone asked that question in 1969 as the Civil Rights Movement, the divisive Vietnam War, and the Sexual Revolution tore at the very fabric of society. Though the Fonda ('Wyatt') and Hopper ('Billy') characters never rise above counter-cultural clichés, Nicholson's 'George Hanson' emerged as so vividly real that a star was born. Laszlo Kovacs' (1933–2007) cinematography accurately captured the diverse regions of the U.S. in a way the pretentious, self-indulgent script did not. Hand-held cameras, ad-lib dialogue and natural lighting, previously confined to The Underground, hit the mainstream and never went away. An incredible irony: Hopper wanted *Easy Rider* to feature an old-fashioned symphonic score. Leo Jaffe, top "suit" at Columbia, insisted on rock!

"WE BLEW IT, BILLY!" The movie that you absolutely had to see during the late summer and early fall of 1969 turned out to be this ambitious art film that had its origins in the less than lofty tradition of earlier biker flicks.

EATING (1990)

Rating: **** ½

Henry Jaglom, dir.; Jaglom, scr.; Judith Wolinsky, pro.; 1.78:1; C; 110 min.; Rainbow Film Co./Breaking Glass.

    As humans, we eat to live. The premise of this odd cult item? In truth, we live to eat! Daily consumption of food takes on significance—intellectual, emotional, spiritual—which most of us remain blithefully unaware of. An upscale L.A. birthday party toasts 'Helene' (Lisa Blake), turning forty and aware of that juncture's difficult meaning to women. When friends of various ages arrive for cake and comfort, a conversation reveals that two other invitees were also born on this day, they thirty and fifty, these also significant ages as to life passages. A one-set movie, *E.* allows us to eavesdrop on subjects ranging from husbands and lovers to work and unfulfilled ambitions, all conversations eventually returning to… *food*. 'Martine' (Nelly Alard) captures everything on film, turning what we see into a movie within a movie. Jaglom (1938–) who served an apprenticeship with Dennis Hopper on *Easy Rider,* has always turned out cultish films. From the first—*A Safe Place,* 1971, with Tuesday Weld, Jack Nicholson, and Orson Welles—his work proved so esoteric that no one much cared. Here then is his long overdue masterpiece.

EATING RAOUL (1982)

Dark comedy cult Rating: **** ½

Paul Bartel cult Rating: **** ½

Mary Woronov cult Rating: *****

Paul Bartel, dir.; Bartel, Richard Blackburn, scrs.; Anne Kimmel, pro.; 1.85:1; C; 90 min.; Bartel Films.

A cult director thanks to his work for Roger Corman, Bartel (1938–2000) set out to bring his own odd vision to the screen. The script he

CANNIBALISM IS FUNNY... WHO KNEW? Paul Bartel and Mary Woronov in another of cult cinema's beloved dark-humor flicks.

and Blackburn penned focuses on 'The Blands': Ozzie and Harriet from the vanilla 1950s attempting to survive in our degenerate contemporary world. The Blands hope to open a retro Country Cookin' place. To make money, they learn from friend 'Doris the Dominatrix' (Susan Saiger) how to advertise sex services in the Personals. Clients are murdered, including 'Raoul' (Robert Beltran, 1953–), a blackmailer. Disposal of his body allows this to qualify as the first cannibalistic comedy. Woronov (1943–), onetime performer at Warhol's The Factory, is inspired as a morally insane "mainstream" woman who would die before committing adultery but feels no guilt murdering slime. P.B. shot the film for $350,000 over a period of two years, buying snippets of film stock when he could afford to. Would have had a sequel, "Bland Ambition." Sadly, the auteur passed away before that reached fruition.

ECSTASY (1933)

Erotic Film Rating: ****

Historic Value: ***** ½

Headley… oops! Hedy! Completist Rating: *****

Gustav Machaty, dir.; Machaty, Frantisek Horky, Jacques A. Korepel, scr.; Horky, Mortz Grunhut, prods.; 1.19:1; B&W; 82 in. (86 min., director's cut), Elekta Film.

 A legend surrounds *Ecstasy*, often considered the first non-porn film to feature a beautiful woman topless. That's hardly true; check out D.W. Griffith's *Intolerance* (1916) or, earlier still, Italy's many ancient-world costumers. The tempest in a cinematic teapot had more to do with the female lead's age; Hedy Kiesler (1914–2000), later redubbed Hedy Lamarr, was a teenager. More incendiary: a depiction of this female in the throes of orgasm; hence, the title. By today's standards the sequence appears mild, the camera close on her face. Czech-Austrian Machaty (1901–1963)—already associated with erotic movies (*Seduction*, 1925)—inspired Hedy's passion by pricking her naked derriere with a pin. 'Eva,' a virgin, marries an older man, then slips off to an Eden-like forest with a youth she calls 'Adam.' Based on a 1929 book by Robert Horky which, like D.H. Lawrence's *Lady Chatterley's Lover* (1928), dared argue that a woman has as much of a right to carnal pleasure as do men. Deeply offended, Pope Pius VII condemned this work as obscene. Hedy become a mainstream sex symbol in such Hollywood films as *Algiers* (1938) and *White Cargo* (1942). Cartoonist Bob Kane (1915–1988) modelled Catwoman on Hedy.

ED WOOD (1994)

Ed Wood Cult Rating: **** ½

Tim Burton Cult Rating: **** ½

Tim Burton, dir.; Scott Alexander, Larry Karaszewski, scr.; Burton, Denise Di Novi, prods.; 1.85:1; B&W; 127 min.; Touchstone.

Before Tommy Wiseau and *The Room*, there was Edward D. Wood, Jr. (1924–1978) and *Plan 9*: The least talented filmmaker of his era producing what many consider the worst movie ever made. To make clear this bio-pic of the cross-dressing auteur would not be mistaken for another colorful surrealist film, T. B. (1958–) shot in B&W, referencing films of the 1950s, even foregoing Danny Elfman's magical scores. Johnny Depp (1963–) plays the would-be Orson Welles of Z budget flicks as a blithe spirit. For his portrayal of Bela Lugosi (1882–2019) Martin Landau (1928–2017) won the Academy Award for Best Supporting Actor. Cult-worthy performers include Sarah Jessica Parker as Dolores Fuller, Jeff Jones as Criswell The Great, Bill Murray as Bunny Breckinridge, Lisa Marie as Vampira, and Vincent D'Onofrio (voice courtesy of Maurice LaMarche) as Welles. From a book by Rudolph Greg. A handful of devout Burton (and Wood) aficionados caught this in theatres. Thanks to home video a broader, wider following developed. The world's first ever cult film about the making of… a cult film.

ELECTION (1999)

Edgy comedy Rating: *****

Alexander Payne, dir.; Payne, Jim Taylor, scr.; Albert Berger, Keith Samples, David Gale, Ron Verxa, prods.; 2.35:1; C; 103 min.; Bona Fide Prods./MTM Films/Paramount.

John Hughes' mega-hit *Ferris Bueller's Day Off* (1986) turned Matthew Broderick (1962–) into a mainstream star; Payne's *Election* transformed him into a cult sensation. A high school teacher is assigned to oversee an election in which 'Tracy Flick' (Reese Witherspoon, 1976–) plans to run unopposed. Motivated less by any desire for democratic competition than abject hatred for the goodie-two shoes suck-up, the advisor convinces an easy-going jock (Chris Klein, 1979–) to enter the race. Here is a contemporary variation on an adage from Woody Allen's *Crimes and Misdemeanors* (1989): Comedy is tragedy plus time, as the obsessed anti-hero learns too late. Payne (1961–) offers us a pessimistic vision of the world masked in the guise of light-hearted comedy. From a novel by Tom Perrotta in which T.F. was consciously intended as a female variation on 'Sammy Glick' from Budd Schulberg's *What Makes Sammy Run?* (1941). Broderick's role collapses Shakespeare's 'Coriolanus' into 'Iago' from *Othello* as Neil Simon might've combined them.

EMERALD FOREST, THE (1985)

Green Moviegoer Cult Rating: *****

Boorman aficionado Rating: **** ½

John Boorman, dir.; Rospo Pallenberg, scr.; Boorman, pro.; 2.35:1; C; 114 min.; Christel Films/Avco Pictures.

"Save the rainforest!" No matter how many times ecologically oriented organizations like Greenpeace or The Sierra Club made this announcement, nothing drives a message home like a great film. T.E.F. offered a fact-based adventure involving a U.S. engineer (Powers Boothe, 1948–2017) assigned to build a state-of-the-art dam in a Third World Country. While there, his son is abducted by an indigenous tribe. For ten years the father searches for his boy. The now-grown youth (Charley Boorman, 1966–), having learned to live in a natural setting, is better off for having been raised far from the madding crowd and modern pollution of resources. Boorman (1933–) had in the past turned out mainstream blockbusters (*Deliverance*, 1972; *Excalibur*, 1981) and unfathomably bad flops (*Zardoz*, 1974; *The Exorcist II: The Heretic, 1977*). T.E.F. is his cult item, a deeply personal project brought to the screen with a delicate balance of passion and intellect. Shot entirely in Brazil.

SAVE THE RAINFOREST: John Boorman managed to bring ecological issues to the public with this engaging action-adventure film.

EMANUELLE NEGRA, aka *BLACK EMANUELLE* (1975)

Bitto Albertini, aka Albert Thomas, dir.; Albertini, Ambrogio Moleteni, scr.; Mario Mariani, pro.; 1.85:1; C; Emaus Films.

The best remembered sequence in *Joys of a Woman*, the superior sequel to *Emmanuelle*, featured Sylvia Kristel engaged in love-making with a breathtaking Eurasian girl, Laura Gemser (1950–). While watching, producer of Italian exploitation flicks M. M. experienced an epiphany: Why not star her in a series as a 'black' (in truth, the actress is light brown) variation? The title/name had been copyrighted. No problem: knock an 'm' out of the spelling! Here was the first in a series, many directed by Joe D'Amato, as a female reporter travels the world (in this instalment to Africa) for photo-shoots, always enjoying free sex with attractive men and women, often in menages. Films of this sort ("If it feels good, *do* it!") came to a swift end during the next decade with the advent of AIDS. There is no official 'time'

THE 1960s SEXUAL REVOLUTION IN 1970s CINEMA: Belatedly, films featuring 'French' (Sylvia Kristel) and 'Black' (Laura Gemser) Em(m)anuelle brought soft-core porn to the arthouse, and then the mainstream, audience at theatres and on pay cable TV.

listed for *E.N.*; while L.G. agreed to a softcore feature, graphic inserts were added to create an alternative hardcore version. The mainstream cut features soft-core eroticism of the type appearing in *Lui/Oui* magazine.

EMMANUELLE (1974)

Erotic value: ** ½

Social impact Rating: *****

Just Jaecken, dir.; Jean-Louis Ruchard, scr.; Yves Rousset-Rouard, pro.; C; 1.66:1; 93 min.; Trinaria Films.

"'X' was never like *this*!" So proclaimed poster-art for this French film when *E.* was released in the U.S. Columbia's PR team hoped to distinguish this from recent porn, particularly *Deep Throat*, with its sleazy reputation. Here, for the first time, was not so much a sex film but a legitimate movie *about* human sexuality. The story derived from a 1969 combination of fiction and fact. Maryat Rolet-Andriane, 1932–2004, aka 'Emmanuelle Arsan,' had married a respected diplomat. In a roman-a-clef she shared her journey from virginal, frigid 19-year old to willing nymph. One female's experiences during the 1960s became a metaphor for the worldwide Sexual Revolution. The film featured luscious locations from Paris to Bangkok, exotic music, and elegant Sylvia Kristel (1952–2012), who became the poster-girl for what Dr. Alex Comfort labelled the Joys of Sex, changing the public's perception of eroticism from a Puritanical negative to delightful pastime. The major liability: Jaecken's (1940–) failure to find the proper tone. A sequel, *Joys of a Woman: Emmanuelle II*; Francis Giacobetti, 1975) is far superior (if less known) in all regards.

EMPIRE (1964)

Andy Warhol Cult Rating: *****

Watch-ability Rating: NO STARS

Andy Warhol, dir.; Warhol, scr.; Warhol, pro.; B&W; 485 mins.; Warhol Films.

Empire is the movie this maestro of Pop sensibility was born to shoot. With fellow Underground auteur Jonas Mekas (1922–2019) as cinematographer, A.W. set a camera on the 41st floor of the Time-Life Building, pointed it at the Empire State Building and, in extreme long-shot (for a sense of objectivity) and slow-motion (adding a counter-point of subjectivity), shot 485 min. of footage. A viewer watches (few if any have been able to stick with it) 8 hrs. 5. mins. of a single stationary shot. The most exciting action occurs when a bird flies by. Most observers considered this madness. For A.W., such claims as "unwatchable" proved that he had succeeded in his purpose of challenging and confounding an audience. 'Do you actually expect people to sit down for this 'show'?" howled most Normals. In fact, *no!* Why not set up a projector in one's home, loop the film so that it will run continuously, and allow visitors to glance at it for as long as anyone cares to—precisely the case if a still picture of the Empire Building were framed on the wall? *E.* begs the question: Why assume that storytelling must be the *only* purpose of such a rich medium?

ERASERHEAD (1977)

David Lynch Cult Rating: *****

Jack Nance Cult Rating: *****

AFI; David Lynch, dir.; Lynch, scr.; Lynch, Fred Baker, pro.; Lynch, mus.; Herbert Candwell, cin.; Lynch, ed.; 185:1; B&W; 89 min.

Born in a small middle-American Montana town, Lynch (1946–) saw the 'normal' world around him from a notably off-kilter point-of-view. First as a graphic artist, then in the realm of avant garde theatre, later with a series of seven short films, D.L. presented an American Everyman's worst secret fears as to the meaninglessness of existence and absurd nature of life. His first feature, *E.* focuses on 'Henry Spencer' (Jack Nance, 1943–1996) who drags himself through a bleak, unrewarding modern world, doing drudge work at a factory; also he must contend with his ever-screaming malformed child. Privately H.S. fantasizes about a girl (Judith Roberts) in an apartment just across the way, though she may be a creation of his sad imagination. Considered by fans of edgy filmmaking to be an indie movie equivalent to the land-breaking/

mind-blowing 1893 painting "The Scream" by Edvard Munch. Largely financed by the American Film Institute. Lynch edited, created the haunting musical score, and oversaw the nightmarish production design.

ESCAPE FROM NEW YORK (1981)

Near Future Dystopian Sci-Fi Rating: **** ½

Carpenter Cult Rating: **** ½

John Carpenter, dir.; Carpenter, Nick Castle, scr.; Debra Hill, Larry Franco, pro.; 2.35:1; C; 99 min. (theatrical release print), 106 min. (director's cut); AVCO-Embassy.

The stupendous success of *Star Wars* motivated all the major studios to green-light sci-fi/fantasy projects in hopes that lightning might strike twice. Mainly, this resulted in big budget bombs like the costly/embarrassingly chintzy *Flash Gordon* (1980). Far more appealing: this tightly budgeted (approximately six million), highly imaginative item from one of the struggling companies that turned out several worthy cult films before their swift demise. Though Carpenter did not get to create the Western he had always hoped to make, he did at least borrow the 'Space Cowboy' concept from *Star Wars*' 'Han Solo' in the person of Kurt Russell (1951–), who would go on to greatness in both epic fantasy and cowboy films. A remarkable cast of character actors included Lee Van Cleef (1925–1989), in a more sympathetic role than 'Angel Eyes' in Sergio Leone's spaghetti westerns; Oscar winner Ernest Borgnine (1917–2012) in a career reviving role as the droll cabbie; music and black exploitation flick superstar Isaac Hayes (1942-2000) adding grit to this tale of a ruined New York City in the year 1997; and Harry Dean Stanton (1926–2017) as his perpetual sad eyed loner self. Last but hardly least: Brit Donald Pleasence (1919–1995) who had scored as 'Sam Loomis' in Carpenter's *Halloween*, here playing the hollow in appearance president in need of immediate rescue by the last American hero, the wonderfully named 'Snake Pliskin.' Despite the title, shot mostly in St. Louis MO to save on expenses.

ETERNAL SUNSHINE OF THE SPOTLESS MIND (2004)

Cult Rating: *****

Mainstream Rating: *****

Michel Gondry, dir.; Gondry, Charlie Kaufman, Pierre Bismuth, scr.; 1.85:1; C; 108 min.; Focus Features/Anonymous Content.

Should I become a painter, an inventor, or a drummer in a rock band? So wondered M.G. (1963–), settling on the latter as he joined 'Oui-Oui.' But when they couldn't afford to hire a pro to make their videos, Gondry volunteered and shortly was doing them for cult star Bjork. A collaboration made in heaven with absurdist author C.K. (1958–) led to a perfect movie: part comedy, part drama; part old-fashioned boy meets girl, boy loses girl, boy gets girl (maybe) romance and part near-future dystopian art film; part cult picture with its devastation of the time-space continuum and part charming mainstream hit. Jim Carrey (1962–) and Kate Winslet (1975–) are near-future lovers who, in an experimental procedure, have their memories of one another erased. Can true love ever be denied? A song by Beck provides the cherry atop this cinematic sundae. Elijah Wood, Kirsten Dunst, and Mark Ruffalo add to the cult appeal. This ties *The Tru-*

A DIFFERENT KIND OF CULT MOVIE: The popularity of Michel Gondry's time-shifting project proved that the American mainstream was at last developing cultish tastes.

man Show (Peter Weir, 1998) as one of the key films proving the line between cult and mainstream becomes ever thinner with each passing year.

EVIL DEAD, THE (1981)

Raimi Cult Rating: ****

Campbell Cult Rating: ****

Sam Raimi, dir.; Raimi, scr.; Raimi, Bruce Campbell, Rob Tapert, Irvin Shapiro, prods.; 1.37:1; C; 85 min.

 Growing up in Royal Oak MI, Raimi (1959–) and friend Bruce Campbell (1958–) shot mini-movies with an eight m.m. camera. During the late 1970s, while living in Detroit, they (like other young aspiring auteurs) were so over-whelmed by the critical and commercial success of *Halloween* they determined to make a supernatural thriller of their own. After three years of scripting, raising money, shooting for two weeks in rural Tennessee, then meticulously editing, the pards completed what they hoped would be an even scarier film than *The Hills Have Eyes*. Five college students (including Campbell as 'Ashley J. Williams') spend spring break at an isolated cabin. They discover an ancient book of the dead which releases wicked spirits from surrounding trees. An edge of your seat gorefest, *T.E.D.* received one thumb way up from horrormeister Stephen King. Not only sequels but comic books and video games led to a full-fledged franchise. One member of the editing team, Joel Coen, convinced his brother Ethan to collaborate on their project, *Blood Simple*.

EXECUTION OF MARY, QUEEN OF SCOTS, THE (1895)

Silent short gorefest Rating: *****

Alfred Clark, dir.; William Heye, scr.; Thomas A. Edison, pro.; 1.33;1; B&W; 21 secs. (apprx.); The Black Maria Co.

 One year before *The Kiss* introduced sex as one of two great ongoing movie subjects, this Edison short did so for violence. In what appears to be a single/continuous shot, 'Mary' (Mrs. Robert L. Thomas) is in 1587 led to the block. There, a mighty executioner raises his axe. Nickelodeon patrons were unaware that the camera had, at this point, temporarily ceased filming so a dummy could be set in her place; as the weapon descended, the cameraman started shooting again. Like viewers of France's Grand Guignol live-theatre, audiences for this early flicker were certain they had witnessed an actual death. E. marks not only the first use of Special Effects in movies (a year before George Melies set to work in France) but rates as the original Snuff film, or so it seemed. In 1899 this was paired with *The Kiss* for the first sex and violence theatrical double bill.

EX MACHINA (2014)

Sci-Fi Neo-Noir Cult Rating: ******

Alex Garland, dir./scr.; Andrew Macdonald, Albon Reich, prod.; 2.35:1; C/B&W; 108 min.; Universal.

Though Danny Boyle won universal acclaim for *28 Days Later...* and *Sunshine* (2007), genre buffs noted the former was based on a novel by Garland (1970–), the latter film adapted from A.G.'s original screenplay. Not surprisingly the gifted author eventually stretched to full auteur-ship with this near-future romantic thriller. In its sense of an ever-surrounding (and threatening) natural coldness, *E.M.* recalls Stanley Kubrick's *The Shining* (1980). A young Internet genius (Domhanall Gleeson) wins an in-house competition, then flies to an isolated fort where the firm's mysterious owner (Oscar Isaac) has created a cyborg called 'Ava' (Alicia Vikander, 1988–). 'She' possesses such a high level of self-conscious intelligence that any line between robot and human all but disappears. The new arrival falls in love with this beautiful machine, as obsessed with 'her' as James Stewart was with Kim Novak in *Vertigo*. Here is 'pure' sci-fi, chronicling the history of tomorrow even as such machines are in development today. Vikander gained a cult stardom that would continue in *The Danish Girl* (2015) and *Tomb Raider* (2018). Eerily erotic, yet disturbingly understated.

EYE OF THE DEVIL (1967)

Sharon Tate Rating: **** ½

Witchcraft Rating: **

J. Lee Thompson, dir.; Robin Estridge, Dennis Murphy, scr.; John Calley, Dennis Murphy, prod.; 1.66:1; B&W; 92 min.; Filmways/ MGM.

Following the mild success of *The Haunting* (1963), producers wondered if perhaps the era of high-quality horror films might be ripe for a comeback. David Niven was cast as owner of a French wine-making chateau called home from England when the crops fail. His wife gradually realizes the simple workers practice Wicca and apparently plan to sacrifice her husband to the ancient gods. All the while an elegant blonde witch in basic black wanders about, mysterious and aloof. Everything that could go wrong during production did, including Kim Novak (originally the wife) leaving under awkward circumstances, Deborah Kerr brought in to replace her. Once in the editing room, the situation worsened: The story made no sense. The forgotten film sat on a shelf at MGM for three years, deemed unreleasable. Then, on the night of 8/09/69, the starlet who had embodied the witch—Sharon Tate, (1943–1969)—died horribly,

BEWITCHING: Sharon Tate's Wiccan movie, a box-office disaster when first released, found a new cult audience following her death at the hands of Charles Manson's killer hippies.

along with her unborn child, during what are called the Manson Murders. Overnight, she became a sensation. The film was released with her name and image prominent on the posters to draw in curious viewers. With renewed interest in S.T. following the release of Tarantino's *Once Upon a Time in Hollywood*, cult interest in this misanthropic movie returned.

F

FASTER, PUSSYCAT! KILL! KILL! (1965)

The Ultimate Drive-In Kinky (Pre-Nudity) Blast: *****

Russ Meyer, dir.; Meyer, Jack Moran, scr.; Meyer, Eve Meyer, pros.; 1.37:1; B&W; 83 mins.; Eve Prods.

One ongoing myth about *F.P.K.K.*, hailed as "The *Citizen Kane* of Camp Cinema," is that this trash flick—shot for under $50,000—earned millions on its initial release to the Drive In/Grindhouse circuit. In truth, Russ Meyer (1922–2004) only reaped mild profits; lowbrow audiences expected nudity from the man who had displayed unrobed, large-breasted

THE PERFECT MID-SIXTIES DRIVE IN FLICK: Feminists of the era debated whether Tara Santana represented the exploitation of big busted girls by a male chauvinist director or offered the strongest, most-self reliant woman, paving the way for a more enlightened future. Maybe it's all in one's own point of view?

women in *The Immoral Mr. Teas* (1959). Not so here, though the outfits worn by strippers 'Varla' (Japan's Tara Santana, 1938–2011), 'Rosie' (Haji, 1946–2013), and 'Billie' (Lori Williams, 1946–) appear appropriately sleazy (black leather, tight jeans, cleavage-revealing tops, etc.). These wild women drive into a south-western desert in a Porsche 356 C, kill a racing driver, and kidnap his virginal girlfriend. Only gradually did F.P.K.K. become a cult fav, particularly at revival houses near college campuses. As feminism arose, middle-class women condemned the exploitation director as The Enemy. In time, though, an edgier element in the Women's Movement decreed this a feminist film, filled with strong females who refuse to obey male-dictated rules of behaviour. They employ sexual allure to reverse the cliche that insists this reduces women to sex objects, rather empowering them to dominate male gazers. On an aesthetic level, R.M. was praised (subject matter aside) as a master filmmaker as to employment of the camera to carry his story.

FAST TIMES AT RIDGEMONT HIGH (1982)

General audience Rating: *** ½

For those who were teenagers in the early 1980s Rating: ****

Phoebe Cates cultists Rating: *****

Amy Heckerling, dir.; Cameron Crowe, scr.; Art Linson, Irving Azoff, prods.; 1.85:1; C; 90 min.

    Cameron Crowe (1957–) based this screenplay on his own book about varied lifestyles of kids in CA's Van Nuys during the early 1980s. Perceptive about the characters, anecdotal in style, this had the potential to do for that era what *American Graffiti* (1973) had for the early 1960s. Sadly, first time director Heckerling (1952–) turned out to be no George Lucas nor did she become 'the first important female director of the post-feminist age.' The best A.H. could manage afterwards was *Look Who's Talking* (1989). Still, this film succeeds in spite of rather than because of her. Sequences involving stoned Surfer Dude 'Jeff Spicoli' (Sean Penn, 1960–) and up-tight older teacher 'Mr. Hand' (Ray Walston, 1914–2001) were so well-written that these bits

HIGH SCHOOL DAZE: Sean Penn became an immediate youth cult star (and, later, an Oscar-winning mainstream actor as well) opposite teacher Ray Walston in *Fast Times at Ridgemont High*.

might have worked without *any* director. Phoebe Cates' (1963–) topless appearance by a swimming pool (in a fantasy sequence) qualifies this as her cult film. The high school and malls, costumes and cars are accurate and evocative. Honors for in-depth acting go to Jennifer Jason Leigh (1962–) as the most complex girl.

FIELD IN ENGLAND, A (2013)

Cult Rating: ** 1/2

Ben Wheatley, dir.; Amy Jump, scr.; Claire Jones, Andrew Starke, pro.; 2.35:1; B&W; 90 min.; Film4.

What begins as an historical picture turns into something else entirely, on one level a stark horror story and, on another, an allegory... though precisely what it has to say is elusive. Maybe that was on purpose? 'Whitehead' (Reese Shearsmith) is one of several deserters fleeing a horrific battle during England 17th century Civil War. Hiding in the high weeds of an odd field, they come across 'O'Neil' (Michael Smiley), an Irish alchemist searching this self-contained little kingdom for... well, let's not allow a 'spoiler' to slip through. The remarkable cinematography will bring to mind the later, and far greater, *Lighthouse*, as well as Ingmar Bergman's costume film dystopia in *The Seventh Seal* (1957), without that masterwork's sure-fire sense of Existential philosophy. This item embraces Nihilism though not necessarily of an intellectual order. Is it profound or merely pretentious? Audiences will certainly enjoy arguing that about this ambitious, uncertain, impactful experiment.

FIGHT CLUB (1999)

David Fincher Cult Rating: *****

Chuck Palahuniuk Cult Rating: *****

Edward Norton Cult Rating: *****

Meat Loaf (Aday) Cult Rating: *****

David Fincher, dir.; Chuck Palahniuk, Jim Uhis, scr.; Art Linson, Ross Grayson Bell, Cean Chaffin, pro.; 2.39:1; C; 1939 min.; Fox 2000.

The anti-prose novels of Charles Palahuniuk (1962–) offer an Existential philosophy that recalls the writings of Soren Kierkegaard filtered through the stylings of Franz Kafka. *Fight Club* (1996), his first, initially appeared unfilmable, a stream-of-consciousness nightmare vision of modern life as seen through the eyes of a loose-cannon narrator. This anti-hero attempts to find solace from a hard, cold, ugly world via sex with a woman quirkier even than he. Also, the friendship of 'Tyler Durden,' a rugged individualist who punches his way toward an odd sort of freedom that borders on nihilism. David Fincher (1962–) refused to compromise the outlandish vision. Here is a sea-green/sickly-blue urban setting that has sunk into unsatisfying consumerism. Edward Norton (1969–) and Brad Pitt (1963–) vividly embody the obscure storyteller and his romanticized image (perhaps a mental creation) of the last American loner. Helena Bonham Carter (1966–) provides a female voice of oblique anti-reason. Budgeted at nearly $70 million, the highly acclaimed post-modernist work returned only a little more than half that. Today? A cult classic.

FISH CALLED WANDA, A (1988)

John Cleese Completist Rating: *****

Python-esque Cult Rating: *****

Charles Crichton, John Cleese, dir.; Cleese, Crichton, scr.; Michael Shamberg, pro.; 1.37:1; C; 108 min.; MGM.

Is there life after Monty Python? More specifically, without Terry Gilliam's genius present? The resounding answer: a happy 'yes' once audiences caught this near-perfect spoof offering both a first-rate heist plot and simultaneously a flat-out burlesque on the caper genre. Everything appears to be mapped out to a perfect nth degree as a cunning collection of English thieves plan to steal diamonds almost as large as the Ritz; then, step by step, everything that can go wrong does, owing to each vile conspirator's scheme to betray all the others. Most memorable performance: Michael Palin (1943–) as a stuttering animal lover, his most loved fish this film's Hitchcockian MacGuffin. Jamie Lee Curtis (1958–) reveals gifts for comedy no one knew she possessed. Her brother and/or lover (Kevin Kline, 1947–) delights as a jerk who can't stand being called stupid because he knows he is. Cleese (1939–) plays 'Archie Leach,' this a reference to Cary Grant's birth name. Collaborator Crichton (1910–1999) was part of the remarkable team of comic talents at England's Ealing studio in the 1950s and 1960s.

FITZCARRALDO (1982)

Werner Herzog, dir.; Herzog, dir.; Herzog, Willi Segler, prod.; 1.85:1; C; 158 min.; Project Filmproduktion.

Like Italy's Franco Zeffirelli, W.H. (1942–) stages operas when not directing films. *F.* may be his most personal work, retelling the tale of Peruvian rubber baron Carlos Fitzcarraldo (1862–1897; Klaus Kinski, 1926–1991). F. oversaw the pushing, pulling, and carrying of a 340-ton

FOR THE LOVE OF OPERA: The great cult star Klaus Kinsky captures the unconditional obsession of genius/madman intent on conquering nature by bringing classical culture to what Joseph Conrad tagged the Heart of Darkness.

steamship over a South American mountain while settling the Madre de Dios basin. In Herzog's version, F.'s self-serving capitalism is balanced by a fanatic dedication to stage a full scale grand opera in the sprawling wilderness. A combination of Herzog's own outrageous artistic ambitions and the historical figure's blind-sighted sense of mission underscores this epic about what W.H. has referred to as a "conquistador of the useless." Shrill cello crescendos and madcap violin strings serve the same purpose that they would in an over-the-top operatic live performance. The film also serves as a thinly disguised autobiography. Jack Nicholson and Jason Robards were approached for the lead. Yet it's difficult to imagine anyone but mad-eyed K.K. as the man who brings cultural imperialism to confused Aguaruna natives.

5,000 FINGERS OF DR. T., THE (1953)

1950s Cult Film Rating: ****

Dr. Seuss Cult Rating: **** ½

ENTER DR. SEUSS: The revolutionary author of post-modern children's books made an uncertain film debut with this fascinating oddity starring Hans Conreid and Tommy Rettig, later of TV *Lassie* fame.

Roy Rowland, dir.; Dr. Seuss, Allan Scott, scr.; Stanley Kramer, pro.; 1.85:1; C; 89 min.; Columbia.

Hollywood's first attempt to adapt the charming child-oriented surrealism of Dr. Seuss, born Theodor Geisel (1904–19991). S. Kramer (1913–2001), a producer noted for 1950s message movies (*The Wild One, High Noon*) found Seuss' odd concept perfect for addressing middle-class suburban Moms as to the horrors they unintentionally visit on their innocent offspring in the name of 'culture.' Bart (Tommy Rettig, 1941–1996; 'Jeff' on CBS' *Lassie*, 1954–1957) is forced by Mary Healy to take piano lessons. The maestro (Hans Conried, 1917–1982), in a role originally intended for Danny Kaye, is a tyrant. The lad suffers through lessons by fantasizing about an alternative world. (This plot eventually 'borrowed' for *Sucker Punch*). The first preview, for an audience not prepared for something so radical, proved a disaster. Columbia execs pruned away its clever sense of cryptic darkness in hopes of Disney-fying the piece. What remains offers a hint of what might have been. 'Sideshow Bob Terwilliger' forever brow-beating 'Bartholomew' on *The Simpsons* is a homage to this film's central conflict.

FLASH GORDON (1936)

The Serial to End All Serials Rating: *****

Frederick Stephani, Ray Taylor, dir.; Stephani, George H. Plympton, Basil Dickey, scr.; Henry MacRae, pro.; 1.37:1; B&W; 245 min. (15 Chapters); Universal.

Before TV, most Hollywood studios turned out cliffhangers for the Saturday morning kiddie audience in search of sci-fi adventure. Universal made the best. And the best of the best was this spaced-out retro-future chapter-play based on Alex Raymond's (1909–1956) comic strip. Olympian Larry 'Buster' Crabbe (1908–1983) played the Galahad-like hero, with menacing Charles Middleton (1874–1949) as nemesis 'Ming the Merciless,' a rip-off of Machiavellian 'Fu Manchu' in Sax Rohmer's anti-Asian melodramas. As lily white heroine 'Dale Arden,' Jean Rogers (1916–1991) screams on cue to be saved. Most male viewers preferred Priscilla Lawson (1914–1958) as Ming's sexually over-charged daughter, a throwback to villainesses portrayed by the young Myrna Loy. The semblance of a

THE GOLDEN AGE OF THE THEATRICAL CLIFFHANGER: "To be continued next week!" followed each chapter of this, the greatest serial ever made, when *Flash Gordon* played Saturday matinees in the early 1930s; two decades later, it and most other chapter plays would be "stripped" (shown each weekday) during the early days of TV.

huge budget was achieved via stock footage from Universal feature films. Released to TV in the early 1950s, stripped for a Monday through Friday format, the series charmed children of those original fans. The base of its appeal: Unconscious camp.

FLESH GORDON (1974)

X-Rated With Something Extra Rating: **** ½

Michael Benveniste, Howard Ziehm, dirs.; Benveniste, scr.; Zielm, Bill Osco, prod.; 1.66:1; C; 90 min. (X-rated original version), 73 min. (R-rated follow-up cut); Mammoth Films.

Following the breakthrough success of *Deep Throat* and *Behind the Green Door*, there existed a brief moment in time when the hardcore sex film might have become a staple of mainstream as well as underground entertainment. Here is the third film to suggest the time was right, a sophomoric satire on the camp *Flash Gordon* serials of the 1930s, now back in fashion thanks to the Pop Art movement and nostalgia craze that would shortly lead to *Star Wars* (1977) and *Raiders of the Lost Ark* (1981). Produced on a budget that exceeded $700,000, what we witness is a respectable color B movie sci-fi spoof... but with penetration. While the special effects are not up to the level of a Ray Harryhausen, they are impressive, mounted by talents that would go on to bigger and better things: Jim Danforth, Rik Baker, Dennis Maren, and David Allen. Candy Samples appears to satisfy fans of porn. Successful enough to spawn a small (i.e., cultish) fan base and franchise that included a home video game and several comic book/graphic novel spin-offs. A year and a half later, porn switched to videotape production and become irrelevant other than for hardcore addicts.

FRANK MILER'S SIN CITY (2005)

Nastiest of Nasty Cult Film Rating: **** 1/2

Frank Miller, Robert Rodriguez, dirs..; Miller, scr.; Elizabeth Avellan, pro.; B&W/C; 1.85:1; 124 min.; Dimension Films.

How to top *Pulp Fiction*? With another trilogy of outlandishly cruel tales about streetwise characters, this time set in a neo-noir alternative universe. Acclaimed author/illustrator for Marvel and D.C., Miller (1957–) had transformed Batman into The Dark Knight. In 1990, he struck out on his own with Dark Horse graphic novels: Bus Station books and modern Manga successfully collapsed into one another. Eclectic casting includes Jessica Alba (1981–), Rutger Hauer (1944–), Benicio Del Toro (1967–), Bruce Willis (1955–), Mickey Rourke (1952–) and Rosario Dawson (1979–). Besides directing, Rodriguez (1968–) served as cinematographer and editor, contributing to the musical score. Guest artist Tarantino (1963–) directed the seminal confrontation between Del Toro and Clive Owen (1964–). A ground-breaking virtual reality film. The actors performed before a green screen, settings and backdrops added digitally. The late Brittany Murphy (1977-2009) appears in all anecdotes involving a vengeance obsessed madman, an ordinary guy

COMPUTER ANIMATION NOIR: The golden age of black and white thrillers was enhanced with contemporary F/X in this notably brutal graphic novel based movie.

swept into street crime, and a serial killer. Rodriguez' vow to film all of Miller's *Sin City* stories received a set-back when the sequel *A Dame to Kill For* (2014) bombed.

FREAKS (1932)

All-time classic cult Rating: *****

Tod Browning, dir.; Browning, Irving J. Thalberg, pro.; Clarence Aaron, Willis Coldseck, scr.; B&W; 64 min.; 1.37:1; Metro-Goldwyn-Mayer.

    Amazingly, the first American grindhouse classic of the sound era was released by MGM, self-proclaimed Tiffany of studios. Intellectual Irving G. Thalberg (1899–1936), impressed by the box-office success of Browning's *Dracula* the previous year for Universal, wanted his own horror entry. Believing the short-story "Spurs" by C.A. Robbins might work, I.T. assigned free-lancer Browning (1880–1962) to develop the project. The fable concerns a bad blonde trapeze artist (Olga Baclanova, 1893–1974) who joins a sleazy little circus. She seduces a midget (Harry Earles, 1902–1985) and steals his fortune. When other title characters discover her plot, they gather to transform the haughty lady into a half-chicken 'thing.' Thalberg was aghast at the results, drastically cutting and, following public outrage during initial screenings, hiding the film in his vault. Schlock-meister Dwain Esper (1893–1982) secured the rights, re-distributing *Freaks* on the grindhouse circuit. All the 'unique' characters—human torso, bearded woman, Siamese twins, etc.—are the real deal.

FRIDAY THE 13th (1980)

Sean Cunningham, dir.; Cunningham, Steve Miner, pro.; Victor Miller, scr.; 1.85:1; C; 95 min.; Paramount.

    Were S.C. (1941–) and Wes Craven separated at birth? Though not physical doubles, they paired as twin horror-meisters after reaching Hollywood to offer Drive In audiences *The Last House on the Left* (1973). The opposite of Godard's *Breathless*, here was a grindhouse item inspired by a previous art film, Ingmar Bergman's *The Virgin Spring* (1960). Initially derided as the worst sort of exploitation, the gross-out genre-

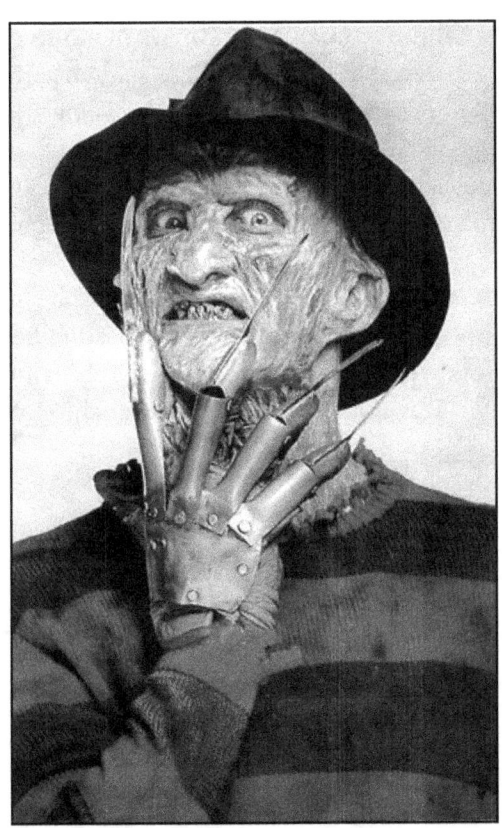

MEET THE MONSTERS, PART I: Freddie Krueger arrived on the horror movie horizon in *A Nightmare on Elm St.* though the iconic 'Jason Voohres' evolved in the seemingly endless string of *Friday the 13th* sequels.

buster went on to become a cult fav and, eventually, a landmark of modern horror. Cunningham unofficially directed at least one chase sequence in *A Nightmare on Elm Street*, then was inspired by Carpenter's *Halloween* to make this thriller set at a long-abandoned summer camp about to be re-opened despite horrific goings on in the past. Kevin Bacon had an early role as a doomed would-be counsellor. The only person who might have been more perfect to play Jason Voohres' mother, a seemingly all-American middle-class lady with murder on her mind, would have been Doris Day. Unlike most other horror franchises, the iconic 'Jason' did not emerge until the first of the follow-ups. For the record, Ari Lehmann (1965–) played Jason here though was not involved in the franchise to follow.

FRITZ THE CAT (1972)

Crumb cultist Rating: *****

Bakshi cultist Rating: ****

Ralph Bakshi, dir.; Bakshi, scr.; Steve Krantz, prod.; 1.37:1; C/B&W; 78 min.; Black Ink.

R. Crumb (1943– ; first name, Robert), contributor of Existential comics to the Underground Press of the 1960s, introduced 'Fritz' in 1965. Here was that beloved old Felix, updated for contemporary hipsters. Illustrator Bakshi (1938–), making his directorial debut, planned a Fritz movie in 1969. It did not reach theatres until the early years of the following decade. Instead of a comment on contemporary issues, *F.* instead 'worked' as a metaphor for a counter-cultural era long since gone. Fritz drops out of a university, joins sex orgies and drug parties, mixes with the Black Panthers and Hell's Angels in an attempt to 'find himself.' To make clear this cartoon was *not* for kids, the ratings board slapped it with an 'X' rather than the R it deserved. Bakshi's later films, including his disastrous animated *Lord of the Rings* (1978), proved hollow, shrill, and disappointing.

FROM DUSK TILL DAWN (1996)

Tarantino/Rodriguez Duel Cult Rating: ****

Salma Hayek Afficionado Rating: *****

Robert Rodriguez, dir.; Robert Kurtzman, Quentin Tarantino, scrs. Meir Teper, Gianni Nunnari, pro.; 1.85:1; C; 100 min.; Dimension Films/A Band Apart/Los Hooligans.

    A Texan of Mexican descent, Rodriguez (1968–) had no idea what to do with his life while growing up in San Antonio until he caught *Escape from New York*. From that moment on, he *had* to be a filmmaker. R.R.'s uneven if interesting picture, the low-budget actioner *El Mariachi* (1992), caught the eye of already established Q.T. 1963–), who took it upon himself to mentor this equally unconventional auteur. Their collaboration on *F.D.T.D.* might best be understood as a double feature of Grindhouse flicks that share the same characters. In the first half the crazed Gecko brothers (Tarantino and George Clooney) embark on a mad crime wave in the southwest: robbing, killing, finally kidnapping a minister (Harvey

OVER THE TOP: Salma Hyak provides 'camp' appeal as a vampire stripper snake-worshipper in a collaboration between Robert Rodriguez and Quentin Tarantino; Carmen Miranda all but invented such outre shenanigans in her Tutti-Fruiti screen vehicles.

Keitel, 1939–) and his kids. At mid-point, they arrive at an isolated biker bar where girls dance in bikinis, their leader (Salma Hayek, 1966–) performing with a boa. To put it accurately if not politically correctly, blood and boobs are on view everywhere. This is a contemporary big budget tribute to low-budget films from the 1970s. Over the hill action stars (John Saxon, Tom Savini, Fred Williamson, Michael Parks, Dany Triejo, etc.) all attest to that via cameo appearances. *F.D.T.D.* embodies the rural crime movies that became popular following *Bonnie and Clyde* with the Vampire stripper genre that began with *Vamp* (1986).

GANG'S ALL HERE, THE (1942)

Busby Berkeley Cult Rating: *****

Carmen Miranda Cult Rating: *****

Gay Subtext Aficionado Rating: *****

Busby Berkeley, dir.; Walter Bullock, Nancy Winkler, George Root Jr., scr.; William LeBaron, pro.; 1.37:1; C; 103 min.; 20th Century Fox.

"Are you a woman?" a U.S.O. girl asks the character played by Carmen Miranda (Muria de Carmo Miranda de Cunha, 1909–1955) in this glossy Technicolor musical. The focus is on Alice Faye (1915–1998) as a demure blonde who falls for a playboy soldier (Phil Baker). The film's agenda was to portray Latin Americans in a positive (if caricatured) light and keep folks in Central and South America from joining the Nazi cause. Though born in Portugal, Miranda represented the zesty, sexy, fun-loving, extroverted image of Brazil's women in such a gleeful way that South of the Border stylings became accessible to members of the U.S. Anglo community. Her signature number, "The Girl in the Tutti-Fruitti Hat," had far-reaching repercussions as to idiomatic American-English. Here, for the first time, the term 'fruit' became synonymous with a gay sensibility, exploding onscreen owing to musical stagings by the legendary Busby Berkeley (1895–1976). His over-the-top choreography had long been a cult fav within the underground (and more recently mainstream) gay community. The line of dialogue quoted above produced raucous laughter, many Americans already convinced Miranda was a male female-impersonator.

GET CARTER (1971)

Neo Noir Rating: ***

Michael Caine Cult Rating: ***

Mike Hodges, dir.; Hodges, Ted Lewis, scr.; Michael Klinger, pro.; 1.85:1; C; 112 min. (director's cut), 103 min. (edited version), MGM-British.

No other Brit-lensed example of the bleak, pessimistic, disturbing, violent, sexualized film genre known as neo-noir comes close to *G.C.* in terms of immediate impact on a viewer. A kingpin of London's Underworld crime scene (Michael Caine, 1933–) learns of his brother's death in their home city of Newcastle. Arriving to attend the funeral, he realizes this will not be a 'sentimental journey': nostalgia gives way to fury as Carter grasps his sibling was murdered by local thugs. Making his directorial debut, M.H. (1932–) was quick to admit that he relied heavily on memories of *Kiss Me Deadly,* bringing its darkness into the post-Production Code era. Caine here recalls Lee Marvin as 'Walker' in *Point Blank,* this film's avenger as cruel to women as men. Playwright and screenwriter John Osborne *(Look Back in Anger, Tom Jones)* appears as a detestable gambler. Britt Ekland's intense phone sex scene so disturbed censors that it was eliminated for many screenings. One of the few important studio films to be branded with an 'X' rating, at the time reserved for obvious pornography.

GHOST WORLD (2001)

Girl-Girl Coming of Age Rating: ** ½**

Thora Birch Cult Rating: ** ½**

Terry Zwigoff, dir.; Zwigoff, Daniel Clowes, scr.; John Malkovich, Lianne Halfon, Russell Smith, pros.; 1.85:1; 111 mins.; Granada/United Artists.

'How I Spent My Summer Vacation': an edgy, self-consciously clever aspiring artist (Thora Birch, 1982–) and a gorgeous cheerleader (Scarlett Johansson, 1984–) form an odd-couple bond. Following graduation, they drift through Portland OR. trying to decide whether to share an apartment.

COMING OF AGE, WITH GIRLS RATHER THAN BOYS FOR ONCE: In only a few years, Scarlett Johansson would be a superstar and Thora Birch a cult sensation.

One of those 'nothing at all happens; everything important happens' films that appear to be chronicling time-wasting on the part of young people "hangin'" while subtly introducing the little things in life that inevitably tear them apart. A plot device involves cult star Steve Buscemi (1957–) as an alienated collector of memorabilia. The film's power derives from a seductive ruse in the first half, encouraging us to believe these iconoclasts ought to be taken at face value. In the second, T.Z. (1949–) reveals how self-deceptive, even shallow, each can be. Adapted from Daniel Clowes' (1961–) cult comic. Birch's best role following *American Beauty* (1999). Her character's sketches were supplied by R. Crumb; Zwigoff in 1994 filmed a documentary about that counter-cultural rebel.

GINGER (1971)

Female Spy Action Rating: NO STARS

Breakthrough Sex & Violence Rating: *** ½

KISS ME QUICK, THEN PASS THE AMMO!: During the 21st century, female assassins no longer exist as disposable badgirls in the James Bond films but, as in the hit *La Femme Nikita*, are presented as sympathetic heroines; not surprisingly, junk movies like *Ginger* with Cherry Caffaro set the pace for first arthouse, then mainstream acceptance.

Don Schain, dir.; Schain, scr.; Ralph Desiderio, pro.; 1.85:1; C; 90 min.; Derio.

    Jennifer Garner (*Electra*, 2005); Angelina Jolie (*Mr. and Mrs. Smith*, 2005); Zoe Saldana (*Columbiana*, 2011); Charlize Theron (*Atomic Blonde*, 2017): major movie stars who sunk their teeth into roles as brainy, beautiful female assassins. Resembling the bad girls in 1960s James Bond films, these lethal ladies play the leads and live to kill again another day. That right-wing feminist concept began with the chintzy (to be most kind) action/sex exploitationer *Ginger*. Cheri Caffaro (1945–) is a spoiled debutante hired by a secret government agency to wipe out drug dealers. 'Ginger McAllister' redirects her deep, dark desires (she's a nymphomaniac-cum-serial killer) for society's good. Sequels include *The Abductors* (1972) and *Girls Are for Loving* (1973), both superior to the cheaper-than-cheap initial entry. Yet this remains the one cultists recall thanks to a jaw-dropping sequence: Ginger ties her male prey to a bed, binds the youth tightly, then tantalizingly strips for him. Next she takes morbid pleasure in castrating the howling preppie 'Rodney.' He's played by J. Calvin Culver (1943–1987) who that same year launched the craze for Gay Hardcore Porn with *Boys in the Sand*, billed as 'Casey Donovan.' C.C.'s husband D.C. (1941–2015) wrote and directed. After their divorce, Schain made family friendly films for the Disney Channel. At most recent sight, C.C. is raising bees.

GIRL CAN'T HELP IT, THE (1956)

Frank Tashlin Cult Rating: *****

Early/Pioneering Rock 'n' Roll Rating: *****

Jayne Mansfield Fan Rating: *****

Frank Tashlin, dir.; Tashlin, Hebert Baker, scr.; Tashlin, pro.; 2.35:1; C; 99 min.; 20th Century Fox.

 In late 1954, two crazes swept America, causing parallel controversies. Blonde bombshell Jayne Mansfield (1933–1967) offered a living cartoon version of Marilyn Monroe so extreme that most middlebrows shuddered. Rock 'n' roll simultaneously made it to mainstream radio. Parents and teachers insisted this was the devil's music. Fox dared combine these seeming threats, not in an exploitation flick (there were indeed many about The Big Beat) but a studio program-picture. A lewd gangster (Edmond O'Brien) hopes to keep his mistress happy; she wants to sing on TV but can't carry a tune. Convinced the new youth music is fit only for the tone deaf, he focuses on that genre. The sadly forgotten Tom Ewell (1909–1994) is fine as her P.R. person. One year earlier, he starred op-

THE DAY JAYNE MANSFIELD DISCOVERED THE BIG BEAT: Two 1950s pop-culture 'inventions' came together in this Frank Tashlin cult classic.

posite M.M. in *The Seven Year Itch*. Performances by Little Richard, Fats Domino, The Platters, Gene Vincent, and Eddie Cochran make this an all-time cult fav for fans of early rock. The Beatles' adoration of this film explains why, when the Fab Four arrived in N.Y. in 1964 and were asked who they wanted to meet, the boys shouted in unison: "Jayne Mansfield!" The cartoonish style was by Frank Tashlin (1913–1972), formerly director of many Warner's 'Looney Tunes.' Note: Politically incorrect!!!

GIRL ON A MOTORCYCLE, THE, aka *NAKED UNDER LEATHER* (1968)

Cult Rating: *

Jack Cardiff, dir.; Cardiff, Ronald Duncan, Gillian Freeman, scr.; Alain Delon, William Sassoon, pro.; 1.66:1; 91 min.; Adel Prods.

BAD BLACK LEATHER BIKER BABES GO TO HELL (BUT HAVE A HELLUVA GOOD TIME ALONG THE WAY!): Ann Margret in *The Swinger* and singer-turned-actress Marianne Faithfull as *The Girl on a Motorcycle*.

During the early days of the Sexual Revolution, no cult novel captured the spirit of the era's young rebel women better than *The Motorcyle* (1963) by Andre Preyre de Mandiargues (1909-1991). Brigitte Bardot (1934-) had taken to posing in black leather on big bikes. Purportedly, that inspired the author to tell the tale of a blonde who slips out of the elegant home she shares with her dull husband, roaring across the countryside to meet her illicit lover. Intense porn was related in a surrealist style (the entire book takes place in her mind) causing readers to argue whether this was trash or art. A long-waited film starring Bebe never happened; blues belter/ druggie/Rolling Stones 'pal' Marianne Faithfull (1946-) took on the role once a new freedom of the screen emerged. Yet this proves incredibly dull and uninvolving. Cardiff did not take advantage of censorship's decline so the sex scenes are few, brief, and at best tepid. The film itself, sluggish though prettily photographed; Cardiff (1914-2009) a lousy director, had been a great cinematographer (*The Red Shoes*, 1948). Posed photographs of M.F. in her tight-as-skin catsuit have drawn many to the film. Most go away totally disappointed.

GIRLS TOWN (1959)

Junk Movie Rating: ** ½

Mamie Van Doren Cult Rating: **** ½

Charles Chaplin Jr. Cultists (Are There Any?): *****

Charles F. Hass, dir.; Robert Hardy Andrews, Robert Smith, scr.; Albert Zugsmith, pro.; 1.33:1; B&W; 90 min.; MGM.

Even MGM, the self-proclaimed Tiffany Studio, wanted in on the money 1950s teenagers spent on schlock cinema, explaining why their prestigious label appears on this cheesy Babes-Behind-Bars flick. 'Silver' (Mamie Van Doren, 1931 -), re-negotiating her screen image from Blonde Bombshell for adults to youth-hipster (even as she closed in on age thirty), gets tossed into stir for a minor offense. Indie exploitation filmmaker A.Z. (1910-1993) here continues his bizarre habit of casting fine musical talents in bizarro roles: crooner Mel Torme, trumpet genius Ray Anthony, and teenie-bopper pop-rocker Paul Anka all appear. Adding to the Cast

'THE GIRL WHO INVENTED ROCK 'N' ROLL': Mamie Van Doren referred to herself by that phrase after giving up on traditional movie stardom to embrace junk movie status as the 1950s Queen of Camp in films such as *Girl's Town*.

from Hollywood Hell: sons of comedy greats Harold Lloyd and Charles Chaplin make guest appearances. Gossip-columnist Shelia Graham offers a cameo; The Platters perform some of the coolest rhythm 'n' blues ever. Insuring that the target audience would attend, there is drag-racing by the guys and a no-holds-barred cat-fight. Director Hass had been known before this as a solid studio journeyman whose work included *Star in the Dust* (1956).

GISAENGCHUNG, aka *PARASITE* (2019)

All Purpose Rating: *****

Boon Joon Ho, dir.; Joon Ho, scr.; Joon Ho, Jang Young Hwan, pro.; 2.39:1; C; 132 min.; Studio Baranson E&A.

This film's English-language title might suggest to a casual observer one more of those contemporary monster movies about some stigmata that enters a person's body and destroys him or her from within. In fact, Boon Joon Ho's (1969–) disturbing example of South Korean New Wave Cinema offers something else altogether, though it might well be thought of as a monster movie in the least generic sense of that term. Initially we appear to be experiencing a realistic depiction of the class system in that country. The Ki-Taeck family is composed of losers, 'lovable' at first glance though less so as the tale progresses. They have nothing, not because (as would be the case in a social critique film) the system is stacked against them, rather that they are lazy. Pure and simple. Honest work is anathema to the adults and kids. Dishonest work? That's something else altogether. When Ki-Woo (Woo sik-Choi) has an opportunity to pass himself off as a sophisticated tutor of languages for the daughter of the wealthy and ambitious Park clan, he can't resist the temptation to give it a try. What follows veers from comedic burlesque to intense drama to a surreal vision and then horrific realism. Deep inside this madcap roller coaster ride for a viewer's emotions we find a profound study of 'friendship,' and whether that concept can (or ever has) existed in the world, this perhaps only a nice term for ingratiating oneself with others, then exploiting them. The only cult film ever to win the Best Picture Oscar, further demonstrating the collapse of old barriers between mainstream audiences and Fringe Film Freaks.

GODZILLA VS. MONSTER ZERO (1965)

Japanese Monster Movie Rating: *** ½

Ishiro Honda Cult Rating: *****

Nick Adams Cult following: *****

Ishiro Honda, scr.; Shin'ichi Sekizawa, scr.; Tomoyuki Tanaka, pro.; 2.35;1; C; 74 min.; Toho company.

Often referred to by fans of Japanese monster movies as 'The Father of Godzilla,' Honda (1911–1993) realized that his work was written off by mainstream critics as fodder for the kiddie market. Apparently, that never phased him. Honda firmly believed that beginning with *Gojira* (1954) he had created cinematic art. And someday the world would catch up to his vision. I.H. wasn't surprised, then, when during his twilight years museums chose to screen his once-dismissed "junk." Intellectuals praised his work in film journals as a nightmare vision of post-Hiroshima Japan. Here, two astronauts (Nick Adams, 1931–1968; Akira Takarada, 1934–) deal with arrivals from Planet X (they resemble tall versions of The Greys in alien-conspiracy theories) who ask to briefly borrow Godzilla and Rodan. Acclaimed Asian director Akira Kurosawa saw this and proclaimed Honda a genius. This is the film in which Godzilla transformed from villain to hero.

GODHIRA WAS ONLY THE BEGINNING!: Ishiro Honda created a succession of large monsters every bit as memorable to fans of 1960s horror flicks as Universal's human-sized creatures were in the 1930s and 140s.

GOODFELLAS (1990)

Martin Scorsese Cultists: *****

Cult Crime Film Afficionados: *****

Henny Youngman Completists: *****

Martin Scorsese, dir.; Scorsese, Nicholas Pileggi, scr.; Irwin Winkler, Barbara De Fina, pros.; 1.85:1; C; 146 min.; W.B.

The greatest mainstream Hollywood gangster film of the 20th century's second half was indisputably *The Godfather* (Francis Ford Coppola, 1972). The greatest *cult* crime film: *GoodFellas*. Building on his indie success *Mean Streets* (1973), Scorsese (1942–) here dealt with a real-life gang figure: Henry Hill (1943–2012), a minor-league mobster turned FBI informant. Related in a stream-of-consciousness style then making its way into mainstream filmmaking, *G.F.* begins, ends, and throughout its lengthy running time returns to the legendary Lufthansa robbery (12/11/1978): a small coterie of low-lives ripped off J.F.K. Airport for more than $5 million. Ray Liotta (1954–), in the role of his career as H.H., begins the piece with a now iconic line: "As far back as I can remember, I always wanted to be a gangster." Robert De Niro, Paul Sorvino, and Joe Pesci (1943–) play assorted comrades in crime. Lorraine Bracco (1954–) enacts a nice Jewish girl sucked into an alternative world of danger, violence, risk, addiction, chintzy glamor and endless pasta. Comic Henny Youngman and singer Jerry Vale play themselves. Adapted from Pileggi's book *Wiseguy* (1986), the title was changed to avoid confusion with a popular TV show.

GOOD TIME (2017)

Indie Cult Rating: **** ½

Bennie & Josh Safdie, dir.; Josh, Ronald Bronstein, scr.; Terry Dougas, Oscar Bayson, Sebastian Bear McCloud, pro.; 2.35:1; C; 102 min.; Elara/Rhea.

The title refers to the early release days granted to those in stir who have impressed prison authorities with their admirable behaviour. Here, the term is ironically employed: A rigid and lengthy list of restrictions make it impossible for such a poor soul to spit on the sidewalk without being dragged back to the big house. Connie (Robert Pattinson) must attempt to play the game while also freeing his brother Nick (Bennie Safdie) from the clink after that youth is caught during a botched robbery. The roundabout ways in which Clint must do so recall the wild schemes of a similarly duty-bound cowboy (Kirk Douglas) in the contemporary Western classic *Lonely are the Brave* (1962). The film's success as an indie cult sensation sprung the Safdie brothers into the national limelight, allowing them to attract superstar comic Adam Sandler for the lead in their next film, *Uncut Gems* (2019) More than one critic and/or fan has remarked on the striking sense of tension that characterizes the work.

GRAND BUDAPEST HOTEL, (THE) (2014)

Anderson Afficionado Rating: *****

Wes Anderson, dir.; Anderson, Hugo Guinness, scr.; Anderson, Scott Rudin, Steven Rales, pro.; 1.37:1; C/B&W; 99 min.; Fox Searchlight/ Indian Paintbrush.

Here (finally!) was the W.A. (1969–) film that broke through to mainstream viewers, doing so without any commercialization that might have disappointed loyal cultists. The aesthetic approach involved creating elaborate tabletop miniatures, then through modern technical devices including CGI allow actors to appear to inhabit a make-believe world expressionistically recalling Europe during the two decades between the World Wars. That was the period during which the old order of things necessarily gave way to modernism, for better or worse. Watching *G.B.H.* is a little like getting to see Jean Renoir's *La Regle du Jeu*, 1939) as remade by George 'Puppetoons' Pal. The focus in this brittle combination of comedy and drama remains on an ever deepening friendship between the title establishment's stuffy concierge (Ralph Fiennes, 1962–) and a humble, goofy lobby boy (Tony Revolori). A mystery concerns the disappearance of a valuable Renaissance painting, but to call this a thriller would be as heretical as considering Orson Welles' *Citizen Kane* (1941) a mystery. Constantly changing color schemes (to show, among other things, the passage of time) qualify *G.B.H.* as worth watching multiple times to catch subtleties previously missed. Once in a lifetime cast includes Harvey Keitel, F. Murray Abraham, Adrien Brody, Wilhem Dafoe, Tilda Swinton, and Jeff Goldblum. Live action sequences filmed at Hotel Borse, Gorlitz Germany.

GREY GARDENS (1975)

Cult Documentary Rating: *****

Albert, David, and Muffie Maysles, Ellen Houde, dirs..; Albert and David M., prods.; 1.37:1; C; 94 mins.; Portrait Films.

The Maysles clan of documentarians were considering a project about Princess Lee Radziwell, sister of Jacqueline Kennedy. While researching, they came across a subject so fascinating they abandoned their initial idea. Two relatives, Edith Bouvier Beale (1895–1977) and her daughter Little Edie (1917–2002) had retreated from the surrounding world. Partly, this had to do with the tragic history of their in-laws but also deep personal problems. These attractive American aristocrats abandoned high society, residing alone, other than pets, in an ancient house thought to be haunted. Their odd existence occurs near East Hampton L.I., a fashionable summer retreat. As the film progresses, a viewer becomes spellbound by the give and take, love and hate, and co-dependency of these unique women. Beautiful if sad, harrowing yet strangely uplifting, here is a non-fiction film that studies the process of daily survival in a setting at once upscale and downtrodden. In 2009, a TV film starring Jessica Lange and Drew Barrymore retold the story, as did a stage musical. Quite unlike anything you've ever seen.

GROUNDHOG DAY (1993)

All-purpose Rating: *****

Harold Ramis, dir.; Ramis, Danny Ruben, scr.; Ramis, Trevor Albert, pro.; 1.85:1; C; 101 min.; Columbia.

On February 2, citizens of small-town Punxsutawney PA gather for, as legend has it, a furry creature will determine if winter is at an end or not, depending on whether he spots his shadow. A smarmy Pittsburgh weatherman (Bill Murray, 1950–), a news producer (Andie MacDowell), and a cameraman (Chris Elliott), arrive to cover the event. When a freak blizzard forces them to remain an extra night, the cynic becomes caught in a time-warp, forced to live Groundhog Day over again, and again, and… Ramis (1944–2014), previously associated with broad comedy (*Caddyshack*, 1980; *National Lampoon's Vacation*, 1983) rose to the occasion, turning out a smart film in its *Twilight Zone* approach yet sweetly sentimental (with religious undertones) as well. Tom Hanks, Steve Martin, and John Travolta were considered for the lead. Serendipity occurred with Murray's casting: his character's arc is awesome to watch. A one-joke film, though incredibly each variation on that theme tops the previous ones.

GUN CRAZY (1950)

B Noir Cult Rating: *****

Joseph H. Lewis, dir.; MacKinlay Kantor, Dalton Trumbo, 'Millard Kaufman,' scr.; Maurice King, pro.; 1.37:1; B&W; 86 min.; King Bros. Prods./United Artists.

BANG! BANG! YOU'RE DEAD: Peggy Cummins place a nice small-town girl who goes bonkers whenever she gets her hands on a couple of gats in Joseph Newman's early anti-gun flick.

A classic of the rural gangster genre, this medium-budget noir was the first film to condemn America's culture of violence. John Dall (1918–1971) plays a young man obsessed with shooting since childhood. He would never employ this tool for deadly purposes other than when serving his country. Destiny has him visit a sleazy rural carnival where a pretty blonde (Peggy Cummins, 1925-2020) performs a sideshow's sexy shooting act. A marriage seemingly made in heaven swiftly degenerates; they transform into the couple from hell, releasing each other's worst instincts. No greater example of 'the aesthetics of economic necessity' exists than Lewis' handling of a robbery: Initially to have been filmed with multi-cameras inside and outside the bank, J.HL. (1907–2000) had to make do with a single camera and one continuous shot from within the car. The result is among the most acclaimed sequences in B movie history. Drawing on Fritz Lang's *You Only Live Once* (1937), here is an early predecessor to *Bonnie and Clyde* and *Natural Born Killers* (1994). Exerted a huge influence on Godard's *Breathless*.

HAIRSPRAY (1988)

1960s pop-culture fans: **** ½

Rickie Lake cultists: *****

John Waters' diehard fans: *** ½

John Waters, dir.; Waters, scr.; Robert Shaye, Rachel Talalay, pros.; 1.85:1; C; 92 min.; New Line Cinema.

  In 1962 Baltimore, large-size girl 'Tracy Turnblad' (Rickie Lake, 1968–) wonders why she can't be a featured dancer on the local *Bandstand* TV show. Rather than whine, she sets out to change the pop-culture surrounding her to a more tolerant and acceptant TeenWorld. Waters' (1946–) unexpected but successful shift from forbidden cinema to the mainstream offers warm nostalgia for a bygone era not unlike *American Graffiti* (George Lucas, 1973) and *Grease* (Randall Kleiser, 1978), if never as brilliant as the former or mundane as the latter. *Hairspray* vividly captures the funky early Sixties' sound and a surrounding fashion scene which flourished after Elvis but before the Beatles. Gimmicky dances on display include The Twist, The Mash Potato, and The Fly. On a more serious side, J.W. portrays the era's racial divisions as they existed in the northeast as well the South. Only a touch of the earlier raunchy Waters is on view, when a girl's zit is popped in close-up. Most of what appears is PG, disappointing diehard Waters enthusiasts. A successful stage musical in 2002, an embarrassing remake by Adam Shankman in 2007, and an eventual TV live staging (2016) helped this movie about a social marginal sustain cult status.

192 • *Midnight Matinees: Cult Cinema Classics*

TACKY TO THE LIMIT; LOVE IT OR LEAVE IT: John Waters moved beyond the abject mania of his early work such as *Pink Flamingos* (1972) and stretched cult movies into the mainstream; Rickie Lake became an overnight cult sensation.

HALLOWEEN (1978)

Slasher Horror Rating: *****

John Carpenter Cult Rating: *****

Jamie Lee Curtis Cult Rating: *****

P.J. Soles Mini-Cult Rating: *****

John Carpenter, dir.; Carpenter, Debra Hill, scr.; Hill, prod.; 2.35:1; C; 101 min. (director's cut), 91 min. (theatrical); Compass/Falcon International.

"Movie brats" of the 1970s, Carpenter and Hill (1950–2005) collaborated on this low-budget ($300,000) indie. When it reaped over $150 million a new era in horror began. The tale takes place on a single afternoon, evening, and night. Three high school girls—(Jamie Lee Curtis, 1958- ; Nancy Kyes (Loomis) 1949- , P.J. Soles, 1950-)—prepare to greet kids in costumes. What they don't know: An escapee from a mental institution, 'Michael Myers,' is headed for their small town, Hadenfield, to take up where he left off 15 years earlier. His psychiatrist (Donald Pleasence, 1919–1995) hopes to stop the killings before they begin again. Many critics interpreted this as an anti-Sexual Revolution message-mov-

UNVEILING THE ERA OF YOUTH HORROR: John Carpenter and Jamie Lee Curtis defined a new genre of thriller and unknowingly set the stage for a franchise with *Halloween*.

ie: girls who 'do' end up dead; the sole virgin (Curtis) survives. As 'The Final Girl,' she initiated a staple for many teen-oriented thrillers to follow. Hitch influences abound: Curtis is the daughter of *Psycho* star Janet Leigh; the doctor is named 'Sam Loomis' after that film's lead character. Unlike Norman Bates, Myers (aka The Shape) is not intended to be sympathetic, rather a human equivalent of the shark in *Jaws*. *Friday the Thirteenth* (Sean Cunningham, 1980) and *Scream* were inspired by this, the initial 1970s slasher.

HARD CANDY (2005)

Ellen (now Elliot) Page Afficionado Rating: *****

General Cult Rating: *

David Slade, dir.; Brian Nelson, scr.; Michael Caldwell, Richard Hutton, pro.; 2.35:1; C; 104 min.; Lions Gate.

    On rare occasion, a titular performance by a star in embryo can transform an otherwise failed film into a cult sensation. That's precisely what happened here: Ellen (now Elliot) Page (1987–) is so real, vital, engaged, committed, intense, and convincing as 14-year-old 'Hayley Stark' that her presence caused this otherwise failed piece of social commentary, with a suspense-thriller plot, to become a sensation, still worth returning to for Page fans everywhere. Initially, the plot seems pure genius: An adult predator (Patrick Wilson) employs an online chat-venue to lure an underage girl ('hard candy' is a pedophile's codename for a victim) into his house. He soon grasps that he's been 'ambushed': She carefully planned to teach him a terrible lesson. However engaging as a case study of such a frightfully common experience, the film falls apart. By having the man also be a serial killer reduces this to an over-the-top piece of vengeance exploitation junk. Of course a murderer deserves the worst possible fate. Should a non-violent predator be killed in cold blood or turned over to the police? That's the question this ridiculously plotted piece (the evil-doer escapes at mid-movie, returning for no other reason than so he can again be captured and tortured) should've stuck with and explored in depth.

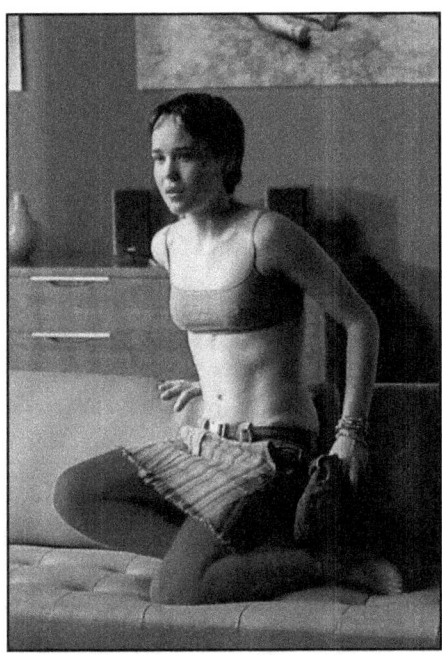

SO YOUNG, SO DEADLY: Brilliant young Ellen (Elliot) Page ran the gamut of emotions from A to the proverbial Z as a female child seeking revenge for a friend's death at the hand of a predator; in the mainstream hit *Kick-Ass*, Chloe Grace Moritz as "Hit Girl" became the youngest professional assassin in movie history.

HARDER THEY COME, THE (1972)

Reggae Fandom Rating: *****

Jimmy Cliff Cult Rating: *****

Perry Henzell, dir.; Henzell, Trevor D. Rhone, scrs.; Henzell, pro.; 1.66:1; C; 103 min.; Xenon Pictures.

    For Reggae fans the world over, there is but one film that not only features this musical genre but completely captures its revolutionary meaning to devotees. *T.H.T.C.* is so ripe with 'the sound' as well as the hypnotically raw quality of its acting, editing, cinematography, and narrative that it has become a cinematic cornerstone for the Reggae Movement world-wide. Henzell (1936–2006) recounts the tragic tale, half Caribbean noir and half modern tragedy, of 'Ivanhoe' (Jimmy Cliff, 1948–), a singing Samurai knight of Jamaica's outback. I. wanders into a Big City and is sucked into 'the sweet life' of money, drugs, crime, and superstardom essential to the local music Biz. He transforms from a performer with a strong social message into the very thing he wanted to expose in his art, then hits the road as a righteous bandit in the tradition of Bonnie and Clyde. An Elvis of Reggae, J.C. performs a music form which had emerged a few years previous with its innovational blend of calypso, African mbira board, and *mento* folk music indigenous to Jamaica. Low-level production values were essential to *T.H.T.C.*'s ability to crystalize a world where widespread poverty imposed by super-wealthy crime lords cannot wipe out the miraculous optimism of street people whose secular religion is inherent in the rhythms of R. Many films have been shot in Jamaica; this was the first produced by local talent. Ironically, it was banned for years there owing to a fear an honest portrait of 'hooligans' would cause teenagers to idolize the onscreen toughs.

HAROLD AND MAUDE (1971)

Bud Cort Cultists: *****

Ruth Gordon Cultists: *****

Offbeat Dramedy Romance Fans: *****

Hal Ashby, dir.; Collin Higgins, scr.; Higgins, Charles B. Mulvehill, pro.; 1.85:1; C; 91 min.; Paramount.

The oddest of all odd couple comedies and the most offbeat romantic film of all time! Harold (Bud Cort) is a rich young man who seems to have everything but obsesses on death. He stages fake suicides which his overly protective and highly pretentious mother (Vivian Pickles) ignores. Harold's hobby is attending funerals of strangers. At one, he meets Maude (Ruth Gordon, 1896–1985), 79 years old, aware her time is swiftly running out yet enjoying life to the fullest every second. Before her passing, will Maude turn Harold on to life, love, passion, and freedom? Though the material all but shouts 'dark comedy,' Ashby films their misadventures in bright lighting, resulting in a freaky feel-good film. Essential to the movie's charm is the pop-folk music by Cat Stevens. Ashby (1929–1988) intended to film a raw sex scene between the tall, gawky Cort (1948–) and diminutive Gordon; Paramount threatened to pull the plug. As proof

Hairspray to *Hugo* • 197

THE GENERATION GAP—IN REVERSE: The wondrously oddball actor Bud Cort played the lover of aged if youthful-in-spirit Ruth Gordon in *Harold and Maude*; note that she's the one who drives the cycle.

of its cult-worthiness, *H.&.M.* played 2,000+ consecutive showings at Edina's MN.'s Westgate Theatre.

HAUSU, aka *HOUSE* (1977)

Outre Cinema Rating: *****

Nobuhiko Obayashi, dir.; Chiho Katsura, Chigumi Obayaski, scr.; Obayashi, Yorihiko Yamada, Tomoyuk Tanaka, pro.; 1.37:1; C; 88 min.; Toho/PSC.

 Here's a predecessor to *Battle Royale* in which the lovely tweenage virgins do not kill one another but band together in hopes of thwarting a force of evil that threatens them 'and then there were none' style. N.O. (1938–2020) was inspired to make this haunted house movie after listening to his daughter describe her deepest, darkest fears. New York-born Kimiko Ikegami (1959–) plays 'Gorgeous,' who convinces her classmates to tag along on a summer trip to visit her old auntie (Yoko Minamida).

What they don't realize (yet): their host is the ghost of that lady, and her grand piano likes to devour pretty little girls whole. The essence of N.O.'s style is deconstruction: He reminds us we are watching a movie constantly. Much of the fierce visual impact was achieved by combining low fidelity video and Chrome Key effects, a first for Asian cinema. Colors constantly change; characters dissolve and reappear; animation of the strangest sort replaces what had seemed a relatively realistic setting. One more of those Asian films considered too daring for U.S. import until the 21st century, though smuggled-in copies made the cult cinema rounds for forty years.

HAXAN, aka *WITCHCRAFT THROUGH THE AGES* (1922)

Historical documentary Rating: *****

Curio/one-shot Rating: *****

Benjamin Christensen, dir.; Christensen, scr.; Christensen, pro.; 1.33;1; B&W; 91 min. (original silent theatrical cut), 122 min. (director's cut); 77 min. (1968 sound re-release); Aljosha Prods./Svensk Films.

The documentary film originated in 1922 with American Robert Flaherty's *Nanook of the North* and Denmark's H. B.C. (1879–1959) forsook on-location realism for an experimental and at the time significantly innovative movie including realistic elements though not limited to them. A former medical student turned cineaste he set out to share the origins of 'Wicca' by including ancient woodcuts and sketches. Reconstructions (B.C. plays both The Devil *and* Jesus) were shot in a studio for total control of imagery, particularly lighting elements, more sophisticated than any seen in previous Silents. Smart scripting that predated the arthouse circuit segues into a preview of the grindhouse yet to come: naked succubi dancing in the moonlight; a child's body slowly roasting over a fire. Such a combination of art and exploitation proved, to put it mildly, controversial. Re-released in 1968 to take advantage of the new freedom of the screen with spoken narration by counter-culture icon William Burroughs. Student filmmakers behind *The Blair Witch Project* named their indie company Haxan in homage to this work.

HEARTBEEPS (1981)

Andy Kaufman Cult Rating: ****

Sci-Fi Offbeat Comedy Rating: *

Allan Arkush, dir.; John Hill, scr. Michael Phillips, pro.; 2.35:1; C; 78 min.; Universal.

THE ANDY KAUFMAN MOVIE: Though the public at large had no interest whatsoever in this modernized sad clown or his film, Kaufman cultists (there are a few) hold this one dear to their hearts.

Of all the remarkably unique stand-up comics who emerged during the late 1970s and early 1980s, one has always been more of a cult figure than a mainstream star: Andy Kaufman (1949–1984), the tall, gawky, clueless (seemingly) child-man who preferred to read *The Great Gatsby* out loud (beginning to end!) rather than tell jokes... until audiences booed him offstage (precisely what A.K. hoped for). The nearest thing to wide popularity came with 'Latka' on TV's *Taxi* (1978–1983). His only starring role was seen by virtually nobody on release. Since Andy's passing, this tale of two cyborgs living in a near-distant future who run away to try and live with love on their own has become a center-piece of Kaufman's small, loyal cult. Objective critics called this "masterfully awful"; fans insist that *H.* be appreciated as a marvelous failure. The charmingly quirky Bernadette Peters (1948–) plays the inamorata of the world's first 'minimalist dada' stand-up comic. Cameos by such cult-worthy performers as Randy Quaid, Christopher Guest, Dick Miller, and Paul Bartel add to this awful film's ongoing fascination.

HEATHERS (1988)

Winona Ryder Cult Rating: **** ½

Michael Lehman, dir.; Daniel Waters, scr.; Denise D. Novi, prod.; 1.85:1; C; 103 min.; New World.

A middle-of-the-road high schooler (Winona Ryder, 1971–) must choose between her edgy friends or a clique (Shannon Doherty, Lisanne Falk, Kim Walker). In the tradition of *Pretty Poison* and *Bad Lands* Veronica falls under the spell of a sexy sociopath (Christian Slater, 1969–). Think: *Mean Girls* as a slasher flick. The film outraged many parents and teachers, not so much owing to such controversial themes as bullying (girl-girl and boy-boy), teen suicide, and high school shootings as the silly, playful tone taken toward those subjects. *Heathers* 'plays' like John Waters' quirky, light-hearted *Hairspray* re-imagined by Sam Peckinpah. Daniel Waters (1962–) originally hoped that Stanley Kubrick might direct, but his script lacked the necessary dark, distinctive tone of *Dr. Strangelove*. Still, the film "speaks" to anyone who ever suffered through the social jungle that is high school, specifically, during that uniquely shattered decade of the 1980s. Lehman's (1957–) hopes to become a key cult director died three years later with *Hudson Hawk* (1991).

HEAVY METAL, aka *HEAVY METAL: THE MOVIE* (1981)

Animated Cult Rating: ****

"Taarna" Sequence Female Warrior Rating: *****

Gerald Potterton, dir.; Ivan Reitman, Leonard Mogel, prod.; Len Blum, Daniel Goldberg, scr.; 1.37:1; C; 90 min.; Columbia.

The relationship between hard rock and sci-fi/fantasy had been cemented by Mogel's *H.M.* magazine, which introduced the adult graphic novel (as opposed to kids' comic books) to Americans. Across Europe and Asia, the G.N. had long since been a part of pop-culture. Reitman (1946–) hoped to add another connection, movies, to an equation between edgy visuals and rock 'n' roll. The result: an anthology of diverse sci-fi short stories, held together by a frame-narrative concerning an 'orb' (green to represent evil). Each sequence was animated by one of Canada's excellent small indie companies, appropriate music supplied by Blue Oyster Cult, Cheap Trick, Black Sabbath, etc. Among the voice talents: John Candy, Joe Flaherty, and Eugene Levy, all veterans of *Second City TV*. An

STRONG IS THE NEW SEXY: The feminist movement gradually went mainstream and as a result Conan the Barbarian types had to make room for Amazonian heroes, from the animated 'Taarna' in *Heavy Metal* to Malin Akerman ('Silk Spectre II') in *Watchmen*.

epic-fantasy tale, "Taarna," introduces a bad-ass babe who sets the pace or many similar live-action screen characters. This finale was scored by old Hollywood hand Elmer Bernstein (*The Magnificent Seven*). The mighty yet sexy woman warrior, previously confined to lowbrow Drive-In items, shortly hit the mainstream big-time.

HEDWIG AND THE ANGRY INCH (2001)

Transgender Community Cult Rating: *****

Wider audience cult Rating: *** ½

John Cameron Mitchell, dir.; Mitchell, scr.; Christine Vachon, pro.; 1.85:1: C; 95 min.; Killer Films/New Line Cinema.

Fifty years ago, *Myra Breckinridge* appeared courageous, daring to bring the transgender experience to mainstream movies. Now, that film disturbs many members of this community owing to its burlesque approach, ridiculing such a weighty decision without revealing a modicum of respect. As the most notable film on the subject during the early 21st century, *H.A.T.A.I.* serves as a corrective. 'Hedwig' (J.C.M., 1963–) is treated with respect as a character rather than presented as a gross caricature, though he/she slips into extreme poses while performing a punk musical act at a chain of inns around the country. Not, however, that this film (based on previous onstage versions and a book by J.C.M. and Stephen Trask) is devoid of humor. Happily, though, there are no cheap shots as we grasp that H.'s club dates are synchronized to those of 'Tommy Gnosis' (Michael Pitt), a one-time confidant who stole Hedwig's songs. Notably intended as entertainment for the mainstream as well as its built-in following, revealing America's more enlightened attitudes.

HELLBOY (2004)

Edgy superhero cult Rating: *** 1/2

Diehard Hellboy aficionado Rating: *** ½

Del Toro Fan Rating: *** ½

Guillermo del Toro, dir.; del Toro, Peter Briggs, scr.; Mike Richardson, Lloyd Levin, Lawrence Gordon, pros.; 1.85:1; C; 132 min. (director's cut), 122 min. (theatrical release print); Starlite/Revolution Studios.

Like father, like son? Not according to graphic novel writer-artist Mike Mignola (1960–), who launched what may be the edgiest superhero ever in 1993: 'Red,' the Devil's spawn. Summoned by Nazis during WWII's twilight hours in a desperate attempt to win by relying on the occult, the rust-colored creature was rescued by Allies, then nurtured to oppose all Forces of Darkness. Wisely, del Toro (1964–) included the character's origins. "You mean, he's *real*?" the pure-of-heart hero (Rupert Evans, 1976–) gasps when, as a long-time fan of Mignola's work, he realizes who this is. A genre innovation has the handsome youth competing with the grotesque creature (Ron Perlman, 1950–), in make-up that took four hours each day to apply, for the hand of Pyro Girl (Selma Blair). A major mistake: toning down the intense of violence to avoid an R, making this more amenable to mainstreamers. Diehard fans were disappointed.

HELLRAISER (1987)

Iconic Serial Killer Rating: **** ½

Clive Barker, dir.; Barker, scr. Christopher Figg, pro.; 1.85:1; C; 94 min. (director's cut), 86 min. (edited version); Cinemarque/Film Futures/New World.

Acclaimed horror author Clive Barker (1952–) wanted to direct the film version of his novel *The Hellbound Heart* (1986) for one reason: to protect his material. This native of Liverpool U.K. was aware of how horribly 'Movie' People can mangle those elements which caused them to want to adapt the piece in the first place. His debut behind the camera concerns a seemingly 'normal' couple (Andrew Robinson, Claire Higgins) who move into a haunted house. Demons residing there ('Cellubites') not only threaten the new owners but cause them to reveal their dark sides. This scored as a cult fav in large part owing to the uniqueness of a Thing that goes bump in the night: 'Pinhead' (David Bradley, 1942–). Barker would have preferred that his own name for the creature, 'Priest,' be used. Extreme issues of sado-masochistic sex allow this an edge that

MEET THE MONSTERS, PART TWO: 'Leatherface' menaces everyone in sight in The Texas Chainsaw Massacre franchise; 'Pinhead' is out for blood in the Hellraiser films.

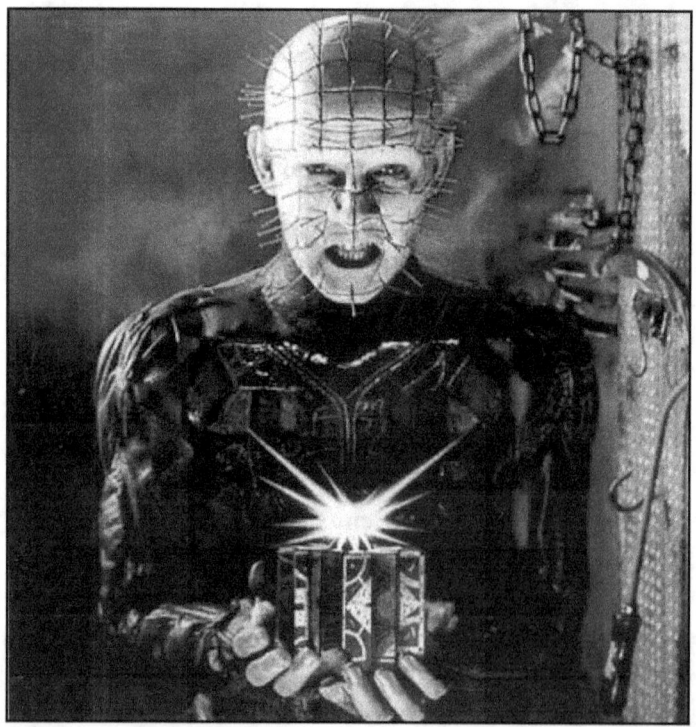

recalls Polanski's *Repulsion* (with its mostly one-set approach) more than such then-popular franchises as *Halloween, Nightmare on Elm Street*, and *The Texas Chainsaw Massacre*. Barker's success suggests that he was more at home with little projects. Such future big films as (*Nightbreed*, 1990) and *Lord of Illusions* (1995) tanked.

HENRY: PORTRAIT OF A SERIAL KILLER (1986)

Serial killer cult Rating: *****

John McNaughton, dir.; McNaughton, Richard Fire, scr. McNaughton, Steven A. Jones, Lisa Dedmond, prods.; 1.37:1; C; 83 min.; Maljack Prods./Greycat Films.

In the unique (and uniquely disturbing) genre of serial killer films, H.P.O.A.S.K. plays second fiddle to none. J.M.N. (1950–) shot his first feature on 16 mm. at a cost of apprx. $100,000 after being hired to helm a fictional slasher flick. He soon sensed that nothing in his imagination could prove so terrifying as actual incidents from the horrific life of Henry Lee Lucas (1936–2001), who killed strangers with a unprecedented venom. A graphic depiction of an entire family done in outdid the sense of terror Richard Brooks had created for an earlier fact-based piece, *In Cold Blood* (1967). Here the gore-factor moved beyond that of Herschell Gordon Lewis's *Blood Feast*. The power of this sequence led to creation of the "home invasion" horror subgenre. Such gruesome subject matter momentarily set aside, this is a noteworthy indie that reveals artistry in every image, cut, and performance, most notably Michael Rooker (1955–) in the title role. One of several films that led to the creation of the NC-17 rating with its overdue admission that a work of art, no matter how intense, ought not to be lumped with worthless hardcore.

HER (2013)

Conventional Rating: *****

Cult Rating: *****

Spike Jonze, dir.; Jonze, scr.; Jonze, Vincent Landry, Megan Ellison, pros.; 1.85:1; C; 126 min.; Annapurna.

Though Spike Jonze (1969–) worked on earlier pictures, *Her*—which he wrote, directed, co-produced, and appears in—marks a notable juncture for an outrageous auteur on the order of Orson Welles' *Citizen Kane* (1941). In a near (and for the most part realistically portrayed dystopian) future, an appealingly geeky guy (Joaquin Phoenix, 1974–), surviving his marital break-up, falls for a Computer Operating System (voiced by unseen Scarlett Johansson). The supporting cast includes such cult-worthy talents as Rooney Mara, Chris Pratt, Olivia Wilde, Bill Hader, and Kristin Wig, the latter two famed *Saturday Night Live* veterans. Shot mostly in Shanghai to insure the setting would appear 'actual' yet simultaneously *exotic*. An initially simple situation broadens and deepens, transforming from an oddball idea into a touching romance, introducing a 21st Century Everyman who arcs from life-loser to an unexpected winner. Jonze effectively employs the color red as Hitchcock did in *Marnie*. Influences include Woody Allen's later films in which characters converse at length within a single shot, and in-print literary work of iconoclastic storyteller Maurice Sendak (1928–2012).

HERCULES UNCHAINED (1959)

Peplum Rating: ****

Steve Reeves cult Rating: *****

Pietro Francisci, dir.; Francisci, Ennio De Concini, scr; Bruno Vailati, pro.; 2.35;1; C; 93 min.; Galatea/Lux.

Movie mogul Joseph E. Levine (1905–1987), a Big Studio type with a taste for vulgar exploitation, noted that the Italian-lensed *Ulysses* (1955) starring Kirk Douglas scored world-wide. To cash in, he hired Francisci (1906–1977), a veteran of Peplums (brief costumes worn by male superheroes) including *Attila* (1954), to come up with something more daring. *Hercules* (1958) featured American muscleman Steve Reeves (1926- 2000) surrounded by international beauties in lingerie-like outfits. The great Mario Bava designed the sets, resulting in a magically colorful world of myth. The lesser-known follow-up outdid the first. Dazzling screen sirens Sylva Koscina (1933–1994) and Syliva Lopez (1933–1959) played

THE BODY BUILDER AS ACTION STAR: The most popular of all Italian mini-epics featured America's Steve Reeves as the legendary Greek Warrior; these were produced on a budget somewhat higher than the run of the mill sand and sandal films (i.e., 'Peplums.'); could Arnold's career have ever been if not for this pioneer?

the hero's demure wife and a bewitching seductress. The screenplay combines shards of Sophocles' and Aeschylus' plays about Oedipus with a lesser known fable concerning ancient-world femme fatale 'Queen Onfale.' Constant action—Reeves wrestles former heavyweight world champ Primo Canara (1906–1967) as 'Anteo'—alternate with giddy sex orgies replete with bondage and torture. A predecessor to *Conan the Barbarian* (1982) and endless other lust-and-violence laden epics to come.

HILLS HAVE EYES, THE (1977)

Cannibal devotee fan Rating: ****

Craven Cult Rating: **** ½

Wes Craven, dir.; Craven, scr.; Peter Locke, pro.; 1.85:1; C; 98 min. (director's cut), 86 min. (theatrical release print); Vanguard.

With the release of *The Last House on the Left*, Craven (1939–2015) was hailed as a cinematic prince of horror. Problem was, he had no idea what to do for an encore. Then he caught *The Texas Chainsaw Massacre*. Inspired, W.C. outlined a similar story with more onscreen gore, employing props left over from *T.T.C.M.* to decorate the home cave of California's cannibals. 'Pluto' (Michael Berryman, 1948–), leader of the atavistic creatures, and his brood prey on normals who veer off the main road. A family that falls into the trap is clearly dysfunctional; Craven had been haunted his entire life by nightmares from a difficult childhood. W.C.'s only regret: he let his crew talk him out of filming a sequence in which a newborn provides a midnight feast. Lead monster star M. Berryman did not require make up, suffering from an incurable illness that caused him to appear horrific. Before *T.H.H.E.*, he played mental patient 'Elis' in *One Flew Over the Cuckoo's Nest* (1975). *T.H.H.E.* set the pace for cannibalism to go mainstream in *The Silence of the Lambs* (1991).

HISTOIRE d'O, aka THE STORY OF O (1975)

S&M Cult Rating: ****

Softcore Porn Rating: * ½

Just Jaecken, dir.; Sebastien Japrisot, scr.; Gerald Lorin, pro.; 1.85:1: X; 105 min. (director's cut), several edited versions; Yang Films/Allied Artists.

MEDIEVAL BONDAGE AS 'THE NEW LIBERATION': An "Underground" literary classic finally made it to the screen during the post-censorship 1970s in a French arthouse film that 'broke through' and played at some mainstream mall theatres.

The box-office success of *Emmanuelle* led not only to sequels and spin-offs but this follow-up. O brought bondage & discipline, sado-masochism, fetishistic costuming, and even anal sex (if by implication) to the mainstream during the Sexual Revolution. Not surprising, *E.*'s director was hired to do the honors again. J.J. (1940–) employs the lush, languid style (seemingly borrowed from French impressionism) to his adaptation of the acclaimed autobiographical if controversial novel by Anne Desclos (1907–1998), writing under the pen-name Pauline Reage. For a tale of a seemingly normal Frenchwoman (Corinne Clery, 1950–) who submits to the pleasure of punishment in a remote castle at the hands of a Marquis de Sade-like master. Screenings failed to evoke horror or eroticism so much as sniggering laughter at the prettiness and pretension. Had a gifted auteur (Francoise Truffaut comes to mind) taken a shot at this, *O* might have proven truly memorable.

HITCH-HIKER, THE (1953)

Rating: ****

Ida Lupino, dir.; Lupino, Collier Young, Robert (L.) Joseph, scr.; Young, Pro.; 1.37:1; B&W; 71 min.; RKO.

    A southwestern noir based on the actual career of Billy Cook (1928–1952), the prison escapee who hitched rides while trying to reach Mexico,

FROM DRIVE IN SUPERSTAR TO MAINSTREAM EXTRA: Isn't that the opposite of how it's supposed to happen?; Candice Rialson (far right) with John Huston in *Winter Kills* (1979).

often murdering the people who stopped to pick him up. In life, and in this economically aesthetic low-budgeter, a narcissist/nihilist sets the pace for 'Chigurh' in the Coen Bros. *No Country for Old Men* (2007). Here, the tale is retold by Ida Lupino (1918–1995), the under-rated actress turned under-appreciated director; how fascinating to note, as many have, that the single noir helmed by a woman is the rare one without a deliciously duplicitous (and anti-feminist) femme fatale. Happily, Lupino was less interested in reworking old action flick clichés than in planning a succession of shots, angles, and camera-movements that would visually convey the inner thoughts of her characters. The only flaw: goodguys O'Brien and Lovejoy have far too many opportunities to escape for their remaining in captivity to be totally believable.

HOLLYWOOD BOULEVARD (1976)

Exploitation Corman Flick Rating: ** ½

Candice Rialson Cult Rating: **** ½

Allan Arkush, Joe Dante, dirs..; Patrick Hobby, aka Danny Opatoshu, scr.; Roger Corman, Jon Davison, prods.; 1.85:1; C; 83 min.; New World.

The Tuesday Weld of our post-Production Code rural Drive In circuit? Candice Rialson (1951–2006), a well-endowed girl-next-door-type willing to do raunchy R-rated nude scenes for Corman's New World. She appeared on the scene at the decade's opening, appearing in such then-daring items as *Candy Stripe Nurses* (1974, one of a continuing series), and the infamous *Chatterbox* (1977), in which her Lolita/Baby Doll-like character was cursed with a talking vagina. Here she's a wide-eyed would-be starlet employed by shoddy Miracle Studio: "If it's a good film, it's a *miracle!*" Her leading role, 'Candy Wednesday,' was partly based on C.R. herself, also on the early Weld image. At decade's end, C.R. appeared briefly in the ambitious *Winter Kills*, then disappeared, dying of liver disease from reported alcoholism. Q.T. has stated that the Bridget Fonda role in *Jackie Brown* (1997) was meant as an homage to C.R. The presences of Mary Woronov and Paul Bartel make clear that the edgy humor was intentional. Dick Miller, not surprisingly, also appears. Followed by a belated (and non-releasable) sequel in 1990.

HOLLYWOOD CHAINSAW HOOKERS (1988)

Self-consciously clever exploitation flick Rating: *** ½

Fred Olen Rey, dir.; Rey ('D.S. Carver'), scr.; Rey, 1.85:1; C; 75 min.; American Independent Prods.; Savage Cinema.

If Linnea Quigley (1958–) hadn't already been recognized as the favorite "Scream Queen" of video-addicted teenage boys, this film crystallized her status. The Iowa-born blonde headed for Hollywood where she starred in several 1970s "Nudies." When mainstream movies absorbed images of nakedness, such actresses had to choose between hard-core porn and low-budget horror. Wisely, Quigley went the latter route. Her ability to be sweet, silly, and when the occasion called for it scary set her apart from other pretty 'B' girls who drifted into this gene. Always, though, she played a victim, not a bold female warrior. Here she isn't one of the title characters but their prey. L.Q.'s classic moment: The bizarre "virgin Dance." Rey (1954–) filmed this for under $23,000, in less than a week. His then wife, Dawn Wildsmith (1963–), also appears. Picked by *Maxim* as one of the best B movie thrillers ever.

HOLLYWOOD SHUFFLE (1982)

Low-budget serious-minded film Rating: ****

Robert Townsend, dir.; Townsend, Keenan Ivory Wayans, Dom Irrera, scr.; Townsend, Carl Craig, pro.; 1.85:1; C/B&W; 78 min. (U.S. theatrical), 81 min. (director's cut); Goldwyn.

"Don't sell out, man!" one Afro-American actor warns a friend in the film that put R.T. (1957–) on the movie map. "Don't play a butler or a slave." While many aspiring black performers complained about the parsity of meaningful roles, Townsend *did* something about it. He and several collaborators (including K.I.W., 1958–), wrote a script on a subject they knew well. R.T. gathered shards of discarded film to avoid the cost of buying expensive stock. Over two years, he brought his cast together when not performing stand-up, financing much of the $100,000 budget by charging expenses to ten credit cards. A bizarre combination of black-exploitation flicks from the previous decade and artistic indie films then coming into popularity. Best bit: 'Bobby Taylor' invents a black fighting machine called 'Rambro.' R.T. would direct studio films like *The Five Heartbeats* (1991). Where there's a will, there's a way!

HONEYMOON KILLERS, THE (1969/1970)

Anti-Romantic Outlaw Films Rating: *****

Leonard Kastle, Donald Volkman, dirs..; Kastle, scr.; Warren Steibel, prod.; 1.85:1; B&W/C; 115 min. (director's cut), 108 (abbreviated theatrical print).

1967: Virtually everyone in America exited *Bonnie and Clyde* in a state of euphoria. One exception: L.K. (1929–2011), a New York musician who believed glamorization of criminals by having them played by gorgeous Hollywood stars in vivid color to be socially irresponsible. Never before interested in making a movie (this his only film), Kastle set to work on a purposefully unsettling piece about real-life killers Martha Beck (Shirley Stoler, 1929–1999), an overweight nurse, and Ray Fernandez (Tony Lo Bianco, 1936–), a sleazy shiek who in the 1950s killed rich lonely ladies. Local censors branded this as 'obscene.' Still, the filmmaker's point: The true obscenity is to make pretty flicks about such lowlives. *T.H.K.* contains little sex or violence, suggesting rather than showing 'the goods.' One of the few films to receive successive releases, first by Corman's A.I.P. as an exploitation flick, then Cinerama as an arthouse item. Each audience perceived the film which it came expecting to see. Among its admirers: Martin Scorsese.

HOUSE OF A THOUSAND CORPSES (2000/2003)

Nasty Cult Flick Rating: ** ½

Rob Zombie, dir.; Zombie, scr.; Andy Gould, prod.; B&W/C; 105 min. (director's cut), 89 min. (theatrical version). Spectacle Entertainment.

The longstanding relationship between raunchy rock 'n' roll and tasteless grindhouse flicks crystalized with this item by musician Zombie (aka Robert Bartleh Cummings, 1965–) turned first-time filmmaker. The plot draws on vivid memories of *The Texas Chainsaw Massacre*: here, two couples, eager to learn if 'Dr. Satan' lives or is only a rural legend, make the mistake of heading down a rough Texas backroad. They become 'guests' of creeps eager to introduce new-comers to rape, cannibalism, devil-worship, and nihilistic violence. Pop-culture references abound: 'Captain Spauling' (bald-pated, bearded horror icon Sid Haig) recalls Groucho's madcap character in *Duck Soup*. A minimum of four other Marx Bros. films are alluded to, also 1950s low-budget thrillers. Zombie attempts to reach the heights (make that depths) of technical incompetence and bad taste that came so naturally to Ed Wood. Zombie's second studio solo album was named for that auteur's 1960 *The Sinister Urge*.

HOUSE OF THE DEVIL, THE (1896)

Silent Cult Horror Rating: *****

Georges Melies, dir.; Melies, scr.; Melies, prod.; 3 mins; B&W/C; Star-Film.

Today, Melies (1861–1938) is best remembered as the father of F/X cinema. *A Trip to the Moon* (1902), from a Jules Verne novel, playfully set actors against an expressionistic cardboard cut-out-world of inspired imagination. Less recalled are his once controversial shorts which at the time caused Melies to be condemned as a Satanist. Moralists went so far as to suggest the then-emerging art of cinema and devil worship were inseparable. In his sixteenth film as director, first as actor, Melies plays Mephistopheles, a role he would return to often (*Sign of the Cross*, 1899; *Feast in Hell*, 1903). Cited as the first authentic horror film, *House* ranks as the origination point for vampire cinema. G.M. transforms from a bat to a human (if a devilish one), summoning scantily clad succubi to serve his unspeakable needs. Today listed as a B&W film, this was hand-tinted in its time. Aka *The Haunted Castle*.

HOUSE ON HAUNTED HILL (1959)

Castle Fan-base Rating: ** ½

William Castle, dir.; Robb White, scr.; Castle, pro.; 1.85:1; B&W; 75 min.; Allied Artists.

When A list director Robert Wise (1914–2005) set to work on *The Haunting* (1963), he announced his intention to reclaim the haunted house genre from the supreme silliness of B items like this. *H.O.H.H.* is one of William Castle's (1914–1977) low-budget "gimmick" thrillers, shunned by suburban adults but adored by 1950s teens. Here, a wealthy man (Vincent Price, 1911–1993) invites five guests to a party in a grand mansion where eight murders have occurred. Once on property, guests find themselves prisoners, warned by the host's wife (Carol Ohmart, 1927–2002) that none are likely to live through the night. One of W.C.'s least effective films (scares are few and far between; the direction is journeyman), *House* stands as the exploitation auteur's most warmly remembered by those who were young when this played matinees in second-string theatres. There's Price's over-the-top acting, which he had mastered while appearing in *House of Wax* (1953) and *The Mad Magician* (1954). The great W.C. 'stunt' this time around: When an onscreen skeleton threatens a blonde (wearing a negligee), a plastic skeleton which Castle had earlier rigged up in the rafters would be drawn on wires over the giddily screaming audience.

HOWLING, THE (1981)

Werewolf Movie Cultists: **** ½

Joe Dante Cultists: **** ½

Joe Dante, dir.; John Sayles, scr.; Jack Conrad, Michael Finnell, pros.; 1.85:1; C; 91 mins.; Embassy.

During the summer of '81, two werewolf films competed for the horror audience. *An American Werewolf in London* (John Landis), Universal's 'A' film, dominated the box office. Offering mild competition: *T.H.*, Embassy's less heralded 'B' picture. Today, afficionados

DEADLIER THAN THE MALE: Ever since Catwoman and the Dragon Lady from *Terry and the Pirates*, wicked women who offer the Kiss of Death have been favorites of cult audiences: The Sex Vampire (Elisabeth Brooks) in *The Howling* and The Erotic Nazi (Dyanne Thorne) in the Ilsa films.

consider the latter superior in every regard other than elaborateness of F/X. For *T.H.*, Rob Bottin (1959–) did the most with what he had; impressive results won him the special effects assignment for *The Thing*. Sayles (1950–) came up with a smart script that set the pace for postmodern monster movies via a horror flick that knows it's a horror flick, such self-awareness communicated through constant references to genre classics. Many cult actors appear in cameos: John Carradine, Dick Miller, and Kevin McCarthy, as well as the avatar of Youth oriented B flicks, Roger Corman. Also J. Forrest Ackerman, publisher of *Famous Monsters of Filmland*, the magazine that in the late 1950s solidified a following for macabre thrillers. The ill-fated Elisabeth Brooks ((1950–1997) creates the prototype for the next generation of femme fatales: a black-leather clad sexual dominatrix. Dante (1946–), a former film critic put to work by Corman on such low-budget projects as *Piranah* (1978), would bring his edgy serio-comic approach to the studio film *Gremlins* (1984). *The Howling*'s theme is expressed in a line originally featured in *The Wolf Man*: "'Little Red Riding Hood' is a werewolf story."

HUGO (2011)

Silent Film Buff Rating: *****

Melies Cultists: *****

Scorsese aficionado Rating: *****

Martin Scorsese, dir.; John Logan, scr.; Scorsese, Johnny Depp, pro.; 1.85:1; C; 126 min.; Paramount/GKF Films.

Deep inside Paris's train station, circa 1931, the title boy (Asa Butterfield), an orphan worthy of Dickens, survives from day to day. Always, he hangs on to a strange automaton, the only reminder of his late clockmaker father (Jude Law, 1972–). Hugo cannot make this mechanical man spring to life until he finds the missing key. This Hitchcock-like MacGuffin may be in the possession of a cranky shopkeeper (Ben Kingsley, 1943–), who sells snacks and cigars to passengers. Gradually, the child realizes this is the ruined genius Georges Melies who, 40 years earlier, initiated the art of fantasy filmmaking. Scorsese (1942–) creates a tone halfway between a realistically believable story and a 20th century fairy-tale, achieved by employing actual locations abetted by state-of-the-art CG technique. The director stated that his employment of color photography within a 3-D context owes much to the classic *House of Wax* (Andre de Toth, 1953). Though Robert Richardson (1955–) won an Oscar for his cinematography, *Hugo* unaccountably lost Best Picture to *The Artist*. As with that film, here was an attempt to reintroduce the glories of Silent Cinema to today's audience. Adapted from *The Invention of Hugo Cabret*, a cult novel by Brian Sellers (1966–). The beloved Christopher Lee (1922–2015) appears briefly.

ICHI THE KILLER (2001)

Asian Off-the-Wall Rating: *****

Takashi Miike, dir.; Sakichi Sato, Hideo Yamamoto, scr.; Akiko Funatsu, Dai Miyazaki, pros.; 1.85;1; C; 129 min. (director's cut), 117 (edited version), Omeaga-Micott Prods.

When *I.T.K.* was screened at the Toronto Film Festival, known for daring choices, this whirlwind-paced adaptation of Hideo Yamamoto's 1998 manga *Koroshiya 1* played only at that witching hour. Barf bags were distributed to the few daring viewers. The story sounds like a conventional crime saga: 'Anjo' is missing, along with a fortune, but none of his Yakuza know whether the leader absconded with the loot or was kidnapped. Any connection to anything else ends there. As the masochistic golden-haired 'Kakihara' (Tedanobu Asano) sets out the learn the truth and encounters his Ultimate Significant Other 'Ichi' (Nao Ohmori, 1972–), a sadistic crybaby, this film runs the gamut of Forbidden Cinema subgenres: Manic Martial Arts, Torture Chic, Rape Revelry, Absurdist Humor, Theatre of Cruelty, S & M, The Pornography of Violence, Asian Noir, Anti-Narrative surrealism, and Self-conscious stylization, to name a few. Beyond the limits of criticism (I.T.K. defies being reviewed in any sane sense), it may be the most purposefully abhorrent film ever made.

IDIOCRACY (2006)

Judge Afficionado Rating: **** ½

Mike Judge, dir.; Judge, Etan Cohen, scrs.; Judge, Elysa Koplovitz, prod.; 1.85:1; C; 84 min.; 20th Century Fox.

Like Judge's *Office Space*, *I.* also became a cult hit if owing to dissimilar reasons. For this is a sci-fi spoof on the order of Woody Allen's *Sleeper* (1973): An ordinary guy (Luke Wilson) is 'hibernated' by scientists, waking 500 years in the future. America has degenerated so completely that his mediocre mind qualifies him as the most intelligent being alive. Sports (like those in the dazzling *Death Race 2000* and dumber-than dumb *Rollerball*, 1975) have de-evolved into thrill-every-moment exercises in sex and violence. Though less than a third of Judge's gags 'work,' this is an important movie. For a decade later, everyone realized it had not taken half a millennia for such a lowering of standards to occur. What had been intended as a parodic projection of what might eventually become the state of our union was transformed, by events no one could foresee in 2006, into a vision of the shape of things to shortly come.

I HEART HUCKABEES (2004)

Oblique Cinema Rating: **** ½

Albert Camus Aficionado Cult Rating: *****

David O. Russell, dir. Russell, Jeff Baena, scr.; Russell, Scott Rudin, pro.; 2.35:1; C; 107 min.; Fox Searchlight.

If a movie's level of sophistication might be determined by the number of theatregoers who at the end have no clue about what they've just seen, then this is the most sophisticated film of the early 21st century. Brilliant to a rare few (particularly those into Existentialism, 1960s style), boring beyond belief to the oblivious masses eager for car crashes, lavish explosions, and general mayhem, this comes closer to watching *My Dinner with Andre* if with husband (Jason Schwartzman) and wife (Naomi Watts) attempting to determine once and for all if anything out there means something beyond its surface value or, as Kurt Weill put it four generations ago, we're all just lost in the stars. Here is a contemporary film that will remind older viewers of those melancholic ballads Frank Sinatra performed saloon style back in the mid-1950s: 'In the wee small hours of the morning.' An eclectic cast (Dustin Hoffman, Talia Shire, Mark Wahlberg, Lily Tomlin, Jude Law) adds to the cult appeal. Russell (1958–) would move beyond cultdom to create such smart popular hits as *Silver Linings Playbook* (2012) and *American Hustle* (2013).

ILSA, SHE WOLF OF THE S.S. (1975)

Politically correct Rating: NO STARS

Sex and Violence Cult classic Rating: *****

Don Edmonds, dir.; John W. Saxton (as 'Jonah Royston'), scr.; David F. Friedman, pro.; 1.66:1; C; 86 min.; Aeteas Film.

"She turned her lovers into lamp-shades!" That was the buzz line for what has been hailed as "the greatest exploitation film ever made" by connoisseurs of 'sick cinema.' Inspired by the historical Ilsa Koch ("The Butcher of Buchenwald," 1906–1960), 'Ilsa' (Dyanne Thorne, 1943–) is the commander of a camp where "medical experiments" are performed on prisoners. A nymphomaniac desperate to reach full orgasm, Ilsa takes male prisoners to bed. After they fail to satisfy her gargantuan libido, she has them castrated by Nazi Babes in black leather, who also torture, abuse, and gleefully disfigure the female captives. Originally rated X, *Ilsa* (minus a few ultra-violent seconds) eventually was altered to an R. Shot on the old *Hogan's Heroes* TV set. Edmonds (1937–2009), a former actor in *Beach Party* films, drew his aesthetic from garish paintings that adorned covers of pulp magazines in the 1950s. Thorne, who had once studied in New York with Stella Adler and Lee Strasberg, appeared in several sequels including *Ilsa, Harem Keeper of the Oil Shiek*s (1976). Today she co-owns a marriage chapel in Las Vegas NV and is a devout born-again Christian.

IMAGINE (1972)

Lennon Cultist Rating: **** ½

John Lennon, Yoko Ono, Steve Gebhardt, dirs..; 1.33:1; C; 70 mins.

When in 1970 John Lennon (1940–1980) left the Beatles, he also abandoned the funky filmmaking style of Richard Lester, who guided the group through *A Hard Days' Night* and *Help!* (1965). John shared his life and music with Yoko Ono (1933–), finding inspiration in her non-narrative approach to cinema. Such an absurdist sensibility is traceable back to Hans Richter's *Ghosts Before Breakfast* (1928) and, more recent-

IN THE CUT: The author visits John Lennon and Yoko Ono during the editing process of *Imagine* in their suite at New York's Pierre Hotel (Photo credit: Richard Brown).

ly, Stan Brakhage's *Eyes* (1971). *Imagine* offers a purposefully surreal combination of far-out fantasy and documentary realism. No attempt was made here to create a Beatle-esque lark to play in neighbourhood movie theatres. This is an Underground/arthouse project! John and Yoko engage in games of chess and pool; they meet and greet fans. Still, the point was not to enhance his old rock-star image but deconstruct it permanently, revealing the person (warts and all) beneath that pop-culture creation. Unrelated incidents (some staged) were interrelated by John and Yoko in the editing suite. Any 'meaning' (existent or imagined) derives from the order in which the collaborators (clearly influenced by Soviet attitudes on editing) decided to place specific sequences. Eclectic guest stars include dance legend Fred Astaire, talk show host Dick Cavett, jazz great Miles Davis, and later disgraced record producer Phil Spector.

INTERVIEW, THE (2014)

Political Burlesque Rating: *** 1/2

Evan Goldberg, Seth Rogan, dir.; Rogan, Goldberg, Dan Sterling, scr.; Rogen, Goldberg, James Weaver, pro.; 2.35:1: C; 112 min.; Columbia.

    Featuring a scrambled fusion of smart satire and sophomoric silliness, the Goldberg/Rogan collaborations (*Pineapple Express*, 2008; *This Is the End*, 2013) project a cultish sensibility. None though so clearly as *T.I.*, originally to have been titled 'Kill Kim Jon-Un,' the movie that might possibly have begun World War III. North Korea threatened full retaliation if this were to be released; the plot concerns 'Skylark' (James Franco), an edgy TV talk show host who learns that the dictator is a huge fan and flies to Pyongyang for an interview. Then, the CIA requests that the goofball assassinate Kim while there. That plot is not as far out as it may seem; evidence exists to suggest that The Company did indeed attempt to eliminate Cuba's Fidel Castro with just such a scheme in the early 1960s, Lee Harvey Oswald perhaps the hit man. Skylark's bonding with Kim is based on an incident involving the dictator and Dennis Rodman. Aims for a *Strangelove* style of dark comedy, if without the twin geniuses of Stanley Kubrick and Terry Southern. An activist group hoped to drop down thousands of copies on North Korea so that citizens, seeing the banned movie, might finally realize how horrible Kim is. A guest on the Skylark show is played by rapper Eminem.

INVADERS FROM MARS (1953)

Early 1950s Sci-Fi Fantasy Rating: **** ½

William Cameron Menzies, dir.; Richard Blake, scr.; Edward Alderson, pro.; 1.37:1; C; 78 min.; 20th Century Fox.

    Following UFO sightings in 1948, movies about 'first contact' proved as plentiful as they were diverse. Cult fascination still surrounds *I.F.M.*, a B-budget item which intensely impacted on young viewers. Here, the flying saucer menace was portrayed from a child's point-of-view. Jimmy Hunt (1939–) is a boy-next-door who spots a craft in his back yard. U.S. born/Brit educated Director Menzies (1896–1957), already renown for

(*Above and next page*) BEFORE AND AFTER: Previous to the Women's Movement of the 1960s, females in sci-fi/horror films were most often portrayed as helpless victims of male invaders; following the impact of feminism, those roles were often reversed.

Ichi the Killer to *I Walked With a Zombie* • 225

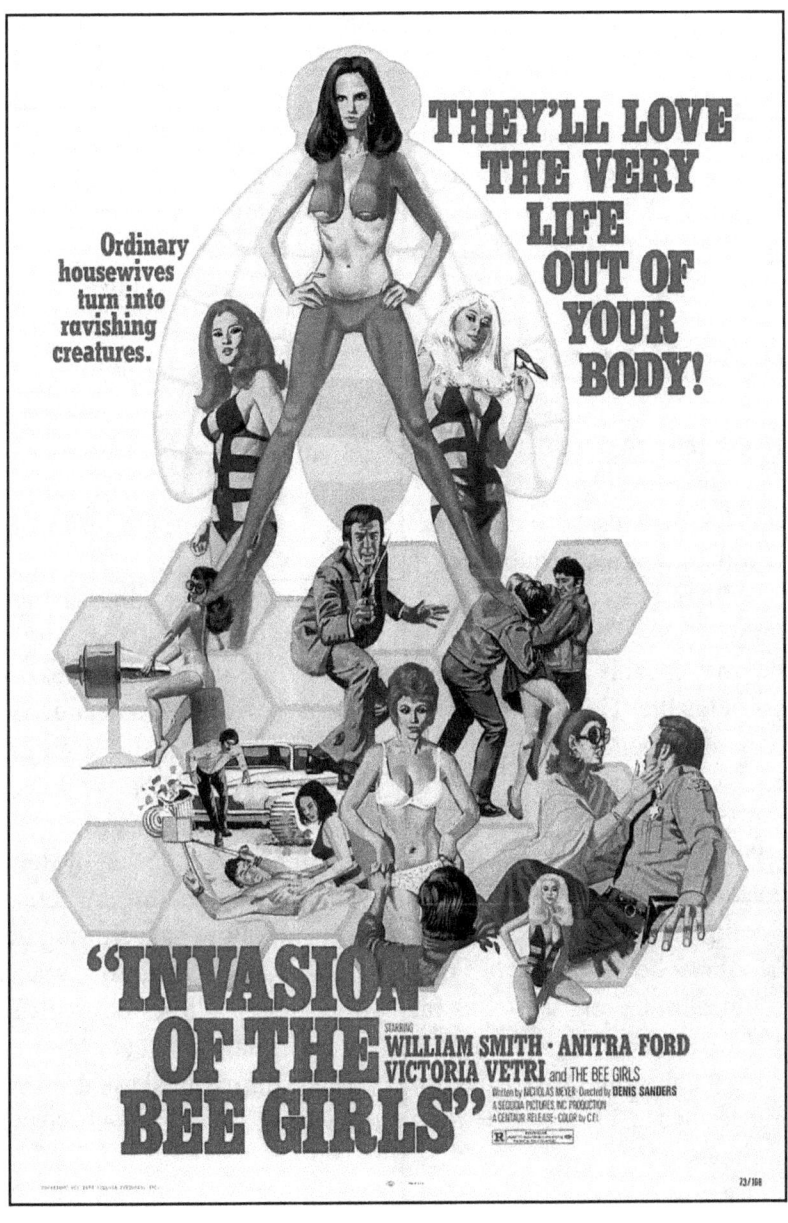

his elaborate film version of H.G. Wells' *Things to Come* (1933), lowered the camera-eye to depict a nightmare-by-daylight as it would appear to a kid. Shifting sands that suck people deep down, Green Mutants lumbering about, a disembodied alien head suspended in a glass frame, garishly bright (and sexual) red clothes worn by a female scientist (Helena Carter), and a sudden transformation of nice TV sitcom style parents (Leif

Ericson, Hillary Brooke) into automatons left a generation of youngsters with bad dreams. The film's disappearance for a decade and a half led many who had seen this in 1953 wondering if they might have dreamed the movie rather than seen it in a theatre, even as the hero wakes to realize all that happened existed only in his mind… or did it? Spielberg references this seminal flick with the late-night rural scenes in *Close Encounters* (1978). Disastrously remade in 1986 by Tobe Hooper.

INVASION OF THE BEE GIRLS (1973)

Camp Cult Appeal: **** ½

Dennis Sanders, dir.; Nicholas Meyer, scr.; Fred Weintraub, pro.; 1.85:1; C; 86 min.; Dandrea/Sequoia Pictures.

Ordinary suburban guys have been dropping like flies during sex encounters with beautiful aliens who literally love them to death. "Just think," one cheaply suited salesman sighs, drinking in a sports bar with others of his ilk: "Coming and going at the same time!" His friends admit they too experience a desire for the fall in the arms of such a gorgeous killer. A smart script by sci-fi writer Nicholas Meyer (1945–) preceded his move to such A list projects as *Time After Time* (1979) and *Star Trek: The Wrath of Khan* (1982). The Queen Bee (literally) is played by demure model turned actress Anitra Ford (1942–). The brawling macho man who conquers her is William Smith (1933–). Following a chilling debut as the village boy in *Ghost of Frankenstein* (1942), he went on to accrue over 300 film/TV credits (thus far), which may well be the world's record. The tragic beauty Victoria Vetri, aka Angela Dorian (1944–), portrays his voluptuous Girl Friday. She was later imprisoned for attempting to murder her lover. So… Aristotle got it wrong? The reverse holds true: life imitates art?

IRREVERSIBLE (2002)

Extreme Cinema Fan Rating: *****

All others: NO STARS

Gasper Noe, dir.; Noe, scr.; Christopher Rossignon, pro.; 2.35:1; C; 97 min. (director's cut); 120 Films/Canal +.

As in ancient tragedy, this contemporary tale concerns one man's (Albert Dupontel) attempt during a 24-hr. period to learn the truth about his little corner of the world. The difference? This is a post-modern tale so, as in *Memento*, the narrative turns back on itself in reverse time. This furthers the connection to Greek myth: Nothing is random. All occurs owing to what has previously happened for an inexorable sense of dark destiny. Monica Bellucci (1964–) is an Italian woman living in Paris with her animal-like lover (Vincent Cassell), they friendly with her more civilized ex. The men set out on a bloody vendetta to discover the identity of a street person who raped and brutally beat 'Alex.' Draws from recent schools as Extreme Cinema (no mercy for the audience as *I.* assaults each viewer) and Cinema du Corps (a stifling focus on human body parts), Argentina's Noe (1963–) delivers a masterpiece of misericordia that's horrifying and heart-breaking, overtly sadistic and inwardly soft-hearted. Low frequency (28 Hz) sound effects are employed to make anyone watching nauseous. No film to play Cannes has had so many walkouts in the first five minutes. An important film, but… be forewarned!

ISLE OF DOGS (2018)

Anderson Cult Rating: *****

Cult Animation Rating: *****

Wes Anderson, dir.; Anderson, Roman Coppola; Jason Schwartzman & Kunichi Nomura, scr.; Anderson, Scott Rudin, prod.; 2.35:1; C; 101 min.; Indian Paintbrush/ Fox Searchlight.

Anderson (1969–) brings stop-motion puppet animation into the 21st century with this personal project, a conventional boy-and-his-dog fable rendered as a one-of-a-kind classic notable for its quirky sensibility, relentless attention to visual detail, and melancholic tone that purposefully does not play to a mainstream audience's expectations. The dystopian-future tale concerns dogs isolated on Trash Island by Japan's cat-loving regime owing to their fear that puppy flu may spread to the human population. Little 'Atari' (Kalyn Rankin) dares search for

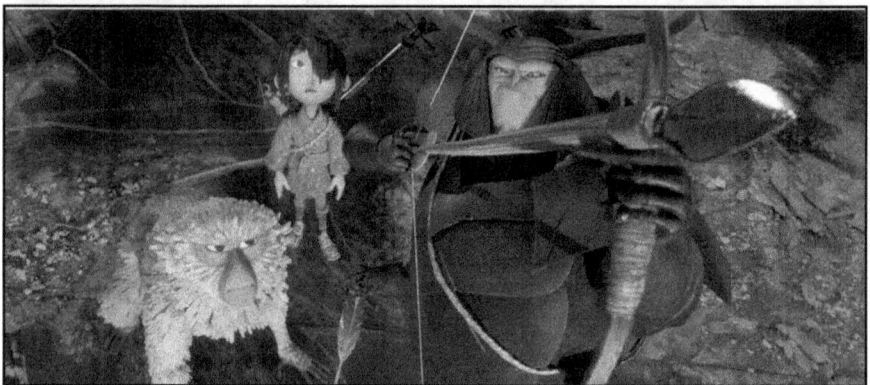

THE NEW FACES OF ANIMATION: Advances in computer technology allow for an ever more sophisticated visualization of Other Worlds, as in *Isle of Dogs* and *Kubo and the Two Strings*.

his 'Spots' with the help of a canine quintet made up of characters as remarkably realized as Disney's seven little people from 1937. Recalls classics by George Pal, Jiri Trinka, and Rankin-Bass, while making use of every recent technical/aesthetic innovation to provide a bountiful as well as innovative feast. Never degenerates into edgy eye-candy, always providing meat for the mind and potent fuel for our emotions, precluding criticism of mere style over substance. Celebrity voices provided by Bill Murray, Scarlett Johansson, and Bryan Cranston, among others. Also highly recommended: a virtual reality companion piece *I.O.D.: Behind the Scenes*.

IT'S ALIVE! (1974)

Ultra-Low-Budget Horror Rating: *****

Larry Cohen, dir.; Cohen, scr.; Cohen, pro.; 1.85:; C; 91 min.; Larco/Warner Bros.

"From da Bronx" L.C. (1936-2019) emerged as a latter day Corman: a lesser known variation on the outsider who 'took' Hollywood by way of low budget/commercially successful genre films. For Cohen, these included black exploitation *(Hell Up in Harlem*, 1973), flying monsters *(Q*, 1982), and contemporary horror *(Wicked Stepmother*, 1989). His greatest effort, *I.A.* presaged the reinvention of the thriller form later in the decade. A seemingly normal suburban couple (John Ryan, Sharon Farrell) head for the hospital where she gives birth not to a baby but a monster, presaging *Alien* (1979). The child's face, briefly glimpsed, strikingly resembles the creature in that later A release. Also like Ridley Scott's masterpiece, most of this movie takes place in shadowy corridors. Val Lewton of R.K.O. noted back in the 1940s that nothing an F/X unit may put up there onscreen will match the nightmares each viewer projects onto an empty dark space. Besides rating as one of the most terrifying movies ever, *L.A.* addresses serious issues: Corruption at drug corporations and the unique relationship between a mother and whatever emerges from her womb.

I WALKED WITH A ZOMBIE (1943)

Cult Horror Rating: **** 1/2

Jacques Tourneur, dir.; Carl Siodmak, Ardel Wray, scr.; Val Lewton, pro.; B&W; 1.37:1; 69 mins.; RKO Radio Pictures.

A magazine story by Inez Wallace about Voodoo rites in the contemporary West Indies and its seduction of Anglo visitors served as a starting point. The storyline borrows from Charlotte Bronte's *Jane Eyre* as a naïve nurse (Frances Dee, 1909–2004) sails to a Caribbean Isle to care for the somnambulist wife (Edith Barrett, 1907–1977) of an elegant plantation owner (Tom Conway, 1904–1967). A female frozen ghost composed of flesh and blood, this blonde zombie hears the call of the wild each night, luring her to a hidden native camp. Once there, she joins

SHADOWLAND: In the R.K.O. thrillers produced by Val Lewton during the 1940s, the monstrous characters were (in comparison to Universal's vividly realized characters) most often heard rumbling through the bushes, just out of sight.

forbidden practices that involve sex and death. These were researched and accurately visualized. Atmospheric, subtly scary, deeply disturbing. 1943's critics found this oddity "dangerously unhealthy." Today it is hailed as a masterpiece of B moviemaking and one of the top examples of Zombie Cinema.

JETEE, LE (1962)

Experimental/Alternative Cinema Rating: ***

Cult Sci-Fi Rating: ***

Chris Marker, dir.; Marker, scr.; Anatole Dauman, pro.; 35 m.m.; B&W; 28 min.; Argos.

A deeply troubled man (Davos Hanich) is chosen by scientists to travel back in time (which they bend), there to create an alternative history and avoid the nuclear war that devastated their world. He remains haunted by a childhood incident: at Orly airport, the boy witnessed an assassination of a man while an enigmatic woman looked on. Decades hence, when the once edgy aesthetics of Left Bank Cinema were adopted by Hollywood, this modest art film would influence such classics as *The Red Spectacles* (Mamoru Oshii, 1987), *12 Monkeys* (Terry Gilliam, 1995), and *The Namesake* (Mira Nair, 2006). A poet-philosopher as well as documentarian, Marker (1921–2012) ranked among those moviemakers who challenged all existing (supposedly set-in-cement) rules about how films ought to be made. For this is an *anti*-movie: C.M. used a still rather than motion-picture camera to capture images, these integrated via an optical printer into a 'photo montage,' accompanied by a minimal amount of voice-over (by Ran Negron) but no dialogue. Like many films by Nouvelle Vague artists (Godard, Truffaut, etc.), *L.J.* contains a homage to Hitchcock: when a couple talk while standing by a tree, the image references James Stewart and Kim Novak visiting the giant redwoods in *Vertigo*.

JEUX D'ENFANTS, aka *LOVE ME IF YOU DARE* (2013)

One of a Kind Rating: *****

Yann Samuel, dir.; Samuel, scr.; Christophe Rossignon, pro.; 1.85:1; C; 93 min.; Nord-Quest/StudioCanal.

"If you are a normal director," Yann Samuel (1965–) claimed, "you hope that people will love your film," which means it will be seen by many viewers worldwide. Understandably, Samuel was not surprised when this, his premiere film, did not become a mainstream hit. A sizable cult developed around an indescribable movie that openly attempted to incite anger, confusion, horror, even hate for its insane narrative and undefinable style. Julien (Thibault Verhaeghe as a child, Guillaume Caret as an adult) and Sophie (Josephine Lebas Joly, Marion Cotillard) are drawn to one another when she, a Polish girl, is abused by the French kids. They commit to everlasting love—so far, so good—which soon turns into something different and far darker: Mad Love. They survive by creating a truth or dare game, less interested in 'truth' than 'dare': When one suggests that the other do some terrible thing to innocent bystanders, the partner can't resist… however horrible the consequences. They are evil, yet we become as entangled in their ever more degenerate tale as we were with the two delightfully sweet kids in *A Little Romance* (1979). This is the film David Cronenberg tried and failed to pull off in *Crash* (1996), a study in a unique form of narcissism that engulfs two otherwise normal (seemingly) people in a love that is everlasting, however vulnerable the participants may be. The color scheme is as purposefully unrealistic as the one in *The Umbrellas of Cherbourg*; here though, the choices are not charming but purposefully disturbing. Theme song: Edith Piaf's "La Vie En Rose." Is it coincidence or destiny that Cotillard (1975–) played that chanteuse in the 2007 biopic?

JOHNNY GUITAR (1954)

Cult Western Rating: *****

Nicholas Ray Cult Rating: *****

QUEEN 'B' OF THE WEST: Onetime Warner Bros. and MGM A list star Joan Crawford moved to a low-rent studio for Nicholas Ray's bizarre Freudian western, *Johnny Guitar*.

Joan Crawford Cult Rating: *****

Gender Transgressive Cult Rating: *****

Sterling Hayden Cult Rating: *****

Nicholas Ray, dir.; Philip Yordan, Ben Maddow (unbilled), scr.; Ray, pro.; 1.66:1; C; 110 min.; Republic.

Leaving RKO after seven years of contract work, Ray (1911–1979) took up the even less prestigious Republic's offer: He had total freedom to make any movie he wished so long as he honed to budget limitations. Ray seized on Roy Chanslor's pulp Western and, with writer Yordan (1914–2003), transformed clichéd characters into living, breathing people onscreen. Maddow (1909–1992), blacklisted at the time, added an attack (camouflaged by period settings) on the House Un-American Committee's insistence that their prey "name names." Fading MGM star Joan Crawford (1906–1977) received above-the-title billing. Sterling Hayden (1916–1986) portrays the title role. His mighty, melancholy presence would in itself assure cult status. Garish color, operatic performances, self-consciously purple-prose, and gender-bending costumes caused critics to dismiss this as vulgar trash. Today? Classic Camp. The love-hate relationship between Crawford's black-outfitted nympho and Mercedes McCambridge's (1916–2004) repressed lesbian qualified this as the key cowboy flick on the 1960s gay midnight movie circuit. Jean-Luc Godard cited *J.G.* as his most revered film.

JOJO RABBIT (2019)

Ultra-original Cult Rating: *****

Taika (Cohen) Waititi, dir.; Waititi, scr.; Waititi, Catherine Neal, Chelsea Winstanley, pro.; 1.85: C; 106 min.; Piki.

Imagine Woody Allen's *Play It Again Sam* (1972) reset in Nazi Germany, with the young, impressionable hero (here, Roman Griffin Davis as the title character) idolizing Adolph Hitler (Watiti) while believing Der Fuhrer himself is omnipresent, offering 'wise' advice as to how the boy ought to proceed. Ah, but here's the rub: JoJo's beloved mom (Scarlett Johansson) is in secret a fervent anti-Fascist, even going so far as to hide a Jewish girl (Thomas McKenzie) in their home—fully aware that if this were discovered, all will be executed. From the refreshing first moment to the surprising finale, everything on view proves cult-worthy, including a take-your-breath-away performance by Sam Rockwell (1968–) as an off-the-wall Nazi. In this case, such humor is sophisticated enough that it never sours and turns offensive, as in the recent *Hogan's Heroes* (1965–

1971) TV series. New Zealand's Watiti (1975–) proves himself an original via wild narrative negotiations between serious drama and goofy comedy, also merciless satire and sweet-spirited sentiment, this may momentarily remind viewers of such iconoclastic film-makers as Terry Gilliam, David Lynch, Billy Wilder, and aforementioned Woody. Johansson is quietly memorable as a de-glamorized character with integrity.

JUNO (2007)

Cute Teen Flick Rating: *** ½

Jason Reitman, dir.; Diablo Cody, Lianne Talfon, pro.; 1.85:1; C; 96 min.; Fox Searchlight.

Moving as far as possible from the intense, unforgiving killer kid in *Hard Candy*, Ellen (now Elliot) Page chose this quirky comedy about a charming, knowing, edgy yet relatively normal 16-year old who finds herself pregnant after a spontaneous 'session' with a good male pal (Michael Cera). Rejecting single parenthood and/or abortion, she decides to give her baby up for adoption to a seemingly 'perfect' super-straight couple… only to learn over the next nine months that anything which seems too good to be true likely is. Page reasserts her acting chops and star quality here, though many viewers grew tired of the endless string of one-liners assigned to Juno by screenwriter Cody (1978–). Cody's apparently soaring career sputtered somewhat when her next effort, the excruciating *Jennifer's Body* (2010) which provided Megan Fox with her first (and last) starring role. Quebec's Reitman (1977–) had already proven his adroitness with bittersweet material by directing the point-on anti-tobacco satire *Thank You for Smoking* (2005). Best performance by far: cult sensation Allison Janey as Juno's mom.

KANASHIMI NO BERADONNA, aka *BELLADONNA OF SADNESS* (1973)

Melancholia Cult Rating: **** ½

Eiichi Yamamoto, dir.; Yamamoto, Yoshiyuki Fukuda, scr.; Osama Tezuka, pro.; 1.33:1; C; 86 min.; Mushi/Spectravion.

What is the process by which an everyday woman transforms into a witch? And might the very idea of *witch* be nothing more than a misguided misconception of one who is in fact a saint? Certainly, that appears to have been the case with Joan of Arc. This subject fascinated French historian/novelist Jules Michelet (1798–1874), who creatively explored the subject in *Sorcere*. Fascinated by that book, E.Y. (1940–), who had co-founded the Mushi animation studio, brought the tale of one such woman—a victim of male patriarchy—who enters into a pact with the devil to exact harsh revenge. This radical feminist vision offers a grim scenario and intense sensuality, as well as a virtual tour through the history of cartooning, from the simplest sort of cut-outs to ultra-realism, incorporating everything from Disney to Ralph Bakshi and the stylings of the beloved Beatles cartoon *Yellow Submarine (1968)*. More a Pink Film (a unique Asian form of softcore porn) than a traditional Animee. Not released officially in the U.S. until the 21st century, though a cult formed over the decades thanks to smuggled-in bootlegs.

KELLY'S HEROES (1970)

Cult Comedy-Action Rating: **** ½

WHY WASN'T THIS FILM A HUGE HIT? Combining the action of *The Dirty Dozen* and the humor of *M*A*S*H*, *Kelly's Heroes* ought to have been a box office bonanza but instead emerged as a cult favorite for Clint Eastwood completists.

Brian G. Hutton, dir.; Troy Kennedy Martin, scr.; Sidney Beckerman, Gabriel Katzka, prods.; 2.35:1; C; 144 min.; MGM.

Canada's Donald Sutherland (1935–), the oddball team member in Robert Aldrich's *The Dirty Dozen* (1967), appeared in yet another WWII actioner as an anachronistic Hippie called… what else? 'Oddball!' The gimmick worked, largely because the period script was informed by a cynical anti-war vision, in tune with the era of release as fighting in Vietnam continued with no end in sight. Here D.S. is an apparent drop-out from the 6th Armored Division who diverts his Sherman M4 tank to aid the title maverick (Clint Eastwood) and other members of the 35th Infantry Division. They sneak past enemy lines not to perform a sefless task (as in *T.D.D.*), rather to rob $16 mill in gold bullion before a general (Carroll O'Connor) can turn it over to our government. Cult figures in the eclectic cast are Telly Savalas (like D.S. a *Dirty Dozen* veteran), comedian Don Rickles, and the great (though then unknown) Harry Dean Stanton. Despite the film's near-perfect blend of dark humor and impactful action,

MGM unaccountably had little faith in its prospects, opening *K.H.* without fanfare. The film flopped, one of the few C.E. action epics to do so.

KICK ASS (2010)

Edgy Cult Superhero Rating: ****

Matthew Vaughn, dir.; Vaughn, Jane Goldman, Matt Millar; Adam Bohling, David Reid, Brad Pitt, Tarquin Park, pros.; 2.35:1; C; 117 min.; Lionsgate/Marv Film.

After *Watchmen*, what? Anyone who believed that 2009 film broke any final barriers of good taste within the superhero genre was in for a surprise. Vaughn (1971–) optioned the rights to John Romita Jr. (1956–) and Mark Millar's (1969–) in-your-face graphic novel, daring to mount an uncompromised film. The premise doesn't sound too different from Disney/Pixar's *The Incredibles* (2004): an average family, sick of street violence, goes the Bruce Wayne route. They don kinky costumes and become righteous avengers, without the blessing of super-powers. What caused every major company in L.A. to turn the project down: 'Hit Girl': an eleven-year-old female assassin. Played by Chloe Grace Moretz (1997–), she proved mesmerizing. And, though few viewers would openly admit it, *sexy*: Lolita on steroids; Hannah Montana in mask and cape on a killing spree. Nicolas Cage's (1964–) awesomely awful over-acting proves effective in the crazy context. For a proper sense of post modernism, characters reference other comic book superheroes, as well as films of John Woo, even pop/op progenitor Andy Warhol. Independently financed and produced, *Kick Ass*'s box-office success proved the 21st century mainstream could no longer be distinguished from what had once been referred to as The Fringe.

KILL BILL, PART I (2003) *KILL BILL, PART TWO* (2004)

Cult Movie to End All Cult Movies Rating: *****

Quentin Tarantino, dir.; Tarantino, Uma Thurman, scr.; Lawrence Bender, pro.; 2.39;1; B&W/C; 111 min. (Part One), 137 min. (Part Two); Miramax.

Waking from a coma, a confused beauty (Uma Thurman, 1960–), her baby kidnapped, vows to even the score with a betraying mentor (David Carradine, 1936–2009). Live-action (with an emphasis on action) fuses with incongruous animation in Q.T.'s celluloid patchwork-quilt of stylized, at times even poetic, violence. U.T.'s 'The Bride' combines every vengeance driven woman from Jeanne Moreau in *The Bride Wore Black* to Meiko Kaji in *Lady Snowblood* and Natsuki Ozawa in *Zero Woman*, with a passing nod to Lucy Lawless in *Xena: Warrior Princess*. Each element—characters, narrative, visuals, music—presents more evidence that while imitation may constitute the highest form of flattery or merely plagiarism, in the unique case of Q.T. the result is contemporary Parallel-Cinema. K.B. offers an apotheosis of adventure movies ranging from the highs of John Ford's elegiac Oaters to the lows of Eddie Romero's Philippines-lensed exploitation flicks. Here, Quentin most relied on the entire oeuvre of 1970s Kung Fu classics with, a touch of Manga tossed in. Even the music references other movies, as each 'song' earlier appeared in one of Q.T.'s favorite films. The same holds true for costuming: Bruce Lee wore the yellow outfit modelled here by U.T. in his final film, *Game of Death* (1978). Why choose between black and white and color when a creative auteur can bounce back and forth from one to the other based on appropriateness for any single sequence? A purposefully eclectic cast of kick-ass femmes includes Lucy Liu (*Charlie's Angels*, 2000), Viveca A. Fox (*Independence Day*, (1996), and Darryl Hannah (TV's *Attack of the 50 Ft. Woman*, 1993). Most of the men (Michael Madsen, *Reservoir Dogs*; Michael Parks, *From Dusk Till Dawn*) are drawn from Q.T's stock company. Chiaki Kuriyama adds a new dimension to *Part II* as the frigid/virgin Asian castrator of men and casual killer of anyone nearby, preferably (but not exclusively) males.

KILLING, THE (1956)

Early Kubrick Rating: *****

Stanley Kubrick, dir.; Kubrick, Jim Thompson, scr.; James P. Harris, pro.; 1.66:1; B&W; 85 min.; United Artists.

Had John Wayne had been born a communist, he'd have been Sterling Hayden (1916–1986). Blacklisted by 'the majors' owing to far left politics, S.D. could no longer win choice roles like his earlier lead in John

TOUGH GUY: Sterling Hayden was born to play the mean streets equivalent to John Wayne's man of wide open spaces in such top noirs as the mainstream classic *The Asphalt Jungle* (John Huston, 1950) and, five years later, Stanley Kubrick's similar heist yarn..

Huston's *The Asphalt Jungle* (1950). So The Big Brute played the lead in young Kubrick's (1928–1999) B budget indie, likewise about a carefully planned robbery gone awry. S.K.'s screenplay featured a fractured-time scheme of the type Q.T., who reveres this film, would employ for *Reservoir Dogs*. Ahead of his time, S.K. was forced to include an over-obvious narration offering a deadly-dull explanations of what is happening as well as when and why. S.K.'s collaboration with top cinematographer Lucien Ballard (1904–1988) reinvented the look of noir thrillers at mid-decade. Concluding shoot-out (guns held close to the heads of criminals) and subsequent piled-high bodies inspired similar images in films by John Woo. Marie Windsor's dying line ("This is like a bad joke without a punch-line!") may be the purest statement of abject cynicism in commercial films… other than Hayden's own two-word closing bit. Timothy Aguilera Carey makes an early appearance as a lumbering racist maniac. From the much admired pulp-fiction novel *Clean Break* (1955) by Lionel White.

KING KONG (1933)

The Greatest Monster Movie Ever Made Rating: *****

Merian C. Cooper, Ernest B. Schoedsack, dirs..; Ruth Rose, James Creelman, scrs.; Cooper, Schoedsack, David O. Selznick, prods.; 1.37:1; B&W; 125 min. (complete cut); 104 min. (semi-restored print); 100 min. (original release), R.K.O.

On the weekend of April 7, 1933, as mainstream Americans lined up to watch 'The Eighth Wonder of the World,' they could not have guessed that they recreated a scene in the upcoming film: similar people eagerly wait to see Kong 'live' onstage. Less known: *Kong* rates as Hollywood's first viable (non-porno) midnight movie. A secret screening for invited guests featured sequences cut from the release print to appease the Motion Picture Production Code, even then being instituted. Missing footage included Kong stomping on shrieking natives, also biting victims in half with his vampirish teeth. A waking woman is tossed to her death from a high apartment building. (The actress, Sandra Shaw, was Gary Cooper's wife). And sex: Kong stripping away Ann's (Fay Wray, 1907–2004) clothes, afterwards smelling his fingers to enhance the experience. Prints featuring 'forbidden' footage circulated Underground for three and a half decades. In time, not only was the excised material restored. Ironically, this expanded version was shown in early evening time slots on 'family-friendly' TV.

GENIUS AT WORK, IV: While family audiences caught the pared down version at open matinee and evening showings, the cult cinema cognoscenti caught an unedited version at private midnight screenings; Willis O'Brien, creating the creatures in his studio.

KING OF KONG: A FISTFUL OF QUARTERS (2007)

Gamer Cult Movie: *****

Seth Gordon, dir., scr.; Ed Cunningham, pro.; 1.85:1; C; 79 min.; LargeLab.

    In the demi-monde of pool, Fast Eddie Felson (Paul Newman) took on Minnesota Fats (Jackie Gleason) in *The Hustler* (1961); as to poker, the title character (Steve McQueen) going up against Lancey Howard (Edward G. Robinson) in *The Cincinnati Kid* (1965). But those were works of fiction, if inspired by fact. Here's the real deal: quiet, hopeful Steve Wiebe daring to challenge Billy Mitchell, the all-time champ at… Donkey Kong. For what might seem a modest form of early 21st century entertainment for the masses became a domain unto itself for marginals living on society's fringe. Gordon gets to the very heart of the matter, revealing how what for the mainstream may be a fun hobby became, to a devoted few, a way of life, combining elements of sport and religion into an all-consuming preoccupation. Every aspect of this alternative universe is distilled for the ardent gamer and the casual viewer wishing for a brief peek into this universe.

KISS ME DEADLY

Robert Aldrich Cultists: *****

Ralph Meeker Cultists: *****

Mickey Spillane Cultists: *****

Robert Aldrich, dir.; A.I. Bezzerides, scr.; Aldrich, pro.; 1.85:1; 104 min. (original theatrical cut); 106 min. (director's cut); Parklane Pictures/UA.

    With *The Maltese Falcon* (1930), Dashiell Hammett (1894–1961) gave the public 'Sam Spade,' the perfect gumshoe for his era: morally altruistic, emotionally distanced. Raymond Chandler's (1888–1959) *The Big Sleep* (1939) replaced him with 'Philip Marlowe,' whose intellectual stoicism/philosophic pessimism made him precisely right for the 1940s. Last (and some would say least) came 'Mike Hammer,' the private eye as vulgar

MEET MIKE HAMMER: Mickey Spillane's brutal detective has been brought to the theatrical and TV screens multiple times, but here's the only film to ever 'nail' the bullyish private eye and his seamy world.

slob: Tennessee Williams' 'Stanley Kowalski' from *Streetcar* packing a rod which he did not, like his predecessors, hesitate to employ. The nasty P.I. first appeared in 1947's *I, The Jury*, by Mickey Spillane (1918–2006), king of pulp paperback hacks. The most successful film treatment of his oeuvre appears is this squalid (that's intended as a compliment) tale of the anti-hero's adventures after confronting a hit-and-run victim (Cloris Leachman, 1926-2021, in her film debut). At the finale, femme fatale 'Lily' (German born Gaby Rodgers, 1928-) opens a contemporary Pandora's

Box filled with the modern scourge, radium. A threatening omnipresent night-world is visualized by Ernest Laszlo (1998–1984). No one would have been a better pick for M.H. than Ralph Meeker (1922–1988), tough as nails. Recent re-releases contain two minutes of sex and violence cut before the initial theatrical release.

KISS, THE (1896)

Silent Cult Cinema Rating: ****

William Heise, dir.; John J. McNally, scr.; Tomas Edison, pro.; 18 secs. (apprx.); The Edison Studio/Black Maria.

During the Victorian era's final days, in America as well as England, public kissing remained illegal. However, a Broadway musical *The Widow* dared include one brief if shocking smooch. In New Jersey, Thomas Edison (1847–1931) busied himself preparing brief flickers as commercial products. This became the first live-theatre-to-film adaptation. Apprehensive audiences lined up at Nickelodeons where this "obscene" work would be screened. The Roman Catholic Church condemned not only *T.K.* but movies in general as anti-Christian, likely to draw humanity back to our "beastly" origins. Magnification on a screen of this single aspect of the play—removed from its context, in close-up—added to the furor over films. For the record, the "kissers" were John Rice (1857–1915) and May Irwin (1862–1938).

KOKAKU KIDOTAI, aka GHOST IN THE SHELL (1995)

Cult Animee Rating: *****

Mamoru Oshii, dir.; Kazunori Ito, scr.; Mitsuhisa Ishikawa, Ken Iyodami, Ken Matsumoto, prods.; 1.85:1; C; 83 min.; Bandai /Kodanasha/Manga Ent.

This near-future Animee from Oshii (1951–) ties *Akira* as the genre's most cult-worthy project. A work of dystopian future sci-fi, the story concerns a special unit of Japan's police known as Section 9 and its most intrepid investigator, 'Maj. Motoko Kashnagi.' The technocracy she lives

AKIRA, MOVE OVER! Mamoru Oshii created the most memorable Asian import to the U.S. (indeed, the international market) with this spooky, suspenseful thriller.

within has reduced her humanity. Moto appears to be an unblinking doll. The Iron Major/Maiden sets out to locate a mysterious villain known as The Puppet Master. Influences on Oshii are many: the careful attention to minute detail of setting recalls vividly created realities in films by John Ford and Sergio Leone; flocks of birds overhead and mirror images reference Hitchcock; a self-aware computer was inspired by H.A.L. in Kubrick's *2001*. As to the reappearing basset hound, that's O's favorite breed of dog. *G.I.T.S.* draws on Oshii's Asian culture but also Christian symbolism, he as a child so raised. The failure of a 2017 remake starring Scarlett Johansson proves that this remains a cult conception, not (yet) ready for the mainstream.

KUBO AND THE TWO STRINGS (2016)

Stop Motion Puppet Animation Rating: *****

Travis Knight, dir.; Mark Harmes, Chris Butler, Shannon Tindle, scr.; Knight, Arianne Sutner, pro.; 2.35:1; C; 101 min.; Focus Features/Laika Studio.

Previous to *Life of Dogs*, this film by former Rapper Knight (as 'Chilly Tee,' 1973–) offered hope to cult connoisseurs of Stop motion puppet animation that the unique art form remains with us still, even if each film's failure to draw in sizable audiences leaves doubts as to a healthy future. The story (if that is the correct term) not only takes place in ancient Japan but moves in narrative fits and starts (purposefully so) imitating bygone tales from that island nation's past. The title character is a boy who, like Luke Skywalker on his home planet, lives in an isolated area, dreaming of adventures, suddenly plunged into one of the greatest quests ever as he learns the true identity of his (seemingly) long-lost father. Another Asian art form, the creative folding of paper known as Origami, motivates the sometimes charming, occasionally dark material to follow. Most kids love it, though the filmmaker's intent was to speak to the primal child deep down in every adult, waiting to be re-awakened. Like *The Never Ending Story*, this is a story *about* stories… particularly the manner in which the age-old oral tradition of conveying legends is the most basic means of keeping memories—which is all that we possess of the past—alive. Kubo's three-stringed guitar-like instrument is known as The Shamisen. As to his '*two* strings,' discover that for yourself.

L

LAST SEDUCTION, THE (1994)

Neo Noir Rating: ****

John Dahl, dir.; Steve Baranick, scr. John Shestak, Nancy Rae Stone, pro.; 1.85:1; C; 110 min. (theatrical), 129 min. (dir. cut), ITC.

    A neo-noir that follows the plot conventions of this revived genre, with suitably garish color and unexpected camera-angles as well as a mood-drenched jazz score. What brought attention to this piece in particular: femme fatale 'Bridget Gregory' as conceived by the writer and director (1956–) and, foremost, played by Linda Fiorentino (1958–). If in the original era of noir the beautiful double-dealing blonde glistened with a hypnotic sense of delicious duplicity (typified by Jane Greer as 'Kathie' in *Out of the Past*; Jacques Tourneur, 1947), in the post-feminist aura such characters appeared retro… irrelevant, even. Now, a villainess does not play little girl games to hide her true nature. Here, 'Bridget' embodies evil incarnate—proud of her cruel nature and willing to reveal it from the first to final betrayal. L.F.'s stark beauty and harsh features served her well in this trend-setting role but limited her ability to earn parts as 'ordinary' women. J.T. Walsh (1943–1998) creates a parallel to the Coen Bros.' *Blood Simple* (1989). Briefly, it seemed that Dahl might become an important cult director. Following this and *Red Rock West* (1993), he slipped into the virtual oblivion of TV grunt-work.

LAST WALTZ, THE (1978)

Rockumentary Rating: *****

Cult for The Band Rating: *****

END OF AN ERA: The Band plays for a final time, their performances punctuated by an outstanding list of guest performers.

Martin Scorsese Aficionado Rating: *****

Martin Scorsese, dir.; Mardik Martin, scr.; Joel Chernoff, Robbie Roberson, pro.; 1.85:1; C; 117 min.; FM Prods.

From a back-up band for rockabilly artist Ronnie Hawkins and then folk-rocker Bob Dylan, Canada's The Band eventually came into its own as a legendary… well… *band!* In San Francisco during Thanksgiving vacation, 1976, following more than fifteen years on the road, the five performed together for the final time: Bassist Rick Danko (1943–1999), drummer Levon Helm (1940–2012), organist Garth Hudson (1937–), key-board/pianist Richard Manuel (1943–1986), and guitarist/lead vocalist Robbie Roberson (1943–). In part owing to his fine editing of the earlier *Woodstock* documentary, Martin Scorsese (1942–) won the honor of recording the moment for posterity. A Who's Who of rock stars join in: Dylan, Eric Clapton, Joni Mitchell, as well as lookin' lost pop-singer Neil Diamond. All reveal their reverence for the cross-genre style of this quintet, influenced by everything from folk and country to 1950s Big Beat and 1960s Motown. M.S. proves less is more, quietly employing his camera to capture the moment's beauty. Generally considered the *Citizen Kane* of rock documentaries.

LAT DEN RATIE KOMMA IN, aka LET THE RIGHT ONE IN (2008)

Ultra-Contemporary Vampire Cult Rating: *****

Thomas Alfredson, dir.; Hoyte Jon Avide Lindquist, scr.; Carl Molinder, John Nordling, prod.; 2.35:1; C; 115 min.; EFTI/Filmpool Nord.

    So you thought *Harold and Maude* took the older woman/younger male romance as far as it could go? In this initially subtle, eventually gore-strewn tale, a 200 year-old succubus who still appears childlike (Lina Leandersson) enjoys a lunar love story with a 12-year old bullied boy (Kare Hedebrath). Sweden's T.A. (1965–) eliminated some of the less conventional aspects of John Avide Lindquist's haunting 2004 novel, along with many of its genre trappings. *L.D.R.K.I.* does dare to flirt with the forbidden theme of pedophilia in the context of a sensitive yet terrifying vampire flick. Hoyte Van Hoyteman's unnervingly understated cinematography and Johan Xoderquist's eccentric music underline an unrelenting vision of a harsh frozen world, located off on the far edge of normal life, unlike anything on the screen since Kubrick's *The Shining* (1980). A first-rate U.S./ U.K. remake—*Let Me in* (2010), directed by Matt Reeves and starring Chloe Grace Moretz—comes close to capturing the original's appeal. Tragically, the gifted Alfredson's career suffered a terrible setback when his horror-movie follow-up, *The Snowman* (2017), proved a self-proclaimed disaster.

LAT SAU SAN TAAM, aka HARD-BOILED (1992)

Asian Neo-Noir Rating: *****

John Woo Aficionado Rating: *****

In Your Face Violence Rating: *****

John Woo, dir.; Woo Barry Wong, scr.; Linda Kuk, Terence Chang, prod.; 1.85:1; C; 128 min.; Golden Princess/Rim.

    Sick of accusations that he glorified gangsters in his Hong Kong action flicks, J.W. (1946–) switched loyalties. Inspired by *Bullitt* (1968) and

THE HIGHEST FORM OF FLATTERY: John Woo employed the Asian action film to convey a nihilistic world-view through unforgettable and iconic images; Quentin Tarantino would pay homage in such movies as *Reservoir Dogs*.

Dirty Harry (1971), he idealized tough cops instead. The plot is borrowed from *Yojimbo* (1961) and Sergio Leone's *A Fistful of Dollars* (1964): two criminal households, both alike in indignity, engage in a gang war. Woo sets his vengeance minded anti-hero (Yun-Fat Chow, 1955–) against a deadly hitman (Tony Chiu-Wai, 1962–), unawares that the youth is an undercover cop. Take-your-breath away fights convey a Peckinpah-like mix of the real and surreal thanks to Woo's eccentric combination of carefully choreographed shots with organic moments of unrehearsed inspiration. Woo was now powerful enough to insist the jazz soundtrack he had begged to include in *A Better Tomorrow* (1986) and *The Killer* (1989) be employed to reference the original golden age of noir. Avoid as you would the Bubonic Plague a 92 min. edited version.

LEON: THE PROFESSIONAL (1994)

International cut: *****

Original release print: **** ½

DELICIOUSLY DISTURBING: The more one learns about the artist's background, the more concerned a viewer becomes about the 'relationship' established here between nymphette Nathalie Portman and hit man Jean Reno.

Luc Besson, dir.; Besson, scr.; Besson, Patrice Ledoux, pros.; 2.35:1; C; 136 min. (director's cut) 110 min.; U.S. release print); (British) Gaumont, Les Films de Dauphin.

"You're a hit man?" a streetwise 12-year-old-girl (Nathalie Portman, 1981–) says to the mysterious loner (Jean Reno, 1948–) after he rescues her from a drug-related massacre. "*Cool!*" That sets in motion one of the strangest relationships in film, as this formerly cold-blooded killer (or 'Cleaner') becomes a tender, loving, devoted foster-father. She's bent on revenge against the killing spree's perpetrator: Gary Oldman (1958–) as an addicted/corrupt DEA cop. 'Leon' insists 'Mathilda' drink her milk and stop smoking while mentoring her as to a variety of 'professional skills': i.e., how to stalk and murder one's prey. As if that weren't disturbing enough, throughout the director's cut there's a sense that Mathilda and Leon are on the verge of becoming lovers. Besson (1959–) based the story on his own early inappropriate relationship with an 11 year old (Maiween Le Besc), who years later, as a young adult, acted in this film.

LIGHTHOUSE, THE (2019)

Psychological horror Rating: *****

Robert Eggers, dir.; Eggers, Max Eggers, scr.; R. Eggers, Youree Henley, pro.; 1.19.1: B&W; 109 min.: A 24 New Regency.

In what may be the most macabre variation on a chamber drama since Edgar Allen Poe's "The Black Cat" (1843) and "the Pit and the Pendulum" (1842), an old sailor (Willem Dafoe) and a young misanthrope (Robert Pattinson) settle on a God-forsaken island to tend its stark lighthouse. What follows is a one-of-a-kind movie that will nonetheless remind long-time cineastes of such memorably grotesque classics as *The Phantom Carriage* (Victor Seastrom, 1921), *Vampyr* (Carl Theodore Dreyer, 1932), Ingmar Bergman's *Persona* (1966) and *Hour of the Wolf* (1968), and *Repulsion* (Roman Polanski, 1965), inter-laced with visual elements from *The Birds* (Alfred Hitchcock, 1963). Like all great alternative-cinema/Underground films, here is an in-your-face cinematic torture chamber full of odd premonitions, confusing red herrings, and unexpected pay-offs, conveyed via striking imagery—these juxtaposed with shrill sounds. Dialogue (when it appears, which is rare) recalls fever-pitch allegorical phrases found in Shakespeare, Melville, Dostoevsky. Even more memorable than *The Witch*. Previously, Eggers contributed the superb production design for Jay Stern's *Spirit Cabinet* (2013).

LIMEY, THE (1999)

Way Over the Edge Brit-Flavored Neo-Noir Rating: *****

Steven Soderbergh, dir.; Lem Dobbs, scr.; John Hardy, Scott Kramer, prod.; 1.85:1; C; 89 min.; Artisan Entertainment.

Vengeance based neo-noir at its most effective and oppressive. A mean-spirited Cockney (Terence Stamp, 1938–) is released from prison and heads for Los Angeles to seek out and likely kill the sleazy record producer (Peter Fonda) who seduced and abandoned the anti-hero's daughter. Initially, this appears to be shaping up as another cruel classic in the tradition of *Get Carter!* (the Brit, *not* the American, version). Then something unexpected but appealing happens. First, the film turns into a fish out of water piece, the seemingly rugged 'Wilson' unable to cope with contemporary lifestyles in pseudo-sophisticated Southern Cal. Avoiding the *de rigeur* action sequences, *T.L.* instead offers a character study of a singular man who would like to kill his own doppelganger to make up for his failures as a father, which drove the girl into this creep's arms. The realization that a new girl is now threatened allows for a Catholic redemption theme. Might Wilson settle the score by saving her? Adding to the strangeness: a quasi-romance with an aging actress who recalls Gloria Swanson in *Sunset Boulevard* (1950). She's played by the underrated Lesley Ann Warren (1946–), introduced as a Disney princess, a cult star when that fizzled.

LIQUID SKY (1982)

Original 'Immediate Impact' Rating on Release: *****

In Retrospect Rating: *** 1/2

Slave Tsukerman, dir.; Tsukerman, Anne Carlisle, Nina V. Kerova, scr.; producer, Kerova; C; 1:33.1: 112 min. Z Films.

A team of talented Soviet filmmakers travelled to New York and produced this outrageous indie which mesmerizingly captures the early 1980s post-punk/pro-New Wave alternative scene in sight and sound. Despite the director's previous renown as a realist and documentarian, Tsuukerman (1940–) chose to include campy 1950s sci-fi clichés. Aliens arrive in Manhattan to score drugs, focusing on two models preparing for an *outre* fashion show at an Underground club of the type briefly popular at this juncture in time. Each is played by perversely beautiful Annie Carlisle (1956–). As 'Margaret,' she recalls Kim Novak in *Vertigo*, only on Acid; and 'Jerry,' a David Bowie clone having a horrible hair day. Heroin chic, the bane of New York in the early 1980s, suffuses the all but impossible-to-follow plot while lending this movie its title. Influenced by Andy Warhol's purposefully bad-taste films and Pink Floyd's enigmatic music. Yuri Neyman's cinematography induces even the straightest viewer to share the surreal experience of a downscale disco's light show enhanced by retro-noir shadings. Individual sequences range from corny comedy to a notably brutal rape. Good? No. Impactful? Yes.

LITTLE MISS SUNSHINE (2006/7)

Ozzie and Harriet go Nutzoid Rating: *****

Jonathan Dayton, Valerie Faris, dir.; Michael Arndt, scr.; Albert Berger, many others, pro.; 2.35:1; C; 101 min.; Fox Searchlight.

A seemingly normal suburban family leave Albuquerque NM on their way cross country to Redondo Beach CA so that seven year old 'Olive' can enter a beauty and talent competition. Little do they know of the erotic dance steps that erratic old grandpa has been secretly teaching her. Alan Arkin (1934–) finally received his long overdue Oscar for a clever and non-cliched performance. An important movie for Steve Carrell (1962–) who here proved that, in addition to a gifted light night TV comedy performer, he was about to emerge as one of our finest character leads. Knockabout comedy for smart audiences who well know the identities of Marcel Proust and Frederick Nietzsche, both of whom dominate much of the proceedings. Auspicious premieres for Abigal Breslin (1996–), who a decade later would play 'Baby' in the TV remake of *Dirty Dancing*, and Arndt (1965–); his future blockbuster screenplays include *Toy Story 3* (2010), *Oblivion* (2013), and *Star Wars: Episode VII – The Force Awakens* (2015)

LITTLE SHOP OF HORRORS, THE (1960)

Sci-Fi Film Rating: NO STARS

Black Comedy Cult Film Rating: *****

Roger Corman, dir.; Charles B. Griffith, scr.; Corman, pro.; 1.85:1; B&W; 72 min.; Santa Clara Prods.

Roger Corman (1926–) bet a friend he could shoot a film in less than two days which would then go on to break box-office records. He won that wager: at a cost of little more than $20,000, *L.S.O.H.* netted over $ 1 ½ million on its theatrical release. Teen audiences loved this spoof of the monster movies they had in the late-1950s adored on a more serious level. 'Seymour Krelborn' (Jonathan Haze, 1929–) is a nerd who creates a deadly plant named after his girl 'Audrey' (Jackie Joseph, 1933–). "Feed me!" the audience of return ticket-buyers called out as that dialogue (Griffith supplied the voice of Audrey II) appeared. They did so again when, as college students, they watched on fraternity house or dorm TVs. Jack Nicholson (1937–) became a cult sensation thanks to his masochistic dental patient who insists "No novocaine! It dulls the pain…" When in the wake of *Rocky Horror* pop culture entrepreneurs realized 'so bad it's good' reigned as the new aesthetic, Howard Ashman and Alan Menken mounted a stage musical, filmed in 1986 by Frank Oz. The original still rules.

LOLITA (1962)

Kubrick cult Rating: *****

Nymphette Cinema Cult Rating: *****

Stanley Kubrick, dir.; Kubrick, Vladimir Nabokov, scr.; James B. Harris, pro.; 1.66:1; B&W; 153 min.; A.A. Prods./Metro-Goldwyn-Mayer.

"How did they *ever* make a movie out of 'Lolita'?" Despite the effectiveness of MGM's advertising mantra, the truth is that 'they' didn't. Vladimir Nabokov's (1899–1977) 1955 cult novel concerned a pedophile who sets out to seduce an oblivious brunette child. Though twelve, the book's 'Lo' could pass for ten. Kubrick's movie focuses on an ordinary guy

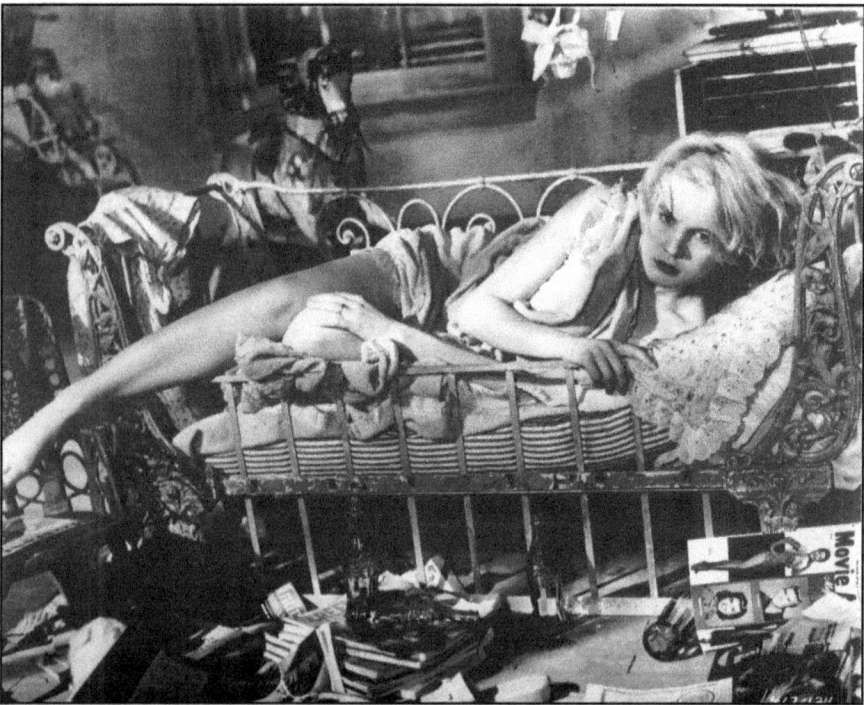

THE YOUNG AND THE RESTLESS: Stanley Kubrick brought Vladimir Nabokov's 'naughty girl' to the screen in the person of Sue Lyon, even as Elia Kazan had earlier done with Tennessee Williams' bad girl as played by Carol Baker in *Baby Doll*.

who falls under the spell of a 15-year-old blonde bombshell (in a bikini, no less). She could pass for seventeen and flirtatiously comes on to him. Among the actors who turned down the 'Humbert' role: Cary Grant, David Niven, Laurence Olivier. James Mason (1909–1984) dared to take the challenge. Hayley Mills of *Pollyanna* fame was offered the title role but her father, Sir John, and Walt Disney would not allow it. Whether Tuesday Weld passed or was passed over has never been determined. Kubrick insisted that while other roles were up for grabs, he would not have shot the film with anyone other than Peter Sellers as the diabolical 'Claire Quilty.' The comic genius came up with the idea (unscripted) for a memorable ping pong game. Though set in America, the film was shot in the UK to avoid censorial interference. Lyon's (1946–2019) heart-shaped sunglasses, essential to the memorable poster, never appear.

LONE WOLF McQUADE (1983)

Cult Action Flick Rating: ****

Steve Carver, dir.; B.J. Nelson, H. Kaye Dyal, John Milius (uncredited), scr; Carver, Yoram Ben Ami, pro.; 1.85:1; C; 107 min.; Orion.

It's all about paying your dues. Early in his career, Chuck Norris (1940–) begrudgingly agreed to lose a martial arts bout with Bruce Lee (1940–1973) in that superstar's *Meng Long guo Jlang*, aka *The Way of the Dragon* (1972). Still, the performance helped America's answer to B.L. win action flick fame in a long (if less than distinguished) line of ultra-low budgeters, all appealing to Norris devotees. One has a cult of its own: *L.W.Mc.* rates as a solid action flick for aficionados of that genre. In it, C.N. plays a Texas ranger out to bring down a drug lord. As he's played by David Carradine (1936–2009), who brought Asian style fighting to TV with *Kung Fu* (1972–1975) \there's a duel of the century knockout finale. No stunt doubles were employed. Some technicians on the set insist at a certain point the stars lost control and the competition became real. This time around, Norris wins. The film's success led to a popular TV series, *Walker, Texas Ranger* (1993–2001). Here, Barbara Carrera (1945–) plays the good/bad girl who must decide which man—and side of the law—she will stand by. Carver visually imitated Sergio Leone's spaghetti Western style.

WHAT COMES AROUND GOES AROUND: Chuck Norris defeats David Carradine in *Lone Wolf McQuade*; perhaps this compensated him for losing a bout with Bruce Lee in *Way of the Dragon*.

LOST IN TRANSLATION (2003)

Sparse Chamber Drama Rating: *****

Sofia Coppola Cult Rating: *****

Bill Murray Cult Rating: *****

Scarjo Cult Rating: *****

Sofia Coppola, dir.; Coppola, scr.; Coppola, Francis Ford Coppola, Rose Katz, pro.; 1.85:1; C; 102 min.; Focus.

Once upon a time… in Tokyo. By coincidence or fate, fast-fading American movie star 'Bob' (Bill Murray, 1950–) comes face to face with 18-year-old 'Charlotte' (Scarlett Johansson, 1984–). A neglected wife, she realizes that the road chosen for her 'journey' may have been the wrong one. Girl meets middle-aged boy/man, girl loses middle-aged boy/man, girl gets (in a manner of speaking) middle-aged boy/man. Anyone who wondered whether S.C. (1971–) might prove to be a one-shot-wonder following the success of *The Virgin Suicides* here encountered proof that this was not the case. An intimate chamber drama about two radically different people who drift into an odd relationship which may lead to offbeat romance or deep friendship—perhaps both or then again maybe neither. There are no guarantees in life, or in films that reflect it so accurately. As with the equally admirable *About Schmidt*, a viewer experiences a moment of fear toward the end when it appears there might be a big, explosive final moment that will destroy the quiet integrity of what has gone before. Happily, that does not occur in either film. A movie that you surrender to emotionally while watching, then intellectually consider by reflecting on the simple surface that contains so many moral complexities deep down beneath. Also present: a BB gun, lots of Sushi, and (yes!) Scarjo's pink panties.

LOVE WITCH, THE (2016)

Updated Velvet Vampire Horror Subgenre Rating: **** ½

Anna Biller, dir.; Biller, scr.; Biller, pro.; 1.85:1; C; 120 min.; Oscilloscope.

Imagine a remake of *Succubus* from a 21st Century feminist perspective. Here is the essence of this rarest of rare contemporary indies in which state-of-the-art digital process is forsaken in favor of retro 35 mm., allowing for an under-stated color scheme that casts a creepy enchantment over relatively realistic settings including a Victorian-era house that has survived the years virtually intact. This is where 'Elaine' (Samantha Robinson, 1991–) resides while seducing a succession of men who either die or fall apart at the seams following their intense sexual bouts. The major difference between this and earlier entries in The Velvet Vampire subgenre: the heroine (or villain, depending on each receiver's viewpoint) is not one more cold-hearted killer who pretends to be in love so that she may inflict pain on male prey but a deeply emotional woman who is so desperate to find true love with a man that she… shall we say… overdoes it each time out? Color schemes occasionally recall Corman's Poe adaptations of the 1960s and Hammer's period pieces from that same decade. Love it or hate it…

L'UCCELLO DALLE PLUME DI CRISTALLO, aka *BIRD WITH THE CRYSTAL PLUMMAGE, (THE)* (1970)

Giallo Cult Rating: **** 1/2

Dario Argento, dir.; Argento, scr.; Salvatore Argento, pro.; 2.35:1; C; 108 min. (director's cut), 98 min. (original international release print); Central Cinema Company.

The term 'Giallo' originally referred to paperbacks published in Italy, an equivalent of sordid Bus Station novels popular with America's underclass readers. Whether the word 'yellow' referenced 'the color of fear,' the lurid cover art, or human liquid waste remains unclear. Hardly the first Giallo film, *B.W.T.C.P.* did confirm Argento (1940–) as the genre's primary avatar. One of the first such genre pieces released in the U.S. Previously, distributors feared gobs of gore (inspired by the shower scene in *Psycho*, (1960) in such an Italianate cinematic context (the gaudiest colors and garish lighting) might offend stateside sensibilities. Not so! At least, not connoisseurs of creepy thrillers. An American (Tony Musante, 1936–2013), at the wrong place at the wrong time, observes what appears a serial killer's latest attempt to mutilate and murder a beautiful woman (Eva Renzi, 1944–2005). Sets the pace for future genre entries thanks to shrill music by Ennio Morricone (1928–2021). Cinematographer Vittorio Storaro (1940–) conveys over-the-top brutality in stylized Neon-inspired visuals. Derived from the same 1958 novel by Frankie Brown that was the basis for *Screaming Mimi*.

LUCKY (2017)

Harry Dean Stanton Cult Rating: *****

John Carroll Lynch, dir.; Logan Sparks, Drago Sumonja, scrs.; Sparks, Sumonja, Steven Behr, Greg Gilreath, Adam Hendricks, pros.; 2.35:1; C; 88 min.; Superlative Films/Divide-Conquer.

"I always thought the one thing we could agree on is what we were lookin' at," the title character says, "but what I see ain't what you see." A finer expression of Post-Modernism—nothing is what it seems, all reality is subjective—does not appear in any previous film. 'Lucky' (Harry Dean Stanton, 1926–2017), a desert rat, lives on the edge of a southwest town. His torn, worn Stetson and omnipresent cowboy boots do not prepare us for a complex personality or existential ideas. A fitting penultimate performance by the acclaimed actor who passed a week before *L.* premiered at a handful of theatres. Only his diehard (in many cases lifelong) followers showed up for this warm-hearted quasi-swan song. Supporting roles here are played by David Lynch (who directed H.D.S. in TV's *Twin Peaks*) and Tom Skerritt, H.D.'s co-star in *Alien*. J.C.L. (1963–), an actor best known for his villainous turns on *American Horror Story*, offers a fine directorial debut with this succession of edgy anecdotes which appear to be random until everything comes together at the end. The final shot is touching, if borrowed from Ingmar Bergman's classic *Wild Strawberries* (1957).

MAD LOVE (1936)

Non-Universal B&W Horror Flick Rating: **** ½

Karl Freund, dir.; Guy Endore, John C. Balderstone, scr.; John W. Considine, pro.; 1.37:1; B&W; 68 min.; MGM.

    For their own foray into thrillers, MGM borrowed the director of Universal's *The Mummy* (1932), Karl Freund (1890–1969). The German emigre brought the same relentless aura of eeriness to this adaptation of Maurice Renard's 1920 novel *The Hands of Orlac*. This version adds Paris' Grand Guignol Theatre of Terrors, later featured in *Interview with the Vampire* 1994). An actress (Frances Drake) nightly performs 'live' as a woman bound and tortured onstage. One customer, 'Dr. Gogol' (Peter Lorre, (1904–1964 here making his U.S. premiere), becomes obsessed with her erotic image. In a macabre variation on the Pygmalion/Galatea myth, he fashions (then worships) a life-like statue. When her pianist husband (Colin Clive, aka 'Henry Frankenstein') loses his hands in an accident, Gogol grafts on those of an executed killer. After seeing this film, Charlie Chaplin insisted the greatest screen actor was not himself but P.L. Photographed in a shimmering black and white style by Gregg Toland (1904–1948), who would shoot *Wuthering Heights* (1939), *The Grapes of Wrath* (1941), and *Citizen Kane* (1941). The final film directed by K.F., who later developed the three-camera setup for shooting TV's *I Love Lucy* (1951–1957).

MAD MAX (1979)

Aussie action cult Rating: **** 1/2

George Miller, dir.; Miller, James McCausland, scr.; Byron Kennedy, pro.; 2.35:1; C; 93 min. (director's cut), 88 min. (original theatrical release);

Kennedy Miller Productions.

A successful Australian doctor, movie buff Miller (1945–) secretly dreamed of becoming a director. As the legend goes, he came home one night, depressed after dealing with victims of motorcycle accidents. For escapism, Miller watched two favorite films back to back on VHS: the

THE LITTLE FILM THAT SPAWNED A BIG FRANCHISE: Squeeze *Hondo* (1953) starring John Wayne together with the B budget *A Boy and His Dog* and you'd get *Mad Max*, the most successful film series ever developed in Australia.

John Wayne Western *Hondo* (1953) and a low-budget dystopian-future indie, *A Boy and His Dog*. Miller then set to work on a script that set the hero of the former into the latter's setting, borrowing one of those real-life bikes. G.M. raised $300,000 to finance the low-budget project. In *M.M.*, Australia's last functioning policeman (Mel Gibson, 1956–) attempts to keep civilization alive by taking on a biker gang modelled on Lee Marvin's in another Miller fav, *The Wild One*. The Aussie auteur hired a gang (The Vigilantes) to play themselves, paying them with all the beer they could drink. The final cut was so shockingly violent, many countries refused to allow bookings. In the U.S., every distributor turned it down so *M.M.* was released as an AIP exploitation item for Drive-Ins. Box office success ($10 million on the international market) initiated a whole new genre of futuristic action flicks set on rural back roads including the hit sequel *Road Warrior* (1981).

MAGICAL MYSTERY TOUR (1967)

Surreal Cinema Rating: NO STARS

Mainstream Beatles' Fan Rating: NO STARS

Music Rating: *****

Beatles Completist Rating: *****

John Lennon, Paul McCartney, George Harrison, 'Ringo Starr' (aka, Richard Starkey, dir., scr., prod.; 1.33:1 ; C; 52 min., BBC Prods./New Line Cinema.

    On the evening of Dec. 26, 1967 ('Boxing Day' in England), the vast majority of English citizens turned their tellies to the BBC. Everyone was eager to catch the premiere of the initial film directed by those four collaborators who had, only a few years earlier, taken their nation and then the world by storm. The Fab Four re-invented music, heralded The Brit Invasion of America, and starred in two commercially and critically hit films for Richard Lester, *A Hard Day's Night* (1964) and *Help!* (1965). Their intent here: as a bus tours ended, spontaneously make a movie that opens as a relatively realistic road trip flick, becoming more surreal (homages to Fellini to Kubrick included) as a means of sharing how crazy things

BEATLEMANIA BOMB: Despite the critical and box-office successes of *A Hard Day's Night* (1964), *Help!* (1965), *Yellow Submarine* (1967), the Fab Four hit rock bottom with this Vanity project acceptable only to hardcore aficionados and Liverputian completists.

had become by the bitter end. The public's (and reviewers') hatred for this mess, self-serving rather than self-revealing, proved so extreme Paul McCartney publicly apologized. In 1974, New Line Cinema revived the piece for a U.S. theatrical showing. Mostly *M.M.T.* played as a midnight cult movie on college campuses.

MAITRESSE (1978)

S&M Cult Rating, 1978: *****

S&M Cult Rating, The Present: NO STARS

Barbet Schroeder, dir.; Schroeder, Paul Voumjargol, scr.; Pierre Andrieux, pro.; 1.66:1; C; 112 mins. (director's cut), 107 (original international print).

A DIFFERENT SORT OF LOVE STORY: Gerard Depardieu and Bulle Ogier star in Barbet Schroeder's purposefully anti-erotic comedy-drama.

Time has not been kind to this onetime shocking cult item from France, the first to present (in a non-exploitive manner) a female dominatrix (Bulle Ogier, 1939–) performing her 'acts' on a boyfriend (Gerard Depardieu, 1948–) as well as numerous clients. The ambition? Set all clichés about 'such people' aside, resulting in an intelligent film despite the graphicness. An arthouse item, *M.* was supposed to humanize those who work in the sex trade by focusing on their everyday lives, not so different from most people's. Were the lead actors less dull, that might have worked. In our current century, when it is not unheard of for respectable female hosts of TV talk shows to wear black leather boots, the sight of a seamy blonde in such legwear has considerably less impact. Maybe the film is a victim of its own success? A single saving grace for modern viewers: masterful cinematography by a then-young Nestor Almendros (1930–1992), who would emerge as a master at his craft with *Days of Heaven* (1978) and *Sophie's Choice* (1982).

MANCHURIAN CANDIDATE, THE (1962)

Hollywood's Most Daring Film Up to That Time: *****

John Frankenheimer, dir.; George Axelrod, scr.; Frankenheimer, Axelrod, scr.; Frankenheimer, Axelrod, pro.; 1.75:1; B&W; 126 min.; United Artists.

Shortly after the assassination of Pres. Kennedy in Nov. 1963, two films—both starring Frank Sinatra (1915–1998), close friend of JFK until a nasty break shortly before that day in Dallas—were pulled from circulation. In *Suddenly,* the star portrayed a presidential assassin. Here, his character tries to halt the killing of presidential candidate by a sniper (Laurence Harvey, 1928–1973). The longer these movies remained unavailable, the more intense their cult fascination became. This innovative interpretation of Richard Condon's paranoid 1959 novel reveals Old Hollywood's desire to create a new form of challenging narrative in tune

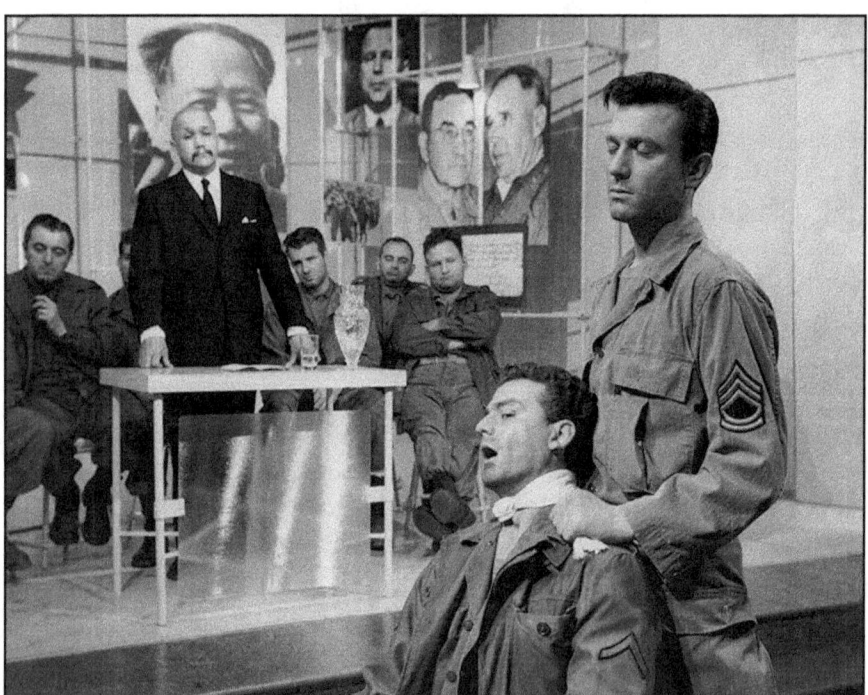

THE REBIRTH OF HOLLYWOOD CINEMA: Laurence Harvey as a captured serviceman brainwashed by the Red Chinese into doing their bidding; with this unique (and in its time oddball) film, a more mature and disturbing sort of Hollywood paradigm was born in the early 1960s.

with the transforming times at a new decade's cusp. Several images are surreal: brainwashing during the Korean War; Angela Lansbury (1925–), purposefully over-the-top as a dominating mother more frightening than any of Hitch's; blonde Leslie Parrish transformed into the Queen of Hearts card; Henry Silva (1928–) offering an early screen presentation of martial arts. A right wing-whacko politician is supported by The Reds if he will allow the communists to overtake us. J.F. went on to film the realistic-political thriller *Seven Days in May* (1964).

MANDINGO (1975)

Historical drama Rating: ** ½

Crazy Cult Film Rating: *****

Richard Fleischer, dir.; Norman Wexler, scr.; C; 1.85: 1: 127 min.; Paramount.
    Case study in how a forbidden book became a mainstream movie: *Mandingo* (1957) by Kyle Onstott sold over five million copies, most in paperback. Eisenhower-era suburbanites would not admit to having read such pulp-trash, a lurid soap-opera about the pre-war south focusing on a wealthy, degenerate white family and their interrelationships, including sexual, with slaves. During Production Code days, this was impossible for Hollywood to film. Nearly two decades later, it was a natural for the old Hollywood hand De Laurentiis, attempting to contemporize his product. In several cities, *Mandingo* was the first film to be booked simultaneously in downtown/urban houses where black exploitation flicks played as well as the then-new mall Megaplexes for suburbanites. Box-office was huge in each, thanks to sex (Anglo Sue George, 1933- , seduces former boxer Ken Norton, 1943–2013) and violence (Norton boiled alive by master Perry King (1948–). The great James Mason delivers a quirky performance a Southern fried patriarch. Mainstream reviews wrote this off as the worst sort of R rated garbage. Yet some academic critics see in it an anti-racist statement by director Fleischer (1916–2006). Tarantino has hailed *M.* as the first true merger of Golden Age studio craftsmanship with lowbrow grind-house mentality.

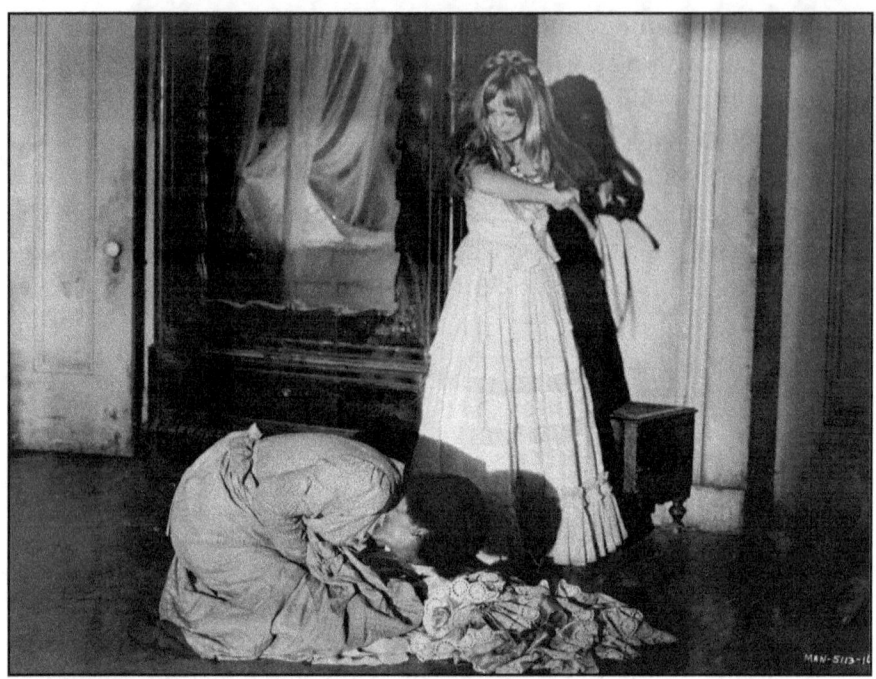

DEPRAVITY IN THE DEEP SOUTH: Plantation mistress Sue George gets her jollies by humiliating slave and husband's mistress Brenda Sykes in the surprise hit *Mandingo*.

MANDY (2018)

Love it or Leave It: Love It Rating: *****

Love It or Leave It: Leave It Rating: NO STARS

Panos Cosmatos, dir.; Cosmatos, Aaron Stewart Ahn, Chris Kelly, scr.; Elijah Wood, Daniel Noah, Martin Metz, pro.; 16:9HD; C; 121 min.; Spectravision.

    Imagine cult auteurs Rob Zombie, Andrei Tarkovsky, and Dario Argento collaborating on a genre-busting, anti-narrative film with Sam Peckinpah and Luis Bunuel watching over the process from above (or gazing up from down below?) The result might resemble this spectacularly great or disastrously awful piece of Extreme Cinema so intense that it will prove 'too much' for most fans. Nicolas Cage (1964–) plays a tender-tough lumberjack who convinces a throwback to a hippie princess (ethereal Andrea Riseborough, 1981–) to join him in an Edenic green world where they achieve a separate peace. An attack force of long-hair bikers resembling the wild ones in *Werewolves on Wheels* (1971) come roaring up and kidnap the girl, setting off a gory vendetta waged with axes, chainsaws, and a crossbow. Possibly a combination of satire and homage to Quentin Tarantino's re-mountings of 1970s Drive In classics. Marvel World references provided by comic book fanatic Cage. "Panaflare" stylistics achieved by the auteur (1974; son of George Pan Cosmatos of *Rambo II* fame) by intensely directing light into the lens of an old-fashioned Panavision Anamorphic camera to achieve what P.C. describes as a "milky" image.

MANHUNTER (1986)

Michael Mann Cultists: **** ½

Hannibal Lecter Cultists: **** ½

Cannibal Cinema Cultists: ****

Michael Mann, dir.; Mann, scr.; Richard Roth, pro.; 2.35:1; C; 120 min.; original theatrical release, 124 min.; (director's cut); De Laurentiis Entertainment.

    It takes a thief to catch a thief. That line takes on a dark new meaning in this oppressive thriller by Chicago-born M.M. (1943–). Originally to have been titled 'Red Demon' after the 1981 Thomas Harris novel, a serial killer coldly murders families in what appear random home break-ins. The agent (William Petersen) out to catch The Tooth Fairy must revisit Dr. Hannibal Lecktor, whom he put away, accepting this man-eater as mentor. Brian Cox (1946–) was chosen over better-known possibilities (Bruce Dern, John Lithgow) to play the role for which Anthony Hopkins (1937–) would win an Oscar in *Silence of the Lambs* (1991). (There, the character's name is spelled 'Lecter.') Some Harris aficionados insist Cox's low-key performance comes far closer to the 'true' H.L. Hopkins returned to the role in a 2002 remake of this film, *Red Drgon*. Dragging cannibalism from the grindhouse and into mainstream theatres, *M.* popularized the term 'Profiler' (a cop who can become at one with a killer's thought processes). Mann's jolting approach to visual storytelling, honed on his *Miami Vice* (1984–1989) TV series, combines the existential Ennui of Antonioni with the streetwise surrealism of Scorsese.

MAN SOM HATAR KVINNOR, aka MEN WHO HATE WOMEN (2009)

Cult Thriller Rating: *****

Niels Adren Oplev, dir.; Nikolaj Arcel, Rasmus Helsterberg, scrs.; Soren Staermore, pro.; 2.35:1; C; 186 min. (ultimate/ collector's cut), 180 (director's cut), 152 min. (original theatrical release); Zdf Enterprises/ Yellow Bird.

When Hollywood undertakes a remake of a highly praised foreign film, the results are often disastrous. That was *not* the case with David Fincher's excellent redux of *The Girl with the Dragon Tattoo* (2011) starring Rooney Mara as a radical, anti-social motorcycle riding computer hacker hired by a reclusive family scion to solve a forty year old mystery. A box-office hit, the film offered proof positive that the 21st century mainstream could stomach (literally!) a work so horrific that it made *Silence of the Lambs* seem tame. *T.G.W.T.D.T.* all but eclipsed the equally superb (some say superior) original from Swedish filmmakers in tune with the Bergman-esque frigid atmosphere of novelist Stieg Larrson (1954–2004). His trilogy furthered an ever-expanding intrusion of what were once considered forbidden themes into the public consciousness. 'Lisbeth' is here played by Salander Nooni who vividly projects melancholia as to her life experiences. The tough but vulnerable girl is sucked into a demi-monde of political/philosophic nihilsm born of bitterness due to our corrupt world.

MAN WHO FELL TO EARTH, THE (1974)

Bowie cultist Rating: *****

Roeg cultist Rating: ** ½

Sci-Fi aficionado Rating: *

Nicholas Roeg, dir.; Paul Mayersberg, scr.; Michael Deeley Barry Spikings, prod.; 2.35;1; C; 139 min.; British Lion/ Cinema 5.

Drawing from a dramatic ploy dating back at least to the sci-fi classic *This Island Earth* (1955), here is the umpteenth variation on the "my planet is dying" theme. 'Thomas Jerome Newton' (David Bowie, 1947–2016) glides down to earth in hopes of acquiring water for his draught-ridden Dune-like world but falls in love with a goofy earth-girl (Candy Clark). The Ziggy Stardust performer claims to have ingested 10 grams of cocaine a day to make it through the shoot because he had no idea what Roeg's (1928–2018) movie was supposed to be about. Cult-worthy celebs who also appear include Rip Torn, Buck Henry, doomed Playboy favorite Claudia Jennings, and Terry Southern. The film makes mincemeat out of the first-class sci-fi novel by Walter (S.) Tevis (1928–1984), whose literary output includes *The Hustler*. Mayersberg had previously written a dreadful 1972 screenplay adapted from Herman Hesse's theological novel *Siddhartha* (1951). Unrelentingly pretentious, unconvincingly hallucinogenic, unpleasantly sexual, self-consciously artsy.

MAN WHO KILLED DON QUIXOTE, THE (2018)

Gilliam Completist Rating: **** ½

Terry Gilliam, dir.; Gilliam, Tony Grisoni, scr.; Amy Gilliam, Gerardo Herrero, Marlela Besuievsky, prod.; 2.35:1; C/B&W; 132 min.; Alacran Pictures/Tomasol Films.

For nearly three decades, T.G. (1940–) attempted to bring his dream projection to fruition: a film based on Cervantes' *Don Quixote* (1605) in which an elderly Spaniard reads one too many tales of bygone knighthood, then sets out to kill dragons and save maidens. Sadly, he only encounters creaky windmills and street whores. Frustrated at every turn (not unlike that now legendary hero), Gilliam at last managed to complete what some have referred to as his autobiographical exorcism in hopes of finally maybe putting the great artistic obsession behind him. An idealistic aspiring-auteur (Adam Driver) returns, as a now-cynical 'creator' of crass commercials, to a spot in Spain where he previously filmed a student-project Quixote film. His current assignment is to shoot an advertisement which employs Cervantes' character in a totally exploitive manner. Then he discovers a humble cobbler (Jonathan Pryce) whom he cast as Quixote, now a local madman, believing he is that would-be knight errant—echoing of course D.Q.'s delusion. Perhaps, though, if you truly believe you are Quixote, you become him—even as that iconic hero 'became' what hoped to incarnate, a knight? A mighty (if often uneven) work of personal expression from the genius filmmaker, as well as a meditation on the idea of what movies mean to those who make them. The documentary *Lost in La Mancha* (2002) chronicles an earlier failed attempt to shoot this film.

MARRIAGE STORY (2019)

Baumbach auteurist Rating: *****

Mainstream/Cult Rating: *****

Noah Baumbach, dir.; Baumbach, scr.; Baumbach, David Heyman, pro.; 1.66:1; C 137 min.; Heyday Films/Netfix.

    Until recently, any motion-picture that cost nearly $19 mill but brought in less than $3 mill at the box-office would be written off as a major commercial failure. But with *M.S.*, this indie is considered a financial as well as critical success—thanks to an emergent and revolutionary release syndrome that may well dominate films during the 2020s. Screenings at key film festivals (Toronto included) created great word of mouth as did a purposefully limited theatrical run. Most viewers, though, discovered this incisive, honest portrait of a divorce, accompanied by a desperate attempt to maintain the essence of 'family,' on Netflix via streaming. A relationship (Adam Driver and Scarlett Johansson are husband and wife) is studied in such minute detail that a vivid sense of realism is consistently conveyed, causing an audience to react as if these truly were 'people' rather than 'characters.' Yet the distinct phases of any break-up are so effectively suggested that the impact is universal: Everyone who has ever survived, or even feared, such an abrupt ending followed by a new beginning will be able to relate. No holds barred in this 'three-handkerchief-weepie' updated for the 21st century, though *M.S.* is hardly devoid of humorous moments. Brooklyn's N.B. (1969–) fulfills the promise of his earlier *Kicking and Screaming* (1995) and *The Squid and the Whale* (2005).

MARNIE (1964)

Conventional Drama Review: **

Hitchcock auteurist review: *****

Alfred Hitchcock, dir.; Jay Presson Allen, scr.; Hitchcock, pro.; 1.85:1; C; 130 min.; Universal.

    Hitch (1890–1980) purchased rights to Winston Graham's novel with the hope of luring Grace Kelly out of retirement. The citizenry of Monaco did not take well to the idea of their princess playing a frigid compulsive thief. Model Tippi Hedren (1930–), her only previous acting credit *The Birds* a year earlier, assumed the demanding role of the blonde emotionally scarred by a violent childhood sexual encounter. At some point in production an explosion occurred between star and director. Rumor has it that Hitch made a rejected pass, the two barely speaking afterwards. The final result is a cold, hard-edged film which critics despised and viewers did not take to. Sean Connery is surprisingly uninvolving as the seemingly sane man Marnie marries but does not sleep with, he her surrogate psychiatrist—until we learn the husband secretly hopes to catch his virginal wife stealing from him, then rape her. Feminists took this as an allegory for spousal abuse by controlling males. To this day, the most divisive Hitch film.

MASK, THE (1994)

Early Jim Carrey Rating: **** ½

Charles Russell, dir.; Michael Fallon, Mark Verheiden, Mike Webb, scr.; Russell, Robert Engelman, pros.; 1.85:1; C; 101 mion. (theatrical release), 114 min. (director's cut); New Line/Dark Horse.

    From the moment Canada's Jim Carrey (1962–) appeared on TV's *In Living Color* (1990), the star in embryo amassed a sizable cult following. Often cast in lowbrow comedies (*Dumb and Dumber*, 1994), J.C. here broke through as an agile rubber-faced talent. This is the old Superman concept as MGM's outlandish cartoonist Tex Avery (1908–1980) might have presented it. Mild-mannered 'Stanley Tokis' transforms into a cool green man (drawing on Gallic mythology) in a banana-yellow 1940s suit after donning a Loki mask. This allows him to pursue a mysterious blonde: Cameron Diaz (1962–), making her debut, achieving immediate stardom. State of the art digital effects allow the already pliable Carrey to become one surreal anthropomorphic animal after another, including Avery's legendary whistling Wolf.

MASHERA DE DEMONIO, LA, aka *BLACK SUNDAY* (1960)

Italian Horror Breakthrough Film Rating: *****

Mario Bava, dir.; Bava, Ennio De Concini, Mario Serandrei, scr.; Massimo de Rita, pro.; 1.66:1; B&W; 87 min.; Galatea/ A.I.P.

In addition to churning out their own low-budget horror films during the 1950s, the original head-honchos at A.I.P.—Lou Rosoff, Samuel Z. Arkoff, James H. Nicholson—perused recent imports for possible U.S. distribution. The three flipped when while watching this Italian-thriller, excitedly agreeing that it represented the tip of a cinematic iceberg for stylish shlock cinema. Mario Bava (1914–1980), son of an early cinematographer in Rome's budding movie industry, followed in his father's foot-steps. And did double duty here, opting for a light-and-shadow approach, drawn from chiaroscuro in the graphic arts, to create an unrelenting atmosphere of creepily erotic death introduced in the prologue: A witch/vampire (Barbara Steele, 1937–) is tortured (in bondage), then buried. A later incarnation of that femme fatale returns to wreak havoc on descendants of the perpetrators. Masters of Italian horror such as Dario Argento and Lucio Fulci insist this movie provided their inspiration. So impressed were the A.I.P. executives that they invited the British-born "skull under the skin" beauty to star opposite Vincent Price in their adaptation of Poe's *The Pit and the Pendulum* (1961). B.S. went on to make some 50 similar (if lesser) films, also cast by Federico Fellini as one of the women in 8 ½. *Black Sunday* is based on an Nicolay Gogol story.

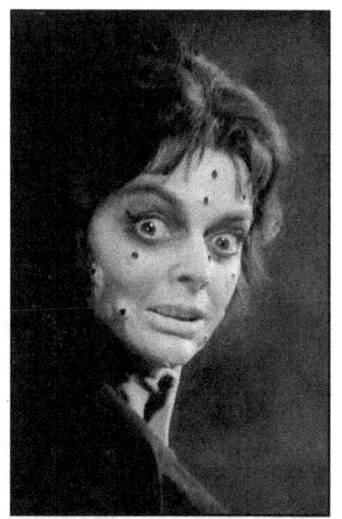

THE MANY MASKS OF HORROR: Barbara Steele emerges from an Iron Maiden almost intact in Mario Bava's first Italian thriller; the cult of Karloff found Boris even creepier than usual in a screen version of one of Sax Rohmer's now politically incorrect potboilers.

MASK OF FU-MANCHU, THE (1932)

Retro Yellow Terror Rating: ****

Politically Correct Rating: MINUS FIVE STARS

Charles Brabin, Charles Vidor, dirs..; John Willard, Irene Kuhn, Edgar Allan Woolf, scr.; 1.31:1; B&W; 68 min.; Cosmpolitan/MGM.

"Kill the white man and take his woman!" When Boris Karloff (as evil Asian 'zDr. Fu Manchu') shouts these orders, he speaks of his own helpless captives. Anglos in the audience grasped a far more disturbing implication: F.M. symbolized the Yellow Peril so many in the west feared would conquer the world. Such prejudice, remarkably vocal in the early 20th century, was fed by author Sax Rohmer (1883- 1959), whose pulp fictions were intended to spark an already smoldering racism. This is the best-remembered among movie versions, thanks in part to B.K. following his monstrous turn in *Frankenstein* with a villain not unlike 'Ming the Merciless' in *Flash Gordon*. There, Buster Crabbe played the all-American boy who opposes monstrous Charles Middleton. Here 'Sir Denis Nayland Smith' (Lewis Stone) embodies the Brit gentleman dedicated to defending King, Crown, and 'Colonies' (the long-since freed U.S.). Scene-stealer Myrna Loy (1905–1993) plays the doctor's daughter 'Fan Lo See,' who craves the body of a young Anglo. While slaves whip the bound fellow, she whirls about in orgiastic delight, experiencing pleasure in his pain. With the initiation of the Production Code, this lurid sado-masochistic sequence was excised. The unexpurgated version became a prime Midnight Movie.

MEAN GIRLS (2004)

High School Expose Rating: **** ½

Mark Walters, dir.; Tina Fey, scr.; Lorne Michaels, prod.; 1.85:1; C; 97 min.; Paramount/M.G. Films.

Every generation has its own cult movie about the horrors of High School, where Darwin's Theory of Evolution is proven over again every day: Survival of the fittest as cliques of 'in' crowders cannibalize the nerdy masses. *Rebel Without a Cause, Fast Times at Ridgmont High*, and *Dazed and Confused* had to make way for a new companion owing to this smart social satire. Based on the book *Queen Bess and the Wannabes* (2002) by recent high school grad Rosaline Wiseman, *M.G.* offered a knowing glance at the then-current variation on spoiled brats who turn everyone's 'happy days' into hell on earth. Lindsay Lohan (1986–), fresh from her brief Disney princess stardom but before her self-inflicted descent into junk movies, is The New Girl. 'Cady' must choose between hanging out with a goth she admires (Lizzie Caplan as 'Janis Ian,' the name borrowed from a sad-faced 1960s singer/songwriter), and 'Regina' (Rachel McAdams), superfi-

THE SHORT, SAD SUPERSTARDOM OF LINDSAY LOHAN: From Disney child star to teen queen, the charismatic actress found her best role in this smart, sexy study of contemporary youth.

cial leader of the pretty Plastics. Lorne Michaels (1944–) of *Saturday Night Live* served as producer. Tina Fey (1970–), one of his most lauded alums, penned a screenplay that maintains a difficult balance between realism and caricature. Surprisingly sexy, considering the P.C. climate at the time.

MELANCHOLIA (2011)

Rating for Devout Depressants/Melancholics: *****

Rating for People Not Contemplating Suicide: NO STARS

Lars von Trier, dir.; von Trier, scr.; Louise Vesth, Foldager Sorenson, pro.; 2.35:1; C; 135 min.; Zentropa Ent.

Near the opening of this, the most depressing film ever made, we watch as the world ends not with a bang, or a whimper, but a deafening blast of silence worse than either possibility that had been proposed by T.S. Eliot. The focus is on a pair of sisters, the older a loving mother (Charlotte Gainsbourg, 1971–), desperately concerned for her vulnerable son, and her sibling (Kirsten Dunst, 1982–) a deep, sad, complex loner not certain whether she should submit to a loveless upper-crust wedding. An immense rogue object inexorably moves ever closer to our small planet. V.T. (1956–) makes maximum use of his camera's ability to swing about, cinema verite style, to the point of maddening viewers. He opts for minimalism in everything else, including dialogue spoken in whispers, much of it inaudible. Lengthy discussions are exhaustingly banal; individual shots, visionary. Tier's great theme is the horror of loneliness. It might be argued that *M.* ends on a slightly hopeful note as three formerly isolated characters hold hands, becoming a community at the last possible moment. Equally describable as 'must see' for avid cineastes who accept the quietly horrific concept, unwatchable for most everybody else. Cult favorites John Hurt, Kiefer Sutherland, and Charlotte Rampling also appear.

MEMENTO (2000)

Christopher Nolan Cult Rating: **** 1/2

Christopher Nolan, dir.; Nolan, scr.; Jennifer and Suzanne Todd, pro.; 2.39:1; C/B&Q; 113 min.; Newmarket.

Leonard (Guy Pearce, 1967– ; of *L.A. Confidential*, 1997) is on a relentless search for whoever killed the former insurance investigator's wife (Jorja Fox). He drives a Jaguar and has plenty of money but there's a stumbling block. L. suffers from a rare but real form of amnesia, known in medical circles as "anterograde": short term memory loss makes it impossible to recall anything from fifteen minutes ago. Nolan (1970–) confounds matters further by having his story-sequences run backward. Though other films employ this approach, none do so as effectively as *M.*, in part owing to C.N.'s decision to shoot certain sequences in color, others in black and white. Though this may cause further confusion for viewers on an initial screening, in retrospect (and after many revisits) the decision as to which is employed at any moment remains consistent with the narrative's meaning. Terrific scene-stealing performances by Carrie-

SHORT TERM MEMORY: Guy Pearce had one of his earliest and greatest roles in Christopher Nolan's genre-busting semi-surreal Neo Noir.

Ann Moss (1967–), Trinity in *The Matrix* films, as a mystery woman; and character actor Joe Pantoliano (1951–) playing a corrupt cop. From a short-story by Nolan's younger brother Jonathan (1976–).

MENG LONG GUO JANG, aka *WAY OF THE DRAGON, THE* (1972)

Asian Martial Arts Rating: ****

Bruce Lee Cult Rating: *****

Bruce Lee, dir.; Lee, scr.; Lee, Raymond Chew, pros.; 2.35;1; C; 113 min. (director's cut), 110 min. (U.S. theatrical), 86 min. (1edited for TV print); Concorde/Golden Harvest.

Casual fans of Bruce Lee (1940–1973) remember him best for *Enter the Dragon* (1973), Hollywood's big-budget showcase for the martial arts master. Dedicated followers prefer this less grandiose piece, B.L.'s initial

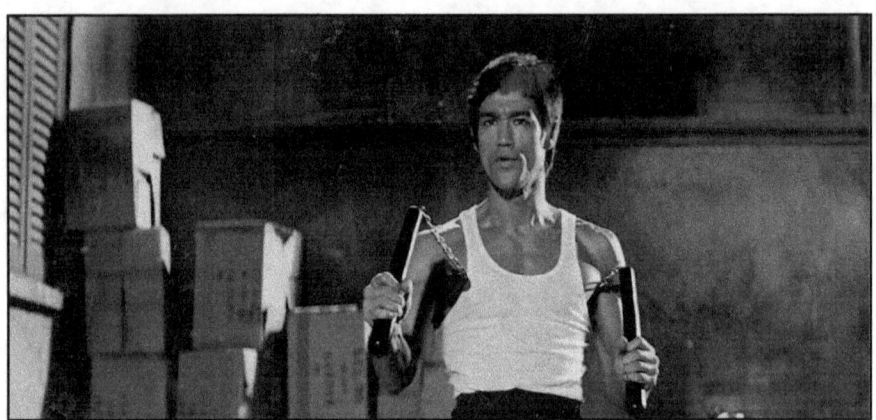

THE UNCHALLENGED KING OF KUNG FU: No one else ever came close (and likely no one ever will) to unseating Bruce Lee as the master of the form.

opus as total filmmaker, his own most loved among a handful of staring vehicles. Lee plays The Dragon, traveling from China to Rome to defend relatives who own an Asian restaurant coveted by the Mafia. In an intriguing twist, Sicilians mobsters hire Japanese hitmen to eliminate Lee. The film is little more than an elongated prologue to the set-piece with which it concludes: A duel to the death between Lee and his greatest opponent, U.S. karate champ Chuck Norris (1940–). Their combat in the Coliseum (which lasts fifteen minutes onscreen and took 50 hours to film) plays as choreography of synchronized brutality. One of the first (if not *the* first) film to feature 'nunshucks.'

METROPOLIS (1927/1984)

Sci-Fi Classic Redux Rating: *****

Fritz Lang, dir.; Thea von Harbou, scr.; Erich Pommer, pro.; 1.33:1; B&W; 210 min. (premiere theatrical screening), various others since; 80 min. (1984 Giorgio Moroder version.

As the Golden Age of German cinema reached its end, husband-and-wife team Lang (1890–1976) and von Harbou (1888 -1954) collaborated on the Ufa/Berlin studio's most daring and costly undertaking: an enormous science-fiction project and first-ever dystopian future film. When a singular woman (Brigitte Helm, 1906–1996) attempts to restore humanity

THE SHAPE OF THINGS TO COME: As the Master of our Futureworld listens to a mad scientist explain the theory of robots, our world moves from human interaction to a pre-*Blade Runner* Cyborgland.

via a return to Christian values, the city's dictator allows a mad scientist to replace her with a robot—the first such cyborg in movie history. Von Harbou adapted her own 1925 novel. Team members included cinematographer Karl Freund (1890–1969) and visual-design genius Eugen Schufftan (1893–1977), whose 'process' allowed cast members to seemingly inhabit table-top models. While filming, Lang (who was half-Jewish) tried to turn *M.* into a warning against creeping fascism. His wife (though they shortly divorced) set out to create a pro-Hitler movie. He hurried off to England, then America; she joined The Reich. In 1984, musician Giorgio Moroder (1940–), avatar of electronic dance music, oversaw a redux with garish color tints and a score featuring stars Pat Benatar, Adam Ant, and Freddie Mercury. A hit with mid-1980s Youth, this version suffered from Future Shock: In a few years, the international music scene had drastically altered. Now G.M.'s *Metropolis* seemed hopelessly dated owing by his attempt to update the piece for 'today.'

MICKEY ONE (1965)

1960s Arthouse to Mainstream Breakthrough
Rating: *****

Arthur Penn, dir.; Alan Surgal, scr.; Penn, John G. Avildsen, pro.; 1.85:1; B&W; 93; Florin/Tatira/Columbia.

"I'm guilty of not being innocent." Any of Kafka's anti-heroes could claim that. The line is spoken by Warren Beatty (1937–) in *M.O.*. He plays a stand-up comic (apparently based on Lenny Bruce) who goes underground in Chicago after learning there's a mob hit out for him, though he has no idea why. *M.O.* begins as a noir, step by step disengaging from relatively realistic thriller as surreal visions gradually appear and then overpower the work. Influenced by experimental European cinema of that era by Fellini, Bunuel and Godard, among others. Penn had previously stretched the Western's aesthetic boundaries with *The Left-Handed Gun* (1958) starring Paul Newman as Billy the Kid. M.O.'s soundtrack includes musical choices as disparate as Bela Bartok's rhapsodies and improvisational jazz from Stan Getz. An early 1960s attempt to collapse Cinema Verite with Hollywood craftsmanship. Columbia Pictures, flabbergasted at the results, wasn't sure if this should be released to the arthouse or grindhouse circuits. Paved the way for *Bonnie and Clyde* two years later. David Lynch and Martin Scorsese have hailed *Mickey* One as a seminal influence and movie milestone.

MIDSOMMAR (2019)

Ari Aster Cult Rating: *****

Anti-Ari Aster Detractors Cult Rating: NO STARS

Ari Aster, dir.; Aster, scr.; Patrick Andersson, Lara Knudsen, pro.; 2.00:1; C; 171 min. (director's cut); 147 min. (general release print); Square Peg.

At first glance *Midsommar* appears to be shaping up as a modern rendering of the Romantic Movement that can be traced back at least to William Wordsworth (1770–1850). That English poet insisted the world is too much with us. Modern city people ought to abandon the clogged, dirty metropolises that pollute those who live within them. The answer: Go back to Nature, a lovely, free, charming realm in which the sun shines down on endless flowers. There, and there alone, we can achieve splendour in the grass. This is precisely what a New York couple, experiencing problems with their relationship owing to daily pressures of society, hope to do when they set off to visit Harga, an isolated village in rural Sweden. Locals welcome them to their upcoming festival, a celebration of all that is real and true… until the forest turns out to be a jungle. An emotional darkness encompasses the proceedings even though daylight reigns, and we (simultaneous with the leads) realize that, as in that classic *Twilight Zone* episode, the smiling residents truly do want "to serve man." The genius of the piece, for those who can stomach it (not many will be able to do so) comes in allowing us to discover (along with the leads) what is actually going on; sublime happiness and absolute horror are two sides of the same coin. Aster's fans consider this to be art; his detractors see it as empty-headed exploitation so disgusting that not even the lowest grindhouse would agree to show the film that makes *Cannibal Holocaust* resemble a Disney family flick.

MISFITS, THE (1961)

A Budget Contemporary Western Rating: ** ½

Gable/Monroe/Clift Doomed Stars Rating: *****+

John Huston, dir.; Arthur Miller, scr.; Frank E. Taylor, pro.; 1.66:1; B&W; 125 min. (original theatrical cut); U.A.

Though Clark Gable (1901–1960) rates alongside Spencer Tracy, Humphrey Bogart, Cary Grant and John Wayne as one of Golden Age of Hollywood's greatest male stars, he (as an ongoing A list legend) never achieved cult status. Not so his co-stars, Marilyn Monroe (1926–1962) and Montgomery Clift (1920–1966), whose downward spirals were chronicled in *Confidential*. C.G, playing a contemporary cowboy (oddly enough named 'Gay'), stressed himself so for director Huston (1916–1985) while doing the pony round-up sequence that he like M.M. delivered his swan song here. Her character, 'Roslyn Taber,' is a "what if?" portrait of Norma Jean had she *not* become a movie star. Husband Arthur Miller (1915–

LONELY ARE THE LOST: Montgomery Clift and Marilyn Monroe finally paired onscreen in one of each sad star's most memorable vehicles.

2005) wrote the self-indulgent if deeply moving script even as they broke up (Kevin McCarthy impersonates him here). A melancholy, pretentious, unsatisfying, irresistible example of bad cinema on the highest possible level of utter failure. M.M. dazzles in a wordless sequence, dancing up and down the steps of a small middleclass home, ecstatic at the thought that she may finally experience a 'normal' life. Clift embodies his sad latter-day screen image: lonely, mother-dominated, attempting to deny deep, gnawing insecurities through manly action.

MONDO CANE (1962)

Cinematic Curio Rating: ****

Paolo Cavara, Gualtiero Jacopetti, dirs..; Cavara, Jacopetti, scrs.; Angelo Rizzolo, pro.; C; 1.37:1; 108 min., 91 min. (highly edited), Cinerz.

Before the release of this oddity from Italy, most moviegoers considered the documentary a boring cinematic form. Then came the first modern "shockumentary," composed mostly of stock footage combined with several sequences filmed specifically for *M.C.*, aka 'A Dog's Life.' An interconnecting theme between episodes: Despite strides made by civilization, humans remain bestial at heart. Images range from men massaging the rear ends of cattle to a bull locked in a deadly struggle with a matador. Turtles roasting on a radioactive beach appear onscreen long enough to induce nausea; forbidden sexual rituals in the far corners of our world follow. A cinematic encyclopedia of what the critics labelled "sensational," "eccentric," "mind-opening," "sleazy," "hideous," "perverse," and "degenerate." As narrator Stefano Sibaldi states: "Behold. The best of the worst." Did the concept of Camp begin here? And is this what the world hungers for? As reality-TV has proven, the frightening answer is 'yes!'

MONSIEUR VERDOUX (1947)

Postwar Paranoia Rating: *****

Charles Chaplin, dir.; Chaplin, Orson Welles, scr.; Chaplin, pro.; B&W; 1.37:1; 124 min., United Artists.

The onetime cockeyed-optimist Chaplin (1889–1977) hisses the most cynical indictment of society at large at film's end when his character is found guilty of marrying, then cold-bloodedly murdering, a string of unwary women. Facing the guillotine, he bitterly sums

CHARLIE CHAPLIN… SERIAL KILLER? In his darkest days during the period of mistrust that was the McCarthy era, the once optimistic Little Tramp took on the guise of a nihilistic Bluebeard type who marries and murders complacent women.

up memories of the Allies' atomic bombings of Japan: "One murder makes a villain. Millions? A *hero*." (This line is in fact a quotation from Beilby Porteus, 1731–1809). C.C.'s words predate Orson Welles' infamous Ferris Wheel speech a year later in *The Third Man*. Indeed, Welles suggested *M.V.* to C.C. and contributed to the screenplay. An embittered Charlie was even then burdened by two paternity suits and attacks from Joe McCarthy's anti-communist campaign. The Hays/Breen Production Code office refused to grant *M.V.* a "respectable" certificate. Verdoux's excuse for such Bluebeard activities—he did it to feed his 'real' family—raised issues of subjective morality which the public couldn't handle, resulting in a box-office bomb. Chaplin considered this his finest work.

MONTY PYTHON AND THE HOLY GRAIL (1975)

Gilliam/Python Rating: *****

Cult Classic to Cinema Classic Rating: *****

Terry Gilliam, Terry Jones, dirs..; Jones, Gilliam, Graham Chapman, Eric Idle, Michael Palin, scrs.; Mark Forstater, Michael White, prods.; 1.66:1; C; 91 min.; Cinema 5/EMI.

Five British upper-class clowns from Oxford and Cambridge teamed with an American genius (Gilliam, 1942–) to create a comedy troupe that combined elements of the goofy Beatles, the off-the-wall intellectual Marx. Bros, and a sense of the absurd from England's radio reposit of smart zaniness, *The Goon Show*. A BBC series, *Flying Circus* (1969–1974), was followed by film projects including this, their second and most popular. Funded in part by various musicians from Led Zeppelin, Pink Floyd, and Genesis, all appreciative of the team's rock 'n' roll sensibility, *M.P.A.T.H.G.* filtered Arthurian legend through the artistic meat grinder of broad burlesque: Part physical crudeness not un-

GENIUS AT WORK, V: The amazing Terry Gilliam cooks up another cinematic potpourri of intellectualized Brit buffoonery.

like the U.K.'s Benny Hill (or America's Stooges), part brilliant banter of the sort characterized by the Algonquin Round Table from the 1930s. Combining grotesque violence that had become a standard of 1970s drama with dark humor, if played with a paradoxically light touch, this expanded the cult-following that had formed during the *Flying Circus* U.S. run on PBS. An eventual Broadway musical, *Spamelot* (2006), revealed the degree to which their Something To Offend Everyone approach had gone mainstream. As to the members, they believe that this pales in comparison to their later, greater achievement, *The Meaning of Life*. True!

MOONRISE KINGDOM (2012)

Anderson Cult Rating: **** ½

Wes Anderson, dir.; Anderson, Roman Coppola, scr.; Anderson, Jeremy Dawson, Steve Dales, pro.; 1.85: C; 94 min; Ascot Elite.

The premise, as W.A. (1969–) conceived of this piece, was to present a sincere romance between a pair of children in which their emotions are never written off as first love, rather appreciated as young people perceive such an emotional bond: Once and forever commitment. Succeeding, he provided the most masterful variation on this theme since *A Little Romance* (George roy Hill, 1979). Like most of us, W.A. perceives our country's golden age as the era he just missed, in his case the early 1960s, before the JFK assassination shattered American innocence. Sam (Jared Gilman) and Suzy (Kara Hayward) run away from home to live out Thoreau's vision of achieving heightened spirituality by existing close to nature. Always, though, they hope to find a Shangri-La that allows for the film's title: a fountain of youth on a New England island where people can indeed live happily after. Society comes looking for them, threatening to turn the dream into a nightmare. W.A. employs carefully selected colors to suggest an enchanted place where desires, as well as fears, take physical shape. A once in a lifetime cast includes Bruce Willis, Tilda Swinton, Bill Murray, Frances McDormand, and Edward Norton. As Shakespeare said, *life is but a dream…*

MS. 45 (1981)

Feminist Vengeance Flick Rating: *****

Abel Ferrara, dir.; Nicholas (Oliverio) St. John, scr.; Mary Kane, pro.; 1.85:1; C; 80 min.; Navaron Films.

   Imagine *Death Wish* (Michael Winner, 1935-2013) with Charles Bronson as a Dark Knight avenger out to kill the sort of street slime that raped his wife—here reimagined from a radical feminist point of view. A (double) rape victim—Zoe (Lund) Tamerlis, 1962-1999)—silently sets out for a reckoning by walking the mean streets in eroticized garb, shooting any man who shows the slightest hint of aggressiveness. But as she surrenders to madness, other men—including those without such threatening inclinations—may also become targets. Is there validity to a vulnerable modern woman fearing that all those of the opposite gender present a potential threat? This early film by the Bronx's leading cult director (1951-) does not offer simplistic answers to such a question, forcing a viewer to consider these disturbing ideas after watching… and then hopefully discuss the implications with others. As compared to M.W.'s flat, exploitive mainstream manner of filming, A.F. startlingly allows us to comprehend not the current state of "Thana's" deteriorating mind as the piece turns ever more phantasmagoric in its presentation of violence. The haunting young star (a writer, artist, and political activist as well as actress), a heroin addict, died in Paris at age 37.

MULHOLLAND DRIVE (2001)

Lynch Cult Rating: *****

David Lynch, dir.; Lynch, scr.; Neal Edelstein, Tony Krantz, Mary Sweeney, prods.; 1.85:1; C; 147 min.; Les Films Alain Sarde/Universal.

   A horrific car crash occurs on that infamously winding road. What initially resembles a neo-noir then roars off in so many directions that the results unfold as a surrealist's attack on the very concept of story—bringing to the mainstream the old Dali/Bunuel avant-garde belief that at its purest, the art of cinema is more naturally a vehicle for Freudian dream theory than literary narrative. If there is a focus, it's on the relationship between a wide-eyed blonde (Naomi Watts) who arrives in L.A. with that grand dream of becoming a big star, and an older, jaded brunette (Laura Herring) whose torrid past dissipates with a combination of metal, oil, and smoke that propels her into amnesia. Lynch (1946–) teams with composer Angelo Badalamenti to insure sight and sound totally fuse, as such true to the aesthetic of 'the talking picture.' The color scheme for Peter Demling's mesmerizing cinematography recalls those crazed/inspired palettes of Douglas Sirk. Cameos by such cult-worthy stars as Tarantino favorite Robert Forster (1941–2019) and old-time Hollywood headliner Ann Miller (1923–2004) add to an implied critique of Tinseltown rivalling Nathaniel West's novel *The Day of the Locust* (1939). Shot as the pilot for an unrealized *Twin Peaks* type TV series, which explains why *M.D.* doesn't so much 'end' as it simply 'stops.'

MUMMY'S GHOST, THE (1944)

Chaney Jr. Cult Rating: ****

Tom Tyler Cult Rating: ****

Ramsay Ames Cult Rating: *****

Reginald Le Borg, dir.; Griffin Jay, Henry Sucher, Brenda Weisberg, scr.; 1.37:1; B&W; 61 min.; Universal.

The Mummy (Karl Freund, 1932) rates, like *Frankenstein* and *Dracula*, as a genre classic. Sequels were cheaply produced, relying on stock footage from the original (a flashback to the ancient rite of mummification reappears in most). All provide fun on a campy level; one developed a cult. *T.M.G.* concerns a High Priest (George Zucco) who appears to be slightly less Egyptian than, say, Tab Hunter) who journeys to America. There he must locate 'Princess Ananka' (Ramsay Ames, 1919–1988); her lover 'Kharis' (Lon Chaney Jr., 1916–1973) has other ideas. This film's uniqueness stems from intriguing details: 1) rumors abound that top-billed L.C. never appears onscreen, footage of Tom Tyler from 1940's *The Mummy's Hand* reused; 2) every time the Mummy comes in contact with the Princess, her black hair gains another touch of silver (until she recalls Elsa Lanchester in *Bride of Frankenstein*) though no one appears to care; and 3) in an example of

Mad Love to *Mystery Train* • 295

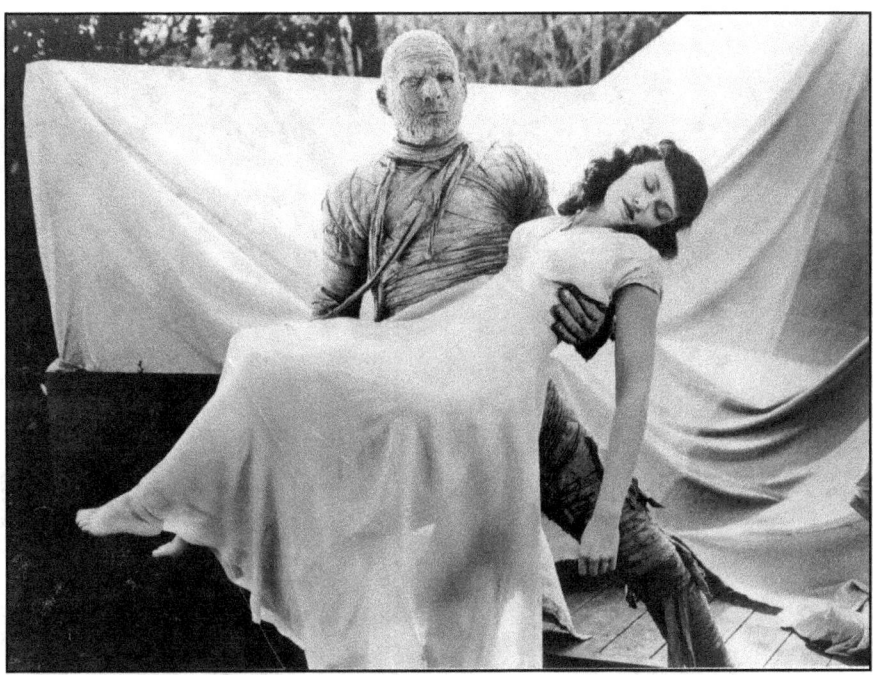

STARRING LON CHANEY JR.... OR MAYBE... NOT? That's either Creighton or Tom Tyler abducting Ramsay Ames, later to play a sweet little ol' lady enjoying her 'morning cup' on TV coffee commercials.

deconstruction based on the denial of audience expectations. When the beast carries the beauty into the swamp, for once the hero does not arrive in time to save her.

MUNCHHAUSEN, aka *ADVENTURES OF BARON MUNCHAUSEN* (1943)

Experimental Cinema Rating: **** ½

Josef von Baky, dir.; Erich Kastner, scr.; Eberhard Schmidt pro.; 1.37:1; C; 134 min. (director's cut), 119 min. (international version; UFA.

    Realizing the tide of WWII had turned against Hitler, Reich Minister of Propaganda Joseph Goebbels had an inspiration: Reach back to charming stories for children by author Rudolf Erich Raspe (1937–1794) in which real life braggart Baron Karl Friedrich von Munchhau-

MODES OF FANTASY: Germany's oft-told folktale of an odball Baron was designed to deliver an anti-Hitler message.

sen (1720–1797) was transformed into a colourful Prussian folk hero, actually living out tall tales he enjoyed spinning. Transform this rich material into a fantasy-spectacle on the level of those then being produced in America (*The Wizard of Oz*, 1939) or England (*The Thief of Bagdad*, 1940), now with an undercurrent of fascist ideology that would rally the citizenry. But the project fell into the hands of UFA's J.F.B. (1902–1966), an anti-Hitler activist. Basky turned the writing over to Erich Kastner (1899–1974), who was Jewish, he assisted by literary light Bertolt Brecht. They devised an elaborate, zany, glitzy fable in which M. (Hans Albers) journeys from Branschweig to the moon by way of Constantinople. He encounters celebrities ranging from Casanova to Catherine the Great, as well as a moon woman's decapitated but talkative head. The implications are anti-Nazi; J.G. and the top brass were apparently too stupid to pick up on that. Highly sexualized; definitely *not* for impressionable kids.

MY DINNER WITH ANDRE (1981)

Creative cinema Rating: *****

Wally Shaun cult Rating: *****

Louis Malle, dir.; Malle, Wallace Shaun, Andre Gregory, scr.; George W. George, Beverly Karp, prods.; 1.66;1: C; 110 min.; Sage Prods.

    A diminutive actor, arriving late, hurries into a restaurant and is seated with his friend, a theatre director. *M.D.W.A.* rates as one of the greatest single-set films ever, and one of the finest shot in 'real-time.' Each character bears the name of the actor playing him. Yet Shaun (1943–) and Gregory (1934–) do not portray themselves, only fictional characters who share the actors' names. The piece appears, on first viewing, spontaneous, organic, improvised. In truth, everything we see and hear was carefully scripted. As the odd couple ramble on about personal demons, social problems, cultural issues and philosophical problems, a viewer alternately conceives of them as brilliant or delusional, enlightened or self-possessed. Gregory portrays an alienated intellectual who has dropped out; Shaun, still eager to rejoin the good fight. Friends claim that in real life they are precisely the opposite. The underrated Malle (1932–1995) is better known for *Lacombe, Lucien* (1974), *Atlantic City* (1980) and *Au Revoir Les Enfants* (1987). They stand tall as his true film classics. This? His cult film.

MY LITTLE CHICKADEE (1940)

1940s Hollywood Edgy Studio Film Rating: *** ½

Edward F. Cline, dir.; Mae West, W.C. Fields, scr.; Lester Cowan, Jack J. Gross, pro.; 1.37:1; B&W; 83 min.; Universal.

    "Is that a gun in your pocket," a playful Mae West (1892–1980) inquires of W. C. Fields (William C. Dunkenfield, 1880–1946) as the knock-kneed plump fellow awkwardly approaches her on a train, "or are you just happy to see me?" That's the best line in the screenplay these two naughty clowns collaborated on, but don't hold your breath waiting to hear it in *M.L.C.* Censors honed in on these irascible humourists (in particular,

WHEN LEGENDS MEET: The most iconoclastic stars of the 1930s finally brought their con artist screen personas together; unfortunately, censors hacked away some of their best mutual gags.

the woman born Mary Jane) more than others among the 1930s madcap iconoclasts. Each represented middle-America's deepest, darkest fears: a wily con-artist, arriving in a 'respectable' village to make mincemeat of marriage, law and order, education, religion, and all other pillars of society. As 'Flower Belle,' M.W. offers an apotheosis of her brash taker of men (other women's husbands included) she honed to perfection in such previous classics as *I'm No Angel* and *She Did Him Wrong* (both 1933). W.C.F. allows us a glimpse of his cynical gentlebums yet to come in *The Bank Dick* (1940) and *Never Give a Sucker an Even Break* (1941). A burlesque of Westerns, as such a forerunner of Mel Brooks *Blazing Saddles* (1974), this isn't half as good as it should be, owing to gags left on the cutting room floor. For cultists of one star or the other (or both), it is but one step short of heaven.

MYSTERY TRAIN (1989)

Jarmusch Cult Rating: *****

Elvis Afficionado Cult Rating: *****

Jim Jarmusch, dir.; Jarmusch, scr.; Jim Stark, pro.; 1.78:1; C; 110 min.; JVC Ent.

Varied people may exist at the same moment in time and in the same city (the same hotel, even) while seeming to inhabit parallel universes… until something as simple as a single pistol shot ties their seemingly unrelated lives together. Here the place is Memphis, captured by cinematographer Robby Mueller as a ghost town on some other world entirely. Those who spend an apparently 'ordinary' day in what ought to be the Jerusalem of Rock 'n' Roll—but, as portrayed in Jarmusch's minimalist piece, is the least inspirational spot on the planet—are so entwined in their own agenda that they barely notice the others who pass by constantly: A dry desk clerk and his stoic young assistant; a pair of Asian teenagers who never get around to paying respect at Graceland (but briefly visit Sun Records Studio); three wild and crazy guys who enter into a film noir-like robbing and killing spree; and two-mismatched women (A European visitor and a street person who briefly become roommates. The film, which travels elliptically in time, apparently inspired by Edward Hopper's legendary painting "Nighthawks"; likewise, Jarmusch's low-key masterpiece appears to have impacted on varied auteurs including as the Coen Brothers (Steve Buscemi appears to be warming up for his *Big Lebowski* role) and Quentin Tarantino (The Ghost of Elvis haunting *Pulp Fiction*). Subtly dazzling.

NAKED KISS, THE (1964)

Shock/Schlock Rating: **** ½

Samuel Fuller, dir.; Fuller, scr.; Fuller, Leon Fromkess, Sam Firks, pros.; 1.85:1; B&W; 90 min.; Allied Artists.

With junk films, production costs were so small that self-expression and taboo themes could only help at the box-office. No one understood this better than Fuller (1912–1991); *T.N.K.* rates as one of his mini-masterpieces. A pre-credit sequence features camerawork unlike anything previously seen in an American movie, if identical to what Godard and The New Wave were experimenting with in Paris: All tripods tossed aside for a Cinema Verite-style movement. A hooker (Constance Towers, 1933–), locked in a brutal fight with her pimp, is revealed to be bald as her wig flies off. When 'Kelly' tries to kick-start her life in a charming New England village, she faces evil beyond anything in her earlier sleazy demi-monde. One kiss from town playboy (Michael Dante) and she instinctually senses that he is a child molester, this the first Hollywood film to deal honestly with that issue, preceded only by Britain's *The Mark* (1961).

NAKED PREY, THE (1965)

Indie Action Flick Rating: **** ½

Cornel Wilde, dir.; Clint Johnson, Don Peters, scr.; Wilde, Sven Persson, prods.; 2.35:1; C; 96 min.; Theodora Prod.

When Hollywood studios began eliminating long-term contracts during the 1960s, most medium-level stars opted for American TV shows or travelled to Europe in search of work. Unique among his contemporaries, Cornel Wilde (1912–1989), onetime Fox headliner, set up his own indie production company. Owing to a fascination with the tale of mountain man John Colter (who in 1808 was captured by the Blackfeet, stripped, and allowed to run for his life), C.W. commissioned a script. But filming in Wyoming would have proven too costly. An African company, eager to lure Hollywood business, made Wilde an offer he could not refuse, explaining the change in time-period and locale. The stunning location work led to a seminal movie in which old-fashioned "adventure" narratives gave way to the first modern "action" film, dialogue and character downplayed in favor of the stark visualized conflict from beginning to end. In Carl Reiner's 1970 dark comedy *Where's Poppa?*, several inner city youths, having seen this, force George Segal to make 'the run' in Central Park.

NAPOLEON DYNAMITE (2004)

One of a Kind Cult Rating: **** ½

Jared Hess, dir.; Hess, Jerusha (Demke) Hess, scr.; Chris Wyatt, Sean Covel, pro.; 1.85:1; C; 92 min. (theatrical cut), 96 min., director's cut); Fox Searchlight/Paramount.

The Horrors of High School Hell, Gen-X variation on the theme. A small-town in rural Idaho surrounds the title character (Jon Hedder, 1977–), a slacker-era nerd who maintains his sanity by living in an alternative world of medieval myth. Finally, he decides to re-enter the real world by helping his only pal—Aaron Ruell (1976–) as 'Kip,' a fish-out-of-water Mexican kid who may be less accepted even than Napoleon—win the upcoming high school election over the most spoiled among the gorgeous Mean Girls, 'Summer' (Haylie Duff, 1985). Among the film's many plusses: a low-key sardonic sense of humor rather than the broad burlesque of, say, *Fast Times at Ridgmont High*; a knowing eye toward the substance-less style of late 1980s/ early 1990s youth that recalls the acclaimed *Welcome to the Doll House*; and perceptive comedy based on the occurrence of chat rooms, leading to obsessive behaviour by all too many out of work young adults. The combination adds up to a definitive statement. Consider *N.P.* the Time Capsule movie for its unique period.

NATIONAL LAMPOON'S ANIMAL HOUSE (1978)

Gross-out SNL Comedy Rating: *****

Politically Correct Film Rating: NO STARS

John Landis, dir.; Harold Ramis, Douglas Kenney, Chris Miller, scr.; Ivan Reitman, Matty Simmons, pro.; 1.85:1; C; 109 min.; Universal.

In its original conception, this was to have been the initial *Saturday Night Live* (which premiered three years earlier on TV) movie with Chevy Chase as cool guy 'Otter,' Dan Aykroyd as biker 'D-Day,' Bill Murray the nearly-normal 'Boone,' and John Belushi playing goofball 'Bluto.' Only J.B. (1949–1982) appeared: Tim Matheson, Bruce McGill, and Peter Riegert filled in the other parts. The great surprise occurred when this 'risky' little film proved to be a box-office phenomenon. Wicked satires on straight society (*Caddyshack*, 1980) and slob comedies about wild teens (*Meatballs*, 1979) were 'in.' By the late 1970s, elements of the 1960s Counterculture had been absorbed into a New Normal. People watched this endlessly on Home Video and Pay Cable. But if things change, they always change again. With the advent of political correctness, many sequences came to seem less funny than offensive: the seduction of an under-age girl; an African American roadhouse; Bluto's 'male gaze' into the sorority dorm; the killing of a horse among them. Though the above-mentioned sequences are still included, another has been excised: The Deltas fire a weapon at the Homecoming Parade and the huge bullet passes through a float resembling JFK's head. The moment is gone but not forgotten.

NEAR DARK (1987)

Rural Vampire/Outlaw Flick Rating: **** ½

Kathryn Bigelow, dir.; Bigelow, Eric Red, scr.; Charles-Stanley Jaffe, pro.; 1.85:1; C; 94 min.; Joint Venture.

An ever-extending legion of fans appreciate that in her second directorial effort (the first was The Loveless, 1981, starring Willem Dafoe), her first as a solo artist, K.B. (1951–) revealed a Lynch-like ability to en-

WAS JESSE JAMES A WILD WEST VAMPIRE? Long before her Oscar win, Kathryn Bigelow directed this cross-genre cult classic starring Adrian Pasdar and Jenny Wright.

vision living dreams that seemingly occur in an alternative earth. Here she, and co-scripter Red (who wrote *The Hitcher*, 1986) combined four distinct genres: The Road Movie, the Vampire Film, the Biker Flick, and the Western. Late one night, a cowboy (Adrian Pasdar, 1965–) meets a mysterious stranger (Jenny Wright, 1962–). Seemingly, they enjoy a one-night stand. Next day, he suffers from an AIDs-like disease. The girl's cohorts have less in common with traditional vampires than film images of Quantrill's Raiders during the Civil War; the leader (Lance Henriksen, 1940–) is enticingly named Jesse. An electronic-synth musical score by Germany's Tangerine Dream adds an aura of weird sensuality. The human and vampire lovers (this long before the *Twilight* franchise) are a believable pair of sympathetic marginal teenagers. Though Wright found few other films worthy of her melancholic beauty (she resembles a Poe-heroine come to life), this remains her legacy film. Bigelow would be the first woman to win the Best Director Oscar for *The Hurt Locker* (2008). Two warnings: a) avoid the 84 min. cut as you would the plague; b) be prepared even with the full-length film for a disappointing cop-out ending.

NEME-YE NAZDIK, aka *CLOSE-UP* (1990)

Documentary Rating: *****

Anti-documentary Rating: *****

Abbas Kiarostami, dir.; scr.; 1.37:1; C/B&W; 98 min.; Kanun Parvaresh Fekr; Kanun Parvaresh.

Director 'Mohsen Makhmalbaf' approaches an upper-middle class Tehran home, requesting to film a documentary. Thrilled, they speak openly about all aspects of their life. Problem: their guest is not whom he claims to be, rather an utter unknown, Hossain Sabzian (1957–). During the trial, filmed by A.K. (1940–2016), the accused insists he has not committed a crime as he never wished to financially defraud these innocent dupes, only wondering what it might be like to feel important for once. A.K then persuaded those involved to re-enact earlier incidents for the first half of his own film. But are the principles are non-actors recreating what actually occurred, or performers essaying roles based on their own identities, as set down by A.K. in his carefully designed (therefore, artistic and in a sense fictive) script? Should we refer to *C.U.* as a documentary, a docu-drama, a dramatized documentary or a creative work with strong ties to reality? No music appears as this might diminish the illusion of 'truth,' whatever this may be. Indeed, this is *C.U.*'s theme: Even the most realistic movies are only illusions. As such, dangerous since they are not what they purport to be, though we are inclined to believe them… even as we do this.

NEVERENDING STORY, THE (1984)

Family film Rating: *****

Cult Cinema Rating: *****

Wolfgang Petersen, dir.: Petersen, Herman Weigel, scr.; Bernd Eichinger, Dreta Geissler, prods.; 2.35:1; C; 94 min. (release print), 102 min. (director's cut); Bavaria Studios.

    In our modern world, a bullied boy (Barrett Oliver, 1973–) takes refuge in a strange book about a mythic child (Noah Hathaway, 1971–) attempting to keep the magical realm of Fantasia from being overcome by Nothing-ness. A West German production, *T.N.S.* was shot in English to insure distribution in the U.S. The most expensive film produced in that country since *Metropolis* (adjusted for inflation). Appealing creatures are hand-made puppets, the case with *The Dark Crystal*, (1982), Legend (1985) and *Labyrinth* 1986), previous to the popularity of C.G. F/X. A companion piece to *The Princess Bride*, *T.N.S.* combines a contemporary coming-of-age tale with philosophic fantasy. Despite critical accolades and commercial success, novelist Michael Ende (1929–1995) disliked the results and sued to have his name removed. For those who were young during the 1980s *T.N.S.* ties Spielberg's *E.T.* (1982) as the era's greatest fantasy film. A 1990 sequel by George Miller, covering the book's second half, disappointed fans/cultists.

NIGHTMARE ALLEY (1947)

Realistic Horror Rating: **** 1/2

Edmund Goulding, dir.; Jules Furthman, scr.; George Jessel, pro.; 1.37:1; B&W; 110 min.; 20th Century Fox.

    Long before the term *Geek* became synonymous with nerdy teen-age boys, it hinted at the sleaziest backwater carnivals touring the Deep South. In such an act, an alcoholic would in exchange for whiskey bite off and sometimes swallow the head of a living chicken. William Lindsay Gresham (1909–1981) had dared write a novel about the descent of a normal man to such a low state. His point: There but for the grace of God

The Naked Kiss to *The Nutty Professor* • 307

THE DARK SIDE OF THE SCREEN: Each Hollywood noir took mainstream viewers on a walk on the wild side, often into strange corners of the Deep South that suburbanites know little of: The A budget *Nightmare Alley* visited the seediest of backwoods circuses; the low-rent *Thunder Alley* allowed 'respectable' people to peer into the lifestyle of mountain moonshiners.

goes you or I. While studio boss Darryl F. Zanuck was distracted, producer George Jessel (1898–1981, better known as a stand-up comic, slipped this into production. Goulding (1891–1959) included graphic scenes of an actual geek practicing his profession. When Fox's boss-man saw the finished film he feared this might ruin the career of box-office star Tyrone Power, embarrassing Fox as *Freaks* had MGM. Zanuck cut the most offensive sequences before mainstream release. Later, he locked the negative in his vault. Illegal prints ran as midnight movies for decade continue the search. Remade (as a mainstream movie!) in 2020.

NIGHTMARE ON ELM STREET, A (1984)

Craven Cult Rating: *****

Wes Craven, dir.; Craven, scr.; Robert Shaye, pro.; 1.85:1; C; 91 mins. (theatrical release), 101 min. (director's cut); New Line Cinema/Smart Egg Prods.

Of all the post-Halloween slasher flicks, *A.N.O.E.S.* rates as the most important and influential. Craven (1939–2015), a former English prof. at Clarkson Univ., brought his in-depth studies of "primal fears" (universal to all human cultures) and knowledge of Shakespeare, *Hamlet* specifically ("this sleep of death"), to the re-imagined horror genre geared to the Youth audience. Heather Langenkamp (1964–) plays a variation on the Virgin as Survivor initiated by Carpenter with Jamie Lee Curtis in *Halloween*. Here, the killer is less a mindless murder machine than a Loki-like "trickster" from mythology, exuding glib humor via one-liners. Referencing Rod Serling's *The Twilight Zone,* he enters into dreams of sleeping people. As 'Fred(dy) Kreuger," Robert Englund (1947–) sports a Fedora as well as a red and green sweater, the colors associated with evil in Western culture. Future star Johnny Depp (1963–) made his feature premiere while John Saxon (1935–2020), veteran of movies ranging from A productions to Z quickies, identifies the piece with the nouveau thriller: movies about movies and the knowledge of pop culture a hip/knowing audience boasts. Devotees note that Charles Belardinelli, who did the F/X, plays F.K. in one scene.

NIGHT OF THE HUNTER, THE (1955)

All Time Cult Classic Rating: ***** +

Charles Laughton, dir.; James Agee, scr.; Paul Gregory, pro.; 1.66:1; B&W; 92 min.; United Artists.

When negative reviews poured in and few showed up at theatres, U.A.—desperate to market this serial killer noir—sent it out on the Kiddie matinee circuit. Eventually, *T.N.O.T.H.* became a cult fav for young adults still suffering bad dreams from their initial viewing. Children (Billy Chapin, Sally Jane Bruce) in rural Depression-era Appalachia realize stepfather 'Harry Powell' (Robert Mitchum, 1917–1997), is a murderer. A faux preacher, he married their mother (Shelly Winters, 1920–2006) in hopes of discovering money the late husband/father (Peter Graves, (1926–2010) stole. With 'l-o-v-e' tattooed on the fingers of his right hand, 'h-a-t-e' on the left, Powell pursues the children across a sometimes realistic, alternately surreal landscape. Actor C.L. (1899–1962) had never directed a film. He and cinematographer Stanley Cortez (1908–1997) present the horror as if this were a Grimm fairy-tale set in 1930s America. The great Lillian Gish (1893–1993) plays an elderly lady who, armed with goodness and a shotgun, takes on Mitchum's iconic portrait of evil. Based on a 1953 cult novel by Davis Grubb (1919–1980), who drew his narrative from America's Jack the Ripper Herman Drenth, aka 'Harry Potter' (1892–1932).

NIGHT OF THE LIVING DEAD (1968)

Zombie Cannibal Rating: *****

George A. Romero, dir.; Romero, John (A.) Russo, scr.; Karl Hardman, Rusell Streiner, prods.; 1.37:1; B&W; 96 min.; Image Ten/Walter Reade Organization.

In the long history of *Reader's Digest*, most mainstream of all conventional American publications, only once did the editors feel the need to warn readers away from a new film for fear it might incite mass cannibalism. Soon, a sea change in popular culture derived from *N.O.T.L.D.* and its unexpected popularity. Likely, *R.D.*'s dire prophecy ironically resulted

THE DEAD WALK AT DAWN: George Romero's independently produced horror item caught on nationally and changed the face of zombie cinema forever.

in publicity that caused an exploitation flick shot for about $100,000 to bring in more than $30 million at the box-office. Shot near Pitsburgh PA, here's a chilling Drive In flick about a Zombie Apocalypse, though the creatures are never referred to as that. They chase 'Barbra' (Judith O'Dea) from a cemetery where she visits her mother's grave to an abandoned farmhouse. She and an African American (as a result of Duane Jones' casting; in the script, 'Ben' was not so identified) attempt to survive this long night's journey into day. The sight of monsters consuming parts of our human anatomy, previously portrayed in such little-seen flicks as *Blood Feast*, became a sensation with the new audience then emerging. When this creepy masterpiece was picked by the National Film Registry as an early choice for movies worthy of preservation owing to social significance and artistic worth, the days when such accolades were reserved for works of conventional Good Taste came crashing to an end.

NIGHT TIDE (1961)

Thriller appeal: ****

Dennis Hopper Cult Appeal: **** ½

Curtis Harrington, dir.; Harrington, scr. Aram Kantarian, pro.; 1.66:1; B&W; 85 min; Phoenix Films/A.I.P.

On leave a lonely, sensitive sailor (Dennis Hopper, 1936–2010) wanders to a nearly deserted amusement pier where he meets a lovely brunette (Linda Lawson, 1936–). Shortly, he learns that she plays a mermaid in an attraction; her previous boy friends have all died horribly. The premise was 'borrowed' from Edgar Allan Poe's eerie romance "Annabel Lee" (1849). The youth's obsession with becoming her next victim recalls the "desire for the fall" theme in Hitchcock. Shot in and around Venice Beach and the Santa Monica Pier during off-season on a budget of under $25,000, resulting in a suitably seedy tone. D.H., who earlier appeared with friend James Dean in *Rebel without a Cause* and *Giant*, had been blacklisted by The Majors as too difficult to work with. Unreleased for two years until A.I.P. circulated this on the Drive In circuit, hyped as the sort of shallow thriller that director Harrington (1926–2007) hoped to avoid. C.H.'s autobiography was titled *Nice Guys Don't Work in Hollywood!*

NOTHING BUT THE TRUTH (2008)

Political thriller Rating: *****

Kate Beckinsale Fan Rating: *****

Rod Lurie Cult Auteur Rating: *****

Rod Lurie, dir./scr.; Marc Frydman, prod.; 2.35;1; C; 108 min.; Battleplan Prods.

The story of the year, 2005: journalist Judith Miller was sent to prison after refusing to name the source for a leak that outed Valerie Plame as a secretive CIA operative. Producers scrambled to greenlight a movie or TV project. Israeli-born indie filmmaker Lurie (1962–) got there first with the most: competitors took a 'why bother?' approach once his definitive variation on the theme premiered. Then on the eve of *N.B.T.T.* opening theatrically, its distributor went belly-up. That left this potential classic of the political thriller genre with exposure only to those who searched it out on home video. Kate Beckinsale (1973–) and Vera Farmiga (1973–) deliver their finest performances to date as reporter and prey. This is a fictional work inspired by the event, *not* a simple roman-a-clef. Additionally *N.B.T.T.* rates as one of the great feminist films, not in the didactic sense (this is anything but a message movie), rather owing to a male's artist's ability to grasp specific values women share with one another even when on other sides of a legal issue. Character motivations are probed in a way no longer common. The ending is one of those special 'how did I not see this coming?' turnabouts.

NOT OF THIS EARTH (1988)

Traci Lords 'Legal' Film Rating: *** ½

Jim Wynorski, dir.; Wynorski, R.J. Robertson, scrs.; Wynorski, Roger Corman, Murray Miller, prod.; 1.78:1; C; 81 min.; Miracle Pictures.

Legendary quickie moviemaking auteur J.W. (1950–) bet R.C. he could shoot a remake of the latter's 1957 sci-fi exploitation flick in twelve days. Eleven and a half days later, at a budget slightly over $200,000, Wynorski delivered the goods. Action and F/X bits (particularly during the title sequence) are lifted directly from earlier, bigger R.C. films, notably *Battle Beyond the Star*s (1980). What made this tale of a vampire alien a hit? The casting of Traci Lords (1968–) as a nurse. A veteran of between 80 and 100 hardcore flicks, the woman born Nora Louise Kuzman in Ohio had been underage in all but the last, *I Love You Traci* (1987). Therefore, anyone who watched her videos might be arrested. As Traci agreed to do two memorable nude scenes here (her final ones), this became a collectable. Lords went on to work regularly in theatrical and TV projects, most notably John Waters' *Cry-Baby* (1990) starring Johnny Depp.

NUTTY PROFESSOR, THE (1963)

Jerry Lewis Cultists: *****

Stella Stevens Cultists: *****

Jerry Lewis, dir.; Lewis, Bill Richmond, scr.; Ernest P. Glucksman, pro.; 1.85:1; C; 107 min.; Paramount.

JERK A GO GO!: Jerry Lewis in his most memorable role.

During the early 1950s, Martin and Lewis dominated the silver screen as the era's A-list comedy team, 'Dino' a suave singer and shallow playboy, Jerry ((Jerome Joseph Levitin, 1926–2017) his pathetic nerd/spastic foil. When the duo broke up in 1956, media reports disclosed that Lewis despised (and maybe envied) everything about D.M.'s debonair persona. Some Lewis friends believed that deep down, the reason for Jerry's antipathy had to do with his secretly wishing he had been born Dean Martin. That wish (if true) provided this film's premise: a goofy/ brainy college Prof devises a Dr. Jekyll drink that turns him into Mr. Hyde: 'Buddy Love,' a cynical, seductive crooner. Here was a Martin and Lewis opus with Jerry playing both parts. Buddy's songs (including 'Old Black Magic') were famous Dino standards. Most impressive: Stella Stevens (Estelle Caro Eggleston, 1938–), who shared not only Marilyn Monroe's measurements (36–24-36) but also that star's natural comedic gifts.

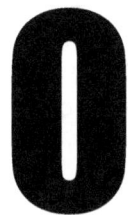

OFFICE SPACE (1999)

Judge Aficionados Rating: *****

Mike Judge, dir.; Judge, scr.; Judge, David Rappaport, Michael Rotenberg, pros.; 1.85:1; 89 min.; 20th Century Fox.

    Before M.J. (1962–) hit the big time with aimed-at-adults animated series like *Bevis and Butt-Head* (1993 -2011) and *King of the Hill* (1997–2010), he labored in a lifestyle known as The White Collar Cubicle: identical offices of companies that manufacture high-tech items, any potential for creativity on the part of employees crippled by a stifling sameness. In *O.S.*, Ron Livingston, Ajay Naidu, and David Herman ferment a palace rebellion against their sadistic czar. The villain steals the show: watching Gary Cole (1956–) as 'Livingston' is akin to getting to see Kevin Bacon impersonate Hitler. A box-office dud, *O.S.* become one of the best-selling videos of the following decade, also a huge hit on cable, inspiring weekly watchings by isolated groups of fans. Judge transcended the software situation by making a movie that spoke to anyone who had ever worked in *any* office, even if the company did not possess that Holy Grails of office equipment, a red stapler.

OLDBOY (2003)

Asian Bizarro Cult Rating: *****

Chan-woo Park, dir.; Park, Nobua Minegish, Garon Tsuchiya, scr.; Syd Lim, Dong-Joo Kim, pro.; C; 2.35:1; 120 min.; Egg Films.

    Drawing from a popular Manga by Minegish and Tsuchiya, Park—(1963–), most renown among South Korean directors—wove this weird tale of an ordinary businessman (Dae-su Oh) drawn into a web of deception and despair. At a bar, the hapless fellow passes out, waking to discover he's been imprisoned in a single room. Released fifteen years later, he sets out to discover who did this and why. *O.* is the middle-work of Park's trilogy on revenge as the darkest human instinct. Like Greek tragedians, Park implies rather than shows violence. The incomprehensible 'world' recalls George Orwell, Lewis Carroll, and Franz Kafka. An outlandish color-scheme references Sirk's *Written on the Wind*. Here is what 20th century Parisian Antonin Artaud (1896–1948) called 'theatre of cruelty': Not a visual depiction of torture so much as a perverse desire to emotionally assault the audience from beginning to end.

ONCE UPON A TIME… IN HOLLYWOOD (2019)

Tarantino Fan Rating: **** ½

Quentin Tarantino, dir.; Tarantino, scr.; Tarantino, David Heyman, pro.; 2.39:1; C; 161 min.; Columbia.

Rumors abound that this will be the last film directed (though not written or produced) by Q.T. Whether that proves true or not, it's difficult to imagine any further extension of his Geek Cinema vision that totally altered movies beginning in the early 1990s. Set in Hollywood and its vicinities even as the Old Studios curl up and die in those transitional times, shortly before *Easy Rider*'s release, an ensemble cast appears in seemingly disparate though ultimately interlocking stories. A fast-fading star (Leonardo DiCaprio) and his stunt double pal (Brad Pitt), apparently modelled on Burt Reynolds and Hal Needham, realize they have hit the barrel's bottom if all that's currently offered is an overseas spaghetti Western. On the verge of stardom, Sharon Tate (Margot Robbie) spends time by hangin' out with weirdos while her husband Roman Polanski is overseas. Charles Manson's deadly hippies plan on killing some of the slick straights. And various superstars (Steve McQueen, Bruce Lee) strut their stuff even as the has-beens, wannabes, and assorted low-lives wander about, each invisibly cocooned in his own personal failure. Smart/perceptive dialogue, violence which exceeds that in Asian action flicks, in-gags which only the most dedicated film buffs will get, presented in a manner posited by the French New Wave's Jean-Luc Godard: "Every film must have a beginning, a middle, and an end—though not necessarily in that order." Like watching an updated remake of Nathaniel West's *Day of the Locust* as directed by Russ Meyer in a *Faster, Pussycat: Kill! Kill!* manner.

ONCE UPON A TIME IN THE WEST (1968)

Ultimate Spaghetti Western Cult Rating: *****

Sergio Leone, dir.; Leone, Bernardo Bertolucci, Sergio Donati, Dario Argento, scr.; Fulvio Morsella, pro. 2.35:1; C; 145 min. (U.S. theatrical), 137 min. (1970 recut); 164 min. (present U.S. version); Refran Cinematografica/Paramount.

    When Leone's (1929–1989) superb spaghetti Westerns *A Fistful of Dollars* (1964), *For A Few Dollars More* (1965), and *The Good, the Bad, and the Ugly* (1966) were released in the U.S. (mostly to Drive-Ins and Grindhouses) in 1965, 1966, and 1968, each proved more commercially successful than the last. In 1969, *O.U.A.T.I.T.W.* was booked into classy theatres where it opened to empty houses. The American mainstream was not (in the pre-Tarantino years) yet ready for edgy sexual violence, couldn't grasp why Clint Eastwood wasn't in it, and didn't get the self-consciously oddball title. Internationally, this was a block-buster, in Paris playing to packed houses at a theatre for two years. When ABC TV began broad-casting *O.U.A.T.I.T.W.* annually on the Sunday following Thanksgiving in the early 1970s, a cult formed around what may be the greatest Western ever made, with its rare combination of spoof and homage. The opening railroad sequence references *High Noon* (1952) and *Johnny Guitar*. This lengthy movie contains images drawn from at least 100 Hollywood oaters, here played with a surreal eye and a sardonic tone. Charles Bronson (1921- 2003) as the loner 'Harmonica' had earlier turned down *The Man With No Name* role. The hauntingly langorous music of Ennio Morricone (1928–2020) parallels Leone's 'pure cinema' (telling the story with his camera while relying as little as possible on dialogue). Leone travelled to America's southwest for a shot of Monument Valley in honor of John Ford's influence on his work. S.L.'s only film to feature a woman (Claudia Cardinale, 1938- ; as 'Jill') in the

ONCE UPON A TIME AT THE MOVIES: Italy's Sergio Leone drew on childhood memories of such Hollywood classics as *High Noon* (1952) and *Johnny Guitar* for his widescreen dream-images of a mythic west and gangster-noir movies like *The Roaring Twenties* and *I Walk Alone* as references in his New York City crime epic.

lead. Henry Fonda (1905–1982) best known for his good guy roles in Westerns (Wyatt Earp in Ford's *My Darling Clementine*, 1946) portrays villainous 'Frank,' deconstructing audience expectations. Note though that he did play Frank (brother of Jesse) James in two Fox Westerns. Woody Strode, Jack Elam, Keenan Wynn, and Lionel Stander add to the cult appeal.

ONCE UPON A TIME IN AMERICA (1984)
Cult Gangster Film Rating: *****

Sergio Leone, dir.; Leone, Leonardo Benvenuti, Stuart Kaminsky, many others, scr; Arnon Milchan, pro; 1.85:1; C; 139 min. (original theatrical print), 229 min. (extended version), 250 min (director's cut), The Ladd Company/Warner Bros.

    What *The Godfather* (1972) was to mainstream crime films, this would be to cultish variations on the same theme. Leone employed Harry Grey's entertaining if minor Bus Station Book *The Hoods* as the basis for a mighty epic that cuts through time and space to tell the tale of a single phone call that may, at the finale, be answered. A gang of criminals, particularly the most sensitive among them (Robert De Niro) and his crass, ambitious pal (James Woods) share a love-hate relationship that lasts for close to half a century. Their earlier years in downtown New York's mean streets recalls James Cagney and Humphrey Bogart in Raoul Walsh's *The Roaring Twenties* (1939); the postwar cynicism that leads to betrayal of the worst sort recalls Byron Haskin's notable noir *I Walk Alone* (1947). Dozens (hundreds) of other gritty flicks are referenced along the way. Tragically, distributor Warner Bros. did not have faith in the piece and cut it down to 2 ½ hrs, set in chronological time. Despite Leone's genius as a visual storyteller, the results were mediocre. Was this all he had been up to? No, not by a long shot. First on VHS, then DVD, ever longer prints allowed Leone cultists and gangster film fans to appreciate the mighty work that also features cult queen Tuesday Weld, performing rare semi-nude scenes. James Russo, Danny Aiello, and the radiant Elizabeth McGovern (in a role that almost went to Brooke Shields) all shine. A masterwork… at least, the second (and third) time around.

ODISHON, aka *AUDITION* (1999)
Off the All Asian Cult Movie Rating: *****

Takashi Miike, Daisuke Tengan, scr.; Satoshi Fukushima, Akema Suyama, prods.; 1.85:1; C; 113 (edited version), 115 (director's cut); Basara/Omega.

    A middle-aged, financially successful businessman wishes to remarry but his shyness makes it difficult to meet women. He and a movie producer friend arrange for girls to "audition" via a faux movie while trying out for his possible second wife. "Words create lies," Ashama (Eihi Shiina) whispers to a helpless victim (Ryo Ishioashi) she is about to torture with long, thin needles. "Pain can be trusted!" Here is the film that brought Miike (1960–) to international attention. Deceptively realistic during its early moments, O. grows ever darker and more paranoid as a romance seemingly develops with what appears to be the perfect woman, a mysterious dream girl. What occurs next could be described as a combination of key motifs from *Vertigo* (1958), *Abres Los Obos*, *Repulsion*, and *Saw*. Not as graphically violent as many of Miike's later movies, most notably *Ishi the Killer* and the 'Dead or Alive' trilogy (1999, 2000, 2002); in its own quiet, oblique manner, every bit as harrowing and by the end horrifying. A towering example of what cultists refer to as 'Extreme Cinema.' The ambiguous ending is prefaced by a key line of dialogue: "The mirror is not big enough for both of us." From an Asian cult novel by Ryu Murakami.

ONLY LOVERS LEFT ALIVE (2013)

Anti-Generic-Vampire-Movie Rating: *****

Jim Jarmusch, dir.; Jarmusch, Marion Bessay, scr.; Reinhard Brundia, Jeremy Thomas, pro.; 1.85:1; C; 123 min. RPC/Pandora.

When is a Vampire movie not a vampire movie? When the piece breaks most essential rules of that genre while subtly satirizing the few that are contained. It's difficult to believe J.J. took so long to get around to portraying the Un-dead in one of his screen oddities, considering that his one Western was called *Dead Man*. The situation here may momentarily remind lovers of succubus cinema of Tony Scott's *The Hunger* (1983). Not that the Jarmusch film contains any of the chillingly chic aspects of that trendy Manhattan macabre-melodrama filled with wildly sexual violent sequences. J.J. is as much a master of the "nothing happens" school of cinema as Anton Chekhov was to live theatre. It's all about character, character, character: Namely Tilda Swinton and Tom Huddleston as melancholic romantics who once opted for eternal life but now detest the ever more dystopian world they inhabit. Playwright Christopher Marlowe (John Hurt) is as essential to this work of profound if indecipherable self-expression as William Blake had been to the earlier Johnny Depp vehicle. The characters names, Adam and Eve, do not refer to the Old Testament but a little-known Mark Twain story. The indie production was shot on the inexpensive Digital form called Art Alexa.

OUTLAW, THE (1943)

Cult Western Rating: *** ½

Jane Russell Cult Rating: *****

Low Camp Rating: ****

Howard Hughes Cultist Rating: *****

Howard Hawks Cult Rating: *

Howard Hughes, Howard Hawks, dirs..; Jules Furthman, scr.; Hughes, pro.; 1.37:1; B&W; 116 min.; RKO.

"HOW'D YOU LIKE TO 'TUSSLE' WITH RUSSELL?": The one and only Howard Hughes 'sold' his adult-oriented Western on sex appeal alone, the first film of this previously conventional genre to be so presented to a startled public.

"How'd you like to tussle with Russell?" That less than subtle come-on line dominated the advertising for what serious-minded writer Furthman (1888–1966) had intended as a re-investigation into the supposed death of outlaw William H. Bonney, aka Billy the Kid, at the hands of Sheriff Pat Garrett in New Mexico, 7/14/1881). Perhaps Hawks (1896–1977), who would later make such classics as *Red River* (1948), was thinking along these lines when he agreed to co-direct. Neither counted on endless problems with producer Hughes (1905–1976), who perceived this as a showcase for his latest 'discovery': Jane Russell (1921–2011), first of the big-breasted female stars. Genius cinematographers Gregg Toland and Lucien Ballard were told to keep their camera-eyes on her chest rather than the gorgeous scenery. In his debut as 'The Kid,' Texas-born Jack Buetel (1917–1989) appears lost and confused. Hughes and Hawks did agree on one thing: adding a hint of homosexual jealousy to the mix between the three male leads. A rape scene in which Billy forces himself on 'Rio,' causing her to stop hating him and fall in love, kept what was supposed to have been a 1941 release locked in a vault for two years. Victor Young's derivative musical score is among the most embarrassingly over-romantic in Hollywood history. Viewers can't determine whether this was meant to be funny. Intriguing, as the noted humourist Ben Hecht did add edgy lines to the script.

PANDORA'S BOX (1929)

Jack the Ripper Rating: *****

Georg Wilhelm Pabst, scr.; Ladislaus Vajda, scr.; 1.33:1; B&W; 133 min. (director's cut), 131 min. (original release print); Nero-Film AG.
Even as The Roaring Twenties drew to a close, German director Pabst (1885–1967) outlined this cautionary fable attacking the recently trendy promiscuity. Though young Marlene Dietrich hungered for the part, Pabst insisted on American actress Louise Brooks (1906–1985). She, like 'Bernice' in an F. Scott Fitzgerald short story, dared to bob her hair! As 'Lulu', L.B. seduces a father and his son, destroying both, then moves on to more conquests. Her life takes a downward spiral; at the end, she realizes the latest man invited into her boudoir is Jack the Ripper. A case study of a film having the opposite effect of the author's intentions: Females in the audience adopted Lulu as a role model, mimicking her garish eye make-up. The film containing this "icon of modernity" (as one critic described L.B.) is masterfully cinematic. Few title cards were necessary as the camera conveys all we need to know. We literally 'see' not only what characters see but also what they think and feel. Brooks, symbol of worldliness, was born and raised in the small town of Cherryville KS!. Most aficionados of serial killer cinema consider this the single greatest example of that morally questionable genre.

PAN'S LABYRINTH (2006)

Del Toro Cult Rating: *****

Guillermo de Toro, dir.; de Toro, scr.; de Toro, Alfonso Cuaron, Bertha Navarro, pros.; 1.85:1; C; 118 min. (director's cut), 112 min. (edited international version); Estudios Picasso.

"A political fable in the guise of a fairy-tale," A.O. Scott of the *Times* wrote, "or maybe it's the other way around?" That phrasing precisely captures the magic of de Toro's (1964–) personal work. In 1944, 'Ofelia' (Ivana Baquero, 1994–)—a child on the verge of womanhood—lives near a Spanish forest with her mother and step-father, a vicious fascist officer. Sensing the ugliness of the Nazi-dominated world around her, Ofelia slips into the woods, entering a labyrinth where she encounters a Faun (Doug Jones, the only American involved with the project). The land beyond recalls Wonderland, Oz, and Narnia while suggesting a bizarre mythic alternative kingdom like no other in CineFantastique history. Recalls legendary tales by the Brothers Grimm and hellish paintings by Francis Bacon (1561–1626). Here the Pale Man barely bothers to hide his lustful hunger for this 'princess.' Co-produced by Cuaron (1961–), who would direct the sci-fi classic *Gravity* (2013). An uproar occurred as parents, mistakenly assuming this would be a family-friendly Disney-like work, expressed outrage when (after bringing their kids to see this) they slipped into culture shock owing to the adult allegory's dark Freudian elements.

PARAPLUIES DER CHERBOURG, LES, aka *UMBRELLAS OF CHERBOURG, THE* (1964)

Revolutionary Cinema Musical Rating: *****

Jacques Demy, dir.; Demy, scr.; Mag Bodard, Gilbert de Goldsmidt, Pierre Lazareff, pro.; 1.66:1: C; 91 min.; Parc Film/Madeleine.

    The whole world fell in love with *La La Land* (2016), Damien Chazelle's musical drama with comedy. Only the most devoted of Cineastes could name the classic that served as inspiration. J.D. (1931–1990) studied art at university, then worked with animator Paul Grimault during Demy's apprenticeship in movies. At this point he became taken with the ability to manipulate tones and hues in a cartoon as compared to films shot in the real world. As this was long before CGI effects, he dreamed of painting the small French town where this bittersweet love story takes place so that ever-changing emotions of characters are always reflected in the setting's visuals. Likewise, the score by Lalo Schifrin (1932–) does not merely provide backdrop but carries the story, as every word is sung. Catherine Deneuve (1943–) emerges as a Gallic Grace Kelly, lighting up the screen. J.D. borrows from French impressionist paintings for pastel moments, then cuts to Gene Kelly style bright lights even as the world surrounding these lovers (Nino Castelnuovo is the guy) shifts with the currents of time. Premiered in U.S. in 1964 and, unlike many other imports, continued to grow in popularity during the following decade.

PARIS, TEXAS (1984)

Rating: **** ½

Wim Wenders, dir.; L.M. Kit Carson, Sam Shephard, scr.; Don guest, Anatol Daumon, pro.; 1.78;1; C; 145 min.; Argos.

A man wanders out from the desert and into the arms of his brother, who attempts to make sense of why the individualistic sibling finally came home—and why *now*? That's the premise of John Ford's *The Searchers* (1956), one of the best Western ever made; also, Wenders' (1945–) *P.T.*, in the minds of many cineastes the finest film to come out of the German New Wave that commenced in the 1970s. This is the modern world, or at least a slightly off-kilter approximation of it. 'Travis' (1926–2017), unlike John Wayne's 'Ethan Edwards,' has no idea where he has been. His brother 'Walt' (Dean Stockwell, 1936–) does sense they must search (again, the remarkable influence of Ford's masterpiece) for his long lost wife (Natassja Kinski). The sort of movie which the term 'character study' was invented to describe. One critic called it an 'anti -romance.' W.W.'s theme, here and elsewhere: We can only know who we are in the present if we learn what we did in the past, however horrible, and resolve ourselves to the people whom we betrayed, intentionally or not. One of only two films to star best friends Stanton and Stockwell; the other is *Midnight Blue* (1997) written especially for them by the author of this book.

PEEPING TOM (1960)

Serial Killer Cult Rating: *****

Michael Powell, dir.; Leo Marx, scr.; Albert Fennell, pro.; 1.66:1; C; 101 min.; The Archers.

Even as Hitchcock's *Psycho* appeared on American movie screens, *P.T.* premiered in England. Simultaneously, these films spawned an upcoming tidal wave of violence in popular culture. Serial killer 'Mark Lewis' (Carl Boehm) puts 'Norman Bates' to shame with his ingenious manner of murdering women. Mark offers to photograph girls but, as he moves in for the close-up, extends a hidden knife from within his camera's tripod. In a nightmare scenario of what feminists refer to as The Male Gaze, he records their deaths while employing a mirror, thereby forcing each victim to witness her own murder. The British public and press reacted with outrage: This "dangerous," "perverted," "vulgar," "sick," "deeply disturbing" movie was repressed for a decade. Observers now beg the question: Is *P.T.* the most horrifically voyeuristic exploitation film of all time, or a perceptive study *of* this syndrome—as such a true (if harrowing) work of art? Powell (1905–1990), whose masterpieces include the great dance musical *The Red Shoes*, 1948), looked deep into his own troubled soul while creating this garish 'entertainment.' His career never fully recovered from the ensuing scandal.

PEE-WEE'S BIG ADVENTURE (1985)

Paul Reubens Cult Rating: *****

Tim Burton Cult Rating: ****

Tim Burton, dir.; Paul Reubens, Phil Hartman, Michael Varhol, scr.; Robert Shapiro, Richard Gilbert (Abramson), pros.; 1.37:1; C; 91; Aspen/W.B.

Growing up in Sarasota FL, Paul Reubens (1952–) ran away to visit the Ringling circus as often as the small, skinny child could. After moving to L.A. to try and break into Show Biz, he joined the legendary Groundlings improv group. Collaborating with *SNL*'s Phil Hartman (1948–1998),

HIGH FLYIN' PEE WEE: Thanks to the directorial talents of Tim Burton, Paul Reubens managed a successful leap from Saturday morning TV celebrity to movie star.

Reubens created a comedy script about an alter-ego, 'Pee-Wee Herman': an optimistic variation on that 98-lb. weakling who suffered sand tossed into his face at the beach by a big bully in ads for muscle-building equipment during the 1950s. A surprise box-office hit, *P.W.B.A.* offered a combination of Vittorio De Sica's *Bicycle Thieves* (1948) and John Wayne's *The Alamo* (1960) in a giddily bright comedy style. One sequence, in which nattily attired Reubens/ Pee-Wee dances to the rock 'n' roll instrumental "Tequila," achieved iconic status. It was Herman's great good-luck to work for Tim Burton (1958–), making his feature debut following acclaimed shorts like *Vincent* (1982) and *Frankenweenie* (1984). When Danny Elfman (1953–) came on board with his non-threateningly eerie approach to musical scoring, a perfect package jelled. Sadly, the good news for P.R. ended there. His much-admired TV show, *Pee-Wee's Playhouse* (1989–1991), ended when this symbol of man-child innocence (recalling the silent era's saddest clown, Harry Langdon), was arrested in a porn theatre.

PERFORMANCE (1970)

Brit Rock Cult Rating: ****

Anita Pallenberg Aficionado Rating: *****

Donald Cammell, Nicolas Roeg, dirs..; Cammell, scr.; Cammell, Sanford Liberson, prod.; 1.66:1; B&W/C; 105 min.; Goodtimes Ent./Warner Bros.

Impressed by the commercial as well as critical success of *Blow-up*, noted celebrity/artist D.C. (1934–1996) determined to outdo Antonioni with an even more daring film that combined a thriller script with cutting-edge rock, concentrating on then current 'chic' experimental sex and hard drug orgies. *P.* begins as a Brit neo-noir on the order of *Get Carter* as a nasty East End gangster (James Fox, 1939–) goes on the lam, hiding out with a former rock star (Mick Jagger, 1943–) and a free-love hippie Anita Pallenberg, 1942–2017). Soon reality gives way to a living nightmare, time and space losing all meaning as this turns into a phantasmagoric menage-a-trois. Each character is performing at being something he or she isn't; sexual performance determines power or the lack thereof; musical performance can take on a philosophical dimension. Held up from distribution for two years owing to controversy surrounding what appeared to be actual (i.e., not 'performed') cocaine and heroin use as well as non-simulated sex. Today, a time capsule of that bygone era.

PHANTASM (1979)

Predecessor to Post-Modern Horror Rating: **** 1/2

Don Coscarelli, dir.; Coscarelli, scr.; Coscarelli, Paul Pepperman, pro.; 1.85:1; C; 88 min.; New Breed Prods./Embassy.

    Yet another among the dazzling nouveau-horror films turned out during the late 1970s/early 1980s by young talents who had no money or Industry connections but were determined to reinvent a tired genre. Young people notice what surrounding adults do not: A fearful figure, here The Tall Man (Angus Scrim, 1926–2016) in black coat with wild white hair, who reanimates corpses of recently deceased neighbors. Coscarelli (1954–) shot on weekends since many cast and crew members worked day jobs. He also served as cinematographer and editor. Influences on D.C.'s funereal vision include Frank Herbert's *Dune* (1965), Vincent Van Gogh's "The Starry Night" (1889), and short stories by Edgar Allan Poe. The piece-de-resistance which insured cult status is an unforgettable bedroom nightmare sequence. Like other youth-oriented horror flicks, this was inspired by a childhood dream, in Coscarelli's case about deadly puppet people and menacing flying spheres.

PHANTOM OF THE OPERA, (THE) (1925)

Silent Horror Rating: *****

Lon Chaney Sr. Cult Rating: *****

Robert Julien, Lon Chaney; Walter Anthony, Elliot J. Clawson, many others, scr.; Carl Laemmle, pro.; 1.33:1; B&W/C; 101 min.; Jewell Prods/Universal.

    "Don't step on that spider," a popular joke of the 1920s insisted. "It might be Lon Chaney" (1883–1930). Known as The Man of a Thousand Faces, the era's greatest dramatic actor played both heroes and villains; he's best remembered for the latter. L.C. provides a bit of each in this adaptation of the remarkably popular novel by France's Gaston Leroux (1968–1927). Here he emerges as a tragic figure, explaining why *T.P.O.T.O.* has always been central to the Chaney cult. Universal head

MEET THE PHANTOMS: Perhaps none, though, offered to a terrified public by the great Lon Chaney (Sr.) proved so memorable (or cult-worthy) as the title character in this grotesque Gallic romantic Beauty and the Beast fable; even today, when this is screened at still-existent old-fashioned movie palaces, accompanied by a live organ score, fans turn out; Brian De Palma effectively updated the piece for the era of rock.

Laemmle announced that cost was no object: An immense recreation of the Paris Opera House was created, complete with pipe organ. Chaney as usual created his own make-up for the once normal composer whose face is scarred in a fire. Years later, he becomes obsessed with a young singer (Mary Philbin, (1902–1990). Facial features frozen mask-like, Chaney relied on his hands for self-expression; as a child he learned sign-language from deaf mute parents. This remains the best filmed adaptation of P.O.T.O., despite a dozen remakes. Boffo box-office convinced Laemmle to arrange for a series of Talking Horror Movies starring Chaney. Had he not passed away, Lon would have portrayed Dracula, Frankenstein's monster, and The Wolfman, all eventually essayed by… Lon Chaney Jr.!

PHANTOM OF THE PARADISE (1974)

De Palma Completist Rating: *****

Extraordinary One of a Kind Flick Rating: **** ½

Brian De Palma, dir.; De Palma, Louisa Rose, scr.; Edward R. Pressman, pro.; 1.85:1; C; 92 min.; Harbor Prods.; 20th Century Fox.

Even those who do not appreciate B.D.P.'s (1940–) archly humourless Hitchcock redo films (*Dressed to Kill*, 1980; *Raising Cain*, 1992, etc.) may enjoy this giddy Tim Burton-esque horror-farce, with emotions that run as deep as those in T.B.'s *Edward Scissorhands* (1990). A gifted composer (William Finley (1940–2012) is physically and emotionally decimated by a monstrous record/concert producer, 'Swan.' The purposefully twisted plot borrows as much from Oscar Wilde's *The Picture of Dorian Gray* as *The Phantom of the Opera*, with the Faust myth thrown in for good measure. And birds, birds, more birds, referencing A.H.'s symbolic inclusion of them. Cult worthy cast members include Jessica Harper (*Suspiria*), Gerrit Graham (*Child's Play*, 1990), George Memmoli (*Mean Streets*, 1973), and *The Twilight Zone*'s Rod Serling as narrator. Also, Paul Williams (1940–), composer of the music for this and other films, playing the outlandish villain. P.W. is best recalled as 'Little Enos' in the 1970s *Smoky and the Bandit* rural comedies as well diminutive monkey man 'Virgil' in *Battle for the Planet of the Apes* (1973). The title was to have been "Phantom of the Fillmore" honouring that rock palace but negotiating legal rights proved too difficult.

PICKUP (1951)

Hugo Hass Cult Rating: ****

Sordid Romantic Melodrama Rating: ****

Hugo Haas, dir.; Haas, Arnold Lipp, scr.; Haas, pro.; 1.37:1; B&W; 78 min.; Forum Prods.

As an actor, H.H. (1901–1968) looked as if he sorely needed a shave even early in the morning after completing that task. This proved true of the movies he made in America: Grindhouse items that were dismissed as "lurid," "cheap," "seedy," "trashy," and "exploitive." Surprisingly, Haas had been considered a true artist in his homeland (Austria-Hungary), leaving even as the Nazis took control. Though he did play character roles in a few fine Hollywood films (notably MGM's *King Solomon's Mines*, 1950), Haas hoped to regain total control and did so with low-budget projects. This, his best-remembered (if low quality in an old-fashioned notion of 'good taste'), had been adapted from one of the era's garish Bush Station Paperbacks by Joseph Kopta. The plot clumsily combines elements of two classics, *The Blue Angel* (1930) and *The Postman Always Rings Twice* (1946) : a trashy female (Beverly Michaels, 1928–2007) enters into a loveless marriage with an older man (H.H.), then plots his murder. Up until then a serious actress, B.M. became typecast. She was only able to win similar parts in other people's pictures: *Wicked Woman* (Russell Rouse, 1953); *Blonde Bait* (Ed Wood, 1956). Wallowing in self-pity, Haas died in virtual poverty, certain his once ripe career had degenerated into a bad joke.

PLAN 9 FROM OUTER SPACE (1959)

Conventional Sci-Fi Rating: NO STARS

Cult Sci-Fi Rating: *****

Ed Wood Cult Rating: *****

Edward D. Wood, Jr., dir.; Wood, scr.; Wood, pro.; 1.33:1; B&W; 70 min.; Reynolds.

"This is the one they'll always remember me for," Ed Wood (Johnny Depp) happily sighs in Tim Burton's bio-pic of 'the worst director who ever lived" after *P.9.F.O.S.* premieres at a third-rate theatre. Naively, Wood (1924–1978) believed this low-budget (slightly over $50,000) tale of aliens raising the dead (the production title: "Grave Robbers from Outer Space") would enshrine him as a genius alongside Orson Welles. The results of his abbreviated shoot (mostly at the home of boxer/ wrestler /'actor' Tor Johnson, 1903–1971) were so bottom of the barrel even distributors of junk movies did not want anything to do with it. Every bit as awful as Corman's *Little Shop of Horrors*, though this is "pure Camp": Wood didn't know he was making one of the worst films of all time. Bela Lugosi appears in footage shot early-on in production. He died without completing his role. Maila Nurmi (TV horror host Vampira, 1922–2008) remains mute because she couldn't bring herself to speak the gauche dialogue without laughing. When in the early 1980s cults began to form about wonderfully awful junk films, *P.9.F.O.S.* was the first so honoured.

PLAY MISTY FOR ME (1971)

Clint Eastwood Completist Rating: **** ½

Pre-Basic Instinct Anti-Feminist Thriller Rating: **** ½

Clint Eastwood, dir.; Jo Heims, Dean Reisner, scr.; Robert Daley, Jennings Lang, pro.; 2.35:1; C; 102 min.; Malpaso/ Universal.

After completing *Dirty Harry* (1971) for Don Siegel (1912–1991), Clint (1930–) announced his intention to direct. Playing the role of a lovable bartender in Carmel CA, D.C. was on the set to mentor Eastwood if this became necessary. A solid (and to a degree the original) erotic-thriller, *P.M.F.M.* concerns a hip late-night radio D.J. who receives a telephone request from a female listener: would you please play the Erroll Garner jazz-noir classic? Shortly, she introduces herself: 'Evelyn Draper,' a gorgeous but psychotic fan who hopes to turn their one-night-stand into a lifetime commitment. When that doesn't work, she out-*Pycho*'s Norman Bates while presaging Glenn Clouse in *Fatal Attraction* (1987). Though not C.A.'s first choice, Jessica Walter (1941–2021) delivers the performance of her career, making this outrageous character believably terrifying yet strangely sympathetic… to a point. Roberta Flack's rendition of

"The First Time Ever I Saw Your Face" included here was a hit record. Newcomer Donna Mills (1940–), later to star in TV's *Knots Landing*, has several memorable nude scenes.

POINT BLANK (1967)

Revolutionary Hollywood Crime Film Rating: *****

John Boorman, dir.; Alexander Jacobs, David & Rafe Newhouse, scr.; Robert Chartoff, Irwin Winkler, Judd Bernard, scr.; 2.35:1; C; 92 min.; MGM.

    P.B. shocked viewers by blending half-forgotten essentials of noir tales with then newly popular psychedelic cinematic stylings. Lee Marvin (1923- 1987), a veteran of *The Big Heat* (1953) and many other noirs, em-

THE BIRTH OF NEO-NOIR: A form considered to be dead since the early 1960s roared back onto theatre screens (with Lee Marvin, star of so many early noirs, top-billed) with John Boorman's psychedelic, free-form variation of classic crime thrillers from the past.

bodied the one-named 'Walker'; A double crossed outlaw out for revenge against the syndicate. Escaping from Alcatraz, he finds himself an anachronism: An animalistic throwback in a business suit, raging through the contemporary world of hippie fashions, gaudy colors, and high tone board-rooms for the contemporary breed of corporate gangster. One sequence, in which a femme fatale (Angie Dickinson, 1931–) employs ordinary kitchen utensils to reduce the tough guy to rubble, stands out amid fine competition throughout this thriller-phantasmagoria. Though the film failed at the box-office, *P.B.* became an Underground sensation. Noir was back; reinvented as neo-noir, it would never again go away. Boorman (1933–) created a mesmerizing sense of the surreal by his odd camera angles for pre-existing locations combined with a fractured time scheme. From a novel by cult crime author David E. Westlake (1933–2008), under the name 'Richard Stark.'

POOR WHITE TRASH, aka *BAYOU* (1957)

Lowbrow Drive-In Sexploitation Rating: NO STARS

Curio Rating: *** ½

Harold Daniels, dir.; Edward J. Fessler, scr.; M.A. Ripps, pro.; 35 mm.; B&W; 83 min.; American National Company.

The unexpected success of *Baby Doll* motivated producers to throw together grindhouse items about underage beauties in the Deep South. First-timer Ripps somehow talked TV/B movie star Peter Graves (1926–2010) into joining his company in Barataria LA. At an isolated Cajun village, they shot a lurid potboiler about an architect from up north who spots a local nymphette (Lita Milan, then 24, utterly breathtaking if unconvincingly cast as a 15-year-old). This angers a local Goliath (Timothy A. Carey as yet *another* wide-eyed maniac). Released by U.A. as *Bayou*, the dull film failed to attract audiences. In 1961, an outfit called Cinema Distributors picked up legal rights, changed the title to *Poor White Trash*, and released this to the lowest level of rural Drive-Ins. Proving that it pays to advertise, full page spreads in local newspapers warned readers that this contained perversion unlike anything heretofore seen in a movie. Theatres turned droves of people away. Each summer this boring, inane, not particularly salacious exploitation item would reappear, accumulating more profits. By 1967, a film shot for $10,000 had netted more than $10 million. The emergence of nudity in movies beginning in 1967 brought that profitability of this mild 'teaser' to an abrupt end.

PRETTY BABY (1978)

Brooke Shields Cult Rating: *****

Trashy Forbidden Cinema Rating: NO STARS

Intelligent Arthouse Item Rating: *****

Louis Malle, dir.; Polly Platt, scr.; Malle, Platt, pros.; 1.85:1; C; 110 min.; Paramount.

In an age before Political Correctness descended on our pop-culture landscape, Brooke Shields (1965–) became a Mondo Bizarro 1970s

QUICK, NOW! IS IT TRASH OR ART?: ARTHOUSE OR GRINDHOUSE? MAYBE MAINSTREAM? Child prostitution, once the domain of early pornographers and exploitation filmmakers, reached the screen as an under-stated masterpiece thanks to the artistry of filmmaking genius Louis Malle.

equivalent to Shirley Temple: A 12-year old star, an icon of youthful beauty consciously marketed as an underage sex-symbol in Calvin Klein jeans ads and a bestselling erotic photo-volume, *The Brooke Book*, Next, naturally, came a movie: B.S. was cast as 'Violet,' a child prostitute in Storyville, the Red Light District of New Orleans circa 1917. This might have led to an exploitation flick but the rising star was lucky to work for Malle 1932–1995), a Gallic genius who previously offered subtle, stylish, sensitive portrayals of 'taboo' subjects. Keith Carradine 1949–) plays Ernest J. Bellocq (1873-1949), a photographer who made one bordello the subject of his artistic fascination. Susan Sarandon (1946–) proved her acting chops as Violet's mother. cult star Barbara Steele appears as a mature prostitute. At one point in pre-production, Jodie Foster and Jack Nicholson were to have portrayed the lovers.

PRETTY POISON (1968)

Tuesday Weld Cult Rating: *****

Edgy Youth-Thriller Rating: **** 1/2

Noel Black, dir.; Lorenzo Semple, Jr., scr.; Black, Marshall Backlar, pro.; 1.85:1; C; 89 min.; Mollino Prods./20th Century Fox.

"Lolita meets Norman Bates!"; that's how devout fans of this box-office flop (which quickly became a cult fav) described the pluperfect casting. Anthony Perkins (1932–1992) portrays a lean, lanky, twitchy character not unlike the one from *Psycho* (1960), now released from an asylum as cured. He spots seemingly normal all-American girl-next-door 'Sue Ann Stepanek' as the high-schooler rehearses cheerleading moves, then intrigues her by pretending to be a spy. Here is an example of 'follie deux': The violence they perpetrate grows out of the relationship rather than inherent in either. Weld's cult queen status, already solid, here crystalized. The shot (un-intended) in which she licks her lips while getting ready to murder her own mother (1950s cult-star Beverly Garland, 1926–2008) remains a classic bit of black comedy. Based on Stephen Geller's novel *She Let Him Continue*. Black (1937–2014) proved to be a one-shot wonder. As to the Weld born Suzanne, here is her greatest performance.

THE TEEN QUEEN OF CULT CINEMA: Why did Tuesday Weld turn down the leads in *Bonnie and Clyde, Cactus Flower, True Grit, Macbeth* and other ambitious films to do oddball indie items like this? Only she knows for certain!

PRINCESS BRIDE, THE (1987)

Conventional Rating: *****

Family Viewing Rating: *****

Rob Reiner, dir.; William Goldman, scr.; Reiner, Andrew Scheinman, pros.; 1.85:1; C; 98 min.; Act III Communications, 20th Century Fox.

Popular screenwriter Goldman (1931-2018; *Butch Cassidy and the Sundance Kid*, 1969) wrote a children's book especially for his daughters. *T.P.B.* drew on literature from an earlier era, when kids still believed a virgin princess named 'Buttercup' (Robin Wright in the film) could share true love with a humble farmer (Cary Elwes) while foregoing the attentions of a wealthy/cruel prince (Chris Sarandon). Familiar material, to be sure. Yet in print and later as a film, the piece particularized each stock character (and a dozen delightful supporting ones) for fuller verisimilitude while adding a knowing sense of tongue in cheek satire. An unexpected dose of New York Jewish humor appears by way of Billy Crystal (1948–) under Reiner's (1947–) smart direction. The narrative frame features a wise grandfather (Peter Falk, 1927–2011), reading to a bedridden boy (Fred Savage, 1976–). Reiner shot on location in England to avoid the papier-mache look of 1950s studio films. An extended sword fight between Elwes and Mandy Patinkin is the longest since the warmly remembered one in *Scaramouche* (1952).

PULP FICTION (1994)

Tarantino Cult Rating: *****

Cinema Altering Rating: *****

Quentin Tarantino, dir.; Tarantino, Roger Avery, scr.; Danny De Vito, Lawrence Bender, prod.; 2.39:1; C; 178 min. (original director's cut), 154 min. (severely edited print); Miramax/A Band Apart/Jersey Films.

"Trash masterpiece" is the term employed by numerous critics to describe this ensemble example of para-cinema: A collusion rather than collision of Drive-In junk with arthouse stylings. Tawdry tales borrowed from Bus Station books of the late-1940s interconnect as an assassin (John Travolta) is seduced by the boss' wife (Uma Thurman) to the tune of Chuck Berry's "You Never Can Tell"; an over-the-hill club boxer (Bruce Willis) unwisely takes a fall; the hit man and his partner (Samuel L. Jackson) discuss French variations on American fast food; a pair of white trash lovebirds (Tim Roth as 'Pumpkin' and Amanda Plummer as 'Honey Bunny') go on a killing spree. Settings range from a greasy thumb diner to an upper-level faux 1950s 'gourmet comfort food' eatery. A MacGuffin (the suitcase) makes the rounds while maintaining the secret of its sought-after contents. Lowbrow indie sliminess as to subject matter meets the experimental camera techniques of France's Nouvelle Vogue. When *P.F.* enjoyed box-office success at mall venues, the era in which the lowest level of film junk and the highest form of cinematic artistry could serve as the top and bottom slices of bread, mainstream entertainment providing the meat in-between, A New Wave in commercial cinema premiered.

GENIUS AT WORK VI: More than any other filmmaker, Quentin Tarantino has collapsed Grindhouse flicks on one extreme side of 'The Movies' with arthouse items on the other into mainstream product for middle Americans and citizens of the world; John Travolta and Samuel L. Jackson take aim (and this time not at Big Macs as they are re-named in Paris) in *Pulp Fiction*.

PUPPETOON MOVIE, THE (1987)

Pal Cult Rating: **** ½

Arnold Leibovit, dir., scr., pro.; Arnold Leibovit, prod.; 35 m.m.; C; 90 min.; Image Entertainment.

Today, most George Pal cultists focus on his ingenious full length sci-fi/fantasy films: *War of the Worlds* (1954), *Tom Thumb* (1958), and *The*

AN AUTHENTIC AFRICAN AMERICAN FOLK HERO: Though George Pal is criticized today for his 'Sambo' creation of a politically incorrect stereotype, he also be lauded for bringing to the screen one of the great icons of black power.

Time Machine (1960) all ranked high on that list. Thankfully, A.L. chose to assemble some of the remarkable short subjects that initially introduced the concept of 'Pupppetoons' (marionettes without strings, though never 'hand-puppets') created specifically for the special magic only stop-motion animation can provide. Born in Austria/Hungary as Gyorgy Marczincsak, G.P. (1908–1980) studied to be an architect but brought his learned skills to the creation of alternative worlds for *cinema-fantastique*. Leaving Berlin's legendary UFA studio to escape Hitler, Pal entered Hollywood and shortly provided a viable alternative to the genius of Disney. "Tubby the Tuba" (1947) introduces a uniquely charming character as lovable as any devised by Uncle Walt's team. 'Hot Lips Jasper,' caricaturing an African child, will today offend anyone who cannot accept that this series was a product of its times. "John Henry and the Inky Poo" (1946) brings that black folk hero to life with gospel music and lovingly incarnates a long-gone sub-culture of the South. There exists no more moving short anti-war film than "Tulips Still Grow" (1942). A ticket to a once in a lifetime ride.

QUADROPHENIA (1979)

Rock 'n' Roll Angry Youth Rating: *****

Franc Roddam, dir.; Roddam, Pete Townshend, Dave Humphries, Martin Stellman, scr.; Townshend, Keith Moon, John Entwistle, Roger Daltrey, Roy Baird, Bill Burbishley, pro.; 1.85:1; C;120 min.; The Who Films/Polytel.

In every decade, members of 'The Crowd' diligently head for work early each morning, wearing a cheap suit, earning paltry sums for doing routine work, dream about escaping from such a status-quo. Why not chuck it all, buy a bike, and surrender to an instinct that hungers for freedom? In 1965 London, 'Jimmy' (Phil Daniels, 1958–) grows sick of his dead-end existence and attempts to live out such dreams, if with disastrous results. Townshend (1945–) and The Who were not out to romanticize a time when Mods and Rockers ruled, rather—thanks to the wise directorial eye of F.R. (1946–)—present this realistically in contrast to such previous fantasies as *A Hard Day's Night* (1964). The result: A mini-masterpiece, favourably compared to *Rebel Without a Cause* for America during the 1950s. In a scene-stealing role as 'Ace Face,' Sting (Gordon Matthew Sumner, 1951–) transitioned from a performer with The Police into a star. A remarkable film in that for once, a band (in this case The Who) create a filmed tribute to their loyal audience that does not set out to please or offend such people, rather honestly cause them to gaze deep into their souls, perhaps for the first time.

SLUTS IN SPACE: Apologies in advance for the unavoidable politically incorrect caption, but what else could capture the unique appeal of this unique sub-genre of cheesy sci-fi flicks? Zsa Zsa Gabor (NOT in the title role) holds earthguys (including *Rawhide*'s Eric Fleming, far right) captive while, half a decade earlier, earth girl Marie Windsor finds herself captured by The Hollywood Dream Girls.

QUEEN OF OUTER SPACE, (THE) (1958)

Flamboyant Sci-Fi Rating: *****

Generic Sci-Fi Rating **

Edward Bernds, dir.; Charles Beaumont, Ben Hecht, scr.; Ben Schwalb, pro.; 2.35;1; C; 80 min.; Allied Artists.

'Unintentionally funny' is how critics described this oddball tale of three astronauts who land on a planet dominated by man-hating women. But the credits reveal legendary wit Ben Hecht (1894–1964) co-authored. Might the humor have been intentional, this not one more 1950s space-opera but a smart satire on them? An early predecessor to *Blazing Saddles*' spoof of Westerns, Q.O.O.S. burlesques what filmmaker John Landis might tag the 'Amazon Women on the Moon' sci-fi subgenre, *Catwomen of the Moon, Devil Girl from Mars (1954),* and *Fire Maidens of Outer Space* (1956) among them. The casting of Grand Guignol blonde Zsa Zsa Gabor (1917–2016, not in the title role but as a leftish revolutionary fighting for the rights of Real Girls to be objectified by men) adds to the Camp appeal. The spaceman costumes are leftovers from *Forbidden Planet*. Expressionistic set designs in grotesque colors would influence the aesthetics of the original *Star Trek*. Laurie Mitchell (1928–) plays the masked queen. If the male leads recall The Three Stooges, note that Bernds (1905–2000) directed their shorts.

RE-ANIMATOR (1985)

Cult/Bondage Horror Rating: ****

Stuart Gordon, dir.; Gordon, Dennis Paoii, William Norris, scrs.; Brian Nuzna, pro.; 1.85:1; C; 93 min. (uncut/unrated print), 93 min. (R-rated), 86 min. (trimmed for mainstream viewing); Empire Pictures.

In the early 1980s Charles Band (1951–) set out to become the next generation's Roger Corman, overseeing production of low- budget horror films. He assigned Gordon (1947–2020), of Organic Theatre Company, to film the old H.P. Lovecraft story "Hebert West, Re-Animator." Originally G.S. hoped to do it in black and white for (hopefully) another *Night of the Living Dead*. C.B. persuaded him to use color and include as much blood and guts as possible. The result resembles a collaboration between Hershel Gordon Lewis and David Cronenberg. A med student (Bruce Abbott) allows his new roommate (Jeffrey Combs, 1954–) to include him in a Frankenstein-like experiment. The Beautiful Blonde caught in the middle is played by Barbara Crampton (1958–), previously a performer in New York City Shakespearean productions. Following her fully nude bondage scene, B.C.'s career was re-directed to cult sensation via *Chopping Mall*, 1986), *Puppetmaster* (1989), and *Castle Freak* (1995). Many of the film's loyal followers see it less as a horror flick with weird comedy than a spoof of the Body Parts Thrillers.

REBEL WITHOUT A CAUSE (1955)

All Purpose Rating: *****

Nicholas Ray, dir.; Ray, Stewart Stern, Irving Shulman, scr.; David Weisbart, pro.; 2.55:1; C; 111 min.; Warner Bros.

"You're tearing me apart!" 'Jim Stark' (James Dean, 1931–1955) shrieks at his parents (Ann Doran, Jim Backus) in the living room of their upper-middleclass home. All across America, teens living in upscale neighborhoods responded to a film that dared express their anger, frustration, and confusion in the post–war world of suburban conformity. Ray (1911–1979) originally called his script "The Last Run" until Weisbart suggested they use the title of a book about criminal psychology W.B. had optioned years earlier. The Youth film that defined a generation: 'Jimbo' and 'Judy' (Natalie Wood, 1938–1981) embodied the first true American 'teenagers.' Central to the James Dean cult, *Rebel* provided those "between twelve and twenty," as singer Pat Boone put it, with a symbol for The New Youth… i.e., themselves. Released to theatres less than a month after Dean's death in an automobile accident. Key sequences proved seminal to 1950s culture: The switch blade fight, the chickie race, and confrontations with clueless parents. Missing element: Rock 'n' roll. The film was shot shortly before Fifties' Youth discovered 'their *own* music' via Chuck Berry, Bill Hayley, and Elvis Presley.

REEFER MADNESS (1936)

'So Bad It's Great' Rating: *****

All Other Ratings: NO STARS

Louis J. Gasnier, dir.; Lawrence Meade, Arthur Hoerl, Paul Franlin, scrs.; Dwain Esper, pro.; B&W; 1.37:1; 66 min.; G & H (George A. Hirlman) Prods.

In 1933, Victor Lacata of Florida murdered his family while apparently under the influence of marijuana. Though Lacata was a schizophrenic with homicidal tendencies, the authorities and press presented the situation as something that could happen to anyone who smoked reefer. Always on the lookout for a new subject that could be commercially exploited in one of his lurid 'educational' projects, Esper (1893–1982) seized on this emerging 'threat.' By reputation, this drama is so bad that it's irresistible. French director Gasnier (1875–1963) made his reputation in the silent era directing famed clown Max Linder. Carlton Young, who plays Jack the Dealer, went on to bigger and better things as member of John Ford's legendary stock company. Original title: "Tell Your Children."

YESTERDAY'S PROPAGANDA, TODAY'S CAMP: In the late 1960s, college hippies took great delight in lighting up while watching this anti-drug flick from three decades earlier.

A cult item on the college campus circuit during the late 60s as students gleefully lit up.

REPO MAN (1984)

Edgy Cult Rating: **** ½
Alex Cox, dir.; Cox, scr.; Peter McCarthy, Jonathan Wacks, pros; 1.85:1; C; 92 min.; Edge City/Universal.

The movie that most fully and accurately captured the early 1980s punk scene in L.A.'s marginal outer-limits, where aspiring young musi-

A CULT HERO FOR THE POSTMODERN AGE: Harry Dean Stanton emerged from obscure character actor to superstar of edgy movies with *Repo Man*.

cians mingled with old alcoholic losers. The latter are embodied by Harry Dean Stanton (1926- 2017, in a role intended for Dennis Hopper), as a bitter William S. Burroughs type reduced to professional car re-possessing; the former, a cynical spiked-hair punk (Emilio Estevez, 1962–) mentored by the older man. Part documentary of that bizarre line of work (Cox held just such a job before entering filmmaking), part science-fiction flick (a glowing spaced-out 1964 Chevy plays host to alien visitors), part philosophical tract (Cox's views on "the cosmic unconscious" are shared with his target hipster audience). Music by The Circle Jerks, Iggy Pop, and The Sex Pistols. Visual style influenced by R. Crumb's Underground comics of the late Sixties. Sadly for Cox (1954–), this one-shot success didn't lead to a true career. Later works like *Straight to Hell* missed the mark.

REPULSION (1965)

Cinema of Confinement Rating: *****

Roman Polanski, dir.; Polanski, Gerard Brach, scr.; Gene Gutowski, pro.; 1.66:1; B&W; 105 min.; Compton Films.

Swinging London, at that moment when the Beatles ruled with records, teens danced in the street (most often, Carnaby), and the New Morality exploded everywhere. Except inside a single 'bird': Recent emigre from Belgium 'Carol' (Catherine Deneuve, 1943–) recoils at the ugliness around her: Leering men on the streets; hideous women in the beauty parlour where she works; vegetables left uneaten that grow into twisted ugly things. Suddenly, the walls crack in her apartment and monstrous arms attempt to grab her. Sex appals the frigid female, so much so that when a handsome, likeable young man attempts to break through her shell and help Carol out of an increasingly nightmarish life, he dooms himself. Polanski (1933–), in his first English-language film, encouraged musician Chico Hamilton and D.P. Seamus Flannery to create odd sights and bizarre sounds so that we share, rather than merely watch, a human being's disintegration into madness. The opening image: an eye that recalls the one with which Hitchcock's *Vertigo* (1958) begins. Polanski's debt to that filmmaker is clear in this tale's relationship to *Psycho* (1960), as well as its thematic resemblance to *Marnie*, about a similar threatened virgin.

SURREAL CINEMA GOES MAINSTREAM: The appeal of Catherine Deneuve as a gorgeous Gallic version of Hitch's 'Norman Bates' allowed *Repulsion* to find a large audience in America.

REQUIUM FOR A DREAM (2000)

Aronofsky Aficionado Rating: *****

Darren Aronofsky, dir.; Aronofsky, Hubert Selby, Jr. scr.; Palmer West, Eric Watson, pros.; 1.37;1; C; 102 min.; Artisan Entertainment.

Four disparate people living in Coney Island have many ties, none so strong as their addictions. An aging woman (Ellen Burstyn, 1932- ; in her greatest role ever) is hooked not only to TV giveaway shows but weight loss pills. Her son (Jared Leto, 1971-) has become a full-fledged heroin junkie, stealing from his mother to feed his habit. His girlfriend (Jennifer Connelly, 1970-), an upscale former deb, fell for this bad boy, picked up his habit, and prostitutes herself to fund their hits. Their best pal (Marion Wayans, 1972-) hopes to move from user to dealer, gaining a shot at the big time. The power of this piece derives from Aronofsky's (1969–) auteurial approach. He begins sequences in a relatively realistic style, allowing images to grow ever more surreal, indicating that a member of this quartet has passed from full consciousness into hallucinations. This profoundly pessimistic work offers one ray of sunlight: Wayans' character may survive the trauma. Seemingly set in 1978, the case with Selby's cult novel.

REQUIEM POUR UN VAMPIRE, aka *CAGED VIRGINS* (1971)

European Classy/Trashy Succubus Rating: **** ½

Jean Rollin, dir.; Rollin, scr.; Sam Selsky, pro.; 1.66:1; C; 83 min. (U.S. dubbed grindhouse version), 95 min. (U.S. subtitled arthouse cut); Les Films ABC.

France's J.R. (1938–2010) achieved cult fame as an auteur of the erotic (some would say pornographic) vampire films that exploited (there are those who insist *art*fully so) the then-new freedom of the screen. His bizarre pan-cinema works combine the graphic bloodletting of Herschell Gordon Lewis with the elegant orgiastic frenzy of Radley Metzger, unwinding at a snail's pace that recalls early 1960s Antonioni. Underage virgins (Mireille Dargent, Marie-Pierre Castel) enjoy dressing in clown costumes and killing people. Like many other pretty victims in slash-cinema, they find themselves captives in a vampire's castle. The terrific irony: They prove to be more far dangerous to him than he to them. Could this then be a thinly disguised feminist statement about 'fighting back'? Images that fall just short of Triple 'X' involving bondage and beatings mixed with lesbian sex are surrounded by lovely pastel landscapes which recall high-tone European flicks like *Elvira Madigan* (1967). Another irony: The American Drive-In cut contains *less* nudity that the arthouse-circuit version.

RESERVOIR DOGS (1992)

Tarantino Cult Rating: *****

Steve Buscemi Cult Rating: *****

VIRGIN VAMPIRES, EUROPEAN STYLE: S & M—always inherent in horror films in general, vampire movies in particular—reached a new level of in your face atrocity with Jesus Franco's *Succubus* and Jean Rollin's *Requium*.

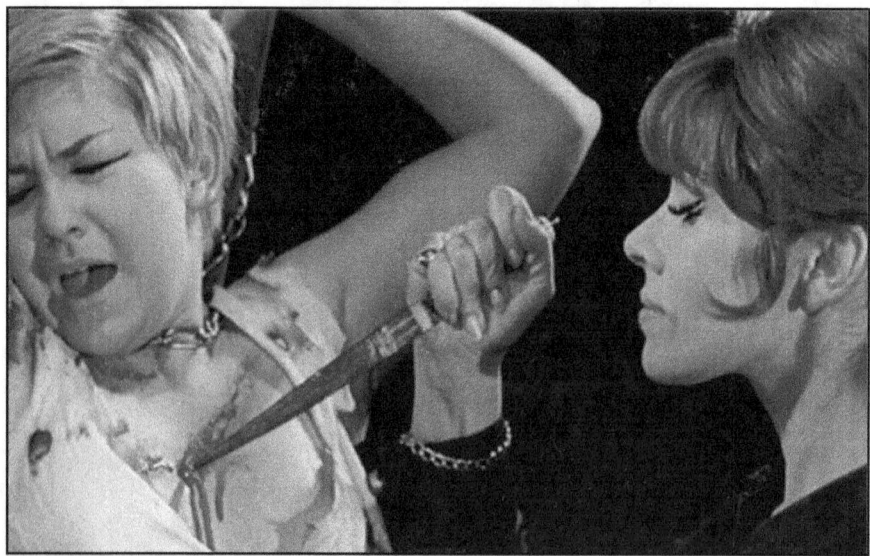

Ultra-Violent Neo Noir Rating: *****

Date Night for Normals Rating: NO STARS

Quentin Tarantino, dir.; Tarantino, Roger Avery, scr.; Lawrence Bender, pro.; 2.35:1; C; 99 min.; Live Ent./Dog Eat Dog Prods./Miramax.

    Crime films fall into one of two categories: pre-Q.T. and post-Q.T. In his first theatrical project, the former video rental store movie mavin combined elements of two 1950s heist flicks, John Huston's classic *The Asphalt Jungle* (1950) and Kubrick's cult film *The Killing*. Sterling Hayden starred in each and if alive would have been first choice for old 'Joe Cabot.' Lesser-known noir actor Lawrence Tierney received the part. Q.T. featured an arthouse-style fractured time sequence overlaid on the raw grindhouse material *without* the voice-over narration S.K. had been forced to add to his film. Already on their way to cult status, Harvey Keitel (1939–), Tim Roth (1961–), and Steve Buscemi (1957–) were catapulted into edgy icon status. No one who has seen Michael Madsen's torture of a bound policemen will be able to hear "Stuck in the Middle with You" again without

MARCHING TO THE BEAT OF A DIFFERENT DRUM: Quentin Tarantino combined elements of John Huston's *The Asphalt Jungle* (1950) and Stanley Kubrick's *The Killing* in his commercial breakthrough, which brought the 'referencing' approach of Sergio Leone's *Once Upon a Time...* films to Hollywood.

thinking back to *R.D.*'s harrowing midpoint. The opening diner discussion between assembled thieves without honor as to Madonna's "Like a Virgin" and the morality of proper tipping were a word-for-word combination of two such conversations Q.T. once overheard.

RETURN TO GLENNESCAUL, aka *ORSON WELLES' GHOST STORY* (1953)

Welles' Completist Rating: **** ½

Hilton Edwards, dir.; H.E., Michael MacLiammoir, scr.; H.E., M.M., Orson Welles, pro.; 1;37:1; B&W; 23 min.; Dublin Gate.

While Rod Serling (1924–1975) and CBS were developing *The Twilight Zone* series (1959–1965), that award-winning screen-writer initially resisted serving as the show's narrator. In his mind, Orson Welles (1915–1985) would be the best choice. Though that did not happen, O.W. did indeed serve such a role for this *Zone*-like short, completed on a break during the shooting of *Othello* (1951). The Genius collaborated with two Shakespearean actors from the cast. While driving to Dublin, O.W. stops during the dead of night, out in the middle of nowhere, to pick up a stranded motorist. We then are treated to a story within the story about this man's strange meeting with two ethereal women on this very road long, long ago… Though Welles is not officially credited, aficionados who seek out this once lost film insist that all his directorial touches are in evidence, allowing this 'ghost story' to be analysed as an extension of his official body of work. Short and splendid.

RIDER, THE (2017)

One of a Kind 'Serious' Film Rating: *****

Chloe Zhao, aka Zhao Ting, dir.; Zano, scr.; Zano, Mollye Asher, Sacha Ben Harroche, prod.; 2.35:1; C; 104 min.; Caviar/ Highwayman Films.

While researching a project about contemporary Native people, Zhao (1982–) met Brady Jandreau, an authentic cowboy and one of a dying breed: A rodeo rider who suffered a cranial injury following a fall. Zano realized that a fictionalized version of this person's life would allow her to explore the mythos of the American male. Jandreau plays his alter ego, 'Brady Blackburn.' Members of the Jandreau family portray corresponding characters. As to the subject-star, B.J. is a natural: the most photogenic real-life rodeo rider since the great Casey Tibbs (1929–1980). Most significant is the approach taken by this Chinese woman to the world of the traditional Western U.S. male: Why would an injured fellow continue to pursue life on the circuit knowing even a slight concussion could result in death? C.Z. neither celebrates nor criticizes a profession that many feminists consider to be ludicrously machismo, instead analyzing everything on view in such a wise manner that *T.R.* replaces Nicholas Ray's *The Lusty Men* (1952) and Sam Peckinpah's *Junior Bonner* (1973) as the film for fans of this uniquely American sport. Zhao (1982-) would go on to win an Oscar as Best Director for *Nomadland* (2020).

ROADIE (1980)

Rock 'n' Roll Music-Movie Rating: *** ½

Alan Rudolph, dir.; Rudolph, Zalman King, Big Boy Medlin, others, scr.; Carolyn Pfeiffer, pro.; 1.85:1; C; 106 min.; Alive/Vivant Productions.

    A small but solid cult developed for the films of A.R. (1943-), mentored by the legendary Robert Altman and auteur of such languid, moody projects as *Choose Me* (1984) and *Trouble in Mind* (1985), appreciated by his devotees. The only one of A. R.'s films to build its own cult-following was this early, atypical, low-budget glance at the raucous southwestern rock-on-the-road lifestyle. Then again, how could a film starring the great Art Carney 1918–2003) as the father of 'Meat Loaf' (Marvin Lee Aday, 1947-) not win such status? The latter plays a humble Texan (named 'Travis' after the Alamo-hero) who falls in love with glitter-groupie 'Lola Boulillibase' (a pre-*Porky's* Kaki Hunter, 1955-) and signs on as an electrician for a modestly talented band called Asleep at the Wheel. More than half of the jokes fall flat. That doesn't bother fans, who concentrate instead on the presence (and in some cases performances) of Alice Cooper (L's dream guy, to whom she wishes to surrender her virginity), Roy Orbison and Hank Williams Jr. (performing a duet, no less), and dazzling Debbie Harry of 'Blondie.'

SHE HAD 'CULT STAR' WRITTEN ALL OVER HER: Deborah Harry of the mainstream punk band Blondie was a natural for rock 'n' roll cult cinema.

ROBOT MONSTER (1953)

Conventional Sci-Fi Rating: NO STARS

Cult Sci-Fi Rating: *****

Phil Tucker, dir.; Wyott Ordung, scr.; Tucker, John Brown, George Barrows, pros.; 1.37:1; B&W; 66 min.; Three Dimension Pictures /Astor Releasing.

    Aspiring filmmaker Tucker (1927–1985) didn't have much money but did possess considerable savvy as to the 1950s pop-culture milieu. Science fiction had become big with the kids as did (briefly) 3-D. Shot in less than four days at little more than $15,000, the first film to combine both elements (as well as early stereophonic sound) earned more than a million on its theatrical release, then scored again the following year on TV. An alien who arrives to eliminate final survivors of a war of the planets becomes obsessed with a pretty girl (Claudia Barrett, 1929–). Ro-Man (George Barrows) is actually a guy in a gorilla outfit wearing a weird helmet, receiving orders from above via a bubble-machine. He hangs out in Bronson Canyon, later to be made famous in *The Searchers* (John Ford, 1956) and *Star Wars* (1977). Lizard/dinosaurs are provided courtesy stock footage from *One Million B.C.* (1940). Elmer Bernstein (1922–2004), later of *Magnificent Seven* fame, did the score. Male lead George Nader (1921–2002) would shortly be 'outed' by *Confidential* magazine. His TV show: *The Man and the Challenge*.

ROCK 'N' ROLL HIGH SCHOOL (1979)

Cult Rock Rating: **** ½

Allan Arkush, Joe Dante, dirs..; Richard Whitley, Russ Dvonch, Joseph McBride, scr.; Roger Corman, Michael Finnell, pros.; 1.37:1; C; 93 min.; New World.

    The moment that big-budget (if low-quality) *Grease* (1978) scored with kids of all ages, R.C. green-lit this low-budget (high-quality) exploitation item. *R.N.R.H.S.* comes far closer to the tone of the original (and great) stage version of *Grease*, as well as warmly remembered rock exploitation flicks from the Big Beat era: *Rock, Pretty Baby* (1956), *Rock Around*

A RECURRING POSE: In ultra-low budget sci-fi films like *Robot Monster* as in the considerably more ambitious *This Island Earth*, the old Beauty and the Beast theme returns.

the Clock (1957), etc. Most often, they focused on a teenager (Tuesday Weld in *Rock! Rock! Rock!*) who tries to convince super-straight parents that Rockabilly proffers only harmless fun. Here, P.J. faces the meanest principal (villainess Mary Woronov, already a major cult figure) ever, to rule it over Vince Lombardi High School. The pace, attitude, and visual sensibility reflect the music of the Ramones (Johnny, 1948–2004; Dee Dee, 1951- 2002), and Marky (1952–), playing themselves as the most outrageous Punk Rock band on the planet. The great question: why the Goldie Hawn-like actress Soles did not become a major star. Her work in *Halloween* and subsequent turn in *Stripes!* (1981) would suggest a more impressive career than what followed.

ROCK! ROCK! ROCK! (1956)

Mid-fifties Nostalgia Rating: **** ½

All Other Ratings: **

Will Price, dir.; Michael Subotsky, Phyllis Coe, scrs. Subotsky, Max Rosenberg, prods.; 35 mm; B&W; 85 min.; Vanguard.

No sooner had rock 'n' roll swept the airwaves than Hollywood schlockmeisters hurriedly assembled exploitation flicks for the emergent American Teenager: *Shake, Rattle & Rock* (1956), *Mister Rock and Roll* (1957), and *The Big Beat* (1958). None was so shoddily produced or successful as *R!R!R!* Credit the latter to the screen premiere of Suzanne 'Tuesday' Weld (1943–) who had just turned thirteen, exuding a nymphette sex appeal that combined elements of young Marilyn and Brigitte B. in a Lolita-like package. Whenever Tuesday opens her pretty/pouty mouth to sing, the world-class voice of Connie Francis (1937–) appears. *R.R.R.* decimates the connection between rock music and hooliganism. 'Dori' is the best-behaved girl imaginable while Frankie Lymon and the Teenagers perform "No! I'm *not* a juvenile delinquent." Other iconic performers: The Moonglows, the Flamingos, and Chuck Berry (1921–2017). Teddy Randazzo (1935–2003), later a top music producer, plays Dori's boyfriend. Also onscreen: Alan Freed (1921–1965), the d.j. who popularized the term 'rock 'n' roll' but was destroyed in the Payola scandal.

THE ORIGINAL ROCK 'N' ROLL CELEBRITY D.J.: Before clean-cut Dick Clark, there was the more rough-hewn Alan Freed, who introduced white teenagers to the glories of black music; his Big Beat exploitation flicks preceded Elvis' musicals into grindhouse theatres.

ROCKY HORROR PICTURE SHOW, THE (1975)

Cult Musical Rating: *****

Tim Curry Cultist Rating: *****

Jim Sharman, dir.; Sharman, Richard O'Brien, scr.; Michael White, Lou Adler, pros.; 1.85:1; C; 100 min.; 20th Century Fox.

    Growing up 'strange' in New Zealand, O'Brien (1942–) divided his time between two addictions: tacky sci-fi films and raw rock 'n' roll. Falling asleep, the teenager would imagine an ideal combination of the two, filtered through the edgily adolescent humor of *Mad* magazine. As a young adult in England he collaborated with Sharman (1945–) on a production of the rock-opera *Jesus Christ, Superstar*, sharing his vision for a musical that would bring Camp to the London stage. Here, an ultra-straight young couple, their car breaking down in a storm, enter the cryptic home of scientist 'Frank N. Further,' much to their great regret! Premiering in 1973, the play—popular with 'hip' audiences—moved to Broadway a year and a half later. 20th Century Fox agreed to do a movie so long as the risky project could be budgeted at $1 million. When the film opened wide to non-existent response, the company feared they would not make back their investment. By decade's end, *T.R.H.P.S.* returned over $100 million as a Midnight Movie. Devotees would show up in costume and echo the dialogue. Tim Curry (1946–), in his film debut, created an over-the-top rendering of the mad genius. For the record, Peter Hinwood (1946–) embodied the title character. The young innocents were Susan Sarandon and Barry Bostwick.

ROI DE COEUR, LE, aka KING OF HEARTS (1966)

Rating: ****

Philippe de Broca, dir.; Daniel Boulanger, scr.; Michelle de Broca, pro.; 2.35:1; C; 102 min.; Fildebroc.

    "Make love," chanted young people in America during the mid-Sixties, "not war." Shortly before Hollywood responded and began turning out anti-Vietnam films and paeons to the Free Love Movement, this charming little French film became a great favorite (and political rallying point) at many colleges. An early work by P.d.B. (1933–2004), who had served his apprentice-ships working with such New Wave giants as Francoise Truffaut and Claude Chabrol, here is a "gentle fable" that expresses the New Left of that era. During WWI, a clueless soldier (Alan Bates, 1934–2003) wanders into a small town. The citizenry acts strangely, dressing up in esoteric costumes and living the roles of fictional characters, all happy in their individual 'worlds.' What he does not realize (yet) is that they are escapees from a nearby mental asylum, though their approach to the absurdity of war seems far less crazy than that of society at large. Shortly, he is named king, with a beautiful ballet dancer (Genevieve Bujold, 1942–) his love interest. Appealingly colourful, mawkishly sentimental; the film served its purpose for a short period of time, then all but disappeared from sight. And sound.

ROMA (2018)

Arthouse cult Rating: *****

Mainstream Moviegoer Rating: NO STARS

Alfonso Cuaron, dir.; Cuaron, scr.; Cuaron, Nicholas Celis, Gabriela Rodriguez, pro.; 2.39:1; B&W; 135 min.; Esperanto.

 Following the critical and commercial success of the crowd-pleasing sci-fi classic *Gravity* (2013), Mexico's A.C. (1961–) returned to the arthouse approach that established him as a premiere auteur: director, writer, cinematographer, editor, and co-producer. Autobiographical, and filmed in sequence for as natural a sensibility as possible in Mexico City's upscale Cuahtemoc borough, A.C.'s focus is on the disintegration of a well to do family not unlike his own. Events are observed by a maid, 'Cleo' (Yalitza Aparicio), based on the real-life nanny Liboria Rodriguez; she helped the boy survive both familial and political-economic changes that swept his homeland during the turbulent 1970s. (L.R. appeared in A.C.'s early project *Y Tu Mamá También*, 2001). In concept, a coming of age work, yet this plays as a one-of-a-kind movie experience, if vaguely related to *Cinema Paradiso* considering the youth's fascination with films. Critics hailed this as a demanding masterpiece. Mainstream audiences booed out loud at the purposefully slow pace and endless use of the pan shot to reveal causal aspects that exist between seemingly unconnected people and places.

ROOM, THE (2003)

So Unbelievably Bad It's Great Cult Rating: *****

Any Other Imaginable Means of Viewing: NO STARS

Tommy Wiseau, dir.; Wiseau, scr.; Wiseau, pro.; 1.85:1; C; 99 min.; Wiseau-Films/TPW.

"You're tearing me apart!" No one could deliver that line more brilliantly than James Dean in *Rebel Without a Cause*. Likewise no actor could say it worse than T.W. (Piotr Wieczorek), born in Poland, 1955, the year *Rebel* was released. Though *T.R.* resembles a grade Z trash-indie, featuring quasi-professionals and mostly shot in a single room, the maddeningly claustrophobic soap opera (or satire on soaps, intentional or otherwise) had a budget of at least $6 million; Tommy is as independently wealthy as he is talentless. His story concerns 'Jonny' (T.W.) who lives with 'Lisa' (Juliette Danielle) but fears she sleeps with best friend 'Mark' (Greg Sestero). In each successive conversation characters say the same tired lines over and over, actors managing to mouth them in an even more inept manner each time, either hysterical or flat. Dialogue and situations are not to be believed. This film put to an end the long-held belief that Ed Wood was the world's worst director, E.W.'s *Plan 9 from Outer Space* the worst movie of all time.

ROYAL TENNENBAUMS, THE (2001)

Anderson Afficionado Rating: *****

Wes Anderson, dir.; Anderson, Owen Wilson, scr.; Anderson, Barry Mandel, Scott Rudin, pros.; 2.35:1; C; 110 min.; Touchstone.

Royal (Gene Hackman) returns to the wife (Anjelica Huston, 1951–) and children he hasn't visited for decades, insisting he will soon die. Royal hopes for a reconciliation—reckoning, even—which plays differently with each now adult daughter or son. Though all family members are geniuses, most have led bizarre lives owing to dysfunctional childhoods. Such material could make for the most eccentric of comedies or the bleakest of tragedies. In the hands of Anderson (1969–), the project includes elements of both. 'Quirky' is the term most often used to describe this auteur whose original vision is enhanced by great gifts at realizing his sensibility on film. The music of the Rolling Stones, the comic strips of Charles Schulz, the presence of actor Kumar Pallana, and a compulsion to film characters while underwater are a few among his signatures touches. A.'s movies are about the subjectivity of time, its relativity to our mood at any moment. Everything onscreen hints this is an adaptation of a book yet it's an original screenplay, somewhat autobiographical. Nuanced eccentricity.

RUSHMORE (1998)

Early Anderson Rating: ****

Wes Anderson, dir.; Anderson, Owen Wilson, scr.; Anderson, Barney Mendel, pros.; 2.35:1; C; 93 min.; American Empirical Pictures/Touchstone.

Anyone who might have incorrectly believed that *Bottle Rocket* (1996) was an appealingly offbeat one-shot for Anderson and Wilson (1968–) was proven wrong with the release of this equally quirky, even more satisfying blend of comedy and drama. The narrative revolves around 'Max Fischer' (Jason Schartzman, 1980–), the most unique student at the title prep school. Excelling at every extra-curricular activity he's also on the verge of flunking owing to lack of interest in classes. An unlikely friendship with a wealthy industrialist (Bill Murray, 1950–) is tested by growing competition for an intelligent teacher (Cynthia Williams). Anderson based the situation, characters, and sense of place on St. John's Prep School in Houston TX, which he had attended. He filmed most of this movie there. Influences on the style range from the children's stories of Roald Dahl, the unique photographs of France's Jacques-Henri Lartigue, and the early Francis Coppola quasi-autobiographical *You're a Big Boy, Now*. J.S., in his film debut, creates the greatest icon of privileged youth in search of personal identity since 'Holden Caulfield' in *The Catcher in the Rye* (1951). Wry, dry, sweetly sentimental. Cult-worthy co-stars include Luke Wilson, Seymour Cassel, and Brian Cox ('Hannibal Lecktor/Lecter' in *Manunter*).

SAW (2004)

Torture Chic Rating: ****

James Wan, dir.; Wan, Leigh Whannell, scr.; Mark Burg, Greg Hoffman, Oren Koules, pros.; 1.85:1; C; 103 min.; Twisted Pictures.

An Australian filmmaker of Chinese descent, Wan (1977–) made an auspicious premiere as director with this claustrophobic example of The Torture-Porn-Chic Movement. Always, Wan has insisted that was not his intention. However one interprets the piece, two men, a doctor (Cary Elwes) and a street person (Leigh Whannell) wake simultaneously to find they've been kidnapped and imprisoned in a filthy bathroom. Each is chained to an opposing wall. A dead body lies between them. As the ticking clock approaches six, the doctor must murder the hobo or his own wife and daughter will be slaughtered. All the while a detective (Danny Glover) tries to break in, while a frightful puppet and bound-and-gagged girl enter the twisting Jigsaw plot. Wan designed *S.* as an extended homage to Italian Giallos in general, Dario Argento's thriller *Deep Red* (1975) in particular. A film that resulted in public outcry against ever escalating graphic violence in modern movies.

SCARFACE (1983)

Conventional gangster film Rating: *

'Guy Movie' Rating: *****

Brian De Palma, dir.; Oliver Stone, scr.; Martin Bregman, pro.; 2.35:1; C; 170 min.; Universal.

That De Palma (1940–) is capable of making a good (some might say great) gangster epic is clear from *Carlito's Way* (1993). More typical of his approach: *Scarface,* a nominal success on theatrical release, then a huge cult movie on home video/DVD. Pacino (1940–) is 'Tony Montana,' a killer who enters the U.S. in 1980 during The Muriel Exodus from Cuba. In close parallel to Paul Muni's Sicilian (modelled on Al Capone) in the original *Scarface* (Howard Hawks, 1932), Tony works his way up through the ranks of Miami's crime-world, betraying the boss (Robert Loggia, 1930–2015) who gave him his start, seizing that man's mistress (Michelle Pfeiffer) and empire. The violence proved so strong the Ratings Board originally planned to label it 'X.' The 'f' word is repeated 225 times, a record back in pre-Tarantino 1983. Don't take my word; *Count* 'em. *S.* became one of the first 'man cave movies,' viewed on DVD by guys who delighted in the Grand Guignol approach, revelling in the film's sense of cheesiness, objectification of women, and out of control violence.

SCORPIO RISING (1964)

Pioneer Cult Film Rating: *****

Kenneth Anger, dir.; Ernest D. Gluckman, scr.; Gluckman, pro.; 1.37:1; B&W/C; 28 min.; Puck Film.

A former child actor, Anger (1927–) turned his wrath on mainstream movies with his purposefully nasty tell-all book *Hollywood Babylon* (1959). As an indie filmmaker, his mini-master pieces of bad (purposefully) taste culminated with this, Anger's legacy film. Simultaneously screened at grindhouses and arthouses even as the distinction between the two dissipated. Bruce Byron (1959–) plays 'Scorpio,' who models himself on James Dean in *Rebel* by way of Marlon Brando in *The Wild One.* Anger brings to the surface a homo-erotic aspect of each film that had heretofore gone unrecognized. A.'s then-revolutionary approach blended documentary realism with wild fantasies to destroy genre limitations. Graphic inserts of gay sexuality would have earned this an X, though the Ratings System would not be set in place for another two years. Popular rock 'n' roll records provide the soundtrack—a first for 'serious' (i.e., not *Beach Party*) filmmaking. In 1965, several mainstream theatres screened this for curious theatregoers intrigued by what was then called the Underground. David Lynch and John Waters acknowledge the vast influence of Anger on their own work.

SCOTT PILGRIM VS. THE WORLD (2010)

Edgy Youth Film Rating: ****

Edgar Wright, dir.; Wright, Michael Bacall, scr.; Wright, Marc Platt, pro.; 1.85:1; C; 112 min.; Universal.

Actually, it isn't the world *per se* though it might as well be when the eponymous loser (Michael Cera, 1988–) takes on seven former boyfriends of the gorgeous girl he hopes to date. Then again, 'Ramona Flowers' (Mary Elizabeth Winstead, 1984–) is worth such an epic tournament during a contemporary quest for true love in Toronto. Complicating matters: a barely legal age obsessive girlfriend (Ellen Wone) and a would-be rock band that can't get its sound together. The story may sound familiar but that's not true of E.W.'s directorial style. Watching one of his films is akin to being inside a speeding bullet which, fired at high velocity, tears through all surrounding objects, ricocheting, then flying off upside down in a different direction. Think of him as Kevin Smith on bad acid and you'll have a conception of his slacker subjects here portrayed in a colourful world of escape into video game alternative-living.

SCREAM (1996)

Nouveau Horror Rating: *****

Wes Craven, dir.; Kevin Williamson, scr. Cathy Konrad, pro.; 2.35;1; C; 111 min. (theatrical), 103 (severely cut version), Dimension Films.

"What's your favorite scary movie?" 'Ghostface' (wearing a white mask and accompanying black cloak) asks each of his victims the moment before death strike. Even as W.C. created contemporary horror with the ultra-violent *Last House on the Left*, then re-inventing the genre as a conduit of intellectual ideas with *A Nightmare on Elm Street*, here he again re-imagined shock by creating the *sentient* thriller: a horror film that *knows* it's a horror film (thanks to the script by Williamson, 1965–) as assorted young, attractive characters haunted by a menace discuss their individual possibilities for survival by talking about previous flicks they've seen, including Craven's own—as well as *Halloween*, *Friday the Thirteenth*, and others. The virgin 'Sydney Prescott' (Neve Campbell) has

A HORROR FILM THAT KNOWS IT'S A HORROR FILM: Drew Barrymore as the First Girl Victim in Wes Craven's 'aware' and self-referencing teen thriller.

the best chance to be the "final girl." Cult-worthy co-stars include Drew Barrymore as the first victim, also Courtney Cox, David Arquette, Rose McGowan, and Skeet Ulrich. Inspired by a famous painting of modern madness by Edvard Munch (1863–1944). The film that introduced the masses to the concept of caller I.D..

SEARCHING (2018)

One of a Kind Cult Rating: **** ½

Aneesh Chagantry, dir.; Chagantry, Sev Ohanian, scr.; Ohanian, Timur Bekmambetov, prod.; 1.85:1; C; 102 min.; Screen Gems/ Barzeleves.

    So-called 'Reality TV' programs such as NBC's *Dateline*, CBS's *48 Hours*, and ABC's *20–20* often feature factual stories of a parent who, frustrated by the authorities' ability to locate their missing child, set out to solve the crime by way of an intense internet search for 'digital fingerprints.' Hardly surprising that a fictional feature-film would be produced on this timely subject. What did come as a shock (as well as a stroke of genius) was Chagantry's decision to communicate the entire tale of a dad (John Cho) who will not give up trying to locate his daughter (Sara Sohn) via an aesthetic approach that transforms a contemporary thriller into a one-of-a-kind film. Every image which we, watching *Searching* in a theatre or on TV, view is rendered as some aspect of the technology that has become essential to everyday life: super-phones, lap-tops, monitors, etc. The indie filmmakers turn their tale of one such search into an artful means of forcing us to reconsider the manner in which we now observe reality (for better or in the minds of many worse!) by considering everything indirectly rather than actually looking at the world around us. Only weakness: the confusing and less than satisfying finale. Preceded by a similar if lesser work, Le Gabriade's *Unfriended* (2014).

SERBUAN MAUT, aka *DEATH RAID*, aka *THE RAID*, aka *THE RAID: REDEMPTION*, aka *DEADLY ASSAULT* (2011/2012)

Indonesian 'Excessive' Cinema Rating: *****

Gareth Evans, aka Gareth Huw Evans, dir., scr., Ario Sagantoro, pro.; 1.85:1; C; 101 min., release print, 102 min., director's cut; XYZ.

    Wales' Evans first attracted attention with *Samurai Monogatari* (2002), an imaginative mini-epic featuring Japanese students who at the time attended Cardiff University. His unique brand of Anglo-Asian international trans-cultural filmmaking appeared in full-length form here, shot in Jakarta, featuring renown stars of Indonesian martial arts. Imagine John Carpenter's *Assault on Precinct 13* as brought to life by Sam Peckinpah if he were still with us today as a means of approaching what's offered here. The Cinema of Excess style (Evans' most recurring image is of a slit neck bleeding profusely, such tight images sandwiched between far shots that allow for a spectacular view of non-stop combat) reaches a point of horrific saturation; bloodthirsty matches, if seemingly spontaneous, were as carefully choreographed as a top flight staging of the musical *Chicago*. Iko Uwalls (1983–) is police lieutenant 'Rama.' He and his men trapped in a tenement building by thugs loyal to drug dealer 'Tama' (Ray Sahetapy, 1957–). For those able to withstand the stomach-churning approach (in comparison, Tarantino seems like one of Disney's directors), a 2014 sequel managed to top the original as to onscreen carnage if not originality and inventiveness.

SERENITY (2005)

Cult Cinema Rating: **** ½

Joss Whedon, dir.; Joss Whedon, scr.; Barry Mendel, pro.; 2.35:1; C; 119 min.; Universal.

In Earth-year 2517, but existing in another Solar System, a drugged teen named 'River Tam' (Summer Glau, 1981–) attends a virtual school in a memory-induced glade, idyllic to the point of oppressiveness. The individualistic girl, rescued by her brother and several mercenaries, attempts to locate someone or something called 'Miranda.' Circumstances introduced in the earlier TV series allow her to join spaced-out misfits aboard a maverick ship they employ to avoid extremes of their cosmos: a seemingly listless majority, 'Alliance,' and 'The Reavers,' rare rebellious masked marauders on the frontier . The nearest thing to Normalcy—A Sane Middle—exists on the craft, where people experience emotions yet manage to control them. Glau won her role in part owing to balletic training: in action sequences, she creates a choreography that borders on flying. One line—"Eta Koorman Nah Smeah"—provides the greatest sci-fi non-sequiter since "Klaatu bareda nikto" in *The Day the Earth Stood Still* (Robert Wise, 1951). Fresh from success with *Buffy the Vam-*

pire Slayer (1992), Whedon (1964–) devised an offbeat TV show, *Firefly* (2002–2003), cancelled after 14 episodes. He convinced Universal to mount a medium-budget movie. Though not huge at the box-office, *S.* (like *Firefly*) amassed a cult following owing to a delicate balance between intellectualism, spirituality, F/X hardware, and well-staged stunts. Whedon would then reboot *The Avengers* franchise.

SEVEN (1979)

T&A Cult Rating: *****

All Other Ratings: **

Andy Sidaris, scr.; Sidaris, Robert Baird, William Driskill, scr.; Sidaris, pro.; 1.65:1; C; 101 min. (director's cut); 84 min. (mutilated version); American International Pictures.

Sidaris (1931–2007) turned out this sexy actioner for Corman. Seen mostly at Drive-Ins but also some four-wall theatres, here is a contemporary rip-off of *The Magnificent Seven*: A tough loner who formerly worked as a government agent though more recently privately employed as a Hitman (William Smith, 1933–) must do a job that our forces are legally unable to, murdering the crime bosses of Hawaii. To accomplish this, he rounds up a Baker's Half-dozen dangerous operatives. These include beautiful women: Barbara Leigh (1946– , who hoped to play Vampirella in a B movie and did model in costume for some of the magazine's covers; and Susan Kiger (1953–); a *Playboy* model and a veteran of the original T&A comedy, *H.O.T.S.* S.K.'s willingness to shed her bikini top caused A.S. to cast other Playmates in future films he would produce with his wife Arlene: *Malibu Express* (1985), *Hard Ticket to Hawaii* (1987), and *Fit to Kill* (1993), to name a few. Sidaris sensed that the Grindhouse would soon be gone and effectively marketed these via Home Video. At one point, the hero considers fighting a mighty enemy warrior, then shrugs and shoots him. Shortly, Spielberg and Lucas would 'borrow' this for *Raiders of the Lost Ark* (1981).

SE7EN (1995)

Cult Cinema for the New Mainstream Rating: *****

David Fincher, dir.; Andrew Kevin Walker, scr.; Arnold Kopelson, Phyllis Carlyle, prod.; 2.40:1; C; 127 min.; Cecchi Gori Prods./New Line Cinema.

With this film, D.F. (1962-) abandoned his successful career as director of music videos for Michael Jackson, George Michael, and Madonna while escaping the disaster of his *Alien 3* (1992). D.F. breathes rough-hewn life into a remarkable script by Andrew Kevin Walker (1964–), drawing together the fine details that characterize the best police procedurals with the grotesque aspects of grindhouse pictures. An old cop (Morgan Freeman) is uncomfortably teamed with a rookie (Brad Pitt) on a sickening case. A cold-blooded, insane though brilliant (and highly educated) serial killer (Kevin Spacey) is murdering assorted people who have, in his diseased mind, broken one of the Seven Deadly Sins. F. and cinematographer Darius Khondji settled on a bleach bypass process that left a silvery hue over images of constant rain in downbeat New York, causing color film stock to appear as lifeless as the gritty black and white of 1940s noirs. Hints in the dialogue suggest that 'John Doe' is a combination of John Hinckley Jr., twisted admirer of Jodie Foster and would-be assassin of Pres. Reagan, and David Berkowitz, the Son of Sam Killer. That this brilliant film incited no huge controversy and became a box-office hit makes clear how much societal values have changed since *Peeping Tom*.

SEVEN FACES OF DR. LAO, THE (1964)

Cult Rating: *****

Fantasy Film Rating: ****

George Pal, dir.; Charles Beaumont, scr.; Pal, pro.; 1.85:1; C; 100 min.; Metro-Goldwyn-Mayer.

Residents of a nearly deserted Arizona town are delighted when a cryptic Asian (Tony Randall, (1920–2004) arrives with his circus wagon. As they partake of ever stranger late-night shows, locals sense the myth-

MOVIE MAGIC: Thanks to the behind-the-scenes geniuses George Pal and William Tuttle, Tony Randall was able to literally disappear into many guises in a film based on a classic cult novel by Jack Finney.

ic power of these performances as supernatural Lao alters their lives. Based on a National Book Award winner, *The Circus of Dr. Lao* (1935) by Charles G. Finney (1905–1984). Ordinarily family-friendly George Pal (1908–1980; i.e., *Tom Thumb*, 1958) helped set the pace for a future in which fantasy films could appeal to grown-ups as well as teens. Randall's exceptional playing of seven roles (Lao/Merlin/Apollonius/ Pan/Medusa/The Serpent/Abominable Snowman did not win him a Best Actor Oscar though make-up artist William Tuttle (1912–2007) was singled out for an honorary statuette, a category for such skills added by the Academy as a result of this movie's impact. Superb stop-motion animation inspired such future avatars of sci-fi as Steven Spielberg and George Lucas. Screenwriter Beaumont (1929–1967), a gifted veteran of Corman's Poe adaptations and *The Twilight Zone*, was forced by MGM to add an overly conventional romance that diminishes the uniqueness.

7th VOYAGE OF SINBAD, THE (1958)

Ray Harryhausen Cult Rating: *****

Fantasy F/X Cult Rating: *****

Nathan Juran, dir.; Ken(neth) Kob, scr.; Charles H. Schneer, pro.; 1.66:1; C; 83 min.; Morningside Prods./Columbia.

"'The 7th Voyage of Sinbad' is the eighth wonder of the world!" So claimed a loud baritone over thirty-second teaser ads that ran on TV during the child-dominated hours of early afternoon the week before T.7.V.O.S. opened during Spring vacation. This was the first instance of a distributor fully employing that medium's effectiveness to 'sell' a film to the potential youth audience while cannily booking the movie at a time when kids had time on their hands. The title hero (Kerwin Matthews, 1926–2007) joins a wicked magician (Torin Thatcher, 1095–1981) searching for a magic lamp to free a princess (Kathryn Grant (Crosby), 1933–). What set this apart from other Arabian Nights flicks were the special effects, ranging from a monstrous Roc bird to the dazzling snake-woman dancer and the unforgettable non-human Cyclops, designed and created by Ray Harryhausen (1920–2013). Inspired by *King Kong* as a child, he talked his way into a job on the follow-up *Mighty Joe Young* (1949), then oversaw F/X for black-and-white sci-fi films including *The Beast from 20,000 Fathoms* (1953) and *Earth vs. the Flying Saucers* (1956). High-end B pictures, each was budgeted between $100,000 and $200,000. Fortuitously, Schneer (1920–2009) dreamed of bringing state-of-the-art special effects to glorious onscreen life in color and feature them constantly rather than save money by employing F/X sporadically. Columbia backed his vision with a $650,000 budget, film-

GENIUS AT WORK VII: Ray Harryhausen displays some of his iconic creations in his own studio; the table-top miniatures employed for both The Skeleton and Sinbad himself.

ing live sequences on the coast of Spain. Fabulous score by the great Bernard Herman (1911–1975) who provided the music for Hitchcock's *Vertigo*.

SEXY BEAST (2000)

Brit neo-Noir Rating: *****

Ben Kingsley Cultist Rating: *****

Jonathan Glaser Cult Rating: *****

Jonathan Glaser, dir.; Louis Mellis, David Scinto, scr.; Jeremy Thomas, prod.; 2:35:1; C; 89 min.; Chronopolis Films.

They almost got away with it! 'Gall' Ray Winstone (1957–) and four other retired English criminals enjoy their hard-earned sunset years with their wives in sunny Spain. What could ever pull them away from this paradisial existence? Nothing but 'Logan' (Ben Kingsley, 1943–), a London crime boss who will not accept 'no' for an answer. Logan is powerful, threatening, mean-spirited, inconceivably cruel, brutally nasty, and overpowering... his state of abject evil is as impossible to resist as was that of 'Hannibal Lector' in *Silence of the Lambs* (1991). How fascinating then that at one point Anthony Hopkins was considered for the mind-bendingly intense role, though it's now impossible to conceive of anyone but Sir B.K. in the part. As many twists and turns as you would expect from an entry in this crime subgenre, all of them odd, unexpected, and believable. The ferocity of Glaser's filmmaking, on a level with Kingsley's performance (he was nominated for but did not receive the Best Actor Oscar), carries the show from one sordid encounter to the next. A film that literally rubs your face in the filth, then has you (drained) gasping 'thank you for the experience!'

SHADOWS (1959)

Early Manhattan Indie Rating: *****

John Cassavetes, dir.; Cassavetes, scr.; Maurice McEndree, Seymour Cassel, 1.37:1; B&W; 81 min.; Lion Ent.

In the mid-1950s Cassavetes (1929–1989) was among those Method actors hired by Hollywood once Marlon Brando and Montgomery Clift introduced The New American Male of the post-war era (intense, sensitive, lonely). Cassavetes wanted was to direct his *own* cutting-edge movies. That ruled out Tinsel-town. In Manhattan he joined a so-called Underground movement. Employing cheap 16 mm film stock, often working with hand-held cameras rather than a tripod (akin to the French New Wave), choosing improvisational jazz for his soundtracks, Cassavetes focused on the era's Counter Culture: 'Ben' (Ben Carruthers), an African American hipster hoping to discover the meaning of life; Ben's sister 'Leila' (Leila Goldini), an impressionable girl looking for love in all the wrong places; and 'Hugh,' hoping to make it as a musician. Tony Ray, son of director Nick, plays the most significant non-black character. Bobby Darin (1926–1973), pop-star and closet hipster, appears. The grainy look and erratic editing, much criticized then, were key to *S.*'s status as "alternative cinema." An organic film, shot over a three-year period. J.C. regularly screened his work in progress, jotting down reactions from viewers, then refilming scenes. Through this radical process, he gradually *found* his film.

SHAUN OF THE DEAD (2004)

Cult Zombie Flick Rating: **** ½

Edgar Wright, dir.; Wright, Simon Pegg, scr.; Nira Park, pro.; 2.35:1; C; 99 min.; Rogue Pictures/Universal/Working Title.

Though Wright (1974–) is credited as the director, *S.O.T.D.* hardly rates as an auteurist work. Star/co-writer Pegg (1970–) and producer Park had earlier collaborated on edgy Brit TV shows for the BBC2 and Channel Four. Working on the cult TV series *Dr. Who*, they developed sci-fi scripts with a wry/dry sense of humor. This North London-set story concerns life-loser 'Shaun' (Pegg). He works at a dead-end clerking job and spends his free time at the local pub with slacker/dealer pal Ed (Nick Frost), ignoring his serious-minded girlfriend (Kate Ashfield). *S.O.T.D.* is to the Zombie genre in general, George Romero's *Night of the Living Dead* in particular, what *Blazing Saddles* (1974) was to the Western, *Airplane!* (1980) to the airport epics: lovingly satirizing every narrative trope. If that were it, this would rate as a fun film if hardly a cult classic. *S.O.T.D.* also depicts the unsatisfying lifestyle of its downbeat trio with the intelligence a serious drama might offer. *S.O.T.D.* employs (though never overobviously) the Zombie motif as a metaphor for the surrounding situation:

Long before neighbors literally transform into the walking dead, they are soul-less creatures. One of Tarantino's all-time favs.

SHAWSHANK REDEMPTION, THE (1994)

High Quality Cult Rating: *****

Frank Darabont, dir.; Darabont, Stephen King, scr.; Niki Marvin, pro.; 1.78:1; C; 142 min.; Castle Rock/Columbia.

Legendary author Stephen King (1947–) made his transition from pulp-fiction horror to serious literature with this subtly written, deeply touching story. France's F.D. (1959–) transitioned from directing cheap thrillers (*The Fly II*, 1989) to helming A list work. He collaborated with friend S.K. to expand a perfect piece of short fiction into an emotionally charged intimate epic. Banker 'Andy' (Tim Robbins, 1958–) in 1947 is jailed (double life sentences) for murders he did not commit. The American Dream of success gone, he enters prison as an embittered pessimist. Gradually, Andy learns how to survive from older inmate 'Red' (Morgan Freeman, 1937–), admittedly guilty of a murder. In time, each impacts on the other in a manner that can only be called spiritual. A.'s optimism returns when he realizes anyone who is at peace with himself is truly free. A wash-out theatrically, here is the ultimate case of a VHS release transforming an unknown item into a cult film and then a cinema classic. Tom Hanks, the original choice for Andy, worked for King and Darabont in their almost-as-great follow-up, *The Green Mile* (1999). In the original story, Red is not African American but Irish. Clint Eastwood was considered for the part.

SHOWGIRLS (1995)

So Inconceivably Bad It's Great Rating: *****

All Other Ratings: NO STARS

Paul Verhoeven, aka 'Jan Jansen,' dir.; Joe Eszterhas, scr.; 2.35:1; C; 131 min. (NC-17 print), 128 (cut script) Carolco/UA-MGM.

In 1992, collaborators Verhoeven (1938–) and Eszterhas (1944–) marvelled as their *Basic Instinct* scored big at the box-office and, despite in-your-face sexual-violence, received strong reviews. Three years later, *S.* opened to below/beyond dismal reviews and disastrous financial returns (less than $20 million on a $45 mil. budget). Yet in time this 'flop' became one of the most successful home-viewing films ever. Even today, this crass Las Vegas redo of *All About Eve* (1950) receives theatrical bookings. As with *Rocky Horror*, devotees costume themselves: 'Nomi Malone' (Elizabeth Berkley, 1972–), the ambitious lap dancer, and 'Crystal Connors' (Gina Gershon, 1962–), star of exotic Terpsichore whom the young comer would love to replace. *R.H.* embodies Conscious Camp: The team purposefully made a tongue in cheek bad movie. But does that indicate heightened hipness or the worst sort of cynicism? Cultists love to shout out dialogue as actresses shriek those lines onscreen. Tied with *Mommy Dearest* as the most beloved big-budget bad movie ever.

SIDEWAYS (2004)

American Arthouse Cult Rating: *****

Wine Lovers' Rating: *****

Paul Giamatti Cultists: *****

Alexander Payne; Payne, Jim Taylor, scr; Michael London, pro.; 1.85:1; C; 126 min.; Fox Searchlight.

Pinot Noir and The Meaning of Life: That might have worked as an alternative title for this deliberately paced, low-key comedy-drama. Payne (1961–) pitched it as *My Dinner with Andre* goes 'On The Road' in Wine Country. A non-slapstick odd couple composed of mis-matched early middle-aged friends—one a gregarious out-of-work actor who will shortly marry (Thomas Hayden Church), the other a melancholic, neurotic aspiring novelist (Paul Giamatti, 1967-)—drive, eat, play golf, romance a couple of women (Sandra Oh, Virginia Madsen) while on the former's last fling. An idiosyncratic chamber drama set against the big wide-open sky of Northern California takes a philosophical approach to those who try and find themselves when everything important in life appears to have passed them by. Though *S.* won numerous critics' awards for Best Screenplay, much of the dialogue was improvised. The all-time fav film of Wine Lovers everywhere.

SILENT RUNNING (1972)

Dystopian Future Film Rating: *** ½

Douglas Trumbull, dir.; Deric Washburn, Michael Cimino, Steve Bochco, scr.; Trumbull, Michael Gruskoff, pro.; Universal.

GENIUS AT WORK VIII: Following the commercial success of *2001: Space Odyssey*, creative filmmakers like Douglas Trumbull received the 'green light' to address serious social issues in fantasy formats; he is seen here several years later while finalizing the F/X processes for Steven Spielberg's blockbuster *Close Encounters of the Third Kind* (1980).

Rule numero ono in Hollywood, then and now: Everyone would in truth rather direct than whatever else it is they are doing. That included D.T. (1942–), a visual effects genius who brought fantastical concepts to believable onscreen life in such sci-fi classics as *2001: A Space Odyssey* (1968), *Close Encounters of the Third Kind* (1977), and *Blade Runner*. His pet project? This purposefully small message movie that precedes the beloved *WALL-E* (2008) with a warning of what might occur if we do not get around to caring for our environment. In a dystopian future, all flora and fauna has disappeared from the face of the earth. Far off in space, a ship carries beautiful examples of greenery in the manner of a flying museum. When word arrives from our planet that the crew is ordered to ditch such remnants and return home, all members are delighted except one: Bruce Dern as a biologist so devoted to nature that he kills the others and sets off with this last refuge of an otherwise bygone world. The film rings warmly in the memory of those who saw it way back when. Viewed today, *S.R.* is a bit obvious as to theme and tacky in terms of production values. The storyline is uncomfortably close to that of Rolf Forsberg's *Ark* two years earlier. Still, you gotta love those scene-stealing drones Huey, Dewey and Louie.

SLING BLADE (1996)

Billy Bob Cult Rating: *****

Billy Bob Thornton, dir./scr.; David Bushell, Brandon Rosser, prod.; 1.85:1; C; 135 min. (theatrical cut), 148 min. (dir. Cut); Miramax/Shooting Gallery.

In 1994, Billy Wilder (1906–2002) attended a cocktail party and, when other guests proved boring, struck up a conversation with a likeable waiter who spoke of his desire to become a leading man. Noting that the youth lacked conventional good looks, the old-hand suggested that he write a script for himself with a character-lead, its central focus on an off-beat but sympathetic individual. Later that night, B.B.T. (1955–) began work on the project that would make him a star. In *S.B.*, he plays a soft-spoken, low-key, simple (some might claim 'simple-minded') man of the south, recently released from a mental institution following twenty years confinement for killing his mother and her lover. Now, will adjustment be possible? Or will he murder a redneck (Honky tonk singing great Dwight Yoakum) who refers to the fellow as 'retard.'? Robert Duvall (1947–) ought to have received an Oscar nod (Best Supporting Actor) for his nuanced work as the still confused father. Another standout: John Ritter (1948–2003), often written off as a lightweight (*Three's Company* 1976–1984), portrays a gay friend in a non-stereotyped manner.

SMOKE (1995)

Cult Rating: **** ½

Conventional Film Rating: **** ½

Wayne Wang, dir.; Paul Auster, scr.; Kenzo Horikoshi, Greg Johnson, Peter Newman, Hisami Kuroiwa, prods.; 1.85:1; C/B&W; 112 min.; Miramax/Neue Deutsche.

On a Brooklyn street-corner sits Augie's, a tobacco shop where the flotsam and jetsam of contemporary society wander in and out. Augie (Harvey Keitel, 1939–), the philosophic owner, eagerly awaits conversations with alcoholic novelist Paul (William Hurt, 1950–), this ripe performance modelled on the screenwriter. Their small circle of friends includes one-armed garage owner Cyrus (Forest Whittaker, 1961–). In time the lives of disparate people impact on others—perhaps even everyone, everywhere. Wang (1949–) offers an acute observation on the things of life, a dramatically (and often comedic) microscopic study of an invisible magic existing just beneath the seemingly grim surface of daily reality. Keitel's final moments (relating a long but never tiresome Christmas fable) ought to have won him a Best Supporting Actor Oscar. Screenwriter Auster (1947–) directed several sequences. Wang's best film to date.

SONG OF THE SOUTH (1946)

Cult Disney Rating: *****

Willard Jackson, Harve Foster, dir.; Walt Disney, prod.; 1.37:1; C; 94 min.; RKO Radio Pictures.

The only Disney Golden Age project which became a cult film rather than a mainstream classic. This was intended by W.D. (1901–1966) as Hollywood's first post-war pro-Civil Rights movie, setting the pace for a future in which Afro-Americans were portrayed sans the despicable stereotypes of Tinseltown's embarrassing past—most notably, *Gone With the Wind* (1939). Disney drew on the writings of (Anglo) Georgian Joel Chandler Harris (1848–1908), who diligently (and lovingly) recorded the Southern African American community's folklore. Wise old 'Uncle Remus' (James Baskett, 1904–1948) relates moral fables about The Critters, teaching virtue to children, black and white alike. The film was attacked by the N.A.A.C.P., which complained (among many things) that Negro (the polite term at this time) culture had been commercialized by the White Power Structure. It's worth noting, though, that Hattie McDaniel (1895–1952) portrays a former slave in a non-stereotypical manner as to character, if not clothing. Five years earlier she won an Oscar for embodying every stereotype of the plantation Aunt in *G.W.T.W.* With the advent of political correctness, *S.O.T.S.* came to be perceived as 'proof' that Disney was racist, though the final image offers a visual plea for integration of America in general, the South in particular. Pulled from distribution and never officially released on VHS, DVD, or Blue-Ray, this became an Underground classic owing to easily available imported bootleg discs.

SPIDER BABY, OR THE MADDEST STORY EVER TOLD (1967)

Cult Horror Rating: ** ½

Beverly Washburn Afficionado Rating: ****

Jack Hill, dir.; Hill, scr.; Gil Lasky, Paul Moka, pro.; 1.66;1; B&W; 81 min.; Lasky-Monka.

 A terrifying, decrepit mansion resembles the one in William Castle's *House on Haunted Hill* where Carol Ohmart received her just desserts from husband Vincent Price. She's back (he's not), this time dressed in lingerie personally picked out by Hill at then-notorious Frederick's of Hollywood. Also around: Lon Chaney, Jr. as 'Bruno' who in better days drove members of a degenerate family around in their beloved Duesenberg. Now he covers up crimes committed by the final cursed owner. One of Chaney's final horror items and one of Sid Haig's first; the film features a passing of the torch from an old-time star of seedy cinema to his equally creepy successor. Also on hand: Beverly Washburn (–), the cry-on-cue girl from Walt Disney's *Old Yeller* (1957–). Originally to have been titled 'Cannibal Orgy.' Re-released as *The Liver Eaters*.

STAND BY ME (1986)

Nostalgia Rating: **** ½

Rob Reiner, dir.; Raynold Gideon, Bruce A. Evans, scr.; Andrew Scheinman, pro.; 1.85:1; C; 89 min.; Columbia.

One more of the many nostalgia films for the late 1950s and early 1960s turned out during the 1970s and 1980s, this brief (more resemblant of a novella than a novel) coming-of-age tale quietly became a theatrical hit and, ever since, a cult film. Though specifically set in the Pacific North-

'THE BODY': Will Wheaton, River Phoenix, Jerry O'Connell, and Corey Feldman are four friends who set out to discover the title object in Rob Reiner's delightful film from Stephen King's non-horror story.

west, Reiner's (1944–) adaptation of Stephen King's "The Body" (1982) vividly captures the meaning of childhood friendship and the degree to which this cannot be fully appreciated until one reconsiders such bonding from the perspective of an adult. Here, that figure is Richard Dreyfuss (1947–), a professional writer who learns one of his closest buddies has just passed. He recalls an odd long ago odyssey in which he, the deceased, and two other boys (Will Wheaton, Corey Feldman, River Phoenix, Jerry O'Connell play the foursome) set out to recover the remains of a missing child, learning about themselves and the meaning of their relationships along the way. Most memorable sequences: a touching conversation by a campfire; near-death experience on a railroad trestle.

STARSHIP TROOPERS (1997)

Sci Fi Cult Rating: ****

Paul Verhoeven, dir.; Ed(ward) Neumeier, scr.; Jon Davison, Alan Marshall, prods.; 1.85:1; C; 129 min. The Big Picture; Tri-Star Touchstone.

Verhoeven's classic sci-fi films (*Robocp*, 1987; *Total Recall*, 1990) offer in the guise of entertainment a harsh criticism of our immediate world. Surprisingly, the Danish-born director agreed to film Robert A. Heinlein's (1907–1988) novel for male teen readers, celebrating the militarism Verhoeven elsewhere rejects. A futuristic West Point academy transforms white cadets into fascist fighters. P.V. had hoped to undermine R.H.'s view, satirizing what that author presented at face value. Nordic Casper Van Dien (1968–) suggests his character's descent from fleeing Nazis who became the boys in Brazil. Uniforms draw heavily on those worn by Germans during WWII though V. did integrate the film's space cadets as to race and gender. Despite spectacular F/X for and massive battles with arachnids, *S.T.*—budgeted at over $100 mill—disappointed at the box-office. Cable TV/Home Viewing turned it into a cult success. Direct-to-video sequels (2004; 2008), *not* directed by P.V,. revived H.'s ultra-conservative values.

STATKIR, aka STALKER (1979)

Cult Cinema Rating: *****

Arthouse Rating: *****

Science Fiction Film Rating: *****

Philosophy 101 Rating: *****

Andrei Tarkovsky, dir; Tarkovsky, scr.; Alexsandra Demidova, pro.; 1.37:1; C/B&W; 162 min; Mosfilm.

 The title does not refer to a threatening person who haunts others in real-life situations, rather an experienced guide who serves as pathfinder for bold seekers of truth in a faraway future-world. The planet is possibly a de-evolved earth or some far point in the cosmos. He leads the way for a pair of oppositional volunteers: A world-weary writer who hopes that when they reach a legendary 'Room' at the far end of a Zone (like Rod Serling's on American television) he will find metaphysical inspiration. This will restore his long-lost faith in a meaningful existence. Also along: a scientist who wishes to discover a hard, cold, factual explanation of what makes life possible. Deadly opponents guard the secret, philosophical or intellectual, if indeed there is a secret… The best known, most influential Soviet filmmaker since Sergei Einstein a century ago, A.T. (1932–1986) rejects that revolutionary's montage theory. This (like his previous classic *Solaris,* 1972) consists of long shots, encouraging a viewer to reach his own conclusions as to what occurs. However groundbreaking the style, A.T.'s substance is traditional. For here is a drama that obeys the ancient Greek unities of time and space. S. so transcends its science-fiction origins—adapted from the 1972 novel *Roadside Picnic* by Boris & Arkady Strugatsky—that many fans of this appealing combination of Philosophy and Psychiatry believe it should not be characterized as a genre piece.

STEPFORD WIVES, THE (1975)

Feminist Cult Rating: ****

Bryan Forbes, dir.; William Goldman, scr.; Edgar J. Sherick, pro.; 1.85:1; C; 115 min.; Fadsin/Palomar Pictures.

 The young men of Stepford hold executive jobs in Manhattan and take the train home every night to their old-fashioned suburb in Connecticut. All seems rosy. Despite the Women's Movement exploding everywhere else, Stepford's wives are content with being Retro-Women: cooking, cleaning, enjoying bridge games. When a new couple arrives, the independently-minded wife (Katharine Ross, 1940–) senses something sinister beneath the calm surface. The women who once 'were' have been replaced by cyborg-slaves. Terrifyingly, she is next on the list. *T.S.W.* opened poorly. Ross did not have the acting chops of Forbes' original choice, Diane Keaton. And the director (1926–2013), despite fine thrillers from the 1960s (*Séance on a Wet Afternoon*, 1964), delivered the equivalent of an ordinary made-for-TV movie. Imagine what Roman Polanski, who brought novelist Ira Levin's other bestseller *Rosemary's Baby* to the screen, might have done with this! Gradually, *T.S.W.* developed a following among Second Wave feminists who interpreted this as a sci-fi allegory for everything they stood against.

STRIPPED TO KILL (1987)

Erotic Thriller Appeal: **** ½

Kay Lenz Cult Value: *****

Katt Shea, dir.; Shea, Andy Ruben, scr.; Ruben, Roger Corman, Mark Byers, Matt Leipzig, pros.;1.85:1; C; 88 min.; Concorde/ New Horizons.

 In 1985, L.A. based writer-director Shea (1957–) gave in to then-husband Andy Ruben's pleadings and visited a strip club, despite her feminist prejudice against 'the objectification of women.' While watching, she had an epiphany: Uneducated women living on the edge could *empower* themselves as 'ecdysiasts.' Shea wrote a script that dared question whether striptease might be a legitimate blue-collar form of art (Terpsichore). Her film involves a police detective (Kay Lenz, 1953–) assigned to go undercover (as a dancer) and apprehend a killer menacing the girls. Such women are sympathetically portrayed. The lead, who initially resists dancing, not only catches the criminal but becomes hooked: the sense of control a nude dancer has over men has become addictive. Lenz had been singled out for stardom in the 1970s but never found the role to put her on the A list.

STUNTMAN, THE (1980)

One of a Kind Film Rating: *****

Richard Rush, dir.; Rush, Lane B. Marcus; Rush, pro.; 1.85:1; C; 131 min.; 131 min.; 20th Century Fox.

From the moment R.R. (1929–2021), a marginal moviemaker with such credits as Drive In flicks *Hells Angels on Wheels* and *Thunder Alley*

HOLLYWOOD'S HOLLYWOOD: Peter O'Toole as a megalomaniac director and Steve Railsback as the eponymous hero appeared in a box-office disaster that slowly but surely earned a loyal and ever-expanding following.

(both 1967), read Paul Brodeur's remarkable 1970 novel, Rush dedicated himself to bringing this project to the screen. Ten years later, *T.S.M.* was released (more correctly dumped) on the market without fanfare. P.R. people at Fox (like execs at Columbia who earlier declined to green light it) had no idea how to sell this. Was it a grindhouse action flick with an A list star (Peter O'Toole, 1932–2013) top billed? A surreal satire on the order of *Dr. Strangelove* or a big bang extravaganza like *The Bridge on the River Kwai* (1957)? O'Toole did receive an Oscar nomination for his role as 'Eli Cross,' a megalomaniac filmmaker modelled partly on Orson Welles, John Huston, Fritz Lang, Otto Preminger and a host of other self-styled gods of the cinema. Steve Railsback (1945–) plays the title character, a fugitive from the police who passes himself off as a pro stuntman to disappear among a moviemaking crew. One of the great films about film, as a seemingly realistic adventure transforms into a phantasmagoria. A minute though obsessive group of devotees consider this the finest American film of the 1980s.

SUCCUBUS, aka *NECRONOMICON* (1968)

Jess Franco Cult Rating: *****

S&M/B&D Lesbian Vampire Film Rating: *****

Jesus (Jess) Franco, dir.; Pier A. Caminnecci, scr.; Adrien Hoven, pro.; 1.66:1; C; 95 min. (director's cut); 99 min. (original U.S. theatrical release); Aquila Films.

A beautiful redhead (Janine Reynaud, 1930–2018) tortures, then murders a bound girl. But 'Lorna' is a nightclub performer, this a contemporary West German variation on Paris' Grand Guignol. The appeal for audiences: uncertainty as to whether erotic murders are performed or actual. Offstage, Lorna may be a vampire, seducing females (one sequence involving moving mannequins is like nothing previously seen in a film), though this could be Lorna's waking fantasy or a dark dream. To avoid censorship, Spain's Franco (1930–2013) shot this, his first project, outside his homeland. Lorna may be under the control of a disturbing male character (Michel Lemoine, 1922–2013) who recalls the title villain in Fritz Lang's 'Dr. Mabuse' movies. *S.* also resembles *La Dolce Vita*, with its depiction of the 1960s 'sweet life'; *Last Year at Marienbad*, where reality and dream merge into a sensuous out-of-time/out-of-space 'other world'; and Luigi Pirandello's *Six Characters in Search of an Author* (1921), in which differing dimensions of reality are explored.

SUDDENLY (1954)

Cult Curio Rating: ****

Sinatra Aficionado Rating: *****

Lewis Allen, dir.; Richard Sale, scr.; Robert Boosler, pro.; 1.75:1; B&E; 75 min.; Libra Prods.

"Funny name for a town," passers-by comment at the beginning and end of this B thriller, referring to the contrast between a quiet village and its name. Any sense of irony dissipates as a widowed mom (Nancy Gates), her son (Kim Charny), and father-in-law (James Gleason) are approached on their hillside home by a stranger (Frank Sinatra) claiming to be a government agent. Supposedly, he's here to ensure safety for the president, who will pass by on a train. A local police officer (Sterling Hayden) concludes that 'John Baron' is an assassin. Sinatra's performance—a bizarre, over-the-top, mesmerizing combination of claptrap histrionics and psychological realism—is his most memorable. *S.* crystalizes the Norman Rockwell surface of our Eisenhower Era while revealing growing violence just beneath the surface. Lee Oswald watched *Suddenly* three days before the JFK assassination (11/22/63). This (along with *The Manchurian Candidate*) was then pulled from distribution for twenty years.

SUPERMAN VS. THE MOLE MEN (1951)

Mainstream B Movie Rating: ***

Nostalgia Rating: **** ½

Lee Sholem, dir.; Richard Fielding, aka Robert Maxwell, scr.; Barney A. Sarecky, pro.; 1.37:1; B&W; 58 min.; Lippert.

"IT'S A BIRD... IT'S A PLANE... NO, IT'S... GEORGE REEVES": Before the beloved TV series premiered, the producers tested out the viability of their concept with a brief movie programmer later divided into a two-parter for the show.

To test the waters for the *Adventures of Superman* TV series, (1952–1958), a B budget movie was shot and released at kiddie matinees. George Reeves (1914–1959) and Phyllis Coates (1927–) played 'Clark Kent' and 'Lois Lane.' The reporters arrive at an oil-drilling project after hearing rumors about monsters arising from beneath the earth. This was the first feature-length film to be made from a D.C. (then National Publishing) comic, previous releases all serials. The film went over well. A syndicated series appeared the next year. Reruns continued virtually forever. Coates left after season one, replaced by Noel Neill. Sholem's 'get the job done fast' approach won him further TV work including 12 *Superman* episodes. This film was broken down into a two-parter, 'The Unknown People,' in 1953.

SUSPIRIA (1977)

Argento Cult Rating: *****

Dario Argento, dir.; Argento, Daria Nicoldi, scr.; Claudio Argento, pro.; 2.35:1; C; 98 min.; Seda Spettacoli.

    Argento (1940–) is the unofficial master of the Giallo sub- genre of horror; *Suspiria*, his greatest film. Yet it is not a Giallo in the generic sense: No garish ultra-contemporary colors or brazen women's dead-nude bodies on display. This is a more traditional tale (if with gore aplenty for the modern viewer) in the haunted mansion vein. 'Suzy' (Jessica Harper, 1949–) arrives in a rainstorm at a German ballet school and gradually comes to grasp this is a tower of terrors. D.A. cast semi-retired Joan Bennett (1910–1990) to play the academy's Dark Lady as a reference to her work with Fritz Lang, this director's influence on D.A. greater even than that of Hitch. Udo Keir's (1944–) creepy look created a cult for the actor. D.A. had the cast and crew watch Disney's *Snow White and the Seven Dwarfs* (1937) to grasp the mood he wanted. In his mind that was the greatest horror film ever. The use of a Steadicam brings our viewing experience into a more current form of cinematic expression. As the story grows ever more surreal, maggots appear, actual or part of the heroine's nightmare.

SWEET SWEETBACK'S BAADASSSSS SONG (1971)

Radical Counter-Cultural Rating: ****

Melvin Van Peebles, dir.; Van Peebles, scr.; Van Peebles, Jerry Gross, prod.; 1.37:1; C; 97 min.; Yeah/Cinemation.

    Sick of watching Sidney Poitier play 'black apologists' eager to compromise with White America in such films as *Lilies of the Field* (1967) and *Guess Who's Coming to Dinner* (1967), Chicago's M.V.P. (1932–) wrote a script intended to wave a symbolic middle-finger at The Man. He plays the eponymous velour clad anti-hero who hangs with cops until their brutal beating of a Black Panther sets him off on a vengeance spree. When M.V.P. couldn't raise the full half a million necessary to shoot for 19 days, a pre-scandal Bill Cosby advanced him additional funds. Adapting then-revolutionary stylistic approaches from cutting-edge Euro-cinema—jump cuts, hand-held camera, rack-focus, etc.—M.V.P. created the first radical Afro American art indie. To reach a wider audience, distributors transformed *S.S.B.S.* into the initial black exploitation flick. Earth Wind and Fire perform M.V.P.'s musical compositions but were never paid. 'Young Sweetback' is portrayed by Mario Van Peebles. In *Baadasssss!* (2003), a film about the making of this movie, Mario (1957–) plays his father. Even today, some scenes are considered too disturbing for general viewers.

SWITCHBLADE SISTERS (1975)

Cult Rating: **

Jack Hill, dir.; Hill, F.X. Maier, John Prizer, scr.; Prizer, pro.; 1.85:1; C; 91 mins.; Centaur Pictures.

Why does this lightweight entry in the Girl Gang subgenre of juvenile delinquent flicks qualify as a Cult Film? Perhaps an acknowledgement by Q.T. that it's a long-standing fav has something to do with it. But has Quentin seen it recently? No great fun to be had in Hill's uneasy combination of Corman's Bad Girls in Black Leather flicks from the 1950s and Meyer's Wicked Women Drive In classics of the 1960s. Here, a newcomer (Joanne Nail, 1947–) to a rough neighbourhood vies with the top teen thug (Robbie Lee, 1954–) as leader of the pack. Lenny Bruce's daughter Kitty (1955–) plays the pleasingly plump suck-up to each tyrant. The leads, wearing hot pants, look like middle-class Long Island mall-walkers. Lesbian wardens threaten them in jail. The narrative leads to the inevitable catfight. Most interesting element has 'The Debs' dumping their dominating boyfriends to become 'The Jezebels' for 'female empowerment.'

TEEN IDOL... WITH A SECRET: The boy who had all the girls screaming in the early 1950s attempted as best he could to keep his own gayness in the closet.

TAB HUNTER CONFIDENTIAL (2015)

Gay Cult Rating: *****

Jeffrey Schwartz, dir.; Tab Hunter, Eddie Muller, scr.; Allan Glaser, Neil Koenigsberg, prod.; 1.76:1; C/B&W; 90 min.

The All-American Boy as Idealized by Hollywood's Dream Factory… if in the 1940s that had been Sonny Tufts, Troy Donahue in the 1960s, no question that in between them the heart-throb of teenage girls everywhere was that clean-cut fellow born Arthur Keim, Tab Hunter (1931–2018). No wonder, then, that for the better part of a decade, he reigned as the number one choice to play romantic leads opposite Tinseltown's Girl Next Door types in movies and on TV: Natalie Wood, Debbie Reynolds, Jane Powell, Diana Lynn. How did Sandra Dee get left out of the mix? Hunter, however, kept a precious secret that set him apart from his predecessor and replacement: He was gay, sensing this from an early age. Working with the star's full cooperation, drawing from an excellent (and utterly non-exploitive) book by Eddie Muller (1958–), Schwartz (1969–) has created a gem of a documentary that not only reveals the plight of such people 'once upon a time in Hollywood' but an understanding of the American mindset during the 1950s about homosexuality, as well as the manner that arrogant, nasty editors at the infamous *Confidential* magazine (a forerunner of the equally despicable *National Enquirer*) held not only actors but also studios at their mercy.

TAMPOPO (1985)

Food fanatic Rating: *****

Cult Cinema Rating: *****

Juzo Itami, dir.; Itami, scr.; Itami, Seigo Hosogoe, Kumihiko Tamaoki, prods.; 1.37:1; C; 114 min.; New Century Prods.

"The first Ramen Western," posters for *Tampopo* announced when Itami's (1933–1997) second feature-film received distribution beyond Japan's borders. An Asian equivalent to Woody Allen, J.I.'s off-the-wall comedies touch upon the relationship of food to sex as well as the continuum between the two as it impacts on the meaning of life… and death. Here, the title character (Nobuko Miyamoto) supports her son after the husband/father dies by serving noodle soup in a small café. Nothing much happens until magic occurs with the arrival of a wandering Wild West gunslinger (Tsutomu Yamazaki) worthy of *A Fistful of Dollars* (1964). He transforms ordinary food into a metaphysical elixir, revitalizing these lost souls as eternal optimists. Multiple narratives allow us to witness the impact of great sex merged with great food (both involve forms of hunger). Alternately goofy/grotesque and cute-charming. Though a one of a kind movie, *Tampopo* will remind fans of Food on Film of *Like Water for Chocolate* (1992) and *Chocolate*.

TANGARINE (2015)

Future-of-Cinema Cult Status: *****

Sean Baker, dir.; Baker, Chris Bergoch, cr.; Baker, Darren Dean, pro.; 2.35:1; C; 88 min.; Duplass Bros./Through Films.

Just imagine: You're cruising West Hollywood and spot a hooker running around like a madman/woman in pursuit of God only knows what. So you whip out your iPhone 5S smartphone and record what transpires as the scene grows ever more unexpectedly chaotic. An odd personal keepsake to amuse friends once back home. In fact it's a carefully planned, neatly structured narrative film that filmmaker Baker (1971–) unveiled at Sundance with hopes that it might become the biggest indie success story since *The Blair Witch Project*. While that did not happen commercially, here is the movie that proves anyone can, in our age, become an auteur. Baker also involved himself in the editing, cinematography, and all other aspects including the one that gives the film its name and insures that this is not merely on-the-fly documentation but gonzo art: an orange color coordination that initially appears to be imposed on everything for no rhyme or reason but actually draws all other elements of the story together. Kiki Kitana Rodriguez is mesmerizing as a person (that term is important here) recently released from prison and eager to find some form of solidity despite a street lifestyle on that familial moment, Christmas Eve. Running perfectly parallel to the revolutionary approach is a breakthrough theme: Whereas so many indie films of the past attack the limitations of cinema genre, this piece by implication sets out to end all 'old-think' concepts of gender.

TARGETS (1968)

Drive In Movie set in a Drive In Rating: ****

Karloff Cult Rating: *****

Peter Bogdanovich, dir.; Bogdanovich, Polly Platt, Sam Fuller, scr.; Bogdanovich, Roger Corman, pros.; 1.85:1; C; 90 min.; Saticoy Prods./Paramount.

Along with Coppola and Scorsese, Bogdanovich (1939–) was one of those young hopefuls given opportunity to direct low-budget exploitation films by schlock-meister Corman. His deal: make any movie you want, so long as you star Boris Karloff (1887–1969), who owed Corman several days shooting, and include 20 minutes of an earlier B movie, *The Terror*

I LOST IT AT THE DRIVE-IN: Many low budget late-1960s films were shown in Drive-Ins; Peter Bogdanovich's *Targets* concludes there.

(1963). This insured that only 70 mins. of new footage need be shot. P.B. and Platt (1939–2011; a couple at the time) devised a scenario about an over-the-hill monster-movie star attending a retrospective of at the Reseda Drive-In. This is intercut with a contemporary story about a clean-cut teen (Tim O'Kelly) who inexplicably goes on a killing rampage, inspired by two real-life events: Michael Andrews Clark firing at California highway drivers in 1965; Charles Whitman killing fellow students from a tower on an Austin campus in 1966. Ancient 'Byron Orlak' sadly notes that his onetime 'too violent' thrillers seem tame compared to everyday life in our post-JFK-assassination U.S. P.B. wrote his own epitaph as a director when the filmmaker he plays (a variation on himself) watches Howard Hawks' *The Criminal Code* (1931) and sighs: "All the great movies have already been made." Spielberg, Coppola, Scorsese and others would shortly prove that statement untrue.

TARZAN AND HIS MATE (1934)

Rating: *****

Cedric Gibbons, James C. McKay, Jack Conway, dirs.; James Kevin McGuinness, Leon Gordon, scr.; Bernard H. Hymann, pro.; 1.37:1; B&W; 104 min. (complete), 91 min. (original theatrical release), MGM.

An abundance of riches best describes this, the first sequel to MGM's epic *Tarzan the Ape Man* (1932), shot on location in Africa by W.S. Van Dyke. Johnny Weissmuller (1904–1984), an Olympics star, and Maureen O'Sullivan (1911–1998) return as Edgar Rice Burroughs' (1875–1950) 'Lord Greystoke' and wife *(were* they ever officially married?) 'Jane Parker.' Filmed after sophisticated sound recording was introduced at MGM, so T.A.H.M. is not burdened by dated aspects as is its predecessor. Evil ivory hunters encroach on the jungle. Tarzan and monkey-buddy 'Cheetah' to the rescue! At the time, all anyone wanted to talk about: 'Is that *really* Maureen O'Sullivan performing the nude underwater ballet?' Expert swimmer Josephine McKim is her body-double in sub-aqua shots; O'Sullivan appears topless when Jane swims on the surface. Too bad most folks didn't get to see the 21 min. sequence. The film was released *after* the Production Code had been introduced. The uncut version became a cherished midnight movie. The only directorial credit for C.G. (1893–1960) whose 1,059 Art Direction credits include *The Wizard of Oz* (1939).

"ME TARZAN, YOU MATE!": To be politically correct, might a current remake have Jane rescueing Tarzan? Here, Maureen O'Sullivan and Johnny Weissmuller embody the roles.

TAXI DRIVER (1976)

Rating: *****

Martin Scorsese, dir.; Paul Schrader, scr.; Michael and Julia Phillips, pros.; 1.85:1; C; 113 min.; Columbia.

Scorsese (1942–) had already established himself as a great director of Manhattan movies with *Mean Streets* (1973) when hot (for the moment) producers M. and J. Phillips matched him with a script by Schrader

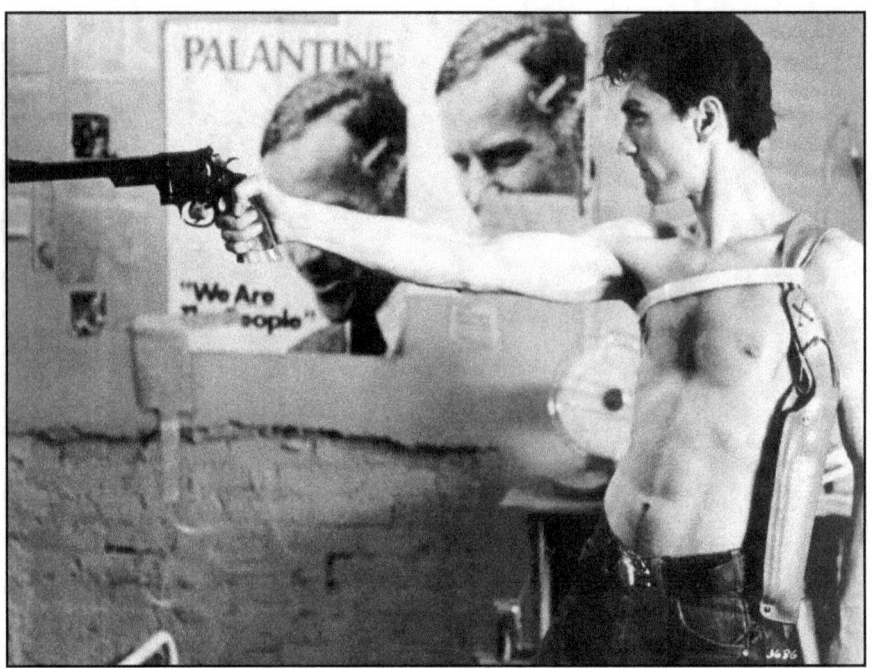

"YOU TALKIN' TO ME?": Martin Scorsese and Robert De Niro reinvented the very idea of American cinema in the 1970s with movies like *Mean Streets* and *Taxi Driver*.

(1946–). In it, a Vietnam War vet returns to discover America went belly-up while he was overseas. A late-night cabbie in a worn Checker, 'Travis Bickle' views the ruined world of drugs and violence with moralistic fervor. In time he becomes obsessed with omnipresent sleaze, particularly porn. Robert De Niro (1943–) endows T.B. with a sense of Scorsese's Catholic guilt *and* Schrader's deeply Calvinistic vision. Travis proves his own worst enemy, treating a society deb (Cybill Shepherd) like a whore and an underage prostitute (Jodie Foster, 1962–) as a society deb. Alienation, nihilism, isolation, and marginalization conspire to transform the title character into a would-be political assassin. How does one more face in the crowd become a deadly stalker? *T.D.* answers this not with dialogue but street-wise vignettes that merge into a portrait of the anarchist as a young man. The violent sequence in which Travis kills the child-whore's pimp (Harvey Keitel) was modelled on a parallel scene near the end of Ford's *The Searchers* (1956). M.S.'s devotion to Hitchcock is obvious in choosing Bernard Herrmann (1911–1975) to create the score (his last). Cult-worthy actors include Peter Boyle. Scorsese appears as a conflicted passenger.

TEASEARAMA (1953)

General Rating: *

Bettie Page Cult Rating: *****

Jerald Intrator, dir.; Alan Bodian, scr.; Intrator, Martin J. Lewis, pros.; C; 1.37:1; running times various; Venus. Productions.

THE ULTIMATE PIN-UP GIRL: While other actress/models grew despondent once they were typecast in B horror and sci-fi film, Bettie (aka Betty) Page would have given anything for such cult status; instead, her movie 'stardom' consisted only of appearances in a pair of lowly 'take it all off' grindhouse flicks, *Teasarama* the better known among her cultists.

"Why now?" the 80-year old woman, living isolated in her small southwestern home, sincerely asked when a *Playboy* reporter arrived in 2002 to determine if she was indeed the notorious Bettie Page (1923–2008): S&M pin-up girl, sometimes stripper who seemingly disappeared off the face of the earth in 1960. Born dirt-poor in a Nashville White Trash shanty, Bettie set off to achieve fame and fortune in Hollywood. Instead, destiny led her to N.Y.C. where edgy photographer Irving Klaw (1910–1966) photographed the cherubic brunette in black bra and matching garter belt, all tied up or gleefully engaging in mild girl-girl action. When mainstream stardom failed to come her way, Page saw the light and became a born-again Christian. What seemed 'bad' (i.e., sleazy) in 1955 became 'the new good' when superstars like Madonna and Lady Gaga emulated Page's act. *Teasarama* is the best (and most beloved) of her take-it-all-off Poverty Row films. A framing device features two male low lives who learn that an ecdysiast pageant will contain every subgenre of dance *but* Burlesque. Crashing the event, they first show stripper films, then bring Page and Lilli St. Cyr (1918–1980) onstage.

TEETH (2007)

Extreme Horror Rating: *** ½

Michael Lichtenstein, dir., scr.; Lichtenstein, Joyce Pierpoline, pro.; 1.78:1; C; 94 min.

How to outdo *Ms. 45* as a feminist-vengeance cautionary fable for men while taking the Kiss of Death/*le petite morte* theme from vampire cinema to its illogical though fitting extreme? Actor turned auteur Michael Lichtenstein (1956–) stunned the folks at Sundance with this depiction of vagina détente: An ancient folk legend that a seemingly sweet and innocent girl might have the title set of pierces deep inside her most private place. Here is a graphic (*beyond* the limit) depiction of castration mixed with social satire on today's confused small-town teens who try and decide between casual sex and total abstinence. The film sounds better (if that's the correct term!) than it plays, owing to an uncertain script that changes directions once too often and a lack of total conviction in the performance. Had Jess Wexler (1981–) as 'Dawn' been more charismatic and convincing as a Lolita-like succubus, likely *Teeth* would have turned her into a cult star. Wexler's follow-up, *Angelica* (2015), disappointed those who believed he might be the next big deal in indie horror.

TESIS, aka THESIS (1996)

Rating: *****

Alejandro Amenabar, dir.; Amenabar, scr.; Amenabar, many others, prods.; 1.85:1; C; 125 min.; Escorpion/Sogepaq.

Had Alfred Hitchcock remade Michael Powell's *Peeping Tom* in Spain, incorporating key elements of Italy's Giallo movement, the result would have been *T*. Chilean born, Madrid raised A.A. (1972–) made his feature film debut with this aesthetically impressive combination of traditional thriller plus an intelligent analysis of a then-emergent situation: the sudden rise of Snuff Films in Spain. A cinema student (Ana Torent, 1966 –), obsessed with violence in the world, sets out to write her university thesis on that subject: Do media images of brutality make us more acceptant of bloodletting in the world around us? She teams with a geeky student (Felix Martinez, 1975–) who has access to forbidden tapes revealing dark secrets about a gone girl. She also becomes attracted to a playboy (Eduardo Noriega, 1973–), despite evidence pointing toward him as the abductor. Fittingly, this film served as A.A.'s own thesis, shot in and around his campus. Nowhere near as dazzling as his later work *Abres Los Obos*, here is a first film that reveals genius on the rise. Hitch homages include a shower sequence (*Psycho,* 1960), a flashing light in darkness (the ending of *Rear Window*, 1954) and a lead who suffers a desire for the fall (*Vertigo*, 1958).

TEXAS CHAIN SAW MASSACRE, THE (1974)

Rural Horror Noir No-Budget Rating: *****

Tobe Hooper, dir.; Hooper, Kim Henkel, scr; Henkel, Hooper, pros.; 1.85:1; C; 88 min. (extended print), 93 min. (release print), 75 min. (director's cut).

In the early 1970s, a teacher in TX found himself waiting to check out at a hardware store. To pass the time, he recalled much-admired movies: Alfred Hitchcock's classic *Psycho* (1960) and *Night of the Living Dead*, which proved any artist could create a great thriller, wherever they lived, even without funds, if the talent and will were there. Dreaming of doing that, Tobe Hooper (1943–2017) glanced up and noticed a long line of chainsaws. He and a friend, Kim Henkel (1946–), developed a story about a brother and sister driving through rural TX, coming face to face with 'Leatherface' (Gunnar Hansen), a masked 'realistic-monster' (he has no supernatural powers). In deference to Hitch, Hooper insisted that little blood be spilled onscreen, inspiring viewers to "see violence in their mind's eyes." Critic Rex Reed hailed this as "the scariest film I have ever seen." Teens agreed, as did Spielberg. He invited T.H. to direct *Poltergeist* (1982) which led to nasty arguments as to that hit film's authorship.

THANK YOU FOR SMOKING (2005)

Cult 'Serious Comedy' Rating: *****

Jason Reitman, dir.; Reitman, scr.; David O. Sacks, pro.; 2.39:1; C; 92 min.; Room 9 Ent.

"For the mortgage!" That's the answer 'Nick Naylor' (Aaron Eckhart, 1968–) offers when anyone asks how he can continue doing what he does: TV spokesperson and D.C. lobbyist for Big Tobacco. A silver-tongued devil, he's the greatest spin doctor alive and is paid well by The Man (Robert Duvall) who doesn't want a liberal senator (Bill Macy) to pass a law that would label each pack with a skull and crossbones. But everything changes when N.N. meets his match: An amoral journalist (Katie Holmes) willing to sleep with her 'prey' to get the story of the century. Possibly the best dark comedy since *Dr. Strangelove* if considerably less cartoonish: J.R. (1977–) manages a smart balance between believable drama and savage satire, refusing to spare anyone in an even-handed view of crass commercialism mixing with sordid politics. Sam Elliott (1944–) incarnates a variation of actor David McLean (1922–1995), who rode the TV airwaves as The Marlboro Man until contracting cancer after becoming addicted to free cigarettes. The moment of truth here: Will this dying cowboy sell out for all the money Naylor offers for his family or do the right thing and speak out? As important a film as it is entertaining. Talk show host Dennis Miller plays himself.

THEATRE OF BLOOD (1973)

Vincent Price Cultists: ****

Douglas Hickox, dir.; Anthony Greville-Bell, scr.; Stanley Mann, John Kohn, pro.; 1.66:1; C/B&W; 104 min.; Harbor Pics.

 Not another horror film of the sort Vincent Price (1911–1993) had appeared in for Corman and others but a companion-piece to such projects as well as a thinly disguised autobiographical statement. Before his phantasmagoric thrillers, Price had been hyped as an American Olivier, likely to make a great name for himself in Shakespearean roles. Instead, he opted to go for the money, losing such early critical support. Here, he is cast as the similarly rejected "Edward Lionheart," a British stage performer who did stick with the Bard but played to 'the back row,' winning audience approval by going over the top yet losing the respect of critics and never being named 'Sir.' Reaching the point of madness, Lionheart schemes to murder each reviewer in a manner recalling the piece which the scribe derided. His enemies are portrayed by a Who's Who of the English actor-elite: Dennis Price, Robert Morley, Jack Hawkins, Robert Coote, and many others including Coral Browne, whom V.P. later mar-

A CARICATURE OF A CARICATURE: If Vincent Price all but gave up his career as an acclaimed character actor to embody over-the-top villains in horror films, here he had the chance to parody his own long-standing screen image.

ried. Diana Rigg (1938-) was cast as his daughter in part owing to the film's tonal similarity to her hit TV series *The Avengers*. Ahead of its time as to onscreen blood and sadism.

THIS ISLAND EARTH (1955)

Retro 1950s Rating: **** ½

Joseph M. Newman, dir.; Franklin Coen, George Callahan, scr.; William Alland, pro.; 1.37:1; C; 86 min.; Universal-International.

"Our planet is dying!" That line ranks as the seminal piece of dialogue from 1950s sci-fi films about doomed aliens landing on earth. Appearing many times in movies and on TV, here is the one in which it originally appeared—spoken by Jeff Morrow (1907–1993) as 'Exeter,' the advanced intellectual visitor (with a high-forehead attesting to his brain-size) and silver hair to suggest his true age. Whenever this appeared on TV for the next decade and a half, those who had seen *T.I.E.* on its initial theatrical run called out those four words even as they appeared on the small screen. With an $800,000 budget, in color and with innovative F/X, this ranked with *When Worlds Collide* (1951), *War of the Worlds* (1953), and *World Without End* (1953) as one of the more ambitious B+ sci-fi/fantasy projects of the era. The skin-tight space suit designed for gorgeous Faith Domergue (1924–1999) took hours to be fitted to her contours each day. 'Metaluna' is the planet's name; its Mutants are truly memorable for their time.

THIS IS SPINAL TAP (1984)

Cult Spoof Rating: *****

Rock 'n' Roll Cult Rating: *****

Rob Reiner, dir.; Christopher Guest, Michael McKean, Harry Shearer, scr.; Karen Murphy, prod.; 1.70:1; C; 82 min.; Embassy.

"No, no, no," the frantic members of Spinal Tap insist when asked if they have lost touch with the Heavy Metal audience, as evidenced by once full concert halls giving way to small venues. "We're simply becoming far more selective as to our audience." An in-denial ability that allows such threatened performers to perceive such disastrous commercial news proves their increasing artistic success is captured here in a satire. The piece plays so convincingly some viewers initially thought this was indeed a forgotten band. Often cited as the first rock "mockumentary," *T.I.S.T.* was preceded by Eric Idle's *All You Need is Cash* (1978), about the Pre-Fab Four, 'The Ruttles.' *T.I.S.T.* was mostly improvised; Guest (1948-), McKean (1947-), and Shearer (1943-) making everything up even as they shot the piece. Cult-worthy stars in cameo roles include Billy Crystal, Brinke Stevens, Paul Shaffer, and Howard Hesseman. The satiric portrait of actual bands—Led Zeppelin, Black Sabbath, et. al.—are so lovingly done that the artists were delighted rather than angered by the results.

THREE CABALLEROS, THE (1944)

Oddball Disney Animation Rating: **** ½

Clyde Geronimo, many other, dir.; Homer Brightman, many others, scr.; Walt Disney, pro.; 1.37:1; C; 77 min. (apprx.); Walt Disney Prods./RKO.

In those days before cable TV and home video, fans of old movies would rent 16 mm prints from companies that specialized in servicing various groups, from church to school to independent. Over time, it became obvious to distributors that then closeted gay groups regularly ordered this Disney anthology about varied sectors of Latin America. Why? In addition to the animated/documentary travelogue, *T.T.C.* can be read as a coming out of the celluloid closet for Donald Duck, once again voiced by the remarkable Clarence Nash (1904–1985). During the film's first half, Donald makes an embarrassing fool out of himself by wildly chasing beautiful women, to the point of appearing to be overcompensating for inner doubts. At mid-movie, he is accidentally kissed by both Panchito and Jose Carioca. At that moment, D.D. joins in with them singing: "we're three Caballeros, three *gay* caballeros…!"

"TWO GUYS KISSED ME... I LIKED IT!" Donald has a bi-curious moment in one of the most bizarre/outlandish/cultish animated films ever turned out by the ordinarily mainstream Walt Disney studio.

THUNDER ROAD (1958)

Moonshin' Movie Rating: *****

Robert Mitchum Cult Rating: *****

Arthur Ripley, Robert Mitchum (uncredited), dir.; Mitchum, Walter Wise, James Arlee Phillips, scr.; 1.66:1; B&W; 92 min.; D.R.M. Prods.; U.A.

    The greatest hillbilly/moonshiner movie ever made. A list star Mitchum (1917–1997) become a one-time auteur with a Z budget quickie. *T.R.* reveals his personal values as no 'respectable' starring vehicle ever did. Korean War vet 'Lucas Doolin' returns to Appalachia, hoping to continue his mountain-folk's family business: distilling and runnin' White Lightning in their 1950 Ford. But the Mob has moved in, attempting to wipe out rugged individualists. A federal man (Gene Barry) hopes to bring Luke in alive. The anti-hero is loved by a moody jazz singer (Keeley Smith, 1928–2017) in her only dramatic role, and a wide-eyed mountain girl (Sandra Knight, 1940- ; then-wife of Jack Nicholson). Mitchum's son

James is cast as his worshipful kid brother. Much frantic action during the moonlight runs; incompetent camera work makes this all the more fun on a junk movie level. *T.R.* ran for more than a decade on the Drive In circuit owing to popular demand. Mitchum wrote and performed the title song, a juke box and radio hit. Only regret: Elvis's manager Col. Parker would not allow Elvis Presley to co-star as the younger Doolin.

TIME BANDITS (1981)

Cult Fantasy Rating: **** ½

Pythonesque Completist Rating: *****

Terry Gilliam, dir.; Gilliam, Michael Palin, scr.; Gilliam, pro.; 1.85:1; C; 103 min. (original theatrical release), 116 min. (director's extended cut); HandMade Films.

Disney's seven dwarfs (minus one) hop aboard H.G. Wells (or is it George Pal's?) Time Machine and tear through wormholes (the wrinkles in time and space) to visit Robin Hood (John Cleese), Agamemnon (Sean Connery), and Napoleon (Ian Holm). Along for the bumpy/bizarre ride through Monty Python's edgy vision of our universe: A ten-year-old boy named 'Kevin' (Craig Warnock, 1970–). Fun, fun, fun for those who 'go with the flow' of Brit humor that manages to be smart and silly, intellectu-

THE SEVEN DWARFS (MINUS ONE) ENTER THE TIME TUNNEL: One of the few Terry Gilliam movies that played to matinee crowds including children eager for an edgy H.G. Wells fantasy.

al and assanine, demented and enlightened all at the same time. The most basic of Gilliam's serious themes is, as always, present. Is there a God? And, if he is indeed benevolent as the New Testament assures us, why then did he invent Spam? (the food product or the email issue). For the record, the little people are 'Randall' (David Rappaport, 1951–1990), 'Fidget' (Kenny Baker, 1934–2016), 'Strutter' (Malcolm Dixon, 1934–2020) 'Og' (Mike Edmonds, 1944–), and 'Wally' (Jack Purvis, 1937–1997). Shakespearean great Ralph Richardson (1902–1983) appears as the Ultimate Power. Former Beatle George Harrison (1943–2001), a lifelong Python fan, served as executive producer.

TOMBSTONE (1993)

Western movie aficionados: **** ½

Val Kilmer Fan Rating: *****

George P. Cosmatos, dir.; Kevin Jarre, scr.; Sean Daniel, James Jacks, Bob Misiorowski, pro.; 2.35:1; C; 130 min. (theatrical release), 134 min. (director's cut); Cinergi/ Alphaville/ Hollywood Pictures.

Representatives of the Disney company would not screen this film in advance for the press, always a certain sign of 'no faith' in one of their own finished products. Screenwriter Kevin James (1954–2011), who earlier penned the historically accurate *Glory* (1989), had been replaced as director during the first week by George P. Cosmatos (1941–2005), best known for mindless actioners like *Rambo II* (1985) and *Cobra* (1993), both starring Sylvester Stallone. Yet some sort of magic occurred during filming: a balance between realistic detail and over-the-top violent sequences led to this B Picture scoring well during the holiday season. Six months later, the ambitious *Wyatt Earp* (Lawrence Kasdan) opened to disappointing reviews and virtually no box-office: Why see the same story twice, particularly when the A picture told it in a mundane, bleak, grating manner, while the first-at-bat version with Kurt Russell (1951–) as Wyatt Earp and Val Kilmer (1959–) as Doc Holliday created the kind of buddy-buddy chemistry that Kevin Costner and Dennis Quaid lacked? A huge hit on home video as well as cable TV, *T.* continues to draw in devoted cultists every time it plays.

A HERO FOR ALL SEASONS: Kurt Russell ably embodied Western hero Wyatt Earp (here seen with Val Kilmer as gambler Doc Holliday) in *Tombstone*; earlier, ha appeared in the near-future thriller *Escape from New York* (from left, Harry Dean Stanton, Adrienne Barbeau, and Russell).

TOMMY (1975)

Rock music cult Rating: **

Ken Russell, dir.; Russell, Pete Townshend, John Entwistle, Keith Moon, scr.; Russell, Robert Stigwood, pro.; 1.85:1; C; 111 min.; Hemsdale.

It's difficult to locate the case of a director less suited to bringing a legendary band's greatest work to film than Alan Parker being as-

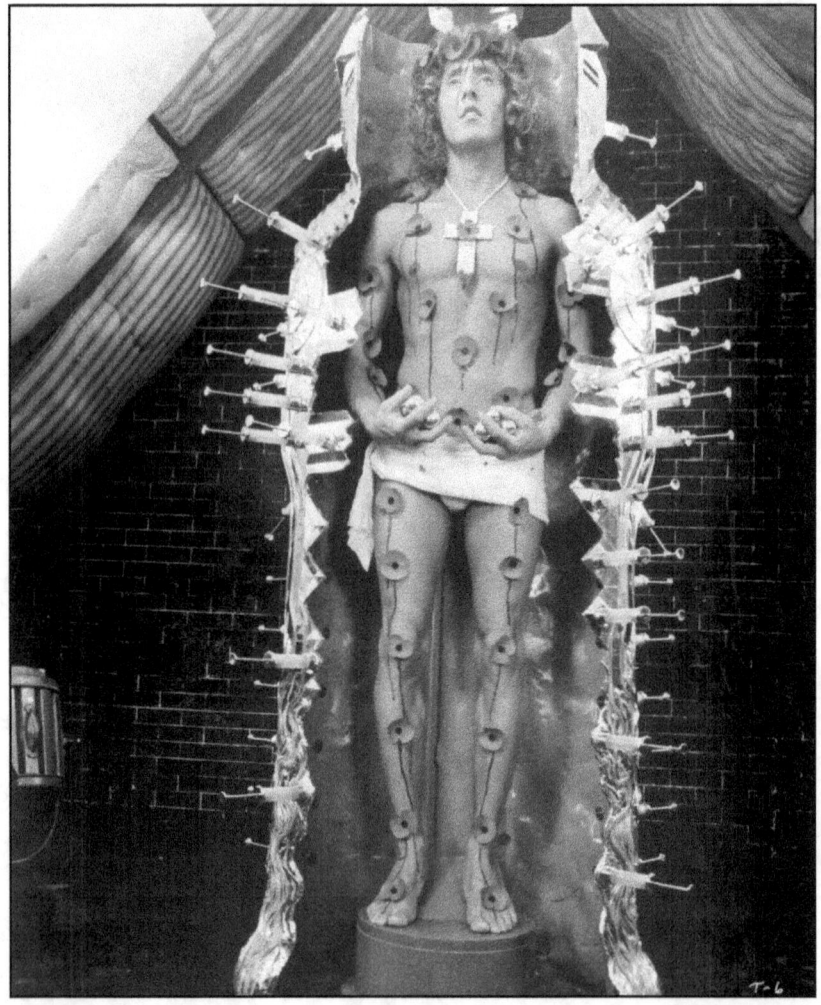

'THE WHO' DESERVED BETTER THAN THIS: Despite the presence of Roger Daltrey in the title role, Ken Russell completely misconceived the rock opera's meaning and replaced it with madness; what might have been the result had Tim Burton or Terry Gilliam directed?

signed to *Pink Floyd: The Wall* (1982), but in truth Russell (1927–2011) mis-interpretation of The Who's rock opera takes the cake. Townshend (1945–) and company employed their fable about a youth (Roger Daltrey in the film) who goes deaf, dumb, and blind when Mummy (Ann-Margret) replaces the boy's absent dad with a moral monster (Oliver Reed). Despite such limitations, Tommy becomes a superstar, allowing The Who to address personal issues, including the fabulous/ frightening cult of celebrity. K.R. turns this work of genius into a nasty burlesque as a Tellie spews forth soap, beans, and chocolate over A.M. Why does this botched project continue to maintain status as a cult fav? Simple: A Who's (pun intended) Who of rock stars, including each member of the band as himself. Also: Eric Clapton, Tina Turner as The Acid Queen, and last but hardly least Elton John in a role he was born to play, The Pinball Wizard. There's also Jack Nicholson who shines (pun intended) in a memorable character role. Yet we can't help but wonder how much closer this might have come to what The Who intended had George Lucas not passed on it.

TOO LATE FOR TEARS (1949)

Down and Dirty Noir Cult Rating: **** ½

Byron Haskin, dir.; Roy Huggins, scr.; Hunt Stromberg, prod.; 1.37:1; B&W; 99 min.; UA/Republic.

An ordinary couple (Arthur Kennedy, Lizabeth Scott) goes for an ordinary drive on an ordinary evening in Southern Cal. Then something extraordinary occurs: Someone in a passing car tosses a bundle of money into their vehicle, mistaking The Normals for their criminal connection. While the husband wants to do the right thing and turn 'the bundle' over to police, his wife transforms from suburban woman-next-door into film noir femme fatale. Here is the catalyst she's been fantasizing about all her life, leading to adventure, romance, a wealthy lifestyle, and death to many an innocent person. Smart, swift-moving, hard-hitting, this small indie thriller was early-on released to TV in a 77 min. cut which sometimes played under the title *Killer Bait*. *T.L.F.T.* turned on the first-generation of 1950s TV addicts to noir before classics like *Out of the Past* (1947) were broadcast. Blonde Scott (1922–2015), born Emma Matzo in a Pennsylvania coal-minin2g town, shimmers with dark desire and over-the-top

BLONDES ARE DEADLY... WHY DIDN'T 'BOGIE' WARN DAN DURYEA?: The tough guy falls prey to Lizbeth Scott in one of the very best B noirs.

'glamour.' Her career suffered when *Confidential* magazine outed L.S. as a Tinseltown lesbian. Dan Duryea (1907–1968), as a tough-guy doomed by a fatal weakness for cheap women, is to die for.

THX 1138 (1971)

Dystopian Future Sci-Fi Rating: * ½**

Lucas Afficionado Rating: ***

George Lucas, dir.; Walter Murch, scr.; Laurence Sturhahn, Francis Ford Coppola, pros.; 2.35;1; C/B&W; 88 min.; American Zoetrope/WB.

    Lucas's (1944–) first theatrical film opens with a shot from the famed serial *Buck Rogers* (1939) as Buster Crabbe 1908–1983) performs in a swashbuckling fantasy. G.L. included this with irony: What follows is a bleak vision of a dystopian world. Drugs keep all citizens (who have numbers, not names) in a sexless state. The protagonist (Robert Duvall, 1931–), yearning for more, escapes the underground existence to reach the surface and observe sunlight. This expansion on G.L.'s own award-winning student (U.S.C.) film was mentored by Coppola, a leading avatar of the New American Cinema. Derivative of many literary works, George Orwell's *1984* in particular, *THX 1138* reveals in retrospect Lucas's attempt to conform to arthouse sci-fi favoured during the early 1970s. A greater irony: in time realizing this was not his forte, he scored big (*very* big!) when he unofficially remade the fun film here employed as a ridiculous 'foil.' *Star Wars* (1977) proved the public still wants old-fashioned popcorn romantic/adventure flicks if now with state-of-the-art F/X and self-referential gags.

TIE ME UP! TIE ME DOWN! (1989)

Odball Almodovar Rating: **

Pedro Almodovar, dir.; Almodovar, scr.; Enrique Posner, pro.; C; 1.85:1; 101 min.; Deseo, El/Miramax.

    A retired hard-core porn star/recovering (perhaps) hard-drug addict (Victoria Abril, 1959–) is kidnapped by a hysterical refuge from a mental institution (Antonio Banderas, 1960–). He slaps her around and ties her to a bed. Rape, however, is not the agenda: He will release her as soon as she agrees to *marry* him. Following protests, she relents, not out of fear but because she's fallen in love. This might seem the nightmare-scenario movie of a macho mentality: 'What women *really* want is to be dominated.' In fact, Almodovar's (1949–) film offers something far broader, wider, deeper; an uncloseted homosexual's vision of the absurdity of heterosexual romantic obsession. Socially significant in that U.S. distributor Miramax refused to accept an 'X' rating, arguing that this (however explicit) was a serious-comedic work of personal expression (as such 'art'). As a result, the long overdue NC-17 rating, for films featuring graphic sex yet clearly not intended as superficial exploitation, was established, the 'X' banished.

TINGLER, THE (1959)

Saturday Matinee Horror film Rating: *** ½

William Castle Cult Rating: **** ½

William Castle, dir.; Robb White, scr.; Castle, pro.; 1.85:1; B&W/C; 92 min.; Columbia.

Lysergic acid diethylamide (L.S.D.) was first distilled in Switzerland, 1938, as a possible cure for mental illness. During the early 1960s, Dr. Timothy Leary (1920–1996) employed the drug to induce hallucinogenic visions. Student experiments became a subject of exploitation movies like Roger Corman's *The Trip* (1967). In truth, L.S.D. made its onscreen debut eight years earlier in what initially seemed merely one more of Castle's (1914–1977) gimmicky low-budget horror items. An over-the-top Vincent Price plays a doctor convinced that some invisible 'thing' inside each of us leads to the "too scared to scream" syndrome. To prove it he uses L.S.D. to stimulate fear in patients/victims. A lurid sequence includes color to approximate a 'trip' added to the phantasmagoria. The film then deconstructs itself: Its conclusion is set in a movie theatre where The Tingler (a velvet worm) wreaks havoc on the onscreen audience. A shameless showman, Castle wired buzzers to seats in theatres where his filmed played. When movie characters shriek, so did viewers whose seats suddenly buzzed. What at the time seemed nothing more than a cheap means of luring in teens is now perceived as the art form of Total Theatre.

TOXIC AVENGER, THE (1985)

Superhero genre Rating: **NO STARS**

Troma Cultist Rating: *********

ALL HAIL TROMA!… ALL 1970s/1980s NERDY GUYS, AT LEAST: The studio created by Lloyd Kaufman and Michael Herz turned out the most popular non-budgeters for the then-new direct to video market, with 'Toxie' their answer to Disney's Mickey Mouse.

Michael Herz, Samuel Wells (aka Lloyd Kaufman), dir.; Kaufman, Joe Ritter, Gay Terry, scr.; 1.85:1; C; 78 min. (R rated), 82 min. (unrated); 91 min. ('extreme' extended cut); Troma.

When Lloyd Kaufman (1945–) and fellow Yale grad Herz opened Troma circa 1975 as the logical successor to A.I.P., everyone understood the post Camp/pro-Cult filmmakers were winking at a knowing audience with their purposefully 'bad' (i.e., great!) exploitation flicks. *T.T.A.* remains their most popular (and only franchised) release: a goofy, violent spoof of super-hero tales. Melvin, aka "Junko" (Mitchell Cohen) is a pathetic wimp reduced to washing floors. When Junko falls into a kettle of chemicals he emerges as 'Toxie.' (The title was an afterthought; the movie shot on the fly, without a script and no idea what they'd eventually call it). Outlandishness not possible in any previous Teen Exploitation Flicks (a child's head is crushed, a pleasant dog shot dead) were chillingly in tune with a new, mean-spirited generation—precisely right for home-media, where rules regarding theatrical features did not apply. Look *real* close and you'll spot future Academy Award winner Marisa Tomei (1964–) as a cute brunette stepping out of a shower. Bikers 'n' babes are *everywhere*.

TO WONG FOO WITH LOVE, JULIE NEWMAR (1995)

Comedy Cult Film Rating: *** ½

Cross Dressing Cult Film Rating: **** ½

Beeban Kidron, dir.; D.C. Beane, scr.; G. Mac Brown, pro.; 1.85:1; C; 109 min.; Universal/Amblin.

Three Manhattan-based drag queens-—African-American 'Noxeema' (Wesley Snipes, 1962–), upscale WASP 'Vida' (Patrick Swayze, 1952–2009), and Spanish 'Chi-Chi' (John Leguizamo, 1964–)—drive cross-country to L.A. where they hope to break into the movie business. Car trouble forces them to remain in a rural town for three days. They transform unenlightened rednecks into eager supporters of The Life. Such unbridled optimism relegates this to a wish-fulfilment film; a number one spot at the box-office on opening week suggested that the mainstream was becoming ever more acceptant. The presence of cult-worthy actresses Melinda Dillon, Stockard Channing, and Blythe Danner add to the appeal, as does Robin Williams in a cameo. The title lady (1933–) plays herself in the finale. 'Wong Foo' was an actual person, a NYC bartender who collected signed photos of celebrity diners and displayed them in his China Bowl Restaurant. U.K. born Kidron (1961–) won the director's seat here thanks to his earlier acclaimed documentary *Hookers Hustlers Pimps and Their Johns* (1993) but could not follow-up.

TRAINSPOTTING (1996)

Boyle Cult Rating: *****

Danny Boyle, dir.; John Hodge, scr.; Andrew Macdonald, pro.; 1.85:1; C; 94 min.; Channel Four/Figment Films.

Four male friends come of age in Edinburgh, talking endlessly about movies, the working-class society they were born into, and their dreams of getting out. Alternately, they perpetrate criminal mischief which ensures their ongoing entrapment here, despondency driving them to heroin addiction. D.B.'s (1956–) work resembles Aronofsky's *Requiem for a Dream*, presenting the viewer with a needle that penetrates human flesh in horrific close-up. *T.'s* style straddles a thin line between realism (on-location shooting) and camera-work that renders such vivid imagery surreal, pushing this in the direction of *A Clockwork Orange*. Other influences: the music of Iggy Pop, novels by Thomas Pynchon, and paintings by Francis Bacon. Ewan MacGregor (1971–), playing 'Renton' (the one lad with a chance of a new start in London) was catapulted to stardom. The title offers an oblique reference to doing drugs. From the novel by Irving Walsh, who insisted that this movie *not* be made in the traditional Brit docu-drama style but reflect his characters' inner lives. Criticized for glorifying drugs by those who did not grasp this is a critical expose of the subculture.

TREMORS (1990)

Cult Horror Rating: **** ½

Kevin Bacon Cult-Fandom Rating: *****

Ron Underwood, dir.; Underwood, S.S. Wilson, Brent Maddock, scr.; Wilson, Maddock, pros.; 1.85:1; C; 96 mins.; No Frills Prods./Universal.

    T. plays as a throwback to low-budget 1950s sci-fi films in which a small number of characters are threatened by some menacing force. The setting here is an isolated area in the southwest; the location is supposedly rural NV though *T.* was shot in Lone Pine CA. The monsters are "Graboids," huge worms with oversized jaws; aka, underground sharks. Among the locals are a pair of lovable loser rednecks—Kevin Bacon, 1958–) and Fred Ward—and a gun-crazy couple (Michael Gross, Reba McIntyre, 1955–). Also: a visiting female seismologist (Finn Carter) who senses sudden 'tremors.' Produced more than thirty years after the golden age of Universal nuclear age thrillers, so rough language, state of-the-art F/X, graphic violence and an undercurrent of glib humor bring the tried-and-true formula in line with a more contemporary sensibility. Great gobs of gore which in the distant past appeared in Forbidden Films such as *Blood Feast* have become matter of fact in current fare. A modest success in theatres; an all-family cult film ever since.

TRIAL, THE (1962)

Orson Welles Cultist Rating: *****

Franz Kafka Cultist Rating: *****

Orson Welles, dir.; Welles, Pierre Cholot, scr.; Alexander & Michael Salkind, pros.; 1.66:1; B&W; 107 min. (cut); 110 min. (director's cut); Astor Pictures.

    From Prague-born Franz Kafka's (1883–1924) dark, posthumously published novel about an ordinary man who wakes to learn that he's been charged with a crime no one will identify. Welles (1915–1985) talked the Salkinds into backing a project that would translate Kafka's literary vision into cinematic terms. Anthony Perkins (1932–1992) brought his post-*Psycho* (1960) association with paranoid characters to a work featuring the darkest of shadows and highest contrast lighting to provide radical shifts from depressing nights to oppressive days. This singular story of a desperate individual, over-powered by the anonymous workings of a dictatorial Establishment, embracing madness as his only escape exerted a huge influence on Terry Gilliam's career, notably *Brazil* (1985). O.W. was the first filmmaker to feature "Adagio in G Minor" by Tomaso Albinoni (1671–1751), soon to become a standard. The actresses—Jeanne Moreau (1928–2017), Elsa Martinelli (1935–2017), and Romy Schneider (1938–1982)—would all shortly became major stars.

TRON (1982)

Sci-Fi Fantasy Rating: ** ½

Steve Lisberger, dir.; Lisberger, Bonnie MacBird, Charles S. Haas, scr.; Donald Kushner, pro.; 2.20:1; C; 96 min.; Disney.

Grasping that traditional animation had become so expensive that profitability of even popular films might be nil, the Disney company won-

ONCE MORE, DISNEY LEADS THE WAY: Long after Uncle Walt's passing in 1966, the Buena Vista team attempted to always be the first to provide new animation forms, including computer animated 'worlds' in *Tron*.

dered if computer animation might prove to be their saviour. That's when indie artist Lisberger (1951–), a graduate of Tufts' fine arts school, pitched the idea of a futuristic film that takes place entirely within an alternative universe. As gaming became ever more popular in the post-Pong era, S.L. sketched out a story about a hacker (Jeff Bridges) as Kevin Flynn/'Clu' who, trapped in cyberspace, joins forces with created super-hero Alan Brady/'Tron' (Bruce Boxleitner) to fight for their freedom. Designed on a computer that featured 2MB memory and 330 MB Storage, the effect that dazzled way back when seem primitive today. That's to be expected and accepted. The huge problem is rather that the characters are never developed and the narrative makes no sense. An at-best minor success theatrically, *Tron* might have landed on the junk heap of popular culture had not the subsequent tie-in game proven popular with teenagers, who then watched the movie. Overshadowed by a belated yet superior 2010 sequel, Tron: Legacy.

28 DAYS LATER… (2002)

Dystopian Future Cult Rating: *** ½

Danny Boyle, dir.; Alex Garland, scr.; Andrew McDonald, pro.; 1.85:1; C; 113 min.; DNA Films.

    A young man (Cillian Murphy, 1976–) comes to consciousness in a hospital room, unable to recall why he is there. Soon 'Jim' realizes that no other patients, or doctors and nurses, are present. Wandering into the empty streets, he grasps what happened: An infection spread throughout London, perhaps all England, causing those exposed to fall into deadly fits of rage. He meets two survivors (Naomi Harris, Noah Huntley) who plan on heading off in search of a rumoured sanctuary where life remains normal. The first half hour is, in a word, remarkable: this plays like a perfect filmed combination of two great dystopian future novels, the classic *I Am Legend* (1954; Richard Matheson) and the lesser known but equally impressive *A Scent of New Mown Hay* (1958; John Blackburn). But once the journey commences, *28 Days* loses steam. The mid-movie events are conventional in a way the opening was not. A big finale, in which our Everman hero turns into a Rambo-clone (who knew?), easily able to defeat one wicked figure after another in personal combat, plays like a spoof of mundane action movies. The director-writer team reveal the innate talents that allowed them to move on to more fulfilling projects.

TWO-LANE BLACKTOP (1971)

Road Movie Cult Rating: **** ½

Monte Hellman, dir.; Rudy Wurlitzer, Will Cory, Floyd Mutrux, scr.; Gary Kurtz, Michael (S.) Laughlin, pros.; 2.35:1; C; 102 min. (U.S. theatrical), 105 min., Universal.

Monte Hellman (1929–2021) made his dream movie owing to *Easy Rider*'s success. Rather than an imitation of its romantic vision of life 'On the Road' for two hipsters, Hellman's film offers an answer to it. Unnamed lead characters—The Driver (James Taylor, 1948–) and The Mechanic (Dennis Wilson, 1944–1983, both played by music stars)—are as lifeless as the astronauts in *2001*. Even as audiences felt more emotional attachment to the computer H.A.L., so do we revel in the outrageously self-important middle-aged 'G.T.O.' (Warren Oates). A redneck in a cheap suit, he serves as a parallel to *E.R.*'s shotgun-wielding crackers at that film's finale. In this new decade, Youth does not symbolize rebellion but lethargy; even crazed yokels are more interesting. A highway competition looks forward to *Death Race 2000* minus its fantastical aura Here the southwest, shimmering with stark beauty in most other films, appears as lifeless as the central characters. Also the film of choice for cultists devoted to Laurie Bird (1953–1979) making her debut as a Hippie hitchhiker; she committed suicide after playing Paul Simon's girlfriend in *Annie Hall* (1977). An appearance by Harry Dean Stanton adds to the cult appeal.

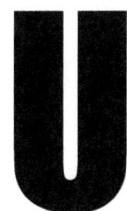

UNDER THE SKIN (2013)

Nouveau Vampire Flick Rating: **** ½

Scarjo Cultists: *****

Jonathan Glazer, dir.; Glazer, Walter Campbell, scr.; Nick Wechsler, James Wilson, pro.; 1.85:1; C; 108 min.; BFI/Film4.

    A beautiful girl (Scarlett Johansson, 1984–) wanders the streets of an isolated small city (in this case, East Lothian in Scotland), always on the lookout for lone males. They soon become her prey, as we realize that she is a vampire-like creature, if in this case sans fangs—at least not ones that are visible. If that sounds conventional enough—one more of the 'sex/succubus' films that became popular in the late 1960s and beyond—think again. For this is latest example of pan-cinema (merging genre expectations with arthouse innovations) from J.G. (1965–), whose previous efforts include the cult classics *Sexy Beast* and *Birth*. Here, there is no narrative in the conventional sense, nor in truth is the piece character-driven. *U.T.S.* is an experiment in transforming style into substance: the dialogue is minimalist (to say the least) yet the other elements—primarily visual, but the employment of sound, both natural and recorded, as well as a shrill, off-putting score by Mica Levi—results in a grandiose feast for us to gaze at without ever degenerating into mere eye-candy. We see things here (including that wet black room) which we have never seen before and will never forget, even if we want to. The female may be an alien or that Scottish figure of myth, a Selkie. Explanations *not* forthcoming. S.J.'s nude scenes were done without use of a body double.

USUAL SUSPECTS, THE (1995)

Edgy Auteurist Rating: *****

Bryan Singer, dir.; Christopher McQuarrie, scr.; Michael McDonnell, pro.; 2.35;1; C; 106 min.; PolyGram/Blue Parrot/Spelling Films.

"The greatest trick the devil ever pulled," the disabled man 'Verbal Kint' (Kevin Spacey, 1959–), tells a police officer (Chazz Palminteri, 1952–), "was to convince mankind (that) he does not exist." Charles Baudelaire (1821–1867) wrote that; collaborators Singer (1965–) and McQuarrie (1968–) insist they were unaware of the source. Director and writer first joined forces two years earlier to make *Public Access*, an uneven indie film that attracted considerable attention. *T.U.S.* combines key elements of *Casablanca* (1942), in which a line spoken by Claude Raines supplies the title; *Citizen Kane* (1941), with its probing listener realizing each story he hears about a legendary figure contradicts the last; and *Double Indemnity* (1944), the most intricately plotted of old film noirs. 'Kane' gives way to 'Keyzer Soze,' a legendary criminal inspired by the real-life case of John List. A career criminal (Gabriel Byrne, 1950–) and his gang embark on an L.A. harbor raid that goes wrong; one survivor (or so it seems) recalls seemingly unrelated events that led to a sudden shoot-out. In a cameo as a N.Y. smuggler, Paul Bartel brings his cult status to the piece; Harry Dean Stanton was initially to have played the role that catapulted Benicio del Toro to stardom.

VALERIE A TYDEN DIVU, aka *VALERIE AND HER WEEK OF WONDERS* (1970)

Cinematic/Aesthetic Rating: *****

Female Coming-of-Age Rating: *****

Jaromil Jires, dir.; Jires, Jiri Musil, Ester Krumbachnova, scrs.; Jiri Becker, pro.; 1.37:1; C; 77 min.; Filmov studio Barandor.

In his seminal book "The Uses of Enchantment" (1976), Bruno Bettelheim argued that fairy-tales are anything but pleasant time killers for kids. Rather, dark and disturbing myths, re-imagined (though not watered down) for children who must learn the way of the world. Full of sex and violence, the spiritual and the sensual, presented in literary codes so as to avoid the more threatening aspects of their adult counter-parts. Few authors have turned such ideology into a coming of age novel as did Viterzslav Nezval, remarkably brought to the screen by a gifted team of Czech artists led by J.J. (1935–2001). Thirteen-year-old V. (Jaraslova Schallerova, dazzlingly impressive) wakes on a summer day in the 19th century to realize she's experienced her first menstruation. During the following week, she simultaneously enjoys the last moments of childhood while embracing adolescence and oncoming adult emotions. Phantasmagorias of color recall paintings by Jean Renoir and the films of Francoise Truffaut for the girl's 'high' moments. Gothic darkness worthy of Luis Bunuel and Orson Welles express her lows. Zombies and vampires hover about, at least in her blossoming imagination ; they are not nearly as horrific as an all too real priest who plans to pluck her cherry. A tour-du-force of cinematic aesthetics.

VIDEODROME (1983)

Sci-Fi Cult Rating: **** ½

James Woods Cult Rating: *****

Cronenberg Cult Rating: *****

Debbie Harry Cult Rating: **** ½

David Cronenberg, dir.; Cronenberg, scr.; Claude Heroux, Pierre David, pros.; 1.85:1; C; 87 min. (theatrical release/USA); 89 min. (director's cut); Filmplan/Canadian Trust/Universal.

    During the early days of cable TV, the owner/manager (James Woods, 1947–) of a small indie station offers 'R' and 'X' rated materials for sleazy audiences. Laughing at moralists who complain he is contributing to the decline of Western civilization, the creepy cat insists he merely provides people with what they want. Then an actual Snuff film causes him to reconsider. Toronto-born Cronenberg (1943–) had established himself as one of the bright lights of nouveau-horror with *The Brood* (1979) and *Scanners* (1983). His approach to grotesque violence (including visualizations of body parts) combines with an undercurrent of post-McLuhan analysis for the age when TV's faux 'reality' became more real to people than everyday life. Debbie Harry (1945–) of the pop-punk-rock group Blondie plays an elusive beauty. *V.* was one of a group of horror/Sci-fi films released by Universal in the early 1980s to initiate a Renaissance for a genre they had all but owned half-a-century earlier. D.C. successfully adjusted his dark vision for a larger audience with his commercial hit *The Fly* (1986).

VIRGIN SUICIDES, THE (1999)

'Serious' Cult Film Rating: **** ½

Sofia Coppola, dir.; Coppola, scr.; Francis Ford Coppola, John Costanzu, Dan Halste, pro.; 1.85:1; C; 97 min.; American Zoetrope/Muse.

    Horny suburban boys sit on a curb, fantasizing about the five beautiful sisters across the street. Then the seemingly have-it-all blondes commit suicide en masse. Were they driven to this by ultra-conservative parents (James Woods, Kathleen Turner, 1954–) who forbade not only sex but even mild rock 'n' roll? Such a case study of the manner in which overprotection can be as destructive as a lack of supervision for vulnerable/confused teenagers, the material sounds like the plot for a didactic Stanley Kramer message-movie or an exploitation flick by Dwain Esper. The subtle, substantial piece is neither. As an award-winning 1993 novel by Jeffrey Eugenides and a 1999 film by Sofia—daughter of Francis—Coppola (1971–), the result is more arthouse than mainstream or grindhouse. An oblique camera-eye precludes moral posturing; a deceptively sensuous style results in a curiously ambiguous work. Coppola and Kirsten Dunst (1982–), as the most enigmatic among the lovely girls) emerged as a sought-after director/actress duo. That ended with the 2006 release of the disastrous historical epic *Marie Antoinette.*

SKINNY DIPPIN': Jenny Agutter transforms from girl to woman in *Walkabout* while surrendering to nature: four decades earlier, much the same thing happened to Hedy Lamar in *Ecstasy*.

WALKABOUT (1971)

Roeg Cult Rating: *****

Australian Cult Cinema: *****

Nymphette Cult Rating: *****

Nicolas Roeg, dir.; Edmund Bond, scr.; Si Litvinoff, pro.; 1.85:1; C; 95 min. (original theatrical); 100 min.; director's cut; Max L. Rabb Prods.

Following *Performance*, this was the second directorial assignment for Roeg (1928–2018), based on an acclaimed 1959 novel by James Vance Marshall. The film opens as a businessman-father drives his children (Jenny Agutter, 1952– ; Luc Roeg) from Sydney into the outback for a 'picnic.' There he attempts to kill them for reasons never explained. They survive, thanks to a bushman (David Gulpilil, 1953–) on a ritual maturation trek. Unable to communicate via words, they do so through eye contact and body language. *W*. plays as quasi-documentary, employing their journeys to capture the stark beauty of Australia's wilds. Agutter's character passes from child to woman while swimming. Her extended nude sequence, surprisingly if sweetly erotic, caused censors to consider an 'X' on what otherwise most resembles a Disney nature film. Should one scene in an otherwise G rated movie qualify it as softcore porn? No film has ever so effectively raised that question.

WARRIORS, THE (1979)

Youth Gang Flick Retro Rating: ****

Walter Hill, dir.; David Shaber, scr.; Lawrence Gordon, pro.; 1.85:1; C; 92 min.; Paramount.

    When Sol Yurick's novel *T.W.* reached bookstores in 1965, the piece already suffered from what Alvin Toffler calls Future Shock: a work intended to show things as they are now, dated owing to the rapidly altering tenor of our times. His tale of late 1950s/early 1960s street gangs referenced the 400 B.C. Anabasis of Xenophon: Athenian warriors trapped behind enemy lines. Here, members of the title gang attempt to make their way from Manhattan to Coney Island after a truce/alliance with others fails. Cult favs Michael Beck (1949–) and James Remar (1953–) are the key Warriors, also at odds with each other. Though much of the film was shot on location in Queens, N.Y., everything appears vaguely artificial. Critics (Roger Ebert included) attacked *T.W.* for its lack of authentic atmosphere, unaware that Hill (1942–) established a fantasy-aura to suggest a dystopian near-future fantasy world. When riots broke out near theatres, a cult formed around the first film to incite street violence since *Blackboard Jungle*.

WASP WOMAN, THE (1959)

Conventional B Horror Rating: *

Cabot Cult Rating: *****

Roger Corman, Jack Hill, dirs..; Leo Gordon, Kinta Zertuche, scr.; Corman, pro.; 1.85:1; B&W; 74 min.; Film Group.

    An aging head of a cosmetics firm grows depressed owing to her diminishing appearance. When a quack doctor brings her a serum derived from the queen wasp's jelly, she momentarily believes a solution is at hand. But there are after-effects, including her transformation into a killer bee. A shameless rip-off of a considerably superior B flick from two years earlier, *(The) She Devil* (Kurt Neumann) with Mari Blanchard in an identical role. Still, Corman's follow-up is the one that became a

THE BEAUTIFUL AND THE DOOMED: Hollywood's most tragic star Susan Cabot went from Universal contract player to Roger Corman Scream Queen… and that's before her life went totally out of control!

cult fav thanks to star Susan Cabot (1927–1986). Survivor of one horrible foster home after another, she crawled up and out owing to her beauty. Universal co-starred her opposite Tony Curtis and Audie Murphy in studio programmers. Her contract concluded, S.C. had nowhere to go but Corman quickies. Injured on the set of this dim thriller, she quit movies to marry King Hussein of Jordan and retire in luxury. On the eve of their wedding he learned that she was Jewish, born Harriet Shapiro, and ended the relationship. Back in the U.S., Cabot married on the rebound and gave birth to a challenged son. Her husband deserted, leaving her to raise the sad child. Friends feared she was going mad. In a shabby apartment her grown son killed her, claiming in court she had attacked him. He walked free. Ever since, her loyal cultists refer to S.C. as 'Queen B.'

WATCHMEN (2009)

Cult Sci-Fi Rating: *****

Superhero Cinema Rating: **** ½

Zack Snyder, dir.; David Hayter, Alex Tse, scr.; Lawrence Gordon, Lloyd Leven, Debrah Snyder, pros.; 2.35:1; C; 162 mi. (theatrical print); 186 (director's cut); 215 (complete); Paramount/Warner Bros./Legendary Ent.

Ordinarily, for a film to gross over $100 million certifies it as a box-office hit. Not so *W.*, which brought in $107 million. That must be measured against a $130 m. investment. Everything about this bleak one-of-a-kind epic suggests cultdom over box-office success. That was true of the 1986-87 limited edition graphic novel. Though distributed by D.C., this was hardly *Superman*. Author Alan Moore (1953–) and illustrator David Gibbons (1940–) created a combination of superhero saga, dystopian fiction, alternative history, dark comedy, hard-edged action, giddy parody, and sci-fi/fantasy with a philosophical edge. Hailed by critics as the comics equivalent of James Joyce's *Ulysses* (1922) as to mythic ambition and intellectual density. Snyder (1966–) brought the heart and soul of the "unfilmable" piece to the screen with innovative C.G. effects. The story (though this is anti-narrative in the tradition *An Andalusian Dog*) begins circa 1986 as a retired superhero, The Comedian, dies. Former fellows reunite to find out who is killing the costumed crusaders, and why someone wishes to unleash World War III. For eye candy, there's Malin Akerman (1978–) as 'Silk Spectre II,' in the most daring female superhero costume ever. The Complete Cut includes a story within the story (what there is of one), a film of the graphic novel "Tales of the Black Freighter," and a smart reference to a dark Lotte Lenya song in Kurt Weill's *The Threepenny Opera* (1928).

WEEKEND (1967)

Godard Cult Rating: *****

Jean-Luc Godard, dir.; Godard, scr.; Godard, pro. (unbilled); 1.66:1; C; 105 min. Comacio/Lira Films.

An upscale Parisian couple (Mirielle Darc, Jeanne Yanne), who have everything consumer culture dictates as valuable but are no longer able to love, feel, or think, hope the cliché of an "idyllic weekend in the country" might fix things. They head off in a luxurious Facella but everything that can go wrong does: traffic back-ups, endless car-crashes, finally casual killing on the streets. This may only be fantasy. Godard's point: What does that matter? It *is* true—for them—as in a post-modern world, reality is entirely subjective. J.L.G. violates all commonly held beliefs about time and space, history compared to the present, lust and love, art and junk, culture and chaos, virtue and evil, anarchy vs. order, optimism/pessimism. He visualizes a world in which nothing means anything, rising above cynicism to achieve the purest pessimism. In a splendid irony, G. encouraged cinematographer Raoul Coutard to capture the most extreme forms of ugliness (a fat pig is butchered alive) in lush, lyrical imagery; Antoine Duhame's sweet score serves such an ironic purpose. "What a lousy movie," Yanne mutters, deconstructing the film he is a part of. Godard asks: Can we trust in *anything*? Then answers his own question: Yes, classic cinema including *Johnny Guitar* and Ford's *The Searchers* (1956).

WELCOME TO MARWEN (2018)

Edgy/offbeat Rating: ****

Mainstream Viewer Rating: *

Robert Zemeckis, dir.; Carole Thompson, scr.; Zemeckis, Steve Starkey, pro.; 2.39:1; C; 116 min.; DreamWorks.

R.Z. (1951–) makes crowd-pleasers that win raves from critics: *Romancing the Stone* (1984), *Back to the Future* (1985), *Forrest Gump* (1994). That had something to do with the domestic and international hatred of *W.T.M.*, which like most Christmas releases cost a fortune (estimated: $40+ million) but earned less than a quarter of that back. Timing proved to be a big problem: Holiday viewers were hardly in the mood for a dark story, no matter how brilliant the F/X might be. Here was a little film (in the *best* sense of that term) with a big budget and no audience: The fact-based tale of Mark Hogancamp of Kingston, NY, beaten nearly to death by rednecks owing to Mark's secret identity as a cross-dresser. His memory gone, unable to relate to the world around him, M.H. (Steve Carrell,

1962–) created a kingdom of his own, designing dolls that recall WWII heroes, playing out fantasies which allowed him an illusion of the power he lacked in life. R.Z. employed motion capture to portray a continuum as to women in M.H.'s life and the fantasy femme dolls he, child-like, played with. Thank heavens for Home Viewing, cable, and newer innovations such as Streaming and Netflix! A small but appreciative cult has now developed.

WELCOME TO THE DOLLHOUSE (1995)

Youth Film Rating: **** 1/2

Todd Solandz, dir.; Solandz, scr.; Solandz, pro.; 1.85:1; C; 88 min.; Suburban Pictures/SONY Classics.

"The horror! The horror!" Dennis Hopper howls toward the end of *Apocalypse Now* (1979) in a dangerous jungle. *W.T.T.D.*'s lead 'Dawn Wiener' (Heather Matarazzo 1982–) might scream those same words everyday as she, an 11-year-old, steps inside her New Jersey High School. The insecure 7th grader is menaced by bullies, male and female, terrified of insensitive teachers and administrators. The wonderful surprise in Solandz's (1959–) movie is that the expected "makeover" (the homely girl turns into a beauty and wins her dream guy) never happens, making this a one-of-a-kind Youth Film. At the end, she's where she began, this a sad if true statement and a daring one for a modern teen movie. As in the classic *Terms of Endearment* (1983) T.S. encourages us to early-on believe this will be a cute comedy, gradually moving through drama to tragedy. The kind of cult-film that opens doors for its filmmaker to do bigger if not necessarily better things in the future.

WHAT EVER HAPPENED TO BABY JANE? (1962)

Hollywood Hag Classic Rating: *****

Robert Aldrich, dir.; Lukas Heller, scr.; Aldrich, pro.; 1.85:1; B&W; 1.85:1; Warner Bros.

THE BIRTH OF "HAG HORROR": The surprise box-office success of this youth-oriented dark comedy featuring Hollywood old-timers led to many imitations during the 1960s.

Way back in Vaudeville days, 'Baby Jane' meant to live theatre what Shirley Temple was to Hollywood movies: the bright and bubbly child star everyone fell in love with at first sight. Sadly, second sight proved to be something else entirely: she was an over-the-top caricature of the adorable little girl. Those who had once purchased Baby Jane dolls for their kids turned their back on her adult performances. Not so her sister 'Blanche,' who became a respected 'serious' actress. Then, a car accident ended all that, leaving Blanche (Joan Crawford) in a wheelchair, cared for in their isolated home by the ever more insane Jane (Bette Davis). The greatest Hollywood Hag melodrama since *Sunset Boulevard* (1950) with Gloria Swanson, Davis' performance as a Grand Dame referencing the role of 'Norma Desmond' on several occasions. Afficionados enjoy this more with each viewing, despite knowing the twist/revelation which is coming. That's quite a compliment. J.C. (1904–1977) hated playing 'old'; B.D. (1908–1989) revelled in it. Her 45 r.p.m. of the theme song became a huge hit.

WHAT'S UP, TIGER LILY? (1966)

Original theatrical release/original videotape: **** ½

Current DVD Release: NO STARS

Woody Allen, dir.; Allen, scr.; 80 min. (original release); 75 min. (contemporary DVD redux); Benedict Pictures/A.I.P.

    Disappointed with the glitzy approach taken by Hollywood's A listers to his initial script, *What's New Pussycat* (Clive Donner, 1965), W.A. (1935–) went indie: securing the rights to a cheapo-cheapo Toho studios imitation James Bond flick, adding original dialogue with the help of friends including then-wife Louise Lasser (1939–). *So Key of Keys* (Senkichi Taniguchi, 1965) was transformed into a spoof about Asian agent 'Phil Moscovitz' search for the world's greatest Egg Salad recipe. At one point, a scantily clad Asian beauty exercises; a voice-over alters whatever her line was to: "Boy, am I great piece!" In our time, Allen's gag-line would be considered sexist and racist. In 1966, at the height of the *Playboy* era, it was considered funny. Rather than hide this 'dated' piece in the vault, most of Woody's laugh-out-loud (if politically incorrect) one-liners were dubbed over again for a new DVD version. Japanese female leads Mie Hama and Senkichi Taniguchi were reunited one year later, opposite Sean Connery, in the Bond film *You Only Live Twice*. At the finale, China Lee (1942– ; *Playboy*'s Miss August, 1964) strips.

WHAT WE DO IN THE SHADOWS (2014)

New Zealand Mockumentary Vampire Flick Rating: **** 1/2

Jermaine Clement, Taika Waititi, dir.; Clement, Waititi, scr.; Clement, Waititi, Emanuel Michael, Chelsea Winstanley, pro.; 1.85:1; C/B&W; 86 min.; Unison Film.

    The traditional vampire is as dead (pun intended) a genre as the conventional Western. If you're going to work in such a time-worn form you've got to re-invent the rules as the surprise mainstream hit *No Country For Old Men* (2007, Joel and Etan Coen.) did for the latter. Here New

Zealander oddball film geeks J.C. (1974–) and T.W. (1975–) explore the one aspect of the succubus lifestyle that has never before been addressed: What does a bloodsucker do when not stalking victims or sleeping the day aware? The answer proves marvelously mundane: Figure out how four flat-mates in modern day Wellington will share the rent, who will do the dishes or scrub the toilet on any particular day, whine about horrible former girlfriends (the true "beasts" to these... well... beasts) and involve themselves in silly spats over absolutely nothing at all, much like the legendary *Seinfeld* gang. As with the best episodes of that show, the great moments here offer deadpan humor and, to continue the comparison, the worst come as (in this final fatal seasons of Jerry's Gang) the comedy turns too broad. Effective use of a mockumentary approach.

WHEN DINOSAURS RULED THE EARTH (1970)

Special Effects Cult Rating: *****

Dinosaur Movie Cult Rating: *****

Victoria Vetri/Angelo Dorian Cult Rating: *****

Val Guest, dir.; Guest, J.GT. Ballard, scr.; Alda Young, pro.; 1.75:1; C; 100 min.; Hammer.

In 1966, Hammer remade the 1940 fantasy *One Million B.C.* in color and widescreen with modern F/X. The movie scored, Raquel Welch (1940–) rocketing to stardom. Her good fortune inspired every starlet to seek a glamour-girl meets dinosaurs vehicle. Victoria Vetri (1944–) seemed made to order. 'Angela Dorian' (her birth name) had been *Playboy*'s Miss September 1967, later chosen as Playmate of the Year. Donning a blonde wig and the skimpiest of bikinis, V.V. proved charming as well as sexy in the most ambitious miniepic of its kind. Jim Danforth (1940–) provided Harryhausen-like stop-motion figurines set against vivid matte paintings. The smart (and surprisingly humorous) script was by J.G. Ballard (1930–2009), whose child-hood WWII reminiscences were brought to the screen by Steven Spielberg as *Empire of the Sun* (1987). S.S. adores *W.D.R.T.E.*, including references to it in *Jurassic Park* (1993). Score another cult triumph

REPUTED TO BE ONE OF SPIELBERG'S FAVORITE PREHISTORIC ADVENTURES: Victoria Vetri joined the ranks of Raquel Welch as a dinosaur fightin' tough gal in this witty and charming Hammer opus.

for Guest (1911–2006), director of *Day the Earth Caught Fire* (1961). Sadly, Vetri failed to find strong roles, suffered a rape attack in her home, and eventually went to prison for shooting her husband. Current DVD/Blue-Ray releases contain nude scenes of V.V. not previously included.

WHERE THE WILD THINGS ARE (2009)

Cult Rating: *****

Mainstream Rating: NO STARS

Spike Jonze, dir.; Jonze, Dave Eggers, scr.; Tom Hanks, Gary Goetzman, Maurice Sendak, prod.; 2.35:1; C; 101 min.; Legendary Pic./ Roadshow Ent./Warner Bros.

A problem child, sent to his room, sails off in his fantasies to an eerie island. There, he convinces the creatures that, if only they proclaim him king, all will live happily ever after. Since the 1963 publication of Sendak's (1928–2012) book, film companies have considered mounting a feature. W.B. greenlighted (if with trepidation) this $100 mill combination of live-action and Henson-esque costumes for the monsters. Critics and audiences expecting a family fantasy were outraged. The problem has less to do with the quality of the work than audience expectations: Jonze did remain true to the original's moribund tone in a way Disney would not have done. S.J. (whose movies are morbidly pessimistic) cut the if not happy than at least bittersweet ending M.S. had provided. Those rare moviegoers who arrived hoping for a Jonze auteurist work found this a fascinating film for adults, *about* if not *for* children. A jazz riff of a movie, flying off in its own weird directions. We do not encounter an adaptation of a much-beloved classic, rather another artist entirely, mounting his own meditation on the way of the world.

WHITE DOG (1982)

In Your Face Rating: ****

Samuel Fuller, dir.; Fuller, Romain Gary, Curtis Hanson, scr.; 1.85:1; C; 90 min.; Paramount.

A Hollywood actress (Kristy McNichol, 1962–) happens upon an abandoned dog, bringing the sad creature home for gentle care. The beast responds with devoted behaviour. Then, an Afro-American passes by and, to the heroine's shock, the 'pet' attacks. The girl gradually realizes a former racist owner paid a trainer to program the hapless creature to abhor people of color. Should she take her friends' advice and have the dog put to sleep or attempt to eliminate such learned behavior? This anti-racist movie was not widely distributed as members of the NAACP (who had not seen it) assumed from the premise that W.D. favoured rather than criticized the situation. In fact, the story is fact-based: this happened to Jean Seberg, wife of co-scripter Romain Gary. Director Fuller (1912–1997) had already achieved legendary status owing to his paperback pulp novels. He is portrayed by Robert Carradine in the World War II drama *The Big Red One* (1980). Ennio Morricone, of spaghetti Western film, created the haunting musical score.

WHITE ZOMBIE (1932)

Cult Rating: *** ½

Victor Halperin, dir.; Garnett Weston, scr.; Edward Halperin, pro.; 1.37:1; B&W; 69 mins.; Halperin Bros./United Artists.

Early in 1932 a Broadway play, *Zombie* by Kenneth Webb, served to introduce these all-but unknown monsters to U.S. audiences. Aware of this and the success Universal enjoyed with its sound -era horror flicks, the Halperin Bros.—who ran an ultra-low budget indie producing company—set about ripping off the play's premise. Victor (1995–1981) and Edward (1898–1981) wrote, produced, and marketed their exploitation item in less than a month. Public domain music (classics by Mussorgsky and others) filled the soundtrack. The result: the first Zombie movie, as such a landmark. Bela Lugosi wildly over-plays the unsubtly named 'Murder Legendre,' evil overseer of a Haitian plantation. He transforms a newlywed (Madge Bellamy) into the walking dead. As Browning had done in *Dracula*, the Halperins featured lengthy close-ups of Lugosi's penetrating eyes, the surrounding face lit to make him appear a devil in the flesh. Most beloved movie ever of hard metal rocker Rob Zombie.

WICKER MAN, THE (1973)

General Cult Rating: **** ½

Wiccan Cult Rating: *****

Robin Hardy, dir.; Anthony Shaffer, scr.; Peter Snell, pro.; 1.37:1; C; 99 min. (complete cut); 88 min. (theatrical cut).

    A stiff, pompous, self-righteous, well-intentioned U.K. police officer (Edward Woodward) receives a cryptic letter. On a tiny Hebrides island off the coast of Scotland, 12-year-old 'Rowen' has mysteriously disappeared. Arriving to investigate, he comes to believe this is no ordinary crime. For here neo-pagans live seemingly normal lives by day, then revert to Druid ways when the full moon shines bright. Likely, they hold this girl for a virgin sacrifice. A well-researched script by playwright/ screenwriter Shaffer (*Sleuth*, 1972 and *Frenzy*, 1973) resulted in the most accurate movie about Wicker, aka Wicca, aka Witchcraft: worship of nature by modern atavists. Christopher Lee, as the isle's 'leading citizen,' was so overwhelmed by the

WITCHCRAFT IN THE MODERN WORLD: Perhaps the most accurate film ever made about the practice of 'dark arts' in hidden corners of our contemporary surroundings.

script that he offered to work without pay. Three top cult actresses—Diane Cilento, Britt Eland, and Hammer's legendary Ingrid Pitt—co-star. Only limitation: Hardy (1929–2016), a writer, here directed for the first time. Sadly, it shows.

WET HOT AMERICAN SUMMER (2001)

Slob Comedy Appeal: * ½

Eclectic Celebrity Cast Appeal: *****

David Wain, dir.; Wain, Michael Showalter, scr.; Howard Bernstein, pro.; 1.85:1; C; 97 min.; Eureka Films.

When this low-budget indie was originally screened at the Sundance Film Festival, no distributor chose to pick it up. When the latter day version of the famed 1979 slob comedy *Meatballs* (with Bill Murray) finally did make its way into theatres, the target audience either ignored this collection of wild vignettes set on the final day of operation for a Maine summer camp back in 1981 or gave a try and despised the foolish rather than truly funny (i.e., *Animal House*) slipshod low-budgeter, as did the critics. Then came home video, and the slow but sure beginnings of a cult following which in time reached the mainstream. Why? One reason has to do with its era; as with the 1950s, 1960s, and 1970s, the 1980s eventually became ripe for nostalgia. This clumsy flick contained just enough fashions, expressions, music, and values of that bygone period to attract grown-ups who had been young then and hungered for reminders of that oddball decade. An incredibly eclectic cast certainly didn't hurt, including Amy Poehler, David Hyde Pierce, Molly Shannon, Paul Rudd, and Jeanine Garofalo, plus co-writer Showalter (1970–), who would emerge as a legitimate auteur with the impressive *The Big Sick* (2017). Wain (1969–) was able to franchise this as the cornerstone of an ongoing set of films and TV series.

WHAT HAPPENED ON 23rd STREET, NEW YORK (1901)

Innovative Filmmaking Experiment: : *****

Edwin S. Porter, dir, scr..; Thomas Edison, pro.; B&W; 13 secs.; Black Maria Company.

It's a whole new century and The Flickers are all the rage at Nickelodeons that line the lower levels of Manhattan Isle's declasse neighborhoods. There, recent immigrants are starved for popular entertainment not hampered by an inability to speak English. One of their favorites: This brief though dazzling image of a suave fellow (AC. Abadie) accompanying a lovely lady (Florence Georgie) on a promenade past the city's newspaper buildings. As they cross over a recently installed hot air shaft, which regularly blasts stale air out of the building, the timing is right or wrong, depending on how you look at things: her dress flies up, revealing shapely legs to all. As these are the final days of the Victorian era, this is shocking enough to lure in viewers eager for a quick peek. In fact, the seeming 'caught on the fly documentary' was scripted, rehearsed, and shot several times. As such, here is what may be the origination point of contemporary Reality TV. The great director Billy Wilder once admitted that seeing this bit of cinema history served as his inspiration for an identical, now iconic, sequence featuring Marilyn Monroe in *The Seven Year Itch* (1955) which has no precedent in George Alexrod's earlier play.

WILD GUITAR (1962)

Hicks Nix Sticks Pix Rating: *****

Ray Dennis Steckler, dir.; 'Nicholas Merriwether,' Bob Whely, Joe Thomas, scr.; Arch Hall Sr., pro.; 35 mm; Fairway International.

Imagine early rock 'n' roller Conway Twitty and Michael J. Pollard as 'C.W. Moss' in *Bonnie and Clyde* collapsed into one another and you have Arch Hall, Jr. (1943–). Once tagged "The Cabbage Patch Elvis," Arch plays 'Bud Eagle,' a good ol' country boy who hears that L.A. big shots are looking for a new Youth Star. He hops on his cycle and heads out to conquer the world, only to crash head-on with the corrupt Music

448 • Midnight Matinees: Cult Cinema Classics

THE KING ELVIS OF THE DEEP SOUTH RURAL DRIVE-IN CIRCUIT: Arch Hall (Jr.); there never was anyone like him and there never will be again!

Biz. The plot steals from Presley's second and third films, *Loving You* and *Jailhouse Rock* (both 1957) and was written (under a pseudonym) by Arch Hall Sr. (1908–1978), who also produced. The elder Hall is portrayed by Robert Mitchum in *The Last Time I Saw Archie* (1960). Ray Dennis Steckler's (1938–2009) shoot resulted in such a mess that one critic wondered if this might be "a naïve form of surrealism." R.D.S. directed several more movie milestones including *The Sadist* (1963, *The Incredibly Strange Creatures Who Stopped Living and Became Mixed Up Zombies!!?* (1964), and *Rat Fink a Boo Boo* (1966). Female lead Nancy Czar (1944–) played the Blonde on the Beach who drives boys mad with lust in Elvis's *Girl Crazy* (1965), then went on to become the U.S. Counsel for Bangladesh. No kidding!

WILD ONE, THE (1953)

Black Leather Jacket/White Hot Chrome Rating: **** 1/2

Laslo Benedek, dir.; John Paxton, Frank Rooney, scr.; Stanley Kramer, pro.; 1.37:1 B&W; 79 mins.; Columbia.

When message moviemaker Kramer planned a film based on the recent (if largely mythic) takeover of Hollister CA by outlaw biker gangs, his goal was to create a cinematic work of social relevance. S.K. hired gang members as extras for additional realism. To his surprise, a mainstream item was transformed into a cult flick by the then-new youth audience. Marlon Brando's (1924–2004) black leather jacket, in truth not yet a fashion choice for bikers, became one overnight. His idea to play the part with sideburns led to James Dean, Elvis Presley, and 1950s suburban adolescents adapting that redneck style. After the Brit rock band The Quarrymen attended a forbidden screening in 1960 (*The Wild One* had been banned in the UK) they changed their name to The Beatles in honor of Lee Marvin's (1924–1987) gang. That actor based his costume on photos of outlaw biker Willie Forkner of the Booze Fighters; after seeing the film, Hell's Angels leader Frank Sadilek began wearing striped shirts. Like *Rebel* two years later, a case of a film produced to mirror a recent phenomenon that changed the country's entire cultural climate and helped create 'The Fifties.'

WILLY WONKA AND THE CHOCOLATE FACTORY (1971)

Family film cult Rating: **** ½

Mel Stuart, dir.; Roald Dahl, David Seltzer, scr.; David L. Wolper, pros.; 1.85:1; C; 89 min. (original theatrical print), 100 min. (final/current cut).

The Howard Hughes of sweets and treats, W.W. (Gene Wilder, 1933–2016) comes out of seclusion to welcome small fry lucky enough to discover gold tickets in his candy bars, entitling each to a factory tour. Among them: poor 'Charley' (Peter Ostrum, 1957–), who shares his happiness with a beloved grandpa (Jack Albertson, 1907–1981). Budgeted at $3 million, this netted a small profit theatrically. Shortly, HBO appeared

YESTERDAY'S YOUTH ICON IS TOMORROW'S DATED JOKE: In the early 1950s, Marlon Brando ruled as 'Johnny' in *The Wild One*; a decade later, Harvey Lembeck burlesqued that image as 'Eric von Zipper' in the Beach Party films.

IF ONLY THE WORLD WORKED AS IT SHOULD: Then Gene Wilder would have received the Best Actor Oscar for this 'sleeper' hit.

as the initial pay-cable outlet. When *W.W.A.T.C.F.* played constantly during the 1970s it became as much a staple as a Disney classic or *The Wizard of Oz*. The results pleased most everyone with the exception of Roald Dahl (1916–1990), who claimed his book *Charlie and the Chocolate Factory* (1967) had been watered down. Still, this introduced a new wave of family films featuring a dark, edgy aura. Never before had boys and girls died horribly in such a feature. Stuart's direction, Harper Goff's art direction, and Logan Frazee's F/X left much to be desired; Tim Burton's 2005 remake offered a brilliant state-of-the-art world of imagination. Yet his movie pales in comparison to the original, owing to G.W.'s depiction of the title character. If Oscars went to the deserving, he would have won Best Actor. Children of the 1970s (and beyond) would, while watching, shout out the words to the Oompa Loompa song.

WITCH, A NEW ENGLAND FABLE, THE (2015)

Nouveaux Horror Tale: *****

Robert Eggers, dir., scr.; Daniel Bekerman, Jodi Redmond, Rodrigo Teixeira, Jay Van Hoy, pro.; 1.66:1; C; 92 min.; Parts and Labor/RT Features.

"Do you want to live *deliciously?*" Say that in public and most people will stare at you as if you've gone crazy. But if a face in the crowd smiles and, with burning eyes, calls out "Black Phillip, The Goat," then you've come in contact with one of those dedicated few who have not only seen *Witch* but become an aficionado. With the most important movie about the subject of Wicca since *The Blair Witch Project* (1999), first-time feature director R.E. (1983–) moved into the frontline of contemporary cult directors. The setting is New England, circa 1634. A devout family of Calvinist farmers attempts to carve an outpost of civilization, commerce, and the Christian faith out of a primeval forest stretching to their west. But something unsettling appears to be moving, if at first invisibly, out of that heart of darkness, into their home and their very souls. Not a generic horror film about witchcraft but a one-of-a-kind eerie, anxiety inducing, slow moving (purposefully!) fable (as the title insists) about nature's massive darkness smothering the human desire to create a small light in the forest. Recalls the Danish classic *Day of Wrath* (Carl Dreyer, 1943) in its horrifying silences.

WITHNAIL AND I (1987)

Brit Droll Humor Rating: * ½

Bruce Robinson, dir.; Robinson, scr.; Paul M. Heller, pro.; 1.85:1; C; 107 min.; Handmade Films.

1969: Hippie era London is alive and well for virtually every resident except the title characters. The upper-crust Withnail (Richard E. Grant, 1957–) and working class Marwood (Paul McGann, 1959–) live in one of the city's worst areas: Camden. There the two failed actors share a room, consuming drugs and alcohol. Then comes an inspiration: Why not pull 'a Thoreau' and slip away to the Brit version of Walden in the Lake District? As in any odd couple comedy, everything that can go wrong does—from rains worse than those back in town to the presence of Uncle Monty (Richard Griffiths, 1947–2013), delivering a scene-stealing performance as the cinema's first "vegetarian homosexual." Brittle humor negates romantic philosophy by Wordsworth, with his "splendour in the grass" and "glory in the flower" musings. Robinson (1946–) drew heavily on the treatise *A Rebours* by Parisian Karl Huysmans (1849–1907), a put-down of Transcendentalism, as well as his own early years as a struggling would-be star. That's Robinson as 'Benvolio' in Franco Zefferelli's *Romeo and Juliet* (1968).

WORKING GIRLS (1986)

Feminist cult appeal: ****

Artistic value: *** ½

Lizzie Borden, dir.; Borden, Sandra Kay, scr.; Borden, Andi Gladstone, pro.; 1.66:1; C; 93 min.; Alternate Current.

Why aren't there more female directors? Feminist film critics angrily asked. Hollywood honchos attempted to answer that by allowing females with media credentials to helm projects. The fascinatingly named Lizzie Borden (1958–), who previously shot several indies, was given the go-ahead for an auteurist project (this time around, one *woman*, one movie). A slice-of-edgy-contemporary-life observes the title characters coming and going during a typical day at a New York office suite. To beg the question: why is this firm different from any other? They are all prostitutes; none cliché, all believable people who have gone into this 'business' for deep personal reasons. Even those who admired this work's sincerity realized L.B. didn't have what it takes; as one critic put it this was "part nudie exploitation, part sociological thesis." Still, given the subject matter, *W.G.* immediately became a cult film for members of the feminist movement. Borden's next, a lacklustre erotic thriller with Sean Young called *Love Crimes* (1992), essentially ended her directorial career.

WRESTLER, THE (2008)

Aronofsky appeal: *** ½

Mickey Rourke appeal: *****

Marisa Tomei Appeal: ***** +

Darren Aronofsky, dir.; Robert D. Siegel, scr.; Aronofsky, Scott Franklin, pros.; 2.35:1; C; 109 min.; Saturn/Protozoa/ Fox Searchlight.

Here is the only film directed by D.A. which he did not write, explaining why it's of least interest to his hardcore cultists but reaches mainstream viewers in a way that, say, *Mother!* (2017) did not. Siegel's observant script believably depicts an over-the-hill professional wrestler,

'Randy Robinson,' aka 'The Ram.' Informed by doctors he must quit the ring or die, Ram realizes he has nothing else to live for... unless he can finally 'connect' with another person. This may be the single mother/lap dancer (Marisa Tomei, 1964–) he falls for, or his estranged daughter (Rachel Evan Wood). Mickey Rourke (1952- } does not so much 'play' Ram, rather inhabiting a character who quirkily resembles the star. The choice of actor transforms the piece into a thinly disguised autobiography. M.R. has known his ups and downs, beginning as a fascinating scene-stealer (*Body Double*, 1984) emerging as a character-lead (*Angel Heart*, 1987), achieving success as a romantic presence (*Wild Orchids*, 1898), reborn as a holy terror in *Sin City*. He has also, like Ram, suffered in the ring as a boxer. The story recalls *Rocky* (1976) if less simplistically optimistic, more realistically bittersweet.

WRESTLING WOMEN VS. THE AZTEC MUMMY, aka *ROCK 'N' ROLL WRESTLING WOMEN VS. THE AZTEC MUMMY* (1964)

Mainstream Rating: NO STARS

Low Camp Rating: *****

Rene Cardona, dir.; Alfredo Salazar, Guillermo Calderon, scr.; Calderon, pro.; 1.37:1; B&W; 85 min.; Cinematografica Calderon.

Before the U.S. mainstream accepted professional wrestling as a legitimate form of entertainment ('Gorgeous George' and his like were strictly for lowbrows) or enjoyed watching strong female leads in action flicks, the Mexican Z movie industry pumped out no-budget genre pieces including both. The title refers to The *Luchadoras*, tough girls who can take on any comers in the ring. 'Loreta' is played by Lorena Velazquez (1937–), Latin America's answer to deliciously deadly dames such as Barbara Steele, Caroline Munro, and Martine Beswick. Her partner in fighting crime as well as a team of Asian King Fu experts is 'Golden Rubi,' portrayed by Elizabeth Campbell (1942–) of Santa Monica. The plot, involving an evil Oriental ('The Dragon') hungry to steal a gold breastplate guarded by shape shifting Xochitl (the Mummy), is as ludicrous as the

Egg Salad recipe in Woody Allen's *What's Up Tiger Lily*? Likely by accident, odd lighting for the B&W cinematography causes this to visually resemble Godard's *Alphaville* (1965), yet another grindhouse/arthouse link. K. Gordon Murry 1922–1979) added a rock 'n' roll soundtrack to create a U.S. TV midnight movie.

WRITTEN ON THE WIND (1956)

Conventional Melodrama Rating: ** ½

Camp/Cult/Unintentional Comedy Rating: *****

Douglas Sirk, dir.; George Zuckerman, scr.; Albert Zugsmith, pro.; 2.00:1; C; 99 min.; Universal-International.

  Among the strange cinematic accomplishments of Sirk (1897–1987), one stands out among all the other glitzy soap-opera moments as so outrageous that it approximates a satire, conscious or not, on the very genre it belongs to. Unable to talk the hard-working executive (Rock Hudson, 1925–1985) of her Texas family-business into marriage, a spoiled nymphomaniac daughter (Dorothy Malone, 1925–2018) of the scion (Robert

IS IT A SERIOUS SOAP-OPERA OR A MEL BROOKS STYLE SPOOF ON THAT GENRE? Dorothy Malone won a Best Supporting Actress Oscar for her over-the-top performance in the film that later inspired TV's *Dallas* and *Dynasty*.

Keith) goes insane. Drunk, she dances like a Burly-Q tramp, then strips to ever wilder music as poor pappy falls down the spiral staircase to his death. Malone won the Best Supporting Actress Oscar. Is this melodrama at its bad taste nadir or a clever satire on such stuff? Accepted at face value on release by mainstream moviegoers, this became a source of ripe humor for hipsters. Grotesque camera angles, impossibly florid color, ripe caricatured acting, and risible dialogue beg the question: Might D.S. have purposefully played such silly stuff that he was assigned in the most preposterous manner? Lauren Bacall (1924–2014) looks lost amidst the absurd sound and fury signifying nothing… except perhaps Camp.

YI YI, aka *ONE (BY) ONE* (2000)

Most Often Viewed Taiwanese Film by Americans:
*****

Edward Yang, dir., scr.; Shin-ya Kawai, many others, pro.; 1.85:1; C; 173 min.; AtomFilm.

"Why is everyday life in the world so very different from what we believe it ought to be like?" one morose character asks in this, the final film from Yang (1947–2000), the Shanghai-born, Taipei located director during most of his career. The teenage girl speaks not only for everyone else in the film, family and friends in particular, but humanity itself as this may be the question to end all questions. How to describe this oblique work about self-absorbed characters? Imagine if the Japanese director Yasujiro Ozu *(Tokyo Story*, 1953) somehow managed to collaborate with Russian playwright Anton Chekhov (*The Three Sisters,* 1900/ 1901) on a study of contemporary middle class Asians so consumed by the endless small dramas during their waking hours that they cannot discover any greater reason to go on? First among equals in this ensemble piece is 'N.J.' (Nien-Jen Wu), a middle-aged man who must sort out the daily details of spouse-hood, father-hood, son-hood, business dealings, and past memories suggesting the existence he might have opted for. Wry, dry humor underlines this slice-of-modern upper-middleclass life portrait of the lonely and listless, as Yang discovers great universal themes in the demi-monde that he knew firsthand and completely understood.

ZERO WOMAN (1995)

Asian Martial Arts Mayhem Rating: *** ½

'Good' Femme Fatale Rating: ****

Daisuke Goto, dir.; Chiaki Hashiba, scr.; Hiroshi Yamaji, Shinsuke Yamazaki, Yoshiniro Chiba, pros.; 1.85:1; C; 99 min.; GAGA.

When Chinese gangsters steal money from a Japanese mob, an invisible arm of the government known as Zero dispatches 'Rei' (model turned actress Natsuki Ozawa, 1972–) to wipe them out. Like *The Chinese Connection* (1972) with Bruce Lee, here is an actioner that takes its premise from long-standing hostilities between the two countries. Technical/aesthetic considerations are nil; that doesn't matter. Like American Z budget classics, the movie's power derives from the lead character's passion for her work. Crazier than a bed-bug one moment, sweet and sentimental the next, Rei exemplifies "the hardboiled Asian babe" who kicks male ass and, now and again, female too. Near-constant nudity is offered by having the heroine enjoy a lengthy shower after each bloody confrontation. Most of the action revolves around rape. Rei pretends to enjoy it; when her latest assailant lets his guard down, she kills him in the cruellest manner. A bizarre combo of Cheri Caffaro's *Ginger* movies and Andy Sidaris' flicks about beautiful women who kill for profit and a perverse sexual release. Kane Kosugi (1974–) adds a modicum of martial arts action. The film's full title is *Zero Woman 2*; this is a semi-sequel to 1974's *Zero Woman: Red Handcuffs*. Based on a manga by Tooru Shinohara.

ZIEGFELD FOLLIES (1940)

Mainstream Kink Rating: **** ½

Cult Animation Rating: **** ½

Vincente Minnelli, many others, dir.; David Freedman, Hugh Martin, Ralph Blume, many others, scr.; Arthur Freed, pro.; 1.37:; C; Metro-Goldwyn-Mayer.

"LUCY, I'M HOME… HONEY, WHERE ARE YOU?" A dominatrix redhead named Ball whips the catgirls into disciplinary positions in the 'family' musical *Ziegfeld Follies*.

During the early years of the 20th Century, Florence Ziegfeld Jr. (1867–1932) brought declasse Vaudeville to the Broadway stage, legitimizing the form that featured comedy and novelty acts. A sophisticated style for idealizing/eroticizing the American Beauty (in a toned-down imitation of Paris' Follies Bergere) reached the screen via MGM's Oscar-winning *The Great Ziegfeld* (1936), William Powell playing the glamourmeister once more; he had already done so in *The Great Ziegfeld* (1936) and *Ziegfeld Girl* (1941). Z.F. follow-up offers a series of sketches, featuring Judy Garland (1922–1969) and 'Funny Girl' Fanny Brice (1891–1951). This emerged as a cult film owing to several sequences: a stop-motion animation opening by Lou Bunin that rivals the best of George Pal; Lucille Ball (1911–1989), she elegantly ladylike in soft pink, wielding a black whip to tame deadly Cat Girls. They, in kinky black costumes, circle Lucy in what may have partly inspired 'Catwoman' in the *Batman* comics. Proof that beneath the family-friendly surface of the era's mainstream entertainment, the dark delights of S&M bubbled.

ZOMBIELAND (2009)

Cult comedy Rating: ****

Woody Harrelson aficionado Rating: **** ½

Reuben Fleischer, dir.; Rhett Reese, Paul Wernick, scr.; Galvin Polone, pro.; 2.35:1; C; 88 min.; Relativity Media/ Pariah/Columbia.

Following an apocalypse that transforms most survivors into flesh-eating fiends, the last normal people in America make their way to a fabled Zombie-free zone. The premise originated in Richard Matheson's novel *I Am Legend* (1954), recycled three times in movie adaptations as well as many films that 'borrow' the idea, from *Panic in the Year Zero* (Ray Milland, 1962) to *28 Days Later*. Here, such a plot is sent up with comedy that never goes over-the-top in a Mel Brooks manner, maintaining enough genre trappings that it also works on a scare level. A smart script has a college student (Jess Eisenberg, 1983–) offering one of those fatalistic voice-overs that have long since become overly familiar, yet works when employed for an ironic contrast in which most such comments are contradicted by what we witness. As a hillbilly survivalist with a penchant for Twinkies, Woody Harrelson (1961–) draws on his role in the Quentin

Tarantino/Oliver Stone collaboration *Natural Born Killers* (1994). A visit to actor Bill Murray's 'mansion' was *not* filmed at his home. The 'Hannah Montana' discussion between J.E. and Emma Stone (1988–) was improvised as a satiric homage to the Madonna dialogue in *Reservoir Dogs*.

About the Author

"MEET THE CULT STARS": The author visits Adrienne Barbeau, Harry Dean Stanton, and Lee Van Cleef of the final day of shooting for *Escape From New York*; a decade and a half later, Stanton would star in the Brode-scripted erotic thriller *Midnight Blue*. Douglas Brode is a novelist, graphic novelist, produced playwright and screenwriter, multi-award-winning journalist and multi-award-winning educator. As to the latter, he created the 'Film Classics' program for The Newhouse School of Public Communications, Syracuse University.

www.ingramcontent.com/pod-product-compliance
Lightning Source LLC
Chambersburg PA
CBHW071940220426
43662CB00009B/922